Paths to College and Career
English Language Arts

Reading Closely and Writing to Learn

CONTENTS

Unit 2   131

Unit 3   309

ABOUT PCG EDUCATION

A division of Public Consulting Group (PCG), PCG Education provides instructional and management services and technologies to schools, school districts, and state education agencies across the United States and internationally. We apply more than 30 years of management consulting expertise and extensive real-world experience as teachers and leaders to strengthen clients' instructional practice and organizational leadership, enabling student success.

As educators engage with rigorous standards for college and career readiness, PCG Education partners with practitioners at all stages of implementation. We work with clients to build programs, practices, and processes that align with the standards. Our team of experts develops and delivers standards-based instructional resources, professional development, and technical assistance that meet the needs of all learners.

In response to a wide range of needs, PCG Education's solutions leverage one or more areas of expertise, including College and Career Readiness, MTSS/RTI, Special Programs and Diverse Learners, School and District Improvement, and Strategic Planning. PCG's technologies expedite this work by giving educators the means to gather, manage, and analyze data, including student performance information, and by facilitating blended learning approaches to professional development.

To learn more about PCG Education, visit us at www.publicconsultinggroup.com.

WHAT IS *PATHS TO COLLEGE AND CAREER?*

Paths to College and Career is a comprehensive English Language Arts (ELA) curriculum that meets the rigorous requirements and instructional shifts of the Common Core State Standards (CCSS). *Paths to College and Career* (for grades 6–8) deeply engages middle-level students in authentic experiences while building their literacy skills and expanding their knowledge of the world around them as they grow toward college and career readiness. *Paths to College and Career* supports teachers' understanding of CCSS-aligned instruction that challenges and engages all students as they read, discuss, and write about complex texts.

Materials and Resources

- **Curriculum maps** that provide a bird's eye view of standards, learning targets, core texts, and assessments across the year, both within each grade and across grades 6–8

- **Detailed plans** for curriculum modules, units, and lessons, with teacher instructional notes and student supports

- **Authentic literary and informational texts** at appropriate grade-level complexity work together to build students' knowledge

- **Supplementary resources** including protocols and practices, graphic organizers, and supports for students with a variety of learning needs

- **Flexibility**, encouraging teacher adaptation and student choice

Intentional Learning Progressions

- **Engaging topics**, and sequencing within topics, that draw students deeply into rigorous reading, writing, and thinking

- Deliberate **year long instructional processes** that develop students' ability to read closely, analyze texts, and synthesize information across multiple texts

- Scaffolded **assignments** that help all students develop skill in evidence-based writing, including argument, explanation, and narrative

- **Regular, consistent writing** for many purposes, both informal and more formal, incorporating the writing process

- **Classroom protocols** that foster rich evidence-based discussions, research, and writing based on evidence from text

---

- **Academic vocabulary** development that builds students' ability to understand sophisticated words and complex language structures
- **Active learning** that encourages students' confidence in their ability to achieve at high levels

Assessment That Informs Instruction

- Daily and ongoing formative assessment opportunities
- Student self-assessment and feedback
- Mid-unit and end-of-unit assessments
- Curriculum-embedded performance tasks for each module in which students synthesize their work to demonstrate their deep learning of skills and content
- CCSS-based rubrics and models of expected student performances

Paths to College and Career provides a complete middle-level ELA curriculum, fully aligned with the Common Core standards and instructional shifts and designed to meet the needs of all students.

Why Do We Need a New and More Rigorous Curriculum?

College and Career anchor standards (CCR) establish literacy expectations for students as they graduate from high school and prepare to enter college or career paths. Grade-specific standards define end-of-year expectations and learning progressions that enable students to meet college and career readiness expectations no later than the end of high school.

The CCSS provide a vision for college- and career-ready students who can

- Independently comprehend and evaluate complex texts
- Construct effective arguments and convey complex information
- Actively listen to, comprehend, and question a speaker
- Engage in productive dialogue
- Demonstrate command of standard English and use a wide-ranging vocabulary
- Be self-directed learners and know how to locate information from a variety of sources
- Build knowledge by engaging with works of quality and substance, reading purposefully, and listening attentively
- Refine and share their knowledge through writing and speaking
- Respond to the varying demands of audience, task, purpose, and discipline
- Be engaged and open-minded—but discerning—readers and listeners
- Cite specific evidence, connecting it through reasoning to their claim, when offering an oral or written interpretation of a text or when making their own point
- Use technology and digital media strategically and capably

- Understand other perspectives and cultures and communicate effectively with people of other backgrounds
- Learn about a variety of periods, cultures, and worldviews by reading great classic and contemporary works of literature

Achieving these high expectations and rigorous goals requires that curriculum and instruction support teachers in preparing students for college and career.

The Standards in Action: The Instructional Shifts and *Paths to College and Career*

The Common Core State Standards for ELA & Literacy set clear, high expectations for what students in each grade need to know as they grow toward college and career readiness. These rigorous expectations require shifts in the content and nature of instruction so that students will achieve the standards. *Paths to College and Career* embodies these instructional shifts.

Shift 1: Building Knowledge through Content-Rich Nonfiction

In college and career, most required reading is nonfiction and informational text. Students need to understand the structure of text and be able to learn independently through text.

- Expanding beyond fiction, students read a true **balance of literary and informational texts**.
- Through carefully selected text sets, students **build knowledge** about the world (domains/content areas) through interactions with **text** rather than through teacher talk or activities.

How does *Paths to College and Career* help teachers and students meet Shift 1?

All modules in *Paths to College and Career* pair literature with rich informational text (including primary source documents and literary nonfiction). Authentic reading materials include full-length books, excerpts, articles, and other texts. In addition, each unit includes a set of sequenced, coherent progressions of learning experiences that build knowledge and understanding of major concepts related to real-world issues and concerns. Students engage in significant topics as they read high-quality literature and fiction. They build expertise on topics and share that expertise with others.

Shift 2: Reading, Writing, and Speaking Grounded in Evidence from Text

The ability to locate and use evidence is a strong indicator of success in college and career. Too often, questions and tasks ask students to answer from their own experience, rather than requiring them to respond with evidence from text. The CCSS expects that most questions and tasks require students to read the text—and to identify what is directly stated and what is inferred. In the classroom, reading, writing, and speaking all emphasize the use of evidence.

- Students engage in **rich and rigorous evidence-based conversation** about text.
- Writing **uses evidence from sources** to inform or make an argument.

How does *Paths to College and Career* help teachers and students meet Shift 2?

Each module of the *Paths to College and Career* curriculum focuses on reading, writing, listening, and speaking in response to high-quality texts. *Paths to College and Career* supports teachers with careful and deliberate sequences of text-dependent questions and tasks that ensure students return to the text for answers. Students use evidence, becoming skilled at asking and answering important text-dependent questions as they read. The curriculum also emphasizes writing from sources and research, matching the emphasis placed on these activities in the CCSS for a variety of purposes. Over the course of the academic year, students regularly write evidence-based informative/explanatory texts as they engage in text analysis. Writing instruction in *Paths to College and Career* frames writing as a recursive and iterative process of planning, drafting, revising, editing, and rewriting. Building the research skills outlined in the CCSS, students learn how to conduct effective, inquiry-based research. Through reading and analysis, students identify topics of interest, formulate questions for searches, assess sources, craft inquiry-based research questions, engage in research and writing, and, finally, analyze and synthesize their research in formal writing pieces.

Paths to College and Career regularly incorporates student discussion in order for students to process orally what they have read and what they will write or have already written in response to a text. Discussions take various forms, some more formal or structured than others. Discussions are student driven and share a common focus on evidence-based claims. Students engage with one another, rather than with the teacher, as they pose questions, build shared knowledge, and support each other. To facilitate classwide engagement, students work in pairs or small groups prior to whole-class discussion. These pair or small-group discussions allow students the space and time to collaboratively build evidence-based understandings of text(s) and share their ideas and understandings.

Students engage in peer-supported and independent research projects of varying lengths and on a range of topics. Using the text as the basis for forming claims and making inferences, students write in multiple contexts. End-of-module performance tasks require students to use textual evidence in authentic contexts.

Shift 3: Complex Text and Its Academic Vocabulary

There has existed a huge gap between the complexity of texts students read and the complexity of texts they need to be able to read to meet college and career expectations. The new standards have raised the overall level of text complexity, with clear expectations for independence at each grade level. One of the greatest factors in text complexity is the academic vocabulary that is more often found in text than in everyday speech. Because of this, teachers need to pay careful attention to building students' vocabulary and helping them learn how to build their own vocabulary in a variety of ways.

- Students **read appropriately complex texts for their grade level**. Instruction and learning centers on those texts. Adequate time allows students to read closely and understand the text fully.

- Students **build the academic vocabulary** they need to access complex texts.

How does *Paths to College and Career* help teachers and students meet Shift 3?

The informational text and literature in each module meet the expected range of quantitative complexity. Students read and review texts for specific purposes. With a gradual release of support, students deconstruct, seek meaning, conduct analysis, define words in context, use and develop background knowledge, and work to understand the text at hand. The *Paths to College and Career* curriculum paces the learning so that students carefully read and reread complex text as they explore ideas, structures, and layers of meaning.

Paths to College and Career emphasizes depth of student understanding rather than the breadth of texts "covered." The process of achieving this depth of understanding includes annotating text. The curriculum frequently asks students to note specific parts of a text that contain important ideas and spark connections to other texts or require additional attention and discussion.

Paths to College and Career builds students' academic vocabulary, the words and language structures more likely to appear in complex literary and informational texts. Through guided practice, students gain familiarity with the words in context or, when appropriate, learn their meaning at point of use as they encounter the word in a text.

Other Features of *Paths to College and Career* That Support All the Instructional Shifts

In addition to directly addressing the instructional shifts, *Paths to College and Career* emphasizes instructional practices that promote achievement of high academic expectations.

Paired and Group Reading/Collaborative Work

Collaboration plays a major role in college and career readiness. The CCSS weave together the four strands of reading, writing, speaking and listening, and language to provide an integrated approach to learning. The lessons and units in *Paths to College and Career* allow students multiple opportunities to collaborate while reading, writing, speaking, and listening. This learning and sharing of insights also benefits students who require additional support in developing these skills.

Scaffolding to Independence

Paths to College and Career scaffolds student learning to promote independence in reading, writing, and speaking about complex texts. Each unit builds on the skills and knowledge students develop in the preceding units, just as each module in a year extends and refines students' work in earlier modules. Over the course of the year and across grade levels, teachers will notice students' increased capacity for independent work. As texts increase in complexity, tasks become more challenging.

Assessment in *Paths to College and Career*

Paths to College and Career provides a full complement of assessments, including ongoing formative assessment practices and protocols in each lesson, unit-level assessments, and a culminating performance task at the conclusion of each module.

- Formative assessment practices and opportunities are embedded in and across lessons. Students self-assess against daily learning targets and receive frequent feedback from the teacher and peers.

- Each unit includes two formal assessments. Mid-unit assessments typically are reading assessments requiring text-based answers. End-of-unit assessments often require using multiple sources in a written essay.

- The final assessment for each module is a performance task. In these culminating projects, students synthesize and apply their learning from the module in an engaging and authentic way. Performance tasks incorporate the writing process, scaffolds for students, and peer critique and revision.

- Assessments offer curriculum-embedded opportunities to practice the types of skills needed on high-stakes assessments and include multiple-item formats:
  - Selected response (multiple-choice questions)
  - Short constructed response
  - Extended response, either on demand or supported
  - Speaking and listening (discussion or oral presentation)
  - Formal argumentative, explanatory, and narrative essays (involving planning, drafting, and revision)

Paths to College and Career Organization and Structure

This curriculum is composed of seven grade levels (6–12). Each grade level includes four primary modules. Each module consists of up to three units, and each unit consists of a set of lesson plans.

Modules are arranged in units comprising one or more texts. The texts in each module share common elements in relation to genre, authors' craft, text structure, or central ideas. Each unit in a module builds on the skills and knowledge students develop in the preceding unit(s). The number of lessons in a unit

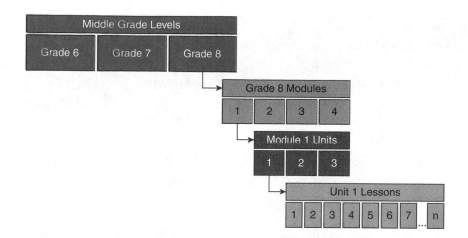

varies based on the length of the text(s). Each lesson is designed to span one class period but may extend beyond that time frame depending on student needs.

The standards assessed and addressed in each module specifically support the study of the module text(s), and include standards in all four domains: reading, writing, speaking and listening, and language. The modules include daily lesson assessments, mid- and end-of-unit assessments, and a culminating performance task in which students are asked to synthesize their learning across the module. The performance task also provides an option for teachers to engage students in writing or discussion of salient excerpts or ideas from the module texts in relation to outside texts, current events, the world writ large, or the human condition.

The *Paths to College and Career* curriculum provides a full year of modules and units, including

- Year long scope and sequence
- Module framing and overview
- Unit-at-a-glance and week-at-a-glance guidance for the teacher
- Performance tasks and other summative and formative assessments
- Lesson plans
- Supporting materials (class work, homework, rubrics, and so on)

Structure of a Year of Instruction

There are four modules per grade level that focus on reading, writing, speaking and listening, and language in response to high-quality texts. Each module lasts one quarter of a school year.

Structure of a Module

Each module provides eight weeks of instruction constituting three units. Each unit includes a set of sequenced, coherent progressions of learning experiences that build knowledge and understanding of major concepts. The modules sequence and scaffold content aligned to CCSS for ELA & Literacy.

Module 1	Module 2	Module 3	Module 4
Close Reading and Writing to Learn	Working with Evidence	Understanding Perspectives	Research, Decision Making, and Forming Positions
Unit 1 Building Background Knowledge	Unit 1 Building Background Knowledge	Unit 1 Building Background Knowledge	Unit 1 Building Background Knowledge
Unit 2 Extended Reading and Research	Unit 2 Extended Reading and Research	Unit 2 Extended Reading and Research	Unit 2 Extended Reading and Research
Unit 3 Extended Writing	Unit 3 Extended Writing	Unit 3 Extended Writing	Unit 3 Extended Writing

Module 1 at each grade level establishes the foundation of instructional routines used throughout the year. Individual modules culminate in an end-of-module performance task, similar to those that students will encounter on high-stakes assessments. This assessment provides information to educators on whether students in their classrooms are achieving the standards.

Modules include daily lesson plans, guiding questions, recommended texts, scaffolding strategies, and other classroom resources. Instructional resources address the needs of all learners. Ancillary resources, including graphic organizers and collaborative protocols and formative assessment practices, apply to all modules.

Paths to College and Career is planned and developed according to the principles of Universal Design for Learning (UDL) to support

- English Language Learners (ELL)
- Students with Disabilities (SWD)
- Accelerated learners
- Students achieving and performing below grade level

Each module is designed to be adapted to a group's specific instructional needs. Lessons are not scripts, but are intended to illustrate how instruction might be sequenced. Lessons are adaptable and allow for teacher preference and flexibility both to meet students' needs and to meet the requirements of the shifts and the standards.

Using *Paths to College and Career*

Paths to College and Career provides strong and engaging instruction and learning experiences in each lesson, throughout each unit and module, and across all grade levels. Students develop expertise in the standards as they practice them with a variety of topics and tasks. The routines and protocols are consistent throughout the lessons, units, and modules, and across grade levels. This predictable structure provides scaffolds for students as they grow toward independence and accountability for their own learning.

Launching a Module

Paths to College and Career provides multiple supports in each module to facilitate instructional planning.

The **Module Overview** provides a road map of the entire module, and includes the module's guiding questions and big ideas, a description of the final performance task, key features of the central texts, the standards addressed and assessed in the module, and long-term "I can" statements that translate the standards into student-centered targets.

The **Week-at-a-Glance Calendar** adds detail to the description provided in the Module Overview, including the instructional focus and a brief description of assessments.

A detailed description in the **Module Assessments** section, including the performance task, further clarifies the trajectory of instruction and the specific skills in context that students will understand by the end of the module.

The **Recommended Texts** chart explains the Lexile (quantitative complexity) measure and text type of each literary and nonfiction work in the module.

These overview documents provide a panoramic view of the module and include the information educators need to make decisions about adapting, enhancing, or changing learning activities.

Teaching a Unit

The **Unit Overview** includes the learning targets and standards addressed in this unit, the texts used in this unit, and a lesson-by-lesson overview. Especially helpful at this level of detail are the lesson-level (supporting) learning targets derived from the long-term targets for the module. "Anchor Charts and Protocols" identifies the introduced and reinforced routines in each lesson.

Inside the Lesson

Each lesson, regardless of the topic or timing within the unit, module, or year, has a dependable structure.

The lesson **Opening** engages students in the work of the lesson and reviews learning targets for the day. The lesson opening builds on the work of the prior lesson.

Work Time comprises the bulk of the lesson and may include close reading, note taking, journaling, teacher modeling, vocabulary development, and partner or group work. As students prepare for a mid-unit or end-of-unit assessment, work time may give them an opportunity to plan, draft, revise, and peer- or self-assess. Work Time varies from day to day according to the learning targets, texts, and tasks.

Closing and Assessment includes a debrief of the lesson and homework instructions. In lessons that do not include a specific assessment, there is a brief formative assessment, such as an "Exit Ticket."

Support for the Teacher

In addition to information provided in the module and unit overviews, support is provided throughout the lesson in sections labeled Teaching Notes and Meeting Students' Needs, as well as in the supporting materials.

Teaching Notes describe protocols used in the lesson, and ongoing practices, such as journaling. They also suggest how to prepare for the lesson. The Teaching Notes also include background information that explains how a concept or routine introduced in this lesson will connect to or build toward other lessons.

Meeting Students' Needs discusses the purpose of particular protocols in the lesson and suggestions for visuals, tools, practices, models, or adaptations for students who may need extra support to achieve lesson goals.

Supporting Materials comprise those materials that might be required for the lesson. These materials may include specific reproducible maps, articles, and graphic organizers. The supporting materials are all collected in the Teacher Resource Book that accompanies each module.

Paths to College and Career is truly a complete and integrated English Language Arts curriculum that ensures teaching and learning to the letter and in the spirit of the new standards and the related instructional shifts.

CURRICULUM MAPS

These grades 6–8 curriculum modules are designed to address CCSS ELA outcomes during a 45-minute English Language Arts block. The overarching focus for all modules is on building students' literacy skills as they develop knowledge about the world.

Taken as a whole, these modules are designed to give teachers concrete strategies to address the "instructional shifts" required by the CCSS.

Structure of a Module

Each module provides eight weeks of instruction, broken into three shorter units. Each module includes seven assessments:

- Six unit-level assessments that are almost always on-demand: students' independent work on a reading, writing, speaking, or listening task
- One final performance task that is a more supported project, often involving research

Structure of a Year of Instruction

There are four modules per grade level: Module 1, followed by Module 2, Module 3, then Module 4. Teachers should begin the year with Module 1, which lays the foundation for both teachers and students regarding instructional routines.

How to Read the Curriculum Maps

The purpose of the curriculum map is to provide a high-level summary of each module and name the standards formally assessed in each module.

Module Focus: Read this first. The "focus" is the same across the grades 6–8 band and signals the progression of literacy skills across the year as well as alignment to the CCSS instructional shifts.

Module Title: This signals the topic students will be learning about (often connected to social studies or science) and aligns with Instructional Shift #1, building knowledge through content-rich nonfiction.

Description: These three or four sentences tell the basic "story" of the eight-week arc of instruction: the literacy skills, content knowledge, and central text(s).

Texts: This lists texts that all students read. The texts in bold are the extended texts for a given module: the texts with which students spend the most time. Remember that texts can be complex based on both qualitative and quantitative measures. Texts are listed in order from most quantitatively complex (based on Lexile® measure) to least quantitatively complex. Texts near the bottom of the list are often complex in ways other than Lexile. Within a given module, the list shows the wide variety of texts students read as they build knowledge about a topic. This aligns with Instructional Shift #1, building knowledge through content-rich nonfiction.

Final Performance Task: This is a culminating project, which takes place during Unit 3 of every module. Performance tasks are designed to help students synthesize and apply their learning from the module in an engaging and authentic way. Performance tasks are developed using the writing process, are scaffolded, and almost always include peer critique and revision. Performance tasks are not "on-demand" assessments. (Note: The End-of-Unit 3 Assessment often addresses key components of the performance task.)

Unit-Level Assessments:

- Each unit includes two assessments, most of which are "on-demand" (that is, show what you know/can do on your own).

- Mid-Unit Assessments typically, though not always, are reading assessments: text-based answers.

- End-of-Unit Assessments typically, though not always, are writing assessments: writing from sources.

- Most assessments have a heavy emphasis on academic vocabulary, particularly on determining words in context.

- Assessments are designed to be curriculum-embedded opportunities to practice the types of skills needed on state assessments.

- The curriculum map that follows lists the title of each assessment, the standards assessed, and the assessment format, of which there are five types.

    - Selected response (multiple-choice questions)

    - Short constructed response (short-answer questions of the type that is scored using a 2-point rubric)

    - Extended response (longer writing or essays of the type that is scored using a 4-point rubric) (either on-demand or supported)

    - Speaking and listening (discussion or oral presentation)

    - Scaffolded essay (involving planning, drafting, and revision)

Standards: In each module, the standards formally assessed are indicated with a check mark.

Grade 8 Curriculum Map

	Module 1	Module 2	Module 3	Module 4
Focus	Reading Closely and Writing to Learn	Working with Evidence	Understanding Perspectives	Research, Decision Making, and Forming Positions
Module Title	Finding Home: Refugees	Taking a Stand	Japanese-American Relations in WWII	Sustainability of the World's Food Supply
Description	Students consider the challenges of fictional and real refugees. They read the novel *Inside Out & Back Again*, analyzing critical incidents that reveal the dynamic nature of Ha, a 10-year-old Vietnamese girl whose family flees during the fall of Saigon. They also read complex informational texts to learn more about the history of war in Vietnam, the historical context of Ha's family's struggle, and the universal themes of refugees' experiences of fleeing and finding home. Students consider how Ha's experience represents	Students continue to develop their ability to closely read text while studying the theme of taking a stand. They read several speeches from real people who took a stand, and then immerse themselves in a study of *To Kill a Mockingbird* by Harper Lee. They engage in a character study of Atticus—analyzing his actions and words, and what others say about him—to better understand his willingness to take a stand for others. Students also consider how the theme of "the Golden	Students study the important yet divergent experiences of war and conflict, specifically WWII, as they read *Unbroken*, which tells the story of Louis Zamperini, an American POW in a Japanese camp, alongside an informational text about Miné Okubo, a Japanese American who was interned in a relocation camp in the United States. To build background knowledge, students read primary source documents. They contrast FDR's response to the Pearl Harbor attack	Students learn how to make evidence-based decisions as they consider the issue of how to best feed all the people in the United States. They analyze Michael Pollan's arguments and evidence (as well as the arguments in other informational texts and videos) to determine whether sufficient and relevant evidence has been used to support the claim. They first read *The Omnivore's Dilemma* to build background knowledge about what happens to food before it gets to

the universal refugee experience of being turned "inside out" and then coming "back again." Students work in research groups to study the experiences of refugees from one of several cultures. Then, using the novel's poems as mentor texts, students write free-verse narrative poems that capture the universal refugee experience.	Rule" is rendered new in the novel, and compare and contrast the novel with poems that have this same theme. Finally, students form groups to create a Readers Theater montage based on key quotes from the text, and write an associated commentary to explain how and why their script remains true to but also veers from the original text.	in his "Day of Infamy" speech with the Japanese response in the "Fourteen-Part Message." Finally, students analyze how Zamperini and Okubo faced others' attempts to make them "invisible" during their imprisonment or internment, and how Zamperini became "visible" after the war. For their culminating writing task, students write a research-based narrative that tells the story of how Okubo, too, regained her life and became "visible" again.	the consumer, and the different choices the consumer can make when buying food. Then, students engage in a robust research project in which they investigate the consequences of each of the food chains and the stakeholders affected, and use an evidence-based process to take a position. For a culminating project, students write a position paper addressing the question: Which of Pollan's four food chains would you choose to feed the United States? Why?
Texts (central texts in bold)*			
• *Inside Out & Back Again*, Thanhha Lai (RL, NL) • "Panic Rises in Saigon, but the Exits Are Few," Fox Butterfield (RI, 1200L)	• *To Kill a Mockingbird*, Harper Lee (RL, 870L) • "Those Winter Sundays," Robert Hayden (RL, Poem, NL) • "Incident," Countee Cullen (RL, Poem, NL) • "Solitude," Ella Wheeler Wilcox (RL, Poem, NA)	• *Unbroken: A World War II Story of Survival, Resilience, and Redemption*, Laura Hillenbrand (RI, NL)	• "Antibiotic Debate Overview," PBS (RI, NL) • "The Economic Impact of the Indiana Livestock Industries," Carlos Mayan and Kevin T. McNamara (RI, 1390L)

- "Genetically Engineered Crops—What, How and Why," Pamela Ronald (RI, 1380L)
- "Understanding Concentrated Animal Feeding Operations and Their Impact on Communities," Carrie Hribar and Mark Schulz (RI, 1360L)
- "Interview with an Organic Farmer," Expeditionary Learning (RI, 1330L)
- "Nitrogen Fertilizer Is Bad Stuff—and Not Just Because It Could Blow Up Your Town," Tom Laskaway (RI, 1300L)
- "Food Deserts," Betsy Dru Tecco (RI, 1250L)
- "The Cultivation of Agricultural Subsidies," PBS (RI, 1080L)
- "Lunch or Junk," Scholastic (RI, 1030L)

- "The President Authorizes Japanese Relocation": Excerpt from Executive Order [and posting] No. 9066 Posting (RI, 1550L), Executive Order (RI, 1310L)
- Excerpt from the Munson Report, "The Fifth Column," Walter Lippmann (RI, 1310L)
- "Miné Okubo," Chelsie Hanstad, Louann Huebsch, Danny Kantar, and Kathryn Siewert (RI, 1280L)
- "Day of Infamy," Franklin D. Roosevelt (RI, 1220L)
- "Fourteen-Part Message," Japanese Foreign Ministry (RI, 1170L)
- "War in the Pacific," Edison McIntyre (RI, 1030L)

- "Equal Rights for Women," Shirley Chisholm (RI, 1240L)
- Excerpts from "The Great Society," Lyndon Johnson (RI, 1090L)
- "Ain't I a Woman?" Sojourner Truth (RI, 790L)
- To Kill a Mockingbird. Dir. Robert Mulligan, Perf. Gregory Peck, 1962 (Film)

- "Hard Times in Sarajevo: Cold Weather Comes Early to Bosnia's War-Torn Capital, Bringing More Hardship, Death," Current Events (RI, 1130L)
- "The Vietnam Wars," Tod Olson (RI, 1120L)
- "Peace Patrol: U.S. Troops Will Stay at Least Another Year in Tense Bosnia," Current Events (RI, 1090L)
- "People without a Land," Scholastic Update (RI, 1080L)
- "Refugee Children in Canada: Searching for Identity," Anne Marie Fantino and Alice Colak (RI, 1050L; excerpt)
- "Meet the Kurds," Vera Saeedpour (RI, 1030L)
- "Refugees: Who, Where, and Why," Catherine Gevert (RI, 1020L)

• Til Gurung, speech at Refugee Transitions' World of Difference Benefit Luncheon, San Francisco, November 3, 2010 (RI, 1000L) • "Town Mouse and Country Mouse," Rachel Lehr (RI, 980L) • "Welcome to Sarajevo," *Skipping Stones* (RI, 930L) • "A Place of Her Own," Andrea Faiad (RI, 910L) • "Children of War," Arthur Brice (RI, 855L) • "I Escaped the Taliban," Kristin Baird (RI, 830L) • "Bosnia: The Children of War," Colin Woodard (RI, 820L) • Transcript: "Forgotten Ship: A Daring Rescue as Saigon Fell," Joseph Shapiro and Sandra Bartlett, NPR (RI, 750L) • "Refugee Writing on the Journey," Karim Haidari (RI, 610L)	• "Riverside's Miné Okubo," Mary H. Curtis (RI, NL) • "The Life of Miné Okubo," Expeditionary Learning (RI, 960L) • "The Report on Japanese on the West Coast of the United States," Curtis B. Munson (RI, 910L)	• *The Omnivore's Dilemma* (Young Readers' Edition), Michael Pollan (RI, 930L) • "Birke Baehr: What's Wrong with Our Food System?" (Video) http://www.ted.com/talks/birke_baehr_what_s_wron g_with_our_food_system. html • "Organic Eggs vs. Conventional Farm Eggs, Free Range Chickens, & Ethical Animal Treatment Vital Farms," Vital Farms (Video)

Performance Task	Free Verse Narrative Poems "Inside Out" and "Back Again" (RI.8.1, RI.8.2, W.8.3.a, b, d, W.8.4, W.8.5, W.8.7, W.8.9, L.8.1, L.8.2, and L.8.6) scaffolded narrative poetry	Readers Theater and Analytical Commentary: Taking a Stand in Maycomb (RL.8.2, RL.8.3, W.8.3, and W.8.4) scaffolded narrative	Narrative Writing: Becoming Visible after Internment Presentation and Reflection (W.8.3, W.8.6, W.8.9.b, L.8.1, L.8.1.b, c, L.8.2, L.8.2.c, and L.8.3) scaffolded narrative	Visual Presentation of Position Paper (RI.8.1, W.8.1, W.8.9, and W.8.9.b) research paper
Lexile®	Common Core band level text difficulty ranges for grades 6–8: 925–1185L			

*Texts listed in order of informational text first, then literature; both categories shown from most to least quantitatively complex (based on Lexile®).

**Supplemental Information for Appendix A of the Common Core State Standards for English Language Arts and Literacy: New Research on Text Complexity http://www.corestandards.org/assets/E0813_Appendix_A_New_Research_on_Text_Complexity.pdf

Unit-Level Assessments (ELA CCSS)

	Module 1	Module 2	Module 3	Module 4
Mid-Unit 1	Getting to Know a Character: What Details in the Text Help Us Understand Ha? (RL.8.1, RL.8.3, RL.8.4, W.8.9, and L.8.4.a) selected response and extended response	Analyzing Excerpts of Lyndon Johnson's Speech "The Great Society" (RI.8.2, RI.8.5, and RI.8.6) selected response and short constructed response	Fishbowl Note-Catcher: Understanding Perspectives on the Pearl Harbor Attack (RI.8.1 and RI.8.9) graphic organizer with short constructed response	Analyzing Author's Purpose in Speech and Text (L.8.4.b–d, RI.8.6, and SL.8.2) graphic organizer
End-of-Unit 1	Examining How Word Choice Contributes to Meaning and Tone in Literary and Informational Texts (RL.8.1, RI.8.1, RL.8.4, RI.8.4, and W.8.9) extended response	Analyzing Author's Craft in *To Kill a Mockingbird* and the Poem "Solitude": Allusions, Text Structure, Connections to Traditional Themes, and Use of Figurative Language (RL.8.4, RL.8.5, RL.8.9, and L.8.5.a) graphic organizer, selected response and short constructed response	Fishbowl Discussion: Comparing Conflicting Accounts of the Pearl Harbor Attack (RI.8.9 and SL.8.1) discussion (using graphic organizer as speaking notes)	Evaluating Claims and Advocating Persuasively (RI.8.8, RI.8.9, W.8.9.b, SL.8.2, and SL.8.3) graphic organizer and discussion

Mid-Unit 2	Analyzing an Informational Text about a Refugee Experience (RI.8.1, RI.8.2, RI.8.3, RI.8.4, L.8.4.a, and W.8.9) graphic organizer, selected response, and short constructed response	Text to Film and Perspective Comparison of To Kill a Mockingbird (RL.8.2, RL.8.6, and RL.8.7) graphic organizer, selected response, and short constructed response	Evaluating and Classifying Primary Sources (RI.8.7) graphic organizer	Research Simulation (W.8.7 and W.8.8) selected response and short constructed response
End-of-Unit 2	Analysis Essay: Explain the Significance of the Novel's Title and Its Relationship to Universal Refugee Experiences and Ha's Character (RL.8.1, RL.8.3, RL.8.4, W.8.2, W.8.4, W.8.5, and W.8.9) scaffolded essay	Argument Essay: "Taking a Stand" (RL.8.1, RL.8.2, RL.8.3, W.8.1, W.8.4, W.8.9.a, and L.8.2.a, b) scaffolded essay	Informational Essay and Commentary: "The Invisibility of Captives during WWII" (W.8.2, W.8.9, L.8.2.c, L.8.3) scaffolded essay	Position Speech: "Which of Michael Pollan's Four Food Chains Would Best Feed the United States?" (SL.8.4, SL.8.5, and SL.8.6) oral presentation
Mid-Unit 3	Best First Draft of "Inside Out" Poem (RI.8.1, W.8.3.a, b, d, W.8.7, and W.8.9) on-demand narrative poem	Readers Theater Scene Selection: Justification (RL.8.1 and W.8.9.a) extended response	Single-Draft Narrative Writing (W.8.3, L.8.1, L.8.1.b, c, L.8.2, and L.8.3) on-demand narrative	Draft Position Paper: "Which of Michael Pollan's Four Food Chains Would Best Feed the United States?" (W.8.1, W.8.1.a, b, e) scaffolded essay
End-of-Unit 3	Best First Draft of "Back-Again" Poem (RI.8.1, W.8.3.a, b, d, W.8.7, and W.8.9) on-demand narrative poem	Readers Theater Commentary (RL.8.2 and RL.8.3) extended response	Analysis of Language Techniques (L.8.1.a, d, L.8.5, L.8.5.b, c) selected response and short constructed response	Final Position Paper: "Which of Michael Pollan's Four Food Chains Would Best Feed the United States?" (RI.8.1, W.8.1.c, d, and W.8.9) scaffolded essay and written reflection

Common Core ELA Standards Formally Assessed, by Module

- In the following tables, any specific CCSS with a check mark indicates that the standard is formally assessed.
- Some standards are formally assessed in multiple modules.
- Because of the integrated nature of the standards, even standards that are not formally assessed are often embedded in instruction throughout every module (for example, RI/RL.8.1).
- Some standards are not applicable in an on-demand assessment context (for example, R.8.10 or W.8.10). In the following tables, these standards are noted as "integrated throughout."
- Some standards (for example, W.8.2) have a main or "parent" standard and then subcomponents (for example, W.8.2.a). Often, students' mastery of the entirety of this standard is scaffolded across multiple modules. Therefore, in the following tables, the "parent" standard is checked only if *all* components of that standard are formally assessed within that particular module. Otherwise, just the specific components are checked.

Reading Standards for Literature

	Module 1	Module 2	Module 3	Module 4
RL.8.1. Cite the textual evidence that most strongly supports an analysis of what the text says explicitly as well as inferences drawn from the text.	✓	✓		
RL.8.2. Determine a theme or central idea of a text and analyze its development over the course of the text, including its relationship to the characters, setting, and plot; provide an objective summary of the text.		✓		
RL.8.3. Analyze how particular lines of dialogue or incidents in a story or drama propel the action, reveal aspects of a character, or provoke a decision.	✓	✓		
RL.8.4. Determine the meaning of words and phrases as they are used in a text, including figurative and connotative meanings; analyze the impact of specific word choices on meaning and tone, including analogies or allusions to other texts.	✓	✓		

RL.8.5. Compare and contrast the structure of two or more texts and analyze how the differing structure of each text contributes to its meaning and style.		✓		
RL.8.6. Analyze how differences in the points of view of the characters and the audience or reader (e.g., created through the use of dramatic irony) create such effects as suspense or humor.		✓		
RL.8.7. Analyze the extent to which a filmed or live production of a story or drama stays faithful to or departs from the text or script, evaluating the choices made by the director or actors.		✓		
RL.8.9. Analyze how a modern work of fiction draws on themes, patterns of events, or character types from myths, traditional stories, or religious works such as the Bible, including describing how the material is rendered new.		✓		
RL.8.10. By the end of the year, read and comprehend literature, including stories, dramas, and poems, at the high end of grades 6–8 text complexity band independently and proficiently.	Integrated throughout.			

Reading Standards for Informational Text

	Module 1	Module 2	Module 3	Module 4
RI.8.1. Cite the textual evidence that most strongly supports an analysis of what the text says explicitly as well as inferences drawn from the text.	✓		✓	✓

RI.8.2. Determine a central idea of a text and analyze its development over the course of the text, including its relationship to supporting ideas; provide an objective summary of the text.	✓	✓		
RI.8.3. Analyze how a text makes connections among and distinctions between individuals, ideas, or events (e.g., through comparisons, analogies, or categories).	✓			
RI.8.4. Determine the meaning of words and phrases as they are used in a text, including figurative, connotative, and technical meanings; analyze the impact of specific word choices on meaning and tone, including analogies or allusions to other texts.	✓			
RI.8.5. Analyze in detail the structure of a specific paragraph in a text, including the role of particular sentences in developing and refining a key concept.		✓		
RI.8.6. Determine an author's point of view or purpose in a text and analyze how the author acknowledges and responds to conflicting evidence or viewpoints.		✓		✓
RI.8.7. Evaluate the advantages and disadvantages of using different media (e.g., print or digital text, video, multimedia) to present a particular topic or idea.			✓	
RI.8.8. Delineate and evaluate the argument and specific claims in a text, assessing whether the reasoning is sound and the evidence is relevant and sufficient; recognize when irrelevant evidence is introduced.				✓
RI.8.9. Analyze a case in which two or more texts provide conflicting information on the same topic and identify where the texts disagree on matters of fact or interpretation.			✓	

RI.8.10. By the end of the year, read and comprehend literary nonfiction at the high end of the grades 6–8 text complexity band independently and proficiently.	Integrated throughout.			

Writing Standards

	Module 1	Module 2	Module 3	Module 4
W.8.1. Write arguments to support claims with clear reasons and relevant evidence.		✓		✓
a. Introduce claim(s), acknowledge and distinguish the claim(s) from alternate or opposing claims, and organize the reasons and evidence logically.		✓		✓
b. Support claim(s) with logical reasoning and relevant evidence, using accurate, credible sources and demonstrating an understanding of the topic or text.		✓		✓
c. Use words, phrases, and clauses to create cohesion and clarify the relationships among claim(s), counterclaims, reasons, and evidence.		✓		✓
d. Establish and maintain a formal style.		✓		✓
e. Provide a concluding statement or section that follows from and supports the argument presented.		✓		✓
W.8.2. Write informative/explanatory texts to examine a topic and convey ideas, concepts, and information through the selection, organization, and analysis of relevant content.	✓		✓	
a. Introduce a topic clearly, previewing what is to follow; organize ideas, concepts, and information into broader categories; include formatting (e.g., headings), graphics (e.g., charts, tables), and multimedia when useful to aiding comprehension.	✓		✓	

b. Develop the topic with relevant, well-chosen facts, definitions, concrete details, quotations, or other information and examples.	✓		✓	
c. Use appropriate and varied transitions to create cohesion and clarify the relationships among ideas and concepts.	✓		✓	
d. Use precise language and domain-specific vocabulary to inform about or explain the topic.	✓		✓	
e. Establish and maintain a formal style.	✓		✓	
f. Provide a concluding statement or section that follows from and supports the information or explanation presented.	✓		✓	
W.8.3. Write narratives to develop real or imagined experiences or events using effective technique, relevant descriptive details, and well-structured event sequences.		✓	✓	
a. Engage and orient the reader by establishing a context and point of view and introducing a narrator and/or characters; organize an event sequence that unfolds naturally and logically.	✓	✓	✓	
b. Use narrative techniques, such as dialogue, pacing, description, and reflection, to develop experiences, events, and/or characters.	✓	✓	✓	
c. Use a variety of transition words, phrases, and clauses to convey sequence, signal shifts from one time frame or setting to another, and show the relationships among experiences and events.		✓	✓	
d. Use precise words and phrases, relevant descriptive details, and sensory language to capture the action and convey experiences and events.	✓	✓	✓	
e. Provide a conclusion that follows from and reflects on the narrated experiences or events.		✓	✓	

W.8.4. Produce clear and coherent writing in which the development, organization, and style are appropriate to task, purpose, and audience. (Grade-specific expectations for writing types are defined in standards 1–3 above.)	✓	✓		
W.8.5. With some guidance and support from peers and adults, develop and strengthen writing as needed by planning, revising, editing, rewriting, or trying a new approach, focusing on how well purpose and audience have been addressed.	Integrated throughout.			
W.8.6. Use technology, including the Internet, to produce and publish writing and present the relationships between information and ideas efficiently as well as to interact and collaborate with others.	Integrated throughout.			
W.8.7. Conduct short research projects to answer a question (including a self-generated question), drawing on several sources and generating additional related, focused questions that allow for multiple avenues of exploration.	✓			✓
W.8.8. Gather relevant information from multiple print and digital sources, using search terms effectively; assess the credibility and accuracy of each source; and quote or paraphrase the data and conclusions of others while avoiding plagiarism and following a standard format for citation.				✓
W.8.9. Draw evidence from literary or informational texts to support analysis, reflection, and research.	✓	✓	✓	✓

	Module 1	Module 2	Module 3	Module 4
a. Apply *grade 8 Reading standards* to literature (e.g., "Analyze how a modern work of fiction draws on themes, patterns of events, or character types from myths, traditional stories, or religious works such as the Bible, including describing how the material is rendered new").	✓	✓		
b. Apply *grade 8 Reading standards* to literary nonfiction (e.g., "Delineate and evaluate the argument and specific claims in a text, assessing whether the reasoning is sound and the evidence is relevant and sufficient; recognize when irrelevant evidence is introduced").	✓		✓	✓
W.8.10. Write routinely over extended time frames (time for research, reflection, and revision) and shorter time frames (a single sitting or a day or two).	Integrated throughout.			

Speaking & Listening Standards

	Module 1	Module 2	Module 3	Module 4
SL.8.1. Engage effectively in a range of collaborative discussions (one-on-one, in groups, and teacher-led) with diverse partners on *grade 8 topics, texts, and issues,* building on others' ideas and expressing their own clearly.			✓	
a. Come to discussions prepared, having read or researched material under study; explicitly draw on that preparation by referring to evidence on the topic, text, or issue to probe and reflect on ideas under discussion.			✓	

b. Follow rules for collegial discussions and decision-making, track progress toward specific goals and deadlines, and define individual roles as needed.			✓	
c. Pose questions that connect the ideas of several speakers and respond to others' questions and comments with relevant evidence, observations, and ideas.			✓	
d. Acknowledge new information expressed by others, and, when warranted, qualify or justify their own views in light of the evidence presented.			✓	
SL.8.2. Analyze the purpose of information presented in diverse media and formats (e.g., visually, quantitatively, orally) and evaluate the motives (e.g., social, commercial, political) behind its presentation.				✓
SL.8.3. Delineate a speaker's argument and specific claims, evaluating the soundness of the reasoning and relevance and sufficiency of the evidence and identifying when irrelevant evidence is introduced.				✓
SL.8.4. Present claims and findings, emphasizing salient points in a focused, coherent manner with relevant evidence, sound valid reasoning, and well-chosen details; use appropriate eye contact, adequate volume, and clear pronunciation.				✓
SL.8.5. Include multimedia components (e.g., graphics, images, music, sound) and visual displays in presentations to clarify information.				✓
SL.8.6. Adapt speech to a variety of contexts and tasks, demonstrating command of formal English when indicated or appropriate.				✓

Language Standards

	Module 1	Module 2	Module 3	Module 4
L.8.1. Demonstrate command of the conventions of standard English grammar and usage when writing or speaking.			✓	
a. Explain the function of verbals (gerunds, participles, infinitives) in general and their function in particular sentences.			✓	
b. Form and use verbs in the active and passive voice.			✓	
c. Form and use verbs in the indicative, imperative, interrogative, conditional, and subjunctive mood.			✓	
d. Recognize and correct inappropriate shifts in verb voice and mood.			✓	
L.8.2. Demonstrate command of the conventions of standard English capitalization, punctuation, and spelling when writing.			✓	
a. Use punctuation (comma, ellipsis, dash) to indicate a pause or break.		✓		
b. Use an ellipsis to indicate an omission.		✓		
c. Spell correctly.			✓	
L.8.3. Use knowledge of language and its conventions when writing, speaking, reading, or listening.			✓	
a. Use verbs in the active and passive voice and in the conditional and subjunctive mood to achieve particular effects (e.g., emphasizing the actor or the action; expressing uncertainty or describing a state contrary to fact).			✓	
L.8.4. Determine or clarify the meaning of unknown and multiple-meaning words or phrases based on *grade 8 Reading and content,* choosing flexibly from a range of strategies.				✓

a. Use context (e.g., the overall meaning of a sentence or paragraph; a word's position or function in a sentence) as a clue to the meaning of a word or phrase.	✓			
b. Use common, grade-appropriate Greek or Latin affixes and roots as clues to the meaning of a word (e.g., *precede, recede, secede*).				✓
c. Consult general and specialized reference materials (e.g., dictionaries, glossaries, thesauruses), both print and digital, to find the pronunciation of a word or determine or clarify its precise meaning or its part of speech.				✓
d. Verify the preliminary determination of the meaning of a word or phrase (e.g., by checking the inferred meaning in context or in a dictionary).				✓
L.8.5. Demonstrate understanding of figurative language, word relationships, and nuances in word meanings.			✓	
a. Interpret figures of speech (e.g., verbal irony, puns) in context.		✓		
b. Use the relationship between particular words to better understand each of the words.			✓	
c. Distinguish among the connotations (associations) of words with similar denotations (definitions) (e.g., *bullheaded, willful, firm, persistent, resolute*).			✓	
L.8.6. Acquire and use accurately grade-appropriate general academic and domain-specific words and phrases; gather vocabulary knowledge when considering a word or phrase important to comprehension or expression.	✓			

ELA Curriculum: Grades 6–8 Curriculum Plan

	Module 1: Reading Closely and Writing to Learn	Module 2: Working with Evidence	Module 3: Understanding Perspectives	Module 4: Reading for Research and Writing an Argument
Topic	Myths: Not Just Long Ago	Rules to Live By	The Land of the Golden Mountain	Insecticides: Costs versus Benefits
Central Texts*	RL—*The Lightning Thief*, Rick Riordan	RL—*Bud, Not Buddy*, Christopher Paul Curtis RI—"Stanford University Commencement Address," Steve Jobs	RL—*Dragonwings*, Laurence Yep RI—"Comprehending the Calamity," Emma M. Burke	RL—*Frightful's Mountain*, Jean Craighead George RI—"The Exterminator," Kristen Weir
Writing Tasks*	• Literary Analysis— Connecting Themes in "Cronus" and *The Lightning Thief* (RL.6.2, W.6.2, W.6.9) • "My Hero's Journey" Narrative (RL.6.3, Writing W.6.3)	• Argument: "How Does Bud Use His Rules: To Survive or to Thrive?" (RL.6.3, W.6.1, W.6.9) • Research/Inform: "My Rule to Live By" (RL.6.3, W.6.2)	• Literary Analysis: How Do the Author's Purposes Affect the Narrator's Points of View? (W.6.2, W.6.9) • Newspaper Article: "How the 1906 San Francisco Earthquake and Fire Affected the People of San Francisco" (W.6.2, W.6.7)	• Research Simulation (W.6.7, 6.8, 6.9) • Position Paper: "Do the Benefits of DDT Outweigh Its Harmful Consequences?" (W.6.1, W.6.9)

GRADE 6

Topic	Journeys and Survival	Working Conditions	Slavery: The People Could Fly	Screen Time and the Developing Brain
Central Texts*	RL—*A Long Walk to Water*, Linda Sue Park RI—"Sudanese Tribes Confront Modern War," Karl Vick	RL—*Lyddie*, Katherine Patterson RI—"Commonwealth Club Address," César Chávez	RI—*Narrative of the Life of Frederick Douglass* (excerpts)	No text purchase required; students will read only articles about the adolescent brain and the effects of technology use, provided in lesson supporting materials.
Writing Tasks**	• Literary Analysis: Writing about the Theme of Survival (RL.7.1, RL.7.2, W.7.2, W.7.9) • Research-Based Two-Voice Poem (RL.7.6, W.7.3, W.7.9)	• Argument: "Should Lyddie Sign the Petition?" (RL.7.3, W.7.1) • "Consumer's Guide to Working Conditions in the Garment Industry" (W.7.2, W.7.6, W.7.7)	• Literary Nonfiction Analysis: Analyzing Douglass's Position in the *Narrative* (RI.7.2, RI.7.6, W.7.2, W.7.9) • Children's Book to Retell an Episode from the *Narrative* (W.7.3, W.7.9)	• Research Simulation (W.7.7, W.7.8, W.7.9) • Position Paper: "Should the American Academy of Pediatrics Raise Its Recommended Daily Entertainment Screen Time from Two Hours to Four Hours?" (RI.7.1, W.7.1, W.7.4, W.7.5)

GRADE 7

Topic	Finding Home: Refugees	Working with Evidence: Taking a Stand	Japanese American Relations in WWII	Sustainability of World's Food Supply
Central Texts*	RL – *Inside Out & Back Again*, Thanhha Lai RI—"The Vietnam Wars," Tod Olson	RL—*To Kill a Mockingbird*, Harper Lee RI—"Equal Rights for Women," Chisholm RI—"Ain't I a Woman?" Sojourner Truth	RI—*Unbroken: A World War II Story of Survival, Resilience, and Redemption*, Laura Hillenbrand	RI—*The Omnivore's Dilemma: The Secrets Behind What You Eat*, Michael Pollan (Young Readers' Edition)
Writing Tasks**	• Literary Analysis: Explain the Significance of the Novel's Title (RL.8.1, RL.8.3, RI.8.1, W.8.2, W.8.9) • Research-Based Free Verse Narrative Poems: "Inside Out" and "Back Again" (RI.8.1, RI.8.2, W.8.3, W.8.9)	• Argument: "Taking a Stand" (RL.8.1, RL.8.2, RL.8.3, W.8.1) • Readers Theater and Analytical Commentary: Taking a Stand in Maycomb (W.8.3)	• Informational Essay: "Invisibility of Captives during WWII" (RI.8.1, W.8.2, W.8.9) • Research-Based Narrative: "Becoming Visible after Internment" (RI.8.1, W.8.3)	• Research Simulation (W.8.7, W.8.8, W.8.9) • Position Paper: "Which of Michael Pollan's Four Food Chains Would Best Feed the United States?" (W.8.1, W.8.9)

GRADE 8

*This plan shows most full-length books all students read and a few key articles. See separate document "Trade Books and Other Resources" for a complete list of resources needed in order to implement the modules.

**This plan shows the two main writing tasks per module and the standards most central to each task. See the curriculum map for the full list of standards assessed (including the writing process and language standards).

MODULE OVERVIEW

Finding Home

Refugees

In this module, students will develop their abilities to read and understand complex text as they consider the challenges of fictional and real refugees. In Unit 1, students will begin reading the novel *Inside Out & Back Again,* by Thanhha Lai, analyzing how critical incidents reveal the dynamic nature of the main character, Ha, a 10-year-old Vietnamese girl whose family is deciding whether to flee during the fall of Saigon. The novel, poignantly told in free verse, will challenge students to consider the impact of specific word choice on tone and meaning. Students will build their abilities to infer and analyze text, both in discussion and through writing. They will then read informational text to learn more about the history of wars in Vietnam and the specific historical context of Ha's family's struggle during the fall of Saigon. In Unit 2, students will build their knowledge about refugees' search for a place to call home. They will read informational texts that convey universal central ideas of refugees' experiences across various times and cultures as they flee and find new homes. As they continue to move through *Inside Out & Back Again,* students will focus on how particular incidents move the story forward and reveal aspects of Ha's character. Unit 2 culminates with students examining how the universal refugee experience causes a refugee's life to be turned "inside out" and eventually turned "back again." In Unit 3, having finished the novel, students will reread critical incidents while also working in research groups to study the experiences of refugees from one of several cultures. Students will use this knowledge to write two free-verse narrative poems that capture the universal refugee experience. They will also reread poems from the novel as mentor texts. **The free-verse narrative poems performance task centers on ELA CCSS RI.8.1, RI.8.2, W.8.3, W.8.4, W.8.5, W.8.7, W.8.9, L.8.1, and L.8.2.**

Guiding Questions and Big Ideas

- What is home?
- How do critical incidents reveal character?
- Which common themes unify the refugee experience?
- How can we tell powerful stories about people's experiences?
- *Critical incidents reveal a character's dynamic nature.*

- *Characters change over time in response to challenges.*
- *Authors select a genre of writing to engage the reader fully.*

Performance Task

Write Free-Verse Narrative Poems: "Inside Out" and "Back Again"

For the final performance task of Module 1, students will draw upon their study of the universal refugee experience to write two research-based poems that reflect the "inside out" and "back again" aspects of a refugee's life. Students will collaborate in teams to research the experiences of refugees of a specific culture. They then will draw upon their research and their study of the novel and the informational texts to write two poems. The first poem, "Inside Out," will be based on the research conducted, and the second poem, the more creative "Back Again," will be aligned with each student's individual interpretation of informational text and his or her own background knowledge and experiences. For the final performance task, the students will have the opportunity to revise, edit, and share their two poems within the classroom and with other research teams. **This task centers on CCSS RI.8.1, RI.8.2, W.8.3, W.8.4, W.8.5, W.8.7, W.8.9, L.8.1, L.8.2, and L.8.6.**

Content Connections

This module is designed to address the CCS English Language Arts (ELA) standards. However, the module intentionally incorporates social studies content, as described below.

Social Studies Connections

Social Studies Themes in Context:

- Individual Development and Cultural Identity
  - Role of social, political, and cultural interactions in the development of identity
  - Personal identity as a function of an individual's culture, time, place, geography, interaction with groups, influences from institutions, and lived experiences
- Development, Movement, and Interaction of Cultures
  - Role of diversity within and among cultures

EXPEDITIONARY
LEARNING

English Language Arts Outcomes

CCSS Assessed in This Module: Reading—Literature	Long-Term Learning Targets
• RL.8.1. Cite the textual evidence that most strongly supports an analysis of what the text says explicitly as well as inferences drawn from the text.	• I can cite text-based evidence that provides the strongest support for my analysis of literary text.
• RL.8.3. Analyze how particular lines of dialogue or incidents in a story or drama propel the action, reveal aspects of a character, or provoke a decision.	• I can analyze how specific dialogue or incidents in a plot propel the action, reveal aspects of a character, or provoke a decision.
• RL.8.4. Determine the meaning of words and phrases as they are used in a text, including figurative and connotative meanings; analyze the impact of specific word choices on meaning and tone, including analogies or allusions to other texts.	• I can determine the meaning of words and phrases in literary text (figurative, connotative, and technical meanings). • I can analyze the impact of word choice on meaning and tone (analogies or allusions to other texts).
• RL.8.5. Compare and contrast the structure of two or more texts and analyze how the differing structure of each text contributes to its meaning and style.	• I can compare and contrast the structure of multiple texts. • I can analyze how different structures impact meaning and style of a text.
• RL.8.6. Analyze full-length novels, short stories, poems, and other genres by authors who represent diverse world cultures.	• I can analyze full-length novels, short stories, poems, and other genres by authors who represent diverse world cultures.
CCSS Assessed in This Module: Reading—Informational Text	**Long-Term Learning Targets**
• RI.8.1. Cite the textual evidence that most strongly supports an analysis of what the text says explicitly as well as inferences drawn from the text.	• I can cite text-based evidence that provides the strongest support for an analysis of informational text.
• RI.8.2. Determine a central idea of a text and analyze its development over the course of the text, including its relationship to supporting ideas; provide an objective summary of the text.	• I can determine the central idea of an informational text. • I can analyze the development of a central idea throughout the text (including its relationship to supporting ideas). • I can objectively summarize informational text.

• RI.8.3. Analyze how a text makes connections among and distinctions between individuals, ideas, or events (e.g., through comparisons, analogies, or categories).	• I can analyze the connections and distinctions between individuals, ideas, or events in a text.
• RI.8.4. Determine the meaning of words and phrases as they are used in a text, including figurative, connotative, and technical meanings; analyze the impact of specific word choices on meaning and tone, including analogies or allusions to other texts.	• I can determine the meaning of words and phrases in text (figurative, connotative, and technical meanings). • I can analyze the impact of word choice on meaning and tone (analogies or allusions to other texts).

CCSS Assessed in This Module: Writing	Long-Term Learning Targets

• W.8.2. Write informative/explanatory texts to examine a topic and convey ideas, concepts, and information through the selection, organization, and analysis of relevant content.
 	
  a. Introduce a topic clearly, previewing what is to follow; organize ideas, concepts, and information into broader categories; include formatting (e.g., headings), graphics (e.g., charts, tables), and multimedia when useful to aid comprehension.
 	
  b. Develop the topic with relevant, well-chosen facts, definitions, concrete details, quotations, or other information and examples.
 	
  c. Use appropriate and varied transitions to create cohesion and clarify the relationships among ideas and concepts.
 	
  d. Use precise language and domain-specific vocabulary to inform about or explain the topic.
 	
  e. Establish and maintain a formal style.
 	
  f. Provide a concluding statement or section that follows and supports the information or explanation presented.
	• I can write informative/explanatory texts that convey ideas and concepts using relevant information that is carefully selected and organized.

• W.8.3. Write narratives to develop real or imagined experiences or events using effective technique, relevant descriptive details, and well-structured event sequences.
 	
  a. Engage and orient the reader by establishing a context and point of view and introducing a narrator and/or characters; organize an event sequence that unfolds naturally and logically.
 	
  b. Use narrative techniques, such as dialogue, pacing, description, and reflection, to develop experiences, events, and/or characters.
 	
  d. Use precise words and phrases, relevant descriptive details, and sensory language to capture the action and convey experiences and events.
	• I can write narrative texts about real or imagined experiences using relevant details and event sequences that make sense.

• W.8.4. Produce clear and coherent writing in which the development, organization, and style are appropriate to task, purpose, and audience.	• I can produce clear and coherent writing that is appropriate to task, purpose, and audience.
• W.8.5. With some guidance and support from peers and adults, develop and strengthen writing as needed by planning, revising, editing, rewriting, or trying a new approach, focusing on how well purpose and audience have been addressed.	• With support from peers and adults, I can use the writing process to ensure that purpose and audience have been addressed.
• W.8.7. Conduct short research projects to answer a question (including a self-generated question), drawing on several sources and generating additional related, focused questions that allow for multiple avenues of exploration.	• I can conduct short research projects to answer a question (including a self-generated question). • I can use several sources in my research. • I can generate additional research questions for further exploration.
• W.8.9. Draw evidence from literary or informational texts to support analysis, reflection, and research. a. Apply *grade 8 Reading standards* to literature (e.g., "Analyze how a modern	• I can use evidence from literary or informational texts to support analysis, reflection, and research.

work of fiction draws on central ideas, patterns of events, or character types from myths, traditional stories, or religious works such as the *Bible,* including describing how the material is rendered new").

b.   Apply *grade 8 Reading standards* to literary nonfiction (e.g., "Delineate and evaluate the argument and specific claims in a text, assessing whether the reasoning is sound and the evidence is relevant and sufficient; recognize when irrelevant evidence is introduced").

CCSS Assessed in This Module: Speaking & Listening	Long-Term Learning Targets
• SL.8.1. Engage effectively in a range of collaborative discussions (one-on-one, in groups, and teacher-led) with diverse partners on eighth-grade topics, texts, and issues, building on others' ideas and expressing their own clearly. a. Come to discussions prepared, having read or researched material under study; explicitly draw on that preparation by referring to evidence on the topic, text, or issue to probe and reflect on ideas under discussion. b. Follow rules for collegial discussions and decision making, track progress toward specific goals and deadlines, and define individual roles as needed. c. Pose questions that connect the ideas of several speakers, and respond to others' questions and comments with relevant evidence, observations, and ideas. d. Acknowledge new information expressed by others, and, when warranted, qualify or justify their own views in light of the evidence presented.	• I can effectively engage in discussions with diverse partners about eighth-grade topics, texts, and issues. • I can express my own ideas clearly during discussions. • I can build on others' ideas during discussions.

CCSS Assessed in This Module: Language	Long-Term Learning Targets

• L.8.1. Demonstrate command of the conventions of standard English grammar and usage when writing or speaking.
 	
  a. Form and use verbs in the active and passive voice.
 	
  b. Recognize and correct inappropriate shifts in verb voice and mood.
	• I can use correct grammar and usage when writing or speaking.

• L.8.2. Demonstrate command of the conventions of standard English capitalization, punctuation, and spelling when writing.
 	
  a. Use punctuation (comma, ellipsis, dash) to indicate a pause or break.
 	
  b. Spell correctly.
	• I can use correct capitalization, punctuation, and spelling to send a clear message to my reader.

• L.8.4. Determine or clarify the meaning of unknown and multiple-meaning words or phrases based on *grade 8 Reading and content*, choosing flexibly from a range of strategies. a. Use context (e.g., the overall meaning of a sentence or paragraph; a word's position or function in a sentence) as a clue to the meaning of a word or phrase.	• I can use a variety of strategies to determine the meaning of unknown words or phrases.

• L.8.5. Demonstrate understanding of figurative language, word relationships, and nuances in word meanings.
 	
  a. Interpret figures of speech (e.g., verbal irony, puns) in context.
 	
  b. Use the relationship between particular words to better understand each of the words.
 	
  c. Distinguish among the connotations (associations) of words with similar denotations (definitions) (e.g., bullheaded, willful, firm, persistent, resolute).
	• I can analyze figurative language, word relationships, and nuances in word meanings.

| • L.8.6. Acquire and use accurately grade-appropriate general academic and domain-specific words and phrases; gather vocabulary knowledge when considering a word or phrase important to comprehension or expression. | • I can accurately use eighth-grade academic vocabulary to express my ideas.
• I can use resources to build my vocabulary. |

Central Texts

1. Thanhha Lai, *Inside Out & Back Again.* New York: HarperCollins, 2011.

2. Tod Olson, "The Vietnam Wars," *Scholastic,* February 24, 1995, 16–20.

3. Joseph Shapiro and Sandra Bartlett, "Forgotten Ship: A Daring Rescue as Saigon Fell," transcript, National Public Radio, August 31, 2010.

4. Fox Butterfield, "Panic Rises in Saigon, but the Exits Are Few," *New York Times,* April 24, 1975.

5. Catherine Gevert, "Refugees: Who, Where, and Why," *Faces: People, Places and Cultures* 19, no. 1 (2002): 6–8.

6. Arthur Brice, "Children of War," *Scholastic,* March 1994.

7. Til Gurung, speech at Refugee Transitions' World of Difference Benefit Luncheon, San Francisco, November 3, 2010.

8. Ana Marie Fantino and Alice Colak, "Refugee Children in Canada: Searching for Identity," *Child Welfare* 80, no. 5 (2001): 587–596.

See the Supporting Materials for Unit 2, Lesson 19, for a complete list of texts students use in their short research project.

EXPEDITIONARY
LEARNING

Week-at-a-Glance Calendar

Week	Instructional Focus	Long-Term Targets	Assessments
Unit 1: War Coming Close to Home			
Weeks 1–3	• Launch study of the novel *Inside Out & Back Again*. • Perform a character analysis of the main character. • Build background knowledge about the history and culture of Vietnam.	• I can cite text-based evidence that provides the strongest support for my analysis of literary text. (RL.8.1) • I can analyze how specific dialogue or incidents in a plot propel the action, reveal aspects of a character, or provoke a decision. (RL.8.3) • I can determine the meaning of words and phrases in literary text (figurative, connotative, and technical meanings). (RL.8.4) • I can analyze the impact of word choice on meaning and tone (analogies or allusions). (RL.8.4) • I can use evidence from literary texts to support analysis, reflection, and research. (W.8.9) • I can use a variety of strategies to determine the meaning of unknown words or phrases. (L.8.4.a)	• Mid-Unit 1: Getting to Know a Character: Which Details in the Text Help Us Understand Ha? (RL.8.1, RL.8.3, RL.8.4, W.8.9, L.8.4.a)
	• Continue with Part 1 of the novel. • Compare historical fiction with informational text: purpose and perspective. • Build background knowledge about the fall of Saigon.	• I can cite text-based evidence that provides the strongest support for my analysis of literary text. (RL.8.1) • I can cite text-based evidence that provides the strongest support for an analysis of informational text. (RI.8.1)	

| Weeks 1–3, continued | • Continue with Part 1 of the novel.
• Listen and read about the fall of Saigon: read-aloud text and transcript.
• Analyze word choice, meaning, and tone. | • I can cite text-based evidence that provides the strongest support for my analysis of literary text. (RL.8.1)
• I can cite text-based evidence that provides the strongest support for an analysis of informational text. (RI.8.1)
• I can analyze the impact of word choice on meaning and tone. (RL.8.4, RI.8.4)
• I can use evidence from literature and informational texts to support analysis, reflection, and research. (W.8.9) | • End-of-Unit 1: Examining How Word Choice Contributes to Meaning and Tone in Literary and Informational Text (RL.8.1, RI.8.1, RL.8.4, RI.8.4, W.8.9) |

Unit 2: Case Study: Why Do People Flee Home?

| Weeks 4–7 | • Analyze unifying central ideas of refugees' experiences.
• Closely read and compare texts; continue reading the novel, paired with informational texts regarding the universal refugee experience. | • I can cite text-based evidence that provides the strongest support for my analysis of literary text. (RL.8.1)
• I can analyze how specific dialogue or incidents in a plot propel the action, reveal aspects of a character, or provoke a decision. (RL.8.3)
• I can cite text-based evidence that provides the strongest support for my analysis of informational text. (RI.8.1)
• I can determine a theme or the central ideas of an informational text. (RI.8.2)
• I can analyze the development of a theme or central idea throughout the text (including its relationship to supporting ideas). (RI.8.2)
• I can analyze the connections and distinctions between individuals, ideas, or events in a text. (RI.8.3)
• I can determine the meaning of words and phrases in text (figurative, connotative, and technical meanings). (RI.8.4)
• I can use a variety of strategies to determine the meaning of unknown words or phrases. (L.8.4) | |

| Weeks 4–7, continued | • Perform close reading of a complex informational text to deepen students' understanding of the universal refugee experience.

• Analyze the significance of the novel's title by connecting the universal refugee experience to *Inside Out & Back Again*.

• Prepare to write an analysis essay by examining a model essay and the essay rubric. | • I can cite text-based evidence that provides the strongest support for my analysis of literary text. (RL.8.1)

• I can analyze how specific dialogue or incidents in a plot propel the action, reveal aspects of a character, or provoke a decision. (RL.8.3)

• I can write informative/explanatory texts that convey ideas and concepts using relevant information that is carefully selected and organized. (W.8.2)

• I can cite text-based evidence that provides the strongest support for an analysis of literary text. (RI.8.1)

• I can determine the central ideas of literary text. (RI.8.2)

• I can analyze the development of a central idea throughout the text (including its relationship to the characters, setting, and plot). (RI.8.2)

• I can analyze the connections and distinctions between individuals, ideas, or events in a text. (RI.8.3)

• I can analyze the structure of a specific paragraph in a text (including the role of particular sentences in developing and refining a key concept).

• I can read above-grade informational texts with scaffolding and support. (RI.8.10)

• I can use a variety of strategies to determine the meaning of unknown words or phrases. (L.8.4)

• I can use evidence from informational texts to support analysis, reflection, and research. (W.8.9) | • Mid-Unit 2: Analyzing an Informational Text about a Refugee Experience (RI.8.1, RI.8.2, RI.8.3, RI.8.4, L.8.4, W.8.9) |

| Weeks 4–7, continued | • Draft, revise, and edit the literary essay.
• Introduce the final performance task and initial research guidelines.
• Closely read critical incidents in the novel related to aspects of the research-based narrative. | • I can cite text-based evidence that provides the strongest support for my analysis of literary text. (RL.8.1)
• I can analyze how specific dialogue or incidents in a plot propel the action, reveal aspects of a character, or provoke a decision. (RL.8.3)
• I can analyze the impact of word choice on meaning and tone. (RL.8.4)
• I can cite text-based evidence that provides the strongest support for my analysis of literary text. (RI.8.1)
• I can write informative/explanatory texts that convey ideas and concepts using relevant information that is carefully selected and organized. (W.8.2)
• I can produce clear and coherent writing that is appropriate to the task, purpose, and audience. (W.8.4)
• With support from peers and adults, I can use the writing process to ensure that the purpose and audience have been addressed. (W.8.5)
• I can conduct short research projects to answer a question. (W.8.7)
• I can use evidence from literary texts to support analysis, reflection, and research. (W.8.9) | • End-of-Unit 2: Analysis Essay: Explain the Significance of the Novel's Title and Its Relationship to Universal Refugee Experiences and Ha's Character (RL.8.1, RL.8.3, RL.8.4, RI.8.1, W.8.2, W.8.4, W.8.5, W.8.9) |

Unit 3: Free-Verse Poems "Inside Out" and "Back Again"

Week 8		
• Undertake structured research and plan for research-based, free-verse narrative poems. • Mentor text writing: select a snapshot of the planned story to write two free-verse, narrative poems, using the novel as a mentor text. • Draft, revise, and edit a research-based narrative.	• I can cite text-based evidence that provides the strongest support for my analysis of informational text. (RI.8.1) • I can conduct short research projects to answer a question (including a self-generated question). (W.8.7) • I can use several sources in my research. (W.8.7) • I can generate additional research questions for further exploration. (W.8.7) • I can cite text-based evidence that provides the strongest support for an analysis of informational text. (RI.8.1) • I can write narrative texts about real or imagined experiences using relevant details and event sequences that make sense. (W.8.3) • I can produce clear and coherent writing that is appropriate to task, purpose, and audience. (W.8.4) • With support from peers and adults, I can use the writing process to ensure that the purpose and audience have been addressed. (W.8.5) • I can conduct short research projects to answer a question (including a self-generated question). (W.8.7) • I can use several sources in my research. (W.8.7) • I can use evidence from informational texts to support analysis, reflection, and research. (W.8.9)	• Mid-Unit 3: Writing Best First Draft of "Inside Out" Poem (RI.8.1; W.8.3.a, b, d; W.8.7; W.8.9) • End-of-Unit 3: Writing Best First Draft of "Back Again" Poem (RI.8.1, W.8.3, W.3.7, W.8.9) • Final Performance Task: Free-Verse Narrative Poems "Inside Out" and "Back Again" (RI.8.1, RI.8.2, W.8.3, W.8.4, W.8.5, W.8.7, W.8.9, L.8.1, L.8.2, L.8.6.)

| Week 8 continued | | • I can use correct grammar and usage when writing or speaking. (L.8.1)

• I can use correct capitalization, punctuation, and spelling to send a clear message to my reader. (L.8.2)

• I can accurately use eighth-grade academic vocabulary to express my ideas. (L.8.6) |

ASSESSMENT OVERVIEW

Final Performance Task

Free-Verse Narrative Poems "Inside Out" and "Back Again"

For the final performance task of Module 1, students will draw upon their study of the universal refugee experience to write two research-based poems that reflect the "inside out" and "back again" aspects of a refugee's life. Students will collaborate in research teams to research the experiences of refugees of a specific culture. They then will draw upon the research as well as their study of the novel and the informational texts to write two poems. The first, an "Inside Out" poem, will be based on the research conducted. The second, the more creative "Back Again" poem, will be aligned with each student's individual interpretation of informational text as well as his or her own background knowledge and experiences. The students will have the opportunity to revise, edit, and share their two poems within the classroom and with other research teams for the final performance task. **This task centers on CCSS RI.8.1; RI.8.2; W.8.3.a, b, d; W.8.4; W.8.5; W.8.7; W.8.9; L.8.1; L.8.2; and L.8.6.**

Mid-Unit 1 Assessment

Getting to Know a Character: Which Details in the Text Help Us Understand Ha?

This assessment centers on standards ELA CCSS RL.8.1, RL.8.3, RL.8.4, W.8.9, and L.8.4.a. Students will read the poem "Birthday Wishes" from the novel and answer selected-response questions to analyze the poem for the author's word choice, tone, and meaning. Questions will include determining word meaning from context. Students then will write a paragraph in response to the following prompt: "Who is Ha? Based on this poem, 'Birthday Wishes,' and one other poem you have read so far in the novel, describe Ha as a character: her traits, values, or beliefs. Write a paragraph in which you explain your current understanding of Ha, using specific evidence from the text of both poems to support your analysis."

End-of-Unit 1 Assessment

Examining How Word Choice Contributes to Meaning and Tone in Literary and Informational Text

This assessment centers on standards ELA CCSS RL.8.1, RI.8.1, RL.8.4, RI.8.4, and W.8.9. For this reading and writing assessment, students will analyze how the tone of each text contributes to the overall meaning. Students will use their strongest evidence from the poem "Saigon Is Gone" from the

---

novel and the audio text "Forgotten Ship: A Daring Rescue as Saigon Fell" to write two paragraphs in which they analyze each text in a paragraph. They will respond to the following prompt: "In this text, what is the message each author is intending to convey about the fall of Saigon? Explain how specific word choices help create a tone that contributes to the text's meaning."

Mid-Unit 2 Assessment

Analyzing an Informational Text about a Refugee Experience

This assessment centers on ELA CCSS RI.8.1, RI.8.2, RI.8.3, RI.8.4, L.8.4.a, and W.8.9. In this on-demand assessment, students will read an unfamiliar informational text about a refugee experience (a speech by Til Gurung, a refugee from Bhutan) and then answer a range of literal and inferential text-dependent questions. The assessment will provide questions in the form of selected-response items, a graphic organizer, and short constructed-response items. Students will cite the strongest text-based evidence to support their answers.

End-of-Unit 2 Assessment

Analysis Essay: Explain the Significance of the Novel's Title and Its Relationship to Universal Refugee Experiences and Ha's Character

This assessment centers on ELA CCSS RL.8.1, RL.8.3, RL.8.4, RL.8.6, W.8.2.d, W.8.4, W.8.5, and W.8.9. For this writing assessment, students will explain aspects of Ha's character. They will respond to this specific prompt: "Consider the meaning of the novel's title, *Inside Out & Back Again*. How does this title relate to the universal refugee experience of fleeing and finding home, and in what ways is Ha's experience an example of this universal experience?" Students will choose the strongest evidence from the informational texts and the novel to construct an informational literary analysis essay.

Mid-Unit 3 Assessment

Writing Best First Draft of "Inside Out" Poem

This assessment centers on ELA CCSS RI.8.1; W.8.3.a, b, d; W.8.7; and W.8.9. Students will use their Research Guides, which outline the research collected through their research teams, and their "Inside Out" poem graphic organizer, which has specific question prompts aligned to the creation of an "Inside Out" poem, to write a first draft of their "Inside Out" poem.

End-of-Unit 3 Assessment

Writing Best First Draft of "Back Again" Poem

This assessment centers on ELA CCSS RI.8.1; W.8.3.a, b, d; W.8.7; and W.8.9. Students will draft their "Back Again" poem about their same fictional refugee moving to a new country, sharing the experiences that the refugee might feel in adapting and mourning while adjusting to his or her new home. As with their "Inside Out" poem, students use a graphic organizer to help them plan.

FINAL PERFORMANCE TASK

For the final performance task of Module 1, students will draw upon their study of the universal refugee experience to write two research-based poems that reflect the "inside out" and "back again" aspects of a refugee's experience. Students will collaborate in research teams to research the experiences of refugees of a specific culture. They then will draw upon their research and their study of the novel and the informational texts to write two poems. The first poem, "Inside Out," will be based on the research conducted, and the second poem, the more creative "Back Again" poem, will be aligned with each student's individual interpretation of informational text and his or her own background knowledge and experiences. The students will have the opportunity to revise, edit, and share their two poems within the classroom and with other research teams for the final performance task. **This task centers on CCSS RI.8.1; RI.8.2; W.8.3.a, b, d; W.8.4; W.8.5; W.8.7; W.8.9; L.8.1; L.8.2; and L.8.6.**

Format

- A well-constructed, research-based, free-verse "Inside Out" poem
- A well-constructed, creative, free-verse "Back Again" poem
- Both poems typed, one-sided, on 8.5-by-11 in. paper

Standards Assessed through This Task

RI.8.1. Cite the textual evidence that most strongly supports an analysis of what the text says explicitly as well as inferences drawn from the text.

RI.8.2. Determine a central idea of a text and analyze its development over the course of the text, including its relationship to supporting ideas; provide an objective summary of the text.

W.8.3. Write narratives to develop real or imagined experiences or events using effective technique, relevant descriptive details, and well-structured event sequences.

W.8.4. Produce clear and coherent writing in which the development, organization, and style are appropriate to the task, purpose, and audience.

W.8.4.a. Produce text (print or nonprint) that explores a variety of cultures and perspectives.

W.8.5. With some guidance and support from peers and adults, develop and strengthen writing as needed by planning, revising, editing, rewriting, or trying a new approach, focusing on how well the purpose and audience have been addressed.

W.8.7. Conduct short research projects to answer a question (including a self-generated question), drawing on several sources and generating additional related, focused questions that allow for multiple avenues of exploration.

W.8.9. Draw evidence from literary or informational texts to support analysis, reflection, and research.

L.8.1. Demonstrate command of the conventions of standard English grammar and usage when writing or speaking.

L.8.2. Demonstrate command of the conventions of standard English capitalization, punctuation, and spelling when writing.

L.8.6. Acquire and use accurately grade-appropriate general academic and domain-specific words and phrases; gather vocabulary knowledge when considering a word or phrase important to comprehension or expression.

Student-Friendly Writing Invitation/Task Description

You are a refugee who has experienced being turned "inside out" upon fleeing from your home, and you have begun to feel as though your life is "back again" as you adjust to your new country. For this performance task, you will research and write poetry to describe these experiences.

Part 1: Research Refugees (in your research team) With your research team, use resources provided to research a specific time and place in history when people have been forced to flee because of war, religious beliefs, political beliefs, or a natural disaster. Gather the strongest evidence and accurate details about this historical situation: What caused people to flee from their home country and find a new home? Use the Research Guide to help you gather sufficient relevant information.

Part 2: Write a Free-Verse Narrative Poetry (on your own) Then imagine that you are a refugee from this specific time and place in history. You, like Ha and the real refugees you have read about, have been forced to flee from your home country for your safety. On your own, write two free-verse poems similar to Ha's diary entries in the novel *Inside Out & Back Again*.

Key Criteria for Success (Aligned with ELA CCSS)

Students must address the following key criteria when completing this task. Specific lessons during the module build in opportunities for students to understand the criteria, offer additional criteria, and work with their teacher to construct a rubric on which their work will be critiqued and formally assessed.

Your free-verse poems will do the following:

- Include figurative language, sensory details, and descriptive words and phrases that convey meaning and tone.

- Make explicit reference to research-based historical details and information that add to the authenticity of the story.

- Adhere to the conventions of standard written English.

- Provide research-based historical details in the context of a realistic scene.

- Align the details in both poems for continuation of the story.

- Maintain a consistent voice throughout both poems.

Options for Students

- Students will learn about dangerous conditions (political, religious, or natural) that would cause a person to make the difficult decision to leave home for an uncertain future. Students will develop narrative writing skills by paying close attention to details, word choice, organization, and conventions.

- Students may be regrouped to discuss countries of similar interest or assigned a country to research. Students may be provided research tasks to support the overall collection of complete information gathering for their poetry writing.

- Consider preselecting countries of interest, allowing fewer research texts to explore, providing texts of various structures or Lexile ranges, and/or isolating information in texts for students with Individualized Education Programs (IEPs) or English language learners (ELL).

Options for Teachers

- Teachers may differentiate research options for students, depending on their experience with the research process.

- Teachers may scaffold the writing process in stages as needed for student success. Keep in mind that the students' best independent drafts of each poem will be used as Mid-Unit and End-of-Unit Assessments in Unit 3.

- Consider research texts for students that offer a range of Lexile measures and structures to provide a rich variety of texts with which students may engage.

- Ask students to share their stories with the class, display them in the school library, or publish them on the school's website.

Resources

Research Texts: See the Supporting Materials for Unit 2, Lesson 19, for a complete list of texts students continue to work with during their short research project.

RECOMMENDED TEXTS

The following table includes both literary and informational texts with a range of Lexile text measures about Vietnam and the fall of Saigon. This list provides appropriate independent reading for each student to help build content knowledge about this topic. Note that districts and schools should consider their own community standards when reviewing this list. Some texts in particular units or modules address emotionally difficult content.

It is imperative that students read a high volume of texts at their reading level to continue to build the academic vocabulary and fluency that the Common Core State Standards (CCSS) demand.

Where possible, texts in languages other than English also are provided. Texts for the grade 8 modules are categorized into four Lexile measures that correspond to Common Core bands: grades 4–5 band, grade 6 band, grades 6–8 band, and above grade 8 band. Note, however, that Lexile measures are just one indicator of text complexity, and teachers must use their professional judgment and consider qualitative factors as well. For more information, see the Appendix.

Common Core Band Level Text Difficulty Ranges:

- Grades 2–3: 420L–820L
- Grades 4–5: 740L–1010L
- Grades 6–8: 925L–1185L

Title	Author and Illustrator	Text Type	Lexile Measure
Lexile text measures in grades 2–3 band level (420L–820L)			
Last Airlift: A Vietnamese Orphan's Rescue from War	Marsha Forchuk Skrypuch (author)	Informational	670
All the Broken Pieces	Ann E. Burg (author)	Literature	680
A Million Shades of Gray	Cynthia Kadohota (author)	Literature	700
Cracker! The Best Dog in Vietnam	Cynthia Kadohata (author)	Literature	730

Why Vietnamese Immigrants Came to America	Lewis K. Parker (author)	Informational	750*
Noodle Pie	Ruth Starke (author)	Informational	770
Goodbye, Vietnam	Gloria Whelan (author)	Literature	810

Lexile text measures in grades 4–5 band level (740L–1010L)

Year of Impossible Goodbyes	Sook Nyul Choi (author)	Literature	840
Echoes of the White Giraffe	Sook Nyul Choi (author)	Literature	870
The Lotus Seed	Sherry Garland (author)	Literature	880

Lexile text measures in grade 6 band level (925L–1185L)

Escape from Saigon: How a Vietnam War Orphan Became an American Boy	Andrea Warren (author)	Biography	930
Hearts of Sorrow: Vietnamese-American Lives	James Freeman (author)	Informational	930
Vietnam Veterans Memorial	Natalie M. Rosinsky (author)	Informational	940
The Fall of Saigon	Mary Englar (author)	Informational	940
Vietnamese in America	Lori Coleman (author)	Informational	940
Refugees & Asylum Seekers	Dave Dalton (author)	Informational	940
Vietnam	Charlotte Guillain (author)	Informational	950

Lexile text measures in grades 6–8 band level (925L–1185L)

The Land I Lost: Adventures of a Boy in Vietnam	Quang Nhuong Huynh (author)	Biography/ Literature	1090
Migration and Refugees	Quang Nhuong Huynh (author)	Biography/ Literature	1090
Vietnamese American	John F. Grabowski (author)	Informational	1100
When Heaven and Earth Changed Places: A Vietnamese Woman's Journey from War to Peace	Le Ly Hayslip with Jay Wurts (authors)	Historical Biography	1100

The Vietnam War	Cath Senker (author)	Informational	1110
Water Buffalo Days: Growing up in Vietnam	Quang Nhuong Huynh (author)	Literature	1120
Refugees	Clarissa Aykroyd (author)	Informational	1150
Lexile text measures above grade 8 band level (over 1185L)			
10,000 Days of Thunder: A History of the Vietnam War	Philip Caputo (author)	Informational	1210
The Vietnamese Americans	Hien Duc Do (author)	Informational	1340
The Vietnamese Boat People: 1954 and 1975–1992	Nghia M Vo (author)	Informational	NoLXL
Boat People: Personal Stories from the Vietnamese Exodus 1975–1996	Carina Hoang (editor)	Informational	NoLXL
Strangers from a Different Shore: A History of Asian Americans	Ronald Takaki (author)	Informational	NoLXL (AD)
Voices of Vietnamese Boat People: Nineteen Narratives of Escape and Survival	Mary Terrell Cargill and Jade Quang Huynh (editors)	Biography	NoLXL (AD)
The Vietnamese	Michelle Houle (author)	Informational	NoLXL (YA)
Weeping under This Same Moon	Jana Laiz (author)	Literature	NoLXL (YA)

Lexile is a trademark of MetaMetrics, Inc., and is registered in the United States and abroad. Copyright 2012 MetaMetrics.

UNIT OVERVIEW

Building Background Knowledge
War Coming Close to Home

In this first unit, students build their close-reading skills as they consider the crisis of war coming close to home. They begin reading the novel *Inside Out & Back Again,* by Thanhha Lai, focusing on how critical incidents reveal the dynamic nature of Ha, the main character, whose Vietnamese family is deciding whether to flee during the fall of Saigon. The novel is poignantly told via diary entries in the form of short free-verse poems. Students consider how text structure, figurative language, and specific word choices contribute to a text's meaning as they closely read selected poems. Their study of the novel is paired with reading a rich informational article, "The Vietnam Wars," which gives students key background knowledge about the history of war in Vietnam. Students build their skills using context clues and also begin the routine of *Quick Writes,* a short piece of written analysis about the text that involves receiving explicit instruction and then practicing writing strong paragraphs in which they effectively cite and analyze text. For their Mid-Unit Assessment, students analyze how key incidents in the novel reveal Ha's character. In the second half of the unit, students continue to read the novel and relevant informational texts as they focus on critical incidents the character experiences leading up to the fall of Saigon. Students begin to examine more carefully how word choice and tone contribute to the meaning of both informational texts and specific poems in the novel. For their End-of-Unit Assessment, students write two strong paragraphs in which they analyze the word choice, tone, and meaning of two texts (an informational audio text and a poem from the novel).

Guiding Questions and Big Ideas

• What is home?

• How do critical incidents reveal character?

• *Critical incidents reveal a character's dynamic nature.*

• *Authors use specific word choice to create tone and enhance meaning.*

Mid-Unit 1 Assessment

Getting to Know a Character: Which Details in the Text Help Us Understand Ha?

This assessment centers on ELA CCSS RL.8.1, RL.8.3, RL.8.4, W.8.9, and L.8.4.a. Students read the poem "Birthday Wishes" from the novel and answer selected-response questions to analyze the poem for

---

the author's word choice, tone, and meaning. Question topics include determining word meaning from context. Students then write a paragraph in response to the following prompt: "Who is Ha? Based on this poem, 'Birthday Wishes,' and one other poem you have read so far in the novel, describe Ha as a character: her traits, values, or beliefs. Write a paragraph in which you explain your current understanding of Ha, using specific evidence from the text of both poems to support your analysis."

End-of-Unit 1 Assessment

Examining How Word Choice Contributes to Meaning and Tone in Literary and Informational Text

This assessment centers on ELA CCSS RL.8.1, RI.8.1, RL.8.4, RI.8.4, and W.8.9. For this reading and writing assessment, students analyze how the tone of each text contributes to the overall meaning. Students use their strongest evidence from the novel's poem "Saigon Is Gone" and the audio text "Forgotten Ship: A Daring Rescue as Saigon Fell" to write two paragraphs in which they analyze each text in a paragraph in response to the following prompt: "In this text, what is the message each author is intending to convey about the fall of Saigon? Explain how specific word choices help create a tone that contributes to the text's meaning."

Content Connections

This module is designed to address the CCSS English Language Arts (ELA) standards. However, the module intentionally incorporates social studies content, as described below.

Social Studies Connections

Social Studies Themes in Context:

- Individual Development and Cultural Identity
  - Role of social, political, and cultural interactions in the development of identity
  - Personal identity as a function of an individual's culture, time, place, geography, interaction with groups, influences from institutions, and lived experiences
- Development, Movement, and Interaction of Cultures
  - Role of diversity within and among cultures

Central Texts

1. Thanhha Lai, *Inside Out & Back Again*. New York: HarperCollins, 2011. (Students read Part 1 during the first unit.)

2. Tod Olson, "The Vietnam Wars," *Scholastic*, February 24, 1995, 16–20.

3. Joseph Shapiro and Sandra Bartlett, "Forgotten Ship: A Daring Rescue as Saigon Fell," transcript, National Public Radio, August 31, 2010.

Unit-at-a-Glance Calendar

Unit 1 is approximately 2.5 weeks, or 14 lessons, of instruction.

Lesson	Lesson Title	Long-Term Targets	Supporting Targets	Ongoing Assessment	Anchor Charts and Protocols
1	Making Inferences: The Fall of Saigon	• I can cite text-based evidence that provides the strongest support for an analysis of literary text. (RI.8.1) • I can effectively engage in discussions with diverse partners about eighth-grade topics, texts, and issues. (SL.8.1)	• I can support my inferences with evidence from text. • I can participate in discussions about the text with a peer, small group, and the whole class.	• Careful listening to students' inferences • Observation of student participation	• Gallery Walk protocol • Turn-and-Talk protocol
2	Launching the Novel: Character Analysis of Ha	• I can cite text-based evidence that provides the strongest support for my analysis of literary text. (RL.8.1) • I can analyze how specific dialogue or incidents in a plot propel the action, reveal aspects of a character, or provoke a decision. (RL.8.3)	• I can make inferences to deepen my understanding of *Inside Out & Back Again*. • I can cite evidence from the novel to explain how incidents reveal aspects of Ha's character.	• Answers to text-dependent questions • Students' notes: "Who Is Ha?"	• Numbered Heads Together protocol • Turn-and-Talk protocol • Things Close Readers Do Anchor Chart

		• I can use a variety of strategies to determine the meaning of unknown words or phrases. (L.8.4) • I can effectively engage in discussions with diverse partners about eighth-grade topics, texts, and issues. (SL.8.1)	• I can use context clues to figure out word meanings. • I can participate in discussions about the text with a peer, small group, and the whole class.		
3	Inferring about Character: Close Reading of the Poem "Inside Out" and Introducing Quick Writes	• I can cite text-based evidence that provides the strongest support for my analysis of literary text. (RL.8.1) • I can analyze how specific dialogue or incidents in a plot propel the action, reveal aspects of a character, or provoke a decision. (RL.8.3) • I can use a variety of strategies to determine the meaning of unknown words or phrases. (L.8.4)	• I can make inferences to deepen my understanding of *Inside Out & Back Again*. • I can cite evidence from the novel to explain how incidents reveal aspects of Ha's character. • I can use context clues to figure out word meanings.	• Answers to text-dependent questions	• Things Close Readers Do Anchor Chart • Think-Pair-Share protocol • Quick Write Anchor Chart

		• I can effectively engage in discussions with diverse partners about eighth-grade topics, texts, and issues. (SL.8.1)	• I can participate in discussions about the text with a peer, small group, and the whole class.		
4	Considering a Character's Relationship with Others: Contrasting Ha and Her Brothers	• I can cite text-based evidence that provides the strongest support for my analysis of literary text. (RL.8.1) • I can analyze how specific dialogue or incidents in a plot propel the action, reveal aspects of a character, or provoke a decision. (RL.8.3) • I can analyze the impact of word choice on meaning and tone (analogies or allusions). (RL.8.4) • I can effectively engage in discussions with diverse partners about eighth-grade topics, texts, and issues. (SL.8.1)	• I can make inferences to deepen my understanding of *Inside Out & Back Again*. • I can cite evidence from the novel to explain how incidents reveal aspects of Ha's character. • I can explain how the specific word choices in the poem "Papaya Tree" create tone and help reveal meaning. • I can participate in discussions about the text with a peer, small group, and the whole class.	• Quick Write 1 (from homework) • Who Is Ha? small-group anchor charts	• Turn-and-Talk protocol • Who Is Ha? Anchor Chart • Numbered Heads Together protocol • Things Close Readers Do Anchor Chart

| 5 | Mid-Unit Assessment: Getting to Know a Character: Which Details in the Text Help Us Understand Ha? | • I can analyze how specific dialogue or incidents in a plot propel the action, reveal aspects of a character, or provoke a decision. (RL.8.3)
• I can cite text-based evidence that provides the strongest support for my analysis of literary text. (RL.8.1)
• I can determine the meaning of words and phrases in literary text (figurative, connotative, and technical meanings). (RL.8.4)
• I can analyze the impact of word choice on meaning and tone (analogies or allusions). (RL.8.4)
• I can use evidence from literary texts to support analysis, reflection, and research. (W.8.9) | • I can make inferences that deepen my understanding of *Inside Out & Back Again*.
• I can analyze how critical incidents in the novel reveal aspects of Ha's character.
• I can cite evidence from the text in my writing that supports my analysis.
• I can participate in discussions about the text with a peer, small group, and the whole class. | • Quick Write 2 (from homework)
• Mid-Unit Assessment: Getting to Know a Character: Which Details in the Text Help Us Understand Ha? | • Who Is Ha? Anchor Chart Gallery Walk protocol |

		• I can effectively engage in discussions with diverse partners about eighth-grade topics, texts, and issues. (SL.8.1)			
6	Building Background Knowledge: Guided Practice to Learn about the History of Wars in Vietnam	• I can determine the theme or central ideas of an informational text. (RI.8.2) • I can use a variety of strategies to determine the meaning of unknown words or phrases. (L.8.4) • I can effectively engage in discussions with diverse partners about eighth-grade topics, texts, and issues. (SL.8.1)	• I can determine the central ideas in one section of the informational text "The Vietnam Wars." • I can use context clues to determine word meanings. • I can participate in discussions about the text with a peer, small group, and the whole class.	• Students' questions and notes for section 1 of "The Vietnam Wars"	• Turn-and-Talk protocol • Think-Pair-Share protocol
7	Building Background Knowledge: Small-Group Work to Learn More about the History of Wars in Vietnam	• I can determine the central ideas of an informational text. (RI 8.2) • I can use a variety of strategies to determine the meaning of	• I can determine the central ideas in one section of the informational text "The Vietnam Wars."	• Students' questions and notes for their assigned section of the text	• Turn-and-Talk protocol • Jigsaw protocol • Things Close Readers Do Anchor Chart

		unknown words or phrases. (L.8.4) • I can effectively engage in discussions with diverse partners about eighth-grade topics, texts, and issues. (SL.8.1)	• I can summarize a portion of an informational text about the Vietnam War. • I can use context clues to determine word meanings. • I can participate in discussions about the text with a peer, small group, and the whole class.		
8	Development of the Plot: Impending Danger and Turmoil	• I can analyze the development of a central idea throughout the text (including its relationship to the characters, setting, and plot). (RL.8.2) • I can cite text-based evidence that provides the strongest support for my analysis of literary text. (RL.8.1) • I can effectively engage in discussions with	• I can make inferences to deepen my understanding of *Inside Out & Back Again*. • I can cite evidence from the text to explain how the central idea develops over the course of the plot of *Inside Out & Back Again*. • I can cite evidence from the text to analyze how	• Quick Write 3 (from homework) • Oral responses to text-dependent questions • Double Arrow Graphic Organizer • Exit Ticket	• Numbered Heads Together protocol • Turn-and-Talk protocol

		diverse partners about eighth-grade topics, texts, and issues. (SL.8.1) • I can use a variety of strategies to determine the meaning of unknown words or phrases. (L.8.4)	various sections of the novel reveal aspects of Ha's character. • I can participate in discussions about the text with a peer, small group, and the whole class.		
9	Building Background Knowledge: Vietnam as a "Battleground in a Larger Struggle"	• I can determine the central idea of an informational text. (RI.8.2) • I can use a variety of strategies to determine the meaning of unknown words or phrases. (L.8.4) • I can analyze the impact of word choice on meaning and tone in informational text. (RI.8.4) • I can effectively engage in discussions with diverse partners about eighth-grade topics, texts, and issues. (SL.8.1)	• I can determine the central idea of two key paragraphs of "The Vietnam Wars." • I can explain how Vietnam was a "battleground in a much larger struggle." • I can use context clues to determine word meanings. • I can participate in discussions about the text with a peer, small group, and the whole class.	• Quick Write 4 (from homework) • Students' annotated texts	• Think-Pair-Share protocol

| 10 | Building Background Knowledge: The Impending Fall of Saigon | • I can determine the central idea of an informational text. (RI.8.2)
• I can analyze the impact of word choice on meaning and tone in informational text. (RI.8.4)
• I can use a variety of strategies to determine the meaning of unknown words or phrases. (L.8.4)
• I can effectively engage in discussions with diverse partners about eighth-grade topics, texts, and issues. (SL.8.1) | • I can determine the central idea of the section "Doc-Lap at Last" in the informational text "The Vietnam Wars."
• I can objectively summarize informational text.
• I can use context clues to determine word meanings.
• I can participate in discussions about the text with a peer, small group, and the whole class. | • Students' annotated texts
• Three Threes in a Row Note-Catcher | • Turn-and-Talk protocol |
| 11 | Character Analysis: How Do Personal Possessions Reveal Aspects of Characters? | • I can analyze how specific dialogue or incidents in a plot propel the action, reveal aspects of a character, or provoke a decision. (RL.8.3)
• I can cite text-based evidence that provides | • I can make inferences to deepen my understanding of *Inside Out & Back Again*.
• I can cite evidence from the poems "Choice" and "Left Behind" to explain how this incident | • Quick Write 5 (from homework)
• Students' annotated text
• Write-Pair-Share
• Jigsaw Recording Form | • Turn-and-Talk protocol
• Jigsaw protocol |

		the strongest support for my analysis of literary text. (RL.8.1) • I can effectively engage in discussions with diverse partners about eighth-grade topics, texts, and issues. (SL.8.1)	reveals aspects of Ha and her family members. • I can participate in discussions about the text with a peer, small group, and the whole class.		
12	Examining How Word Choice Contributes to Meaning and Tone: Close Reading of "Wet and Crying"	• I can cite text-based evidence that provides the strongest support for my analysis of literary text. (RL.8.1) • I can analyze the impact of word choice on meaning and tone. (RL.8.4) • I can effectively engage in discussions with diverse partners about eighth-grade topics, texts, and issues. (SL.8.1)	• I can make inferences to deepen my understanding of *Inside Out & Back Again.* • I can explain how nuances in word meanings contribute to the overall tone of the poem. • I can participate in discussions about the text with a peer, small group, and the whole class.	• Quick Write 6 (from homework) • Write-Pair-Share Note-Catcher with text-dependent questions	• Write-Pair-Share protocol • Turn-and-Talk protocol • Things Close Readers Do Anchor Chart

| 13 | Comparing Meaning and Tone: The Fall of Saigon in Fiction and Informational Text | • I can cite text-based evidence that provides the strongest support for my analysis of literary and informational text. (RL.8.1, RI.8.1)

 • I can analyze the impact of word choice on meaning and tone. (RL.8.4, RI.8.4)

 • I can effectively engage in discussions with diverse partners about eighth-grade topics, texts, and issues. (SL.8.1) | • I can make inferences to deepen my understanding of *Inside Out & Back Again*.

 • I can cite evidence from the poem "Saigon Is Gone" to explain the fall of Saigon and the emotional impact of this news on Ha and the other characters in the novel.

 • I can analyze the word choices of two texts about the fall of Saigon and describe how that word choice contributes to the tone and meaning of each text.

 • I can participate in discussions about the text with a peer, small group, and the whole class. | • Quick Write 7 (from homework)

 • Word Choice, Tone, and Meaning Note-Catcher | • Turn-and-Talk protocol |

| 14 | End-of-Unit Assessment: Examining How Word Choice Contributes to Meaning and Tone in Literary and Informational Text | • I can cite text-based evidence that provides the strongest support for my analysis of literary text. (RL.8.1, RI.8.1)
 • I can analyze the impact of word choice on meaning and tone. (RL.8.4, RI.8.4)
 • I can use evidence from informational texts to support analysis, reflection, and research. (W.8.9) | • I can analyze how the word choice in both informational and literary texts affects the meaning and tone.
 • I can cite evidence from text to support analysis of literary and informational text. | • End-of-Unit 1 Assessment | • Things Close Readers Do Anchor Chart (reviewed) |

EXPEDITIONARY
LEARNING

Building Background Knowledge

War Coming Close to Home

Optional: Experts and Service

Experts

- Invite experts to speak to the class about the history of Vietnam, the Vietnam War, or the fall of Saigon.

- Locate refugees from Vietnam to visit the class and answer questions that students generate.

Service

- Coordinate with a local refugee center to inquire about service opportunities.

Optional: Extensions

- Social studies teachers may complement this unit with a focus on the Guiding Questions for this unit.

Preparation and Materials

- Students keep class notes in a journal. This could be a composition notebook or one section of a binder.

- Throughout this module, students need a folder to collect and store all teacher-provided note-catchers, text-dependent question handouts, and graphic organizers.

- Teachers are encouraged to keep a model journal along with students to model note-taking and Quick Writes.

- Teachers are also encouraged to "test drive" each Quick Write in advance. See Teaching Notes in Lesson 4.

RECOMMENDED TEXTS

The following table includes literary and informational texts with a range of Lexile text measures about Vietnam and the fall of Saigon. This list provides appropriate independent reading for each student to help build content knowledge about this topic.

It is imperative that students read a high volume of texts at their reading level to continue to build the academic vocabulary and fluency that the Common Core State Standards (CCSS) demand.

Note that districts and schools should consider their own community standards when reviewing this list. Some texts in particular units or modules address emotionally difficult content.

Where possible, texts in languages other than English also are provided. Texts for the grade 8 modules are categorized into four Lexile measures that correspond to Common Core bands: grades 4–5 band, grade 6 band, grades 6–8 band, and above grade 8 band. Note, however, that Lexile measures are just one indicator of text complexity; teachers must use their professional judgment and consider qualitative factors as well. For more information, see the Appendix.

Common Core Band Level Text Difficulty Ranges:

- Grades 2–3: 420L–820L
- Grades 4–5: 740L–1010L
- Grades 6–8: 925L–1185L

Title	Author and Illustrator	Text Type	Lexile Measure
Lexile text measures in grades 2–3 band level (420L–820L)			
All the Broken Pieces	Ann E. Burg (author)	Literature	680
Cracker! The Best Dog in Vietnam	Cynthia Kadohata (author)	Literature	730
Why Vietnamese Immigrants Came to America	Lewis K. Parker (author)	Informational	750
Goodbye, Vietnam	Gloria Whelan (author)	Literature	810

EXPEDITIONARY
LEARNING

Lexile text measures in grades 4–5 band level (740L–1010L)			
Year of Impossible Goodbyes	Sook Nyul Choi (author)	Literature	840
Echoes of the White Giraffe	Sook Nyul Choi (author)	Literature	870
Lexile text measures in grade 6 band level (925L–1185L)			
Escape from Saigon: How a Vietnam War Orphan Became an American Boy	Andrea Warren (author)	Biography	930
Vietnam Veterans Memorial	Natalie M. Rosinsky (author)	Informational	940
The Fall of Saigon	Mary Englar (author)	Informational	940
Vietnam	Charlotte Guillain (author)	Informational	950
Lexile text measures in grades 6–8 band level (925L–1185L)			
The Land I Lost: Adventures of a Boy in Vietnam	Quang Nhuong Huynh (author)	Biography/ Literature	1090
Vietnamese American	John F. Grabowski (author)	Informational	1100
The Vietnam War	Cath Senker (author)	Informational	1110
Water Buffalo Days: Growing up in Vietnam	Quang Nhuong Huynh (author)	Literature	1120
Vietnam in Pictures	Stacy Taus-Bolstad (author)	Informational	1170
Lexile text measures above grade 8 band level (over 1185L)			
10,000 Days of Thunder: A History of the Vietnam War	Philip Caputo (author)	Informational	1210
The Vietnamese Americans	Hien Duc Do (author)	Informational	1340
The Vietnamese Boat People: 1954 and 1975–1992	Nghia M Vo (author)	Informational	NoLXL
Boat People: Personal Stories from the Vietnamese Exodus 1975–1996	Carina Hoang (editor)	Informational	NoLXL

LESSON 1

Making Inferences

The Fall of Saigon

Long-Term Targets Addressed (Based on ELA CCSS)

- I can cite text-based evidence that provides the strongest support for an analysis of literary text. (RI.8.1)
- I can effectively engage in discussions with diverse partners about eighth-grade topics, texts, and issues. (SL.8.1)

Supporting Learning Targets

- I can support my inferences with evidence from text.
- I can participate in discussions about the text with a partner, small group, and the whole class.

Ongoing Assessment

- Careful listening to students' inferences
- Observation of student participation

Agenda

1. Opening
   A. Review Learning Targets (5 minutes)
2. Work Time
   A. Gallery Walk/Inferences (10 minutes)
   B. "Mix and Mingle" and Thinking about Details (15 minutes)
   C. Connecting Details and Inferences to Guiding Questions (10 minutes)

---

3. Closing and Assessment

    A. Exit Ticket (5 minutes)

4. Homework

    A. None.

Teaching Notes

- Lesson 1 is designed as an inquiry-based approach to "hook" students into the first unit of Module 1 through pictures, a text-based activity, and a read-aloud. Do not use this lesson to "give away" the first unit (i.e., do not inform them that they are going to read a novel that starts with this particular historical event). Instead, focus on the skill of inferring, helping students understand how their background knowledge helps them make sense of things not directly stated in the text. It is fine at this point if the details are not "adding up" for students; in coming lessons, and throughout the module, they will circle back to many of the ideas that they are initially exposed to in this lesson.

- Preview the slide show of pictures from the *New York Times* of the fall of Saigon (see the link under "Materials"), and prepare specific images from this slide show for the Gallery Walk. Be sure to remove the captions: The purpose of this opening activity is to pique students' interest and get them to "notice" and "wonder" about the images themselves.

- This lesson intentionally includes short excerpts from the full *New York Times* article "Panic Rises in Saigon, but the Exits Are Few." Students do not read the entire text in this lesson; rather, they will read the entire article several weeks from now, during Unit 2. For Teacher Reference only, read the full text for more background information (see Unit 2, Lesson 3, Supporting Materials).

- Remember that it is fine during this engagement lesson if students have lots of questions: That is part of the goal! If students ask for more details, it's a perfect time to say, "Those are great questions!"

- Prepare "sentence strips" (see Unit 2, Lesson 6, Supporting Materials).

- This lesson involves two activities in which students are moving around the room to think and talk with peers. Reinforce expectations throughout, and provide specific positive feedback as students begin these informal collaborative routines.

- Review the Gallery Walk protocol (see the Appendix).

- Note that you spend time deconstructing the learning targets with students at the beginning of this lesson. This gives students a clear vision of the focus of each lesson. This research-based strategy supports struggling learners the most. Using learning targets is also an effective way to teach academic vocabulary.

- This lesson introduces strategies that are used throughout the modules to promote student engagement, collaboration, and self-assessment. Review Cold-Call and the Turn-and-Talk protocol (see the Appendix).

Lesson Vocabulary

inference, infer, panic

Material

- I Notice / I Wonder Note-Catcher (one per student)

- Photographs (without captions) mounted and posted for Gallery Walk, from the *New York Times* slide show: http://events.nytimes.com/learning/general/specials/saigon/110599saigon-pix.1.html

- Sentence strips from "Panic Rises in Saigon, but the Exits Are Few" (two strips per student; see Unit 2, Lesson 6, Supporting Materials)

- Module Guiding Questions (one to display or post on chart or interactive whiteboard)

- Lined paper for Exit Ticket (one per student)

- Examples of nonlinguistic representations of learning target vocabulary (Teacher Reference)

Opening

A. Review Learning Targets (5 minutes)

- This might be the first time students have heard of learning targets. Explain that targets help them understand the specific learning and thinking that a lesson is designed to help them develop. Inform students that you will be sharing targets with them regularly, assessing whether they have met the targets and asking them to self-assess their progress toward targets.

- Read the day's targets aloud to students. Pay particular attention to the word *inference*.

- Explain that an *inference* is "a thought process a reader makes to understand the meaning of text or even an image. When you *infer,* you pay attention to the details in front of you, and you use other information (from the text or your background knowledge) to mentally fill in the gaps between the details that are actually said or shown and what the author expects the reader to understand."

- Inform students that today's work will require them to make inferences based on both images and text.

Meeting Students' Needs

- Learning targets are a research-based strategy that helps all students, but they help challenged learners the most. Post the learning targets where all students can see them.

- Paying careful attention to learning targets engages students in learning, supports their learning, and helps hold them accountable for learning.

- Discussing and clarifying the language of learning targets help build academic vocabulary.

- Support English language learner (ELL) students in making connections with vocabulary. These images can be used throughout the year. Specifically, these can be used in directions and learning targets. (See Supporting Materials for examples of possible nonlinguistic representations for common learning targets, including a few used in this specific lesson.)

Work Time

A. Gallery Walk/Inferences (10 minutes)

- Display and distribute the **I Notice / I Wonder Note-Catcher** and explain the process for the Gallery Walk:

  1. In a moment, students will examine several **photographs** that are posted throughout the room (or along the hallway outside the classroom).

  2. At each photograph, they should pause and capture specific details that they notice (e.g., "Woman is crying," "They are holding on to back of helicopter"), and the things that they wonder about ("I wonder why they are sad?" "What are they getting away from?" "When was this?").

  3. They will have just a minute at each picture, and they might not get to all the pictures.

- You might need to coach your students about your expectations for safe movement and for quiet voices during this work period: "As you move from photograph to photograph, there is no need to engage in side conversations. I expect zero voice levels during this time. Also, please move carefully, taking care not to bump into one another."

- Ask them to begin. Use a timer set to 5 minutes to keep students focused on the gallery. As students complete this activity, circulate to observe and support as needed. You might notice that they are making inferences (e.g., "It's a war" or "The people are escaping"). This is ideal, as such inferences provide the basis for the follow-up conversation.

- Once students have observed the gallery for 5 minutes, ask them to return to their seats.

- Cold-call on several students to share what they "noticed" and "wondered." Once a correct inference comes up, probe the students about why they said what they said (e.g., "You said you saw a war. What specifically did you see that made you think there was a war?" "You used your background knowledge to make an inference that there was a war. No picture has the word 'war' in it, does it?")

- Clarify for students that when they use their background knowledge to add meaning to a picture or text, they are making inferences.

Meeting Students' Needs

Some students may benefit from a more structured I Notice/I Wonder Note-Catcher. You might add sentence stems matched to specific pictures. In addition, the use of a visible timer will help keep students focused on the work at hand.

B. "Mix and Mingle" and Thinking about Details (15 minutes)

- Inform students that the next activity will give them additional information. It may lead them to confirm some of their inferences, revise them, or simply add more details to help them keep making sense of what they saw.

- Give each student two **sentence strips** from **"Panic Rises in Saigon, but the Exits Are Few."** Ask students to read their own sentence strips silently to themselves. Give them 2 minutes or so to do this.

- Ask them to Turn-and-Talk to a peer close by and say what their strips are about.

- Ask the class, "Do you feel like you have the whole story of what is happening in the pictures from these sentence strips?" Students likely will say no.

- Mention that their classmates' strips are different from theirs, and that by mingling and comparing strips, they might be able to collect more information about what is happening in the pictures.

- If needed, reinforce your expectations for movement and noise while they work on the next activity. Give directions:

    - "You will quietly wander for 5 minutes, reading one another's strips. Look for peers who have strips with different pieces of information from yours."

- Gather students in groups of three or four, so that each group has 8 to 10 different pieces of information that might fit together to tell more of the story about what is happening in the pictures in the Gallery Walk.

- Begin the mingle. Set a visible timer for 5 minutes so students know how long they have for this activity.

- Circulate to observe and support as needed. Be sure students are finding peers with sentence strips different from their own.

- Then refocus students as a whole group. Ask them to select an area of the classroom quickly in which to sit with the three or four peers they found who had additional information. Ask students to "huddle" around a desk so that they can talk quietly to one another.

- Ask the groups to take 5 minutes to arrange their strips in an order they think makes sense. Reassure them that there is no "right answer." They are simply thinking about how all these details might fit together. They should end up with a series of strips that they could explain to someone else. Ask, "Why did you put the strips in the order you did?" Emphasize to students that it is fine if they have more questions than answers at this point.

    - After 5 minutes, refocus students as a whole group. Ask them to stay in their same groups and discuss the following question: "Based on the pictures and sentence strips, what can you *infer* has happened?"

- Cold-call on a few students to offer their group's inferences. Follow up by asking, "What specific evidence do you have to back up that inference?"

- Encourage students to use specific details from the sentence strips to support their answers.

Note: It is fine, even good, if students are somewhat unclear at this point and have many questions about what they have read. Remind students that they will have many opportunities to get their questions answered over the coming weeks.

Meeting Students' Needs

- Some students may benefit from having only one strip to read and/or from being guided to a specific place in the room to meet with their group rather than mingling. If this is the case, add "Meet your group at XXX" to the strips of those students.

- Some students may benefit from having a "master copy" of the strips in the right order of the article rather than rearranging while they listen. These students can be told to listen to the read-aloud and to "check" each strip as it is read.

C. Connecting Details and Inferences to Guiding Questions (10 minutes)

- Build on students' inferences to begin to frame the first two **Guiding Questions** for this module.

  - For example, many students likely inferred that there was a war going on and that people had to flee. Point out that often during wars, people have to leave their homes. One question students will be thinking about throughout this module is, "What is home?"

  - For example, many students likely noticed the emotional intensity described in many of the sentence strips ("panic," "suicide," etc.) and may have commented that this must have been very intense for the people involved. Connect this reaction to the second Guiding Question: "How do critical incidents reveal character?" Inform students that throughout the module, they will keep thinking about how the events around us affect who we are.

- Share the module Guiding Questions on a **chart** or your **interactive whiteboard**. Inform students that they will keep returning to these questions as they read more.

- Give students 2 minutes to reread their quotes in their group and identify any that they can connect to the idea of home or showing or revealing character.

- Cold-call on students to respond. Students may suggest such ideas as, "Home is a place you hate to leave. Home is where your family is."

- Potentially, students may also say, "When things get really hard, you show your character," or "Character is who you are even in a terrible time."

- Remind students that they will keep coming back to these big questions.

Meeting Students' Needs

Some students may benefit from being explicitly told which strips to look at when discussing questions.

Closing and Assessment

A. Exit Ticket (5 minutes)

Ask students to write the following on a piece of **lined paper**:

1. One inference you made today

2. A question that you hope to have answered in the coming weeks

Meeting Students' Needs

Students will benefit from your careful reading of these Exit Tickets and making references to their questions as you move through the unit. You might even consider making a chart of the questions, either on chart paper or on your interactive whiteboard, that you can refer to regularly. This type of list validates and reinforces students' thinking/learning.

Homework

No homework.

Note: Review students' Exit Tickets to gauge their initial understanding of the topic and to identify patterns in students' questions that you can informally weave into upcoming lessons.

LESSON 2

Launching the Novel

Character Analysis of Ha

Long-Term Targets Addressed (Based on ELA CCSS)

- I can cite text-based evidence that provides the strongest support for my analysis of literary text. (RL.8.1)
- I can analyze how specific dialogue or incidents in a plot propel the action, reveal aspects of a character, or provoke a decision. (RL.8.3)
- I can use a variety of strategies to determine the meaning of unknown words or phrases. (L.8.4)
- I can effectively engage in discussions with diverse partners about eighth-grade topics, texts, and issues. (SL.8.1)

Supporting Learning Targets

- I can make inferences to deepen my understanding of *Inside Out & Back Again.*
- I can cite evidence from the novel to explain how incidents reveal aspects of Ha's character.
- I can use context clues to figure out word meanings.
- I can participate in discussions about the text with a peer, small group, and the whole class.

Ongoing Assessment

- Answers to text-dependent questions
- Students' notes: "Who Is Ha?"

Agenda

1. Opening
    A. Engaging the Reader: Orienting to the Novel's Text Structure (10 minutes)
    B. Review Learning Targets (5 minutes)

2. Work Time

    A. Introduce Things Close Readers Do Anchor Chart Using "1975: Year of the Cat" (15 minutes)

    B. Answering Text-Dependent Questions: "1975: Year of the Cat" (10 minutes)

3. Closing and Assessment

    A. Debrief: Adding to Our Things Close Readers Do Anchor Chart (5 minutes)

4. Homework

    A. Reread "1975: Year of the Cat," add to notes, and read pages 4–9 for Gist.

Teaching Notes

- This lesson introduces strategies that are used throughout the modules to promote student engagement, collaboration, and self-assessment. Review: Cold-Call, Turn-and-Talk, and Fist-to-Five (see the Appendix).

- This lesson also includes a protocol called Numbered Heads Together: Divide students into groups of four, and assign each student in the group a number from 1 to 4. Numbering students in the group makes it quick and easy to assign group roles, such as note-taker, presenter, timekeeper, or facilitator, and to cold-call on students quickly.

- Throughout this unit, students work in small groups suitable for cooperative learning structures. Use heterogeneous groups in this first unit to support struggling readers and ELL students intentionally. Determine groups ahead of time.

- In this lesson, students are introduced to the concept of "close reading" and begin to build a class Things Close Readers Do Anchor Chart. Throughout this unit, students will add to their practices of close reading and conduct close readings of a more complex text with continued support and feedback from the teacher. They will revisit and add to this chart.

- Students are introduced to one initial way to approach a complex text: to read for the *gist,* or an initial sense of what a text is mostly about. This lays a strong foundation for students to build close-reading skills. Students jot gist statements in their journal, on a sticky note, or in the margins of their text. In subsequent lessons, and with more difficult texts, students add to their repertoire of close-reading practices as they pay close attention to details in the text, and they ask or answer text-dependent questions that help them deepen their understanding beyond the gist. This skill was introduced in Lesson 1 as students looked at images. Here, it is reinforced when students analyze text. This skill is emphasized throughout this unit. Clarify for students that "getting the gist" is preliminary and often tentative—not nearly as formal as determining the main idea.

- Encourage students to use a journal to take notes in class about the novel. Help students understand the importance of ongoing note-taking: They will refer to their notes during Quick Writes and unit assessments.

- Post the learning targets where all students can see them. Using learning targets is an effective way to teach academic vocabulary.

- In advance, preview the Unit 1 Recommended Texts list (a separate document). Lesson 4 includes time to share this list of texts with students.

Lesson Vocabulary

free-verse poetry, stanza, inferences, cite evidence, meaning, gist; lunar, glutinous, foretells

Materials

- *Inside Out & Back Again* (book; one per student)
- Journals (one per student; see preceding Teaching Notes; used throughout module)
- Things Close Readers Do Anchor Chart (new; teacher-created)
- Document camera, interactive whiteboard, and/or chart paper
- Teacher journal for modeling
- Model note-taking (Teacher Reference)
- Fist-to-Five chart (Teacher Reference or to display)

Opening

A. Engaging the Reader: Orienting to the Novel's Text Structure (10 minutes)

- Ask students to gather in small heterogeneous groups of three or four peers (see Teaching Notes). Give each student a number to allow for Numbered Heads Together responses (see the Appendix).

- Once students are in their groups, explain that you will be calling on specific "numbers" to share their group's thinking. For example, if you ask "number 2s" to respond, each student who has been assigned number 2 will speak for his or her group. Explain that this strategy will help the class be sure that a variety of students respond to questions, rather than just a select few.

- Remind students that they looked at images and read some details about the topic of the module the day before. Today they will begin their study of the novel *Inside Out & Back Again* that relates to what they saw and read.

- Do not distribute the book or provide much background about it at this point. Instead, simply orient students to the novel by reading the following quote from the book: "No one would believe me, but at times I would prefer wartime in Saigon over peacetime in Alabama" (page 195). Ask the students:

  - "Based on what you saw and read yesterday, what do you think might have to happen to a little girl to make her say that she would prefer war at home in Saigon (Vietnam) to peace in Alabama (the United States)?"

- Allow students time to discuss this question in small groups as you distribute *Inside Out & Back Again* to each student. Ask the number 4s in each group to share their group's ideas.

- Invite students to browse through the pages of the novel. Ask students to consider these questions one at a time, using a Turn-and-Talk strategy to think and then discuss with a peer the following questions:

  - "What do you notice about how this novel is written?"

- • "How is it like other novels you have read?"

- • "How is it different from other novels you have read?"

- Listen for students to recognize that the novel isn't written in a prose form that they are accustomed to. Ideally, they will notice the dated poems.

- Explain that this is a novel of diary entries and that each entry is written in short *free-verse poetry*. Free-verse poetry doesn't use a regular rhythm or rhyming pattern. It does, however, look like a poem because of its layout and line breaks. Briefly review the word *stanza*: "a group of lines that form the smaller chunks of a poem."

Meeting Students' Needs

- • Mixed-ability grouping of students for regular discussion and close-reading exercises provides a collaborative and supportive structure for close reading of complex texts. Determine these groups ahead of time.

- • Share or ask students to set small-group norms to increase the efficacy of group work. Encourage students to be attentive listeners, to ask questions that are sincere and relevant, and to offer meaningful and constructive ideas to the group discussion.

- • Consider posting the quote from the novel on a chart or by using an interactive whiteboard.

B. Review Learning Targets (5 minutes)

- Post learning targets for student review. Remind them that learning targets enable them to know the focus of the lesson. They will always review the learning targets for the day and then check in at the end of the lesson to assess their progress and determine the next steps.

- Read the first learning target aloud to students: "I can make inferences to deepen my understanding of *Inside Out & Back Again*." Review the term *inferences* (determining meaning based on things not directly stated in the text). Remind students that they were inferring the previous day based on the images they looked at and the sentence strips they read: "When we infer, we use specific information in the text, combined with our background knowledge and/or what the text said earlier, to understand incidents, characters, and theme." *Inside Out & Back Again* leaves many things not directly stated and requires many inferences. Reassure students that they will have lots of support and practice with this skill.

- Read the second target aloud: "I can *cite evidence* from the novel to explain how incidents reveal aspects of Ha's character as she is shaped by war." Discuss the phrase *cite evidence*. Students may be familiar with this term from previous experience. Explain to students that this phrase means they will need to prove what they believe the novel is saying by quoting accurately with words, phrases, and details from the novel.

- Read the last two learning targets aloud: "I can use context clues to figure out word meanings," and "I can participate in discussions about the text with a partner, small group, and the whole class."

- Explain that citing evidence, understanding new vocabulary, and understanding the *meaning* of challenging texts requires a lot of thinking and talking with others. Students will be pairing up for Turn-and-Talk moments as well as thinking and discussing the text in small groups. Remind students to be respectful of others by listening to what their peers have to say, asking polite questions to clarify understanding, and participating in the discussions by offering thoughtful ideas and questions.

Meeting Students' Needs

Consider providing nonlinguistic symbols (e.g., two people talking for *discuss,* a pen for *record,* a magnifying glass for *details,* a light bulb for *main idea*) to assist ELL students.

Work Time

A. Introduce Things Close Readers Do Anchor Chart Using "1975: Year of the Cat" (15 minutes)

- Distribute the book **Inside Out & Back Again**. Ensure that students also have their **journals**.

- Announce: "Today we will get started reading the novel by taking our time and closely reading the first poem, '1975: Year of the Cat.'" This may be the students' first time reading a text with such care. Explain that close reading is important to help the reader fully understand what the author is saying. Often, readers need to reread texts multiple times to understand and appreciate them fully.

- Let them know that, in a moment, they will hear the first poem, "1975: Year of the Cat," read aloud. Remind students that whenever you read aloud, they should read along silently (this promotes fluency). *(Note: This is a teacher, not student, read-aloud. The purpose is to promote fluency generally, and specifically to allow students to hear a sophisticated reader handle the free verse.)*

- Set a purpose: Ask students to think about the *gist* of the poem—just their initial sense of what the text is mostly about.

- Show students the **Things Close Readers Do Anchor Chart**. Explain that throughout this module, they will be charting important learning to help them remember it. They will add to this chart often. On the chart, write the following: "Get the gist—get your initial sense of what the text is mostly about."

- Explain that close reading is just one of many practices that help readers deeply understand a text. They will be practicing getting the gist. Reinforce that getting the gist is preliminary and tentative, and it is particularly useful when text is complex.

- Read aloud "1975: Year of the Cat" as students look at this page and read along silently.

- Then ask students to Turn-and-Talk with a peer in their group: "What is the gist of this poem? What is your initial sense of what it is mostly about?"

- Cold-call on a few student groups to share their thinking.

- Ask students to talk in their small groups about what they notice about the language the author is using. Ask students, "Which details really strike you as you read this poem? Why?"

- Call on the number 1s to share. It is fine to let students merely "notice" at this point; they will continue to study the poem more closely.

- Inform students that in a moment, they will reread this first poem independently and silently. Set a purpose for them. As they read, ask them to think about this question: "What have you learned about Ha in this very first poem?"

- Give students about 5 minutes to reread, asking them to pay attention to details. They don't have to write down anything yet. Display a timer to help keep students focused during this silent reading period.

- Ask students to share with their group details they noticed in the text that helped them learn about Ha. Reinforce norms related to small-group work as needed, particularly naming for students what you see going well (e.g., when you see more talkative students inviting the quieter students into the conversation).

- Inform students that, in a moment, they will record in their journals a few details from the text that helped them learn about Ha. (They will continue this for homework.)

- Model first (for an example, see **Model Note-Taking** in the Supporting Materials). Using a **document camera** or **interactive whiteboard**, orient students to the two-column note-taking chart.

- Explain to students that the word *infer* is an important term: They talked about it in Lesson 1 as well. Being able to infer is one key skill they will develop as readers. They will learn much more in future lessons. Briefly review this general academic vocabulary word: To *infer* means "to take something from the text and combine it with something you already know in order to figure something out." They will infer information about Ha as a character from specific details in this first poem.

- Model writing in your **teacher journal** to show students the types of notes they might take. Be sure to indicate that the first row shows "right there" information (e.g., the text says directly that Ha is 10), whereas the other rows require inferring.

- Then do brief, guided practice. Invite students to share the details that help them learn about Ha. (Encourage them to say in which stanza they find the detail; then take a moment so other students can locate that detail in the text.) As students watch, record this information on the model journal. Probe students to move from a literal to a more inferential analysis of Ha's character, and praise students for this higher-level analysis (e.g., if students say, "Ha is 10," you might probe to ask, "And what can you tell about her as a 10-year-old?").

- Remind them that they will reread this poem as a part of their homework and continue to note details. Give students time to copy the notes from this guided practice so they have a model to support them with their homework.

Meeting Students' Needs

- You might arrange the students in small heterogeneous groups, because they will be practicing paired sharing and small-group discussions. Students will be reading, thinking about, and discussing the book in pairs or small groups throughout the unit.

- Some students may benefit from using a ruler or piece of paper to underline the lines as they are read aloud.

- Some students may benefit from having sentence starters to prompt discussion.

- Some students may benefit from being privately prompted before they are called upon in a cold-call. Although the cold-call is a participation technique that necessitates your random calling, it is important that you set a supportive tone so that the use of the cold-call is a positive experience for all.

B. Answering Text-Dependent Questions: "1975: Year of the Cat" (10 minutes)

Note: In this lesson, most of the text-dependent questions are literal questions that check for understanding. As the unit progresses, the text-dependent questions become more inferential in nature. Below, one inferential question is included as an initial formative assessment about the students' current skills with this type of thinking.

- Explain to students that looking closely at the text to answer questions is an important skill to develop. Ask the following questions one at a time. After reading each question, give students time to think and talk with their group for 2 minutes. Call upon a different numbered heads group member to respond to each question. This strategy provides the opportunity for all students to be accountable for thinking, preparing an answer, and responding.

  1. "Tet is a special day. When is Tet, and which two events are celebrated on Tet?"

     - Listen for students to refer to the first stanza and say that Tet is the first day of the *lunar* calendar. Ask students, "How can we figure out the meaning of the word *lunar*?" Students might be able to connect it to a lunar eclipse or other reference. If needed, explain that *lunar* means "having to do with the moon" and that a *lunar calendar* is "a calendar that is based on the cycles of the moon—a new month begins at the start of the new moon." Listen for students to notice that both New Year's and everyone's birthdays are celebrated on Tet.

  2. "How does the family celebrate Tet?"

     - Listen for the called-upon numbered group members to refer to specific stanzas; reinforce this habit. Students may refer to stanza 4: They must smile. Or stanza 2: Ha's family wears new clothes underneath, eats sugary lotus seeds, and eats *glutinous* rice cakes. (Ask students, "Have you heard of a word sounding like *glutinous*?" Some may have heard of gluten. Gluten refers to a protein in grains, and *glutinous* means "gooey and sticky." Praise this kind of word-solving by reminding students they are meeting the target about using background knowledge and context to figure out word meanings.)

     - Also listen for students to mention stanza 5: no sweeping or splashing water. Ask the class, "Why must the family avoid sweeping and splashing water?" Listen for students to notice that page 1 explains it would mean they are sweeping away hope and splashing away joy. Be sure students recognize that these practices are an outgrowth of the Buddhist tradition, not just "superstitions."

3. "So, how does this special day affect the other days?"

- Listen for the called-upon students to notice that on page 1, the mother says how we act today foretells the whole year. Ask students, "Which two words do you see in the word *foretells*?" Students will notice the words *fore* and *tells*. Point out that *fore* is related to the word "before": *Foretell* means "to tell before, or to predict." When students do this kind of word work, reinforce that they are using background knowledge about words and word roots, plus context clues, to figure out new word meanings.

4. "What does the narrator (Ha) do that might bring bad luck?"

- Listen for students to notice that on pages 2–3, she wakes up before her brothers and taps her toe on the floor first.

5. "What can you infer about the narrator based on this action? In other words, what can you figure out about her, based on what you see in the text and what you already know?"

- Listen for students to comment that Ha might be brave, or stubborn, or not superstitious. Model as needed: "I know from page 2 that her mom says that her brother gets to tap the floor first. But then on the bottom of the page, it says she decides to get up and tap her toe first. So she disobeys her mother. Given that she disobeys, I infer that she and her mother have a difficult relationship."

- Reinforce the process of inferring here—the text does not support those insights about Ha directly. But based on what the text tells us about Tet, and our background knowledge about how people usually respond to traditions, we can infer some things about Ha's character. Remind students that they will continue to practice inferring throughout the module.

- Point out students' strong reading behaviors you observed—in particular, referring to the text to answer questions.

Meeting Students' Needs

- Many students will benefit from seeing the questions posted on an interactive whiteboard or via the document camera; but be sure to reveal the questions only one at a time, so that students stay focused on the question at hand.

- Some students may benefit from having access to "hint cards": small slips of paper or index cards that they turn over for hints about how/where to find the answers to text-dependent questions. For example, a hint card might say, "Check back in the third paragraph on page 7."

- Some students may benefit from having key sections prehighlighted in their texts. This will help them focus on small sections rather than scanning the whole text for answers.

Closing and Assessment

A. Debrief: Adding to Our Things Close Readers Do Anchor Chart (5 minutes)

- Remind students of the Things Close Readers Do Anchor Chart. Share with students that they first read along silently for the gist as the poem "1975: Year of the Cat" was read aloud. Ask that, when they reread the poem, they notice character traits about Ha. When they support these notices with evidence from the text, they are doing something close readers do as well. Add two lines to the anchor chart:
  - Reread
  - Cite evidence
- Preview the homework for students (see the next section). Explain that each night for homework, they will read a portion of the novel or their own independent book.
- Review the day's learning targets with students. Explain that when they returned to the book to answer text-dependent questions, they were citing evidence and learning more about Ha as a character.
- Use the **Fist-to-Five chart** and the Fist-to-Five strategy (see the Appendix) to have students rate how they did with the first learning target. This self-assessment helps students rate themselves on a continuum from 0 (fist), meaning far from the target, to 5 (five fingers), having solidly met the target. Ask students to indicate with their fist if they did not use the text to cite evidence or with five fingers if they consistently used the text to prove their thinking. They can choose to show one to four fingers to indicate whether their use of the text was somewhere in between.
- If time permits, call on a few students to provide evidence for the rating they gave themselves.

Homework

Reread "1975: Year of the Cat." Add at least three more details to your notes that help you learn about Ha. Then complete a first reading for the "gist" of pages 4–9, from the poem "Inside Out" through "Papaya Tree."

Note: Lesson 4 includes time to share the Recommended Texts list with students. Preview this list in advance.

LESSON 3

Inferring about Character

Close Reading of the Poem "Inside Out" and Introducing Quick Writes

Long-Term Targets Addressed (Based on ELA CCSS)

- I can cite text-based evidence that provides the strongest support for my analysis of literary text. (RL.8.1)
- I can analyze how specific dialogue or incidents in a plot propel the action, reveal aspects of a character, or provoke a decision. (RL.8.3)
- I can use a variety of strategies to determine the meaning of unknown words or phrases. (L.8.4)
- I can effectively engage in discussions with diverse partners about eighth-grade topics, texts, and issues. (SL.8.1)

Supporting Learning Targets

- I can make inferences to deepen my understanding of *Inside Out & Back Again*.
- I can cite evidence from the novel to explain how incidents reveal aspects of Ha's character.
- I can use context clues to figure out word meanings.
- I can participate in discussions about the text with a peer, small group, and the whole class.

Ongoing Assessment

- Answers to text-dependent questions

Agenda

1. Opening
   A. Engaging the Reader: The Gist Mix and Share (5 minutes)
   B. Review Learning Targets and Add to the Things Close Readers Do Anchor Chart (5 minutes)

---

2. Work Time

    A.   Close Reading: Poem, "Inside Out" (15 minutes)

    B.   Guided Practice: Quick Write (15 minutes)

3. Closing and Assessment

    A.   Debrief (5 minutes)

4. Homework

    A.   Reread pages 4–9 and complete Quick Write 1.

Teaching Notes

- This lesson introduces a protocol that you will use throughout the modules to promote student engagement, collaboration, and self-assessment. Review the Think-Pair-Share protocol (see the Appendix). For this lesson, pair students of mixed abilities.

- Share small-group and pairing norms to increase the efficacy of group work and working in pairs. In developmentally appropriate ways, give students specific praise when they are listening and contributing (e.g., "Props to this group over here, who I heard really pushing each other to give evidence").

- This lesson introduces students to the routine of Quick Writes (see Work Time, Part B). In advance, prepare the Quick Write Anchor Chart (see Unit 1, Lesson 3, supporting materials). Note the use of the term "focus statement," which is a more specific way of describing a topic sentence that focuses directly on the question being asked in a writing prompt.

- Throughout this module, students write routinely using Quick Writes—sometimes during class, and often as a part of their homework. Based on the needs of your class, determine whether students will do this writing in their notebooks (either as a separate section or chronologically after their various class notes) or on separate sheets of paper. Review the Unit 1 Overview section's Unit-at-a-Glance Calendar, Ongoing Assessment column, to see when and how Quick Writes are used. (You may choose to eliminate one, but understand how this impacts the lesson openings and unit assessments. In Unit 2, you may choose to design similar text-dependent questions to serve as Quick Writes and reinforce the skill of writing strong analytical paragraphs.) If you need scoring guidance in addition to the criteria on the Quick Write Anchor Chart, consider using the 2-point rubric to score students' Quick Writes.

- Model writing a Quick Write in front of the class. To save time, copy the model prompt in advance.

- It is important for students to see this writing done "in real time," rather than just seeing a finished model. However, students will also benefit from having a hard copy to refer to later. A basic Quick Write model is provided (see Unit 1, Lesson 3, supporting materials). If possible, type up the authentic teacher model that you create during class and distribute it to students as well.

- Post the learning targets where all students can see them.

Lesson Vocabulary

gist, inferences; predicts, foretells, fate, destiny

Materials

- *Inside Out & Back Again* (book; one per student)
- Things Close Readers Do Anchor Chart (from Lesson 2)—today's focus: using details to make inferences, using context clues, and talking with others
- "Inside Out" text-dependent questions (one per student)
- Quick Write Anchor Chart (new; teacher-created; see Supporting Materials)
- Document camera
- Teacher journal (for modeling of a Quick Write)
- Quick Write model (one per student and one for display; alternately, type up the "authentic" model that took place during class and distribute that)
- Quick Write 1 (one per student; for homework)

Opening

A. Engaging the Reader: The Gist Mix and Share (5 minutes)

- Inform students that the reading homework is important for the thinking they will do in class in the next lesson. For homework, they completed a "first read" of pages 4–9 and read for the gist. Invite students to open their books and quickly scan pages 4–9 to refresh their thinking.

- Next, ask students to stand up and find a peer to partner with. Each student in the pair will share the gist of the reading homework. Continue to reinforce that *gist* is the "reader's initial sense of what a text is mostly about"; it's okay if it's tentative, incomplete, or inaccurate. These poems may not seem so complex, but it's helpful for students to practice getting the gist.

- Give students 2 minutes to share. Display a timer to help students do this quickly.

- Then ask students to return to their seats for a quick debrief. Ask students:

  - "Was your idea of the gist the same as your partner's? Did you remember something else as you shared and listened?"

- Cold-call on students to offer their insights, and explain that talking about what they are reading is an important way to deepen their understanding of a text. It is a thing close readers do.

B. Review Learning Targets and Add to the Things Close Readers Do Anchor Chart (5 minutes)

- Post learning targets and the Things Close Readers Do Anchor Chart (perhaps on your interactive whiteboard or document camera) for review. Remind students that learning targets allow them to know the learning, thinking, and skills that are the focus of the lesson. Review the learning targets for the day, and check in at the end of the lesson to assess students and to help them assess themselves.

- Cold-call on students to read the learning targets:

  - "I can make inferences to deepen my understanding of *Inside Out & Back Again*."

    - Review *inferences* (from Lessons 1 and 2): Readers determine meaning based on things not directly stated in the text. When we infer, we use details or clues in the text and combine them with our background knowledge to help us understand incidents, characters, themes, and so forth. The book *Inside Out & Back Again* is deceptively simple: It leaves many things not directly stated and requires many inferences. Inform students they will continue to practice inferring in today's lesson.

  - "I can cite evidence from the novel to explain how incidents reveal aspects of Ha's character."

    - Remind students that close readers cite evidence, which means they prove what they believe the novel is saying by referring directly to words, phrases, and details from the novel.

- Read the last two learning targets aloud:

  - "I can use context clues to figure out word meanings."

  - "I can participate in discussions about the text with a partner, small group, and the whole class."

- Remind students that these targets are repeated from Lesson 2.

- Remind students that close reading of complex text includes citing evidence and focusing on word meanings. Talking with others often helps us understand a text more deeply. Add to the anchor chart:

  - Use details from the text to make inferences.

  - Use context clues to figure out word meanings.

  - Talk with others about the text.

- Inform students that today, they will pair up for Think-Pair-Share moments. Remind students to be respectful of others by listening to what others have to say, asking questions to clarify understanding, and participating in the discussions by offering thoughtful ideas and questions.

Work Time

A. Close Reading: Poem, "Inside Out" (15 minutes)

- Pair up students of mixed abilities to work together for this lesson.

- Explain that just as they took their time reading one poem yesterday, they are going to do something similar today, reading the poem "Inside Out" closely. Distribute **"Inside Out" text-dependent questions**. Inform students that they will use a Think-Pair-Share protocol to answer these questions. Explain the process if it is unfamiliar to the class. This is a simple protocol students will use often, in which you will pose a question or prompt and they will do the following:

  1. Take a few seconds to think about the question or prompt and reread the text as necessary. Students may also write down their thinking on the handout.

2. Pair up with another student and take turns sharing their thinking about the question or prompt. Students may revise what they have written on the handout.

3. Share with the whole class any thoughts they have, conclusions they come to, questions they still have, and so forth.

- Invite students to begin by rereading on their own page 4, "Inside Out."

- Ask them to Think-Pair-Share with their partner to discuss the gist of the poem:

  - "What is this poem mostly about?"

- Then read the poem aloud as students read along silently. Ask them to focus on whether their initial understanding of the gist is confirmed or whether they need to revise their thinking.

- Cold-call on a student to share the gist, and briefly clarify understanding for all (e.g., "Ha says war is coming"). Reassure students that it is okay if they have only a very basic understanding of the poem at this point. Part of reading closely involves rereading to deepen understanding.

- Focus students on the first text-dependent question:

  1. "How do the events in this poem connect to the first poem we read, '1975: Year of the Cat,' and the title of the novel, *Inside Out & Back Again*?"

- Remind them to first reread and think on their own.

- Ask students to share their thinking with their partners. Listen for students to make the connection that the first two poems are about predicting good or bad luck for the rest of the year. Students may wonder whether Ha brings bad luck on the family by being the first to rise on Tet instead of her older brother.

- Listen for students to refer to page 4, the first stanza (reinforce this habit of citing page number and stanza): "he predicts our lives will twist inside out."

- Focus students on key words that help link the two poems: *predicts* and *foretells*. Point out the prefix *pre* means "before," and *dict* means "to say or declare." So *predict* means "to tell beforehand." Help students see the direct connection between *predict* in this poem and the synonym *foretell* (from page 1, "1975: Year of the Cat").

- Students also should notice that the poem "Inside Out" is the first part of the novel's title. Inform them that this is one way an author signals importance; they will revisit this poem later in the module.

- Explain that you will repeat this Think-Pair-Share routine with additional questions. Encourage students to return to the text to find specific evidence to help them answer each question.

  2. "What specifically does the fortune-teller *predict* about the family's future?"

     - Listen for students to refer to the first stanza, "our lives will twist inside out." If students don't mention it, identify the word *fate* as meaning "destiny." The fortune-teller is predicting the family's destiny. Point out that *fate* and *destiny* have related meanings: Both mean "events outside of a person's control."

  3. "Ha lives in a war-torn country. How does she hope her life will be turned inside out?"

- Listen for students to refer to the second stanza: She hopes that soldiers will no longer patrol the neighborhood, that she can jump rope after dark, and that she will not have to hide from danger.

4. "Ha knows that 'inside out' probably means something different. What will probably happen?"
    - Listen for students to refer to the very last lines on page 4: "The war is coming closer to home."
- Give specific examples of students you observed rereading and citing textual evidence. Continue to reinforce these reading practices.

Meeting Students' Needs

- Heterogeneous pairing of students for regular discussion and close-reading exercises provides a collaborative and supportive structure for close reading of complex texts. This also provides more talk-time per student when processing and thinking requires more support and collaboration. Consider pairing students within existing small groups for ease in flexing students from pairs to small groups, and vice versa.

- Some students may benefit from using a ruler or piece of paper to underline the lines as they are read aloud.

- Some students may benefit from having sentence starters provided during Think-Pair-Share.

- Many students will benefit from seeing questions posted on interactive whiteboards or via your document camera, but reveal questions one at a time to keep students focused on the question at hand.

- You might arrange the students in pairs, since they will be practicing paired sharing in this lesson. Students will be reading, thinking, and discussing the book in pairs or small groups throughout the unit.

- Some students may benefit from having access to "hint cards," small slips of paper or index cards that they turn over for hints about how/where to find the answers to text-dependent questions. (For example, a hint card might say, "Check back in the second stanza on page 7.")

- Some students may benefit from having paragraph frames as a scaffold for Quick Writes.

B. Guided Practice: Quick Write (15 minutes)

- Inform students that to help them keep track of their thinking or think more carefully about specific sections of the text, they will often complete a Quick Write: a short piece of written analysis about the text. Sometimes they will do this in class, and sometimes they will do it for homework. Quick Writes are a good way for you to know how well each student understands the novel and can connect details from the reading to a writing prompt.

- Post the **Quick Write Anchor Chart** (or use your interactive whiteboard), which will serve as a reminder to students of the criteria for answering the Quick Write prompts. Review the chart:
    - Have I answered the prompt completely?

- Share with students that prompts often have more than one step. They need to read each prompt carefully to understand everything they are being asked to think about:

  - Does my paragraph include the following?

    - A focus statement

    - At least three pieces of specific evidence from the text

    - For each piece of evidence, an analysis or explanation: What does this evidence mean?

    - A concluding sentence

- Explain that most Quick Write prompts are a paragraph in length, and a well-constructed paragraph includes the sentences described above. Any time they do a Quick Write, students will be able to use the novel, graphic organizers, note-catchers, question handout, and notes to help them.

- Inform students that to help them know what a strong Quick Write looks like, you will model for them using the **document camera**. In your **teacher journal**, date the top of the page and write "Quick Write Model." Ask:

  - "Based on what you have read so far in the novel, what can you infer about what will happen to Ha and her family? Be sure to use details from the text to support your answer."

- Refer students to the anchor chart to review what they must include in the Quick Write. Students will notice that they must answer the question completely. Underline or highlight "infer about what will happen to Ha and her family" as the question they must answer. Probe to see whether students can rephrase the word *infer*. Listen for students to remember that to *infer* means "to use their own thinking plus clues in the text to understand the character or incidents."

- Invite students to Think-Pair-Share in response to this Quick Write question. Encourage students to locate clues in the text by asking them:

  - "Will Ha's actions affect the family's future?" (such as Ha's act of disobedience to her mother on Tet, which may bring bad luck)

  - "What might Ha's mother's visit to the fortune-teller have to do with the family's future?" (the fortune-teller's prediction of bad luck)

  - "What does Ha's comment that 'the war is coming closer to home' mean?"

  - "What does the phrase 'inside out' usually mean? Based on what you see in the text, and what you already know about that phrase, what do you infer?"

- Select the best details offered and model writing the focus statement, citing a key detail from the text and explaining the meaning and/or the importance of that detail. Repeat with two more details, again citing evidence and showing students how to explain the evidence. End with a concluding statement.

- Point out that the concluding statement basically sums things up, expressing the main points of the paragraph in a new way. Explain that students will work more on formal conclusions when they begin to write full essays (in Unit 2).

- Distribute hard copies of this Quick Write model for students to refer to when they write their own Quick Write response to a different question for homework.

EXPEDITIONARY
LEARNING

Closing and Assessment

A. Debrief (5 minutes)

- Preview the homework for students (see "Homework"). Remind students that each night for homework, they will read a portion of the novel or their own independent book.

- Review the day's learning targets with students. Explain that when they returned to the book to answer text-dependent questions, they were citing evidence and learning more about Ha as a character.

- Use the Fist-to-Five protocol to have students rate how they did with the first learning target. This self-assessment helps students rate themselves on a continuum from 0 (fist), meaning far from the target, to 5 (5 fingers), having solidly met the target. Ask students to indicate with their fist if they did not use the text to cite evidence or to use five fingers if they consistently used the text to prove their thinking. They can choose to show one to four fingers to indicate whether their use of the text was somewhere in between.

- If time permits, call on a few students to provide evidence for the rating they gave themselves.

Homework

- Reread pages 4–9 of *Inside Out & Back Again* (from "Inside Out" through "Papaya Tree").

- **Quick Write 1: What kind of person is Ha?** Use specific evidence from the text to write a paragraph in which you discuss one of Ha's personality traits. A complete paragraph includes a focus statement, several pieces of textual evidence, explanations about what each piece of evidence shows us about Ha, and a concluding sentence. Use the notes you collected in your journal to help you write this paragraph.

> ## Meeting Students' Needs
>
> You may use a structure or resource other than a journal for collecting student writing.

LESSON 4

Considering a Character's Relationship with Others

Contrasting Ha and Her Brothers

Long-Term Targets Addressed (Based on ELA CCSS)

- I can cite text-based evidence that provides the strongest support for my analysis of literary text. (RL.8.1)

- I can analyze how specific dialogue or incidents in a plot propel the action, reveal aspects of a character, or provoke a decision. (RL.8.3)

- I can analyze the impact of word choice on meaning and tone (analogies or allusions). (RL.8.4)

- I can effectively engage in discussions with diverse partners about eighth-grade topics, texts, and issues. (SL.8.1)

Supporting Learning Targets

- I can make inferences to deepen my understanding of *Inside Out & Back Again*.

- I can cite evidence from the novel to explain how incidents reveal aspects of Ha's character.

- I can explain how the specific word choices in the poem "Papaya Tree" create tone and help reveal meaning.

- I can participate in discussions about the text with a peer, small group, and the whole class.

Ongoing Assessment

- Quick Write 1 (from homework)
- Who Is Ha? small-group anchor charts

Agenda

1. Opening

   A. Engaging the Reader: We Learn More about Ha by How She Speaks about the Papaya Tree, and about Her Brothers (5 minutes)

   B. Review Learning Targets (5 minutes)

2. Work Time

   A. Rereading the Text and Answering Text-Dependent Questions: "Papaya Tree" (12 minutes)

   B. Discuss Quick Write 1 and Create Small-Group Anchor Chart: Who Is Ha? (13 minutes)

3. Closing and Assessment

   A. Debrief (5 minutes)

   B. Preview Unit 1 Recommended Texts List (5 minutes)

4. Homework

   A. Read pages 10–21 and complete Quick Write 2.

Teaching Notes

- This lesson continues to reinforce students' skills with reading closely and continues to attune them to paying close attention to words in general and to an author's word choice in particular. Note the work with the word *critical* in the Opening; this type of work with morphology, and the meaning of words in different contexts, is reinforced throughout these modules.

- Post learning targets in advance.

- Use the visual image of the papaya tree and its fruit to help students visualize this key symbol in the text (see "Materials"). In future lessons, students will consider the symbolic significance of the papaya tree, so do not rush this here in Lesson 4. Of course, if students' comments indicate they are ready to address symbolism, follow their lead.

- This lesson includes the Who Is Ha? Anchor Chart that students will revisit throughout the module. The students' work with the chart in this lesson anchors their initial understandings of Ha and serves as the initial character analysis for the module and review for the Mid-Unit Assessment in Lesson 5. Be sure to have students put their names on their chart, and inform them that you will keep the chart for use in future lessons.

- Prepare the T-chart as a model ahead of time. This will provide the example students need to create their anchor charts for their initial character analysis of Ha.

- Review: Turn-and-Talk, Numbered Heads Together (see the Appendix).

- Students write routinely using Quick Writes—sometimes during class and often as a part of their homework. Consider "test driving" each Quick Write assignment in advance by completing it yourself. This will help you become increasingly clear about the challenges students may face when creating Quick Writes in general or about the specific challenges of citing or explaining evidence to answer a particular Quick Write prompt. If more than one teacher in your building is using the modules, consider comparing your writing to discuss common challenges you anticipate your students may face.

Lesson Vocabulary

cite evidence, infer (review), critical incident, meaning, tone; papaya tree, flicked, vow, witness

Materials

- *Inside Out & Back Again* (book; one per student)
- Things Close Readers Do Anchor Chart (begun in Lesson 2)—today's focus: noticing details, answering questions based on the text
- A photo of a papaya tree, which may be found via a Google Images search
- "Papaya Tree" text-dependent questions (one per student)
- Who Is Ha? Anchor Chart (new, teacher-created, Teacher Reference)
- Chart paper for small-group anchor chart What Do We Know about Ha? (one piece of chart paper per group)
- Markers (four different colors per group)
- Unit 1 Recommended Texts list
- Quick Write 2: How is Ha's life affected by where and when she is living? (one per student; for homework)

Opening

A. Engaging the Reader: We Learn More about Ha by How She Speaks about the Papaya Tree, and about Her Brothers (5 minutes)

- Read the first stanza on page 8 of the poem "Papaya Tree":
  - "It grew from a seed/I flicked into/the back garden."
- Ask students, "What is Ha referring to here?" (Ideally students will realize it is her papaya tree.)
- Draw students' attention to the cover illustration on their *Inside Out & Back Again* books, and ask:
  - "Which images do you notice on the cover of the book?"
- Listen for students to notice a young girl, a red sky, and a tree. Ask students whether they can infer, based on their reading so far, what type of tree this is. Students should realize it is a papaya tree. Reinforce inferring here: "You took something from the text (in this case, the picture on the cover) and something you already knew (based on reading pages 4–9 the past few days), and you put it together." Be sure that students know that a papaya tree is a tropical tree that bears the papaya fruit; clarify if needed.

- Inform students that they will reread the poem "Papaya Tree" on pages 8 and 9 to make inferences. They will be thinking about how Ha's description of the tree helps the reader learn about her and her war-torn country.

Meeting Students' Needs

- Students may benefit from having the stanza and question posted as something they can do while you take attendance or attend to other beginning-of-class chores.
- Some students may benefit from having pictorial representations of learning targets.

B. Review Learning Targets (5 minutes)

- Post learning targets for review. Remind students that learning targets help them know the learning, thinking, and skills that will be the focus of the lesson and that they will review and check learning targets at the end of the lesson.

- Read the first two learning targets aloud to students:

  - "I can make inferences to deepen my understanding of *Inside Out & Back Again*."

  - "I can *cite evidence* from the novel to explain how incidents reveal aspects of Ha's character."

- Students should recognize these targets. Ask students to Turn-and-Talk to review what it means to *infer* and *cite evidence*. Listen for students to state that *infer* and *cite evidence* means that students will need "to use their background knowledge, combined with what the text says, and refer to the language in the novel to prove their thinking."

- Explain that the *critical incident* in the novel they will discuss today is about Ha's papaya tree. "This *incident,* or event, is *critical* (crucial or very important) because Ha pays attention to it a lot and writes about it several times. But we need to infer the meaning of the papaya tree." Be sure to distinguish the meaning of the word *critical* from what this word means in other contexts students might be familiar with (e.g., a negative connotation, such as if a friend is being *critical* of you).

- Read the second target aloud:

  - "I can explain how the specific word choices in the poem 'Papaya Tree' create tone and help reveal meaning."

- Discuss the word *meaning* with students. Ask them to think and then talk with a peer about synonyms for this word. Invite a few students to share out. Be sure students realize that *meaning* refers to "what the text is about" and that *tone* refers to "the emotion or feeling of the text. Tone helps create meaning." Encourage them by saying that they will get smarter about seeing the connection between word choice, tone, and meaning as they continue to read the novel.

Work Time

A. Rereading the Text and Answering Text-Dependent Questions: "Papaya Tree" (12 minutes)

Note: Remember that students will address the symbolic significance of the papaya tree in future lessons. Do not rush it here, but of course, follow students' leads should their comments indicate they are ready to address symbolism.

- Ask students to sit in their small heterogeneous numbered heads groups.

- Display and remind students of the **Things Close Readers Do Anchor Chart**. Invite several students to read the chart, and ask for a Fist-to-Five to check for understanding before moving on to the rereading.

- Ask students to reread "Papaya Tree" silently. Remind them that they are reading for the *gist* of the poem: What is their sense of what it is mostly about? Remind them that *gist* is not as formal as summarizing; it's preliminary.

- After they have read and thought about the poem, invite students to Turn-and-Talk with a peer in their group to share their thinking. Listen for students to notice that Ha has a *papaya tree* growing in her backyard. Her brothers have noticed the tree's blossoms and fruit. Ha wants to be the first one to notice the papaya's ripe fruit.

- Remind them that rereading helps readers notice important details. Then reread the poem aloud, as students read along silently.

- Invite students to share in their groups:

  - "Which new or important details struck you after hearing the poem read aloud again?"

- Encourage students to return to the text, and listen for students to notice details, such as the seed resembles a fish eye ("slippery/shiny/black"), or details about the size and color of the tree ("twice as tall as I stand," and "white blossom"). Point out that such descriptive details often help readers visualize what the writer is describing; students will be paying close attention to this type of language throughout their study of this novel and will often reread key passages to pay particular attention to word choice.

- Show students a **photograph of the papaya tree** and its seeds, blossom, and fruit. Ask students: "Why might the author have chosen this particular tree to focus on?" Cold-call on a few students for response. Listen for students to notice that the tree grows in Vietnam, has sweet fruit Ha can enjoy, and so forth. (Students will return to the symbolic significance of the papaya tree in future lessons.)

- Share the **"Papaya Tree" text-dependent questions** with the students, revealing them one at a time.

- Remind students that they will reread, think, and then talk about these questions. Rereading and talking will help them deepen their understanding of the text:

  1. "How did the papaya tree begin to grow? Was the planting of the tree intentional or a careless act? How do you know this?" (Listen for students to refer to page 8, stanza 1: "Ha *flicked* it into

---

the garden.") Once students have answered, ask: "Why does the author choose the word *flicked* versus *planted*? How do these words differ in meaning and tone?"

- Give students time to reread, think, and talk in their small groups.
- Then use the Numbered Heads Together strategy for whole-group sharing of the answers.

- Repeat this process with the following questions:

2. "From youngest to oldest brother, Ha describes what each brother sees on the tree. What is the pattern she describes?" (Students will notice on pages 8 and 9, stanzas 4–6, that first the blossom is spotted by the youngest, then the small fruit by the middle brother, and the ripened fruit is something Ha hopes to see before her oldest brother.)

3. "Ha *vows* to be the first to *witness,* or observe, the ripening of the papaya fruit. What does the word *vows* mean in this context? Where else do we read that Ha wants to be the first at something instead of her oldest brother?" (Students may recognize *vows* from "wedding vows." Help them notice that in this context, it means "pledge" or "promise." But to help students begin to attend to nuances in word meaning, point out that the word *vow* is stronger than *promise*—a *vow* is "a particularly strong or serious promise.")

- Listen for students to refer back to "1975: The Year of the Cat": Ha wants to be the first one to touch the floor. Remind students that one thing close readers do is return to the text. Model rereading: Have students turn to pages 2 and 3, the last two stanzas of this poem, and notice that Ha is the first to touch the floor on Tet. Then refer to page 2, the third stanza: Her mother wants the oldest son to "rise first to bless our house" and bring good luck to the family on Tet.

4. "What can you *infer* or conclude about Ha's character based on these two poems or critical incidents?" (Students may respond that Ha is competitive, jealous, a fighter, and so forth. Support students with this inference by guiding them with questions and prompts that encourage them to use what they know together with the clues in the text to draw conclusions about Ha.)

Meeting Students' Needs

- Heterogeneous grouping of students for regular discussion and reading exercises provides a collaborative and supportive structure for close reading of complex texts. This also allows for more talk-time per student when processing and thinking requires more support and collaboration. Consider pairing students within existing small groups for ease in flexing students from pairs to small groups, and vice versa.

- Some students may benefit from using a ruler or piece of paper to underline the lines as they are read aloud.

- Some students may benefit from having sentence starters provided to support their participation in group discussions.

- Many students will benefit from seeing questions posted on the interactive whiteboard or via a document camera, but reveal questions one at a time to keep students focused on the question at hand.

- Some students may benefit from having access to "hint cards," small slips of paper or index cards that they turn over for hints about how/where to find the answers to text-dependent questions. For example, a hint card might say, "Check back in the fourth stanza on page 8."

- Some students may benefit from having prehighlighted or otherwise noted details about Ha in their texts.

B. Discuss Quick Write 1 and Create Small-Group Anchor Chart: Who Is Ha? (13 minutes)

- Ask students to remain in their small groups. Distribute **chart paper** and **markers** to each group, and ask them to create a **Who Is Ha? Anchor Chart** (see Supporting Materials).

- Point out to them that this chart looks exactly like the notes they took about Ha in Lesson 2:
  - Detail/Evidence in the left column
  - Page number in the middle
  - Inference/Reasoning in the right column

- Ask students to write their names on their charts using markers in their chosen color. Inform them that you will check their contributions to the chart by tracking how often each color appears.

- Explain that these charts will help them "anchor" their learning about Ha. They will revisit these charts throughout the module. Make sure students also add their group members' names to their chart.

- Give students 10 minutes to create their charts. Encourage them to use their notes from Lessons 2 and 3 and Quick Write 1 responses (from Lesson 3 homework) as well as their classwork from this lesson.

- As students work on the charts, circulate to listen as needed. Encourage students to refer to the text. Encourage and acknowledge students who are citing evidence. Continue to reinforce the small-group norms that make for effective collaboration: listening to others, asking polite clarifying questions, offering meaningful ideas, and so forth. Name the specific behaviors you notice students are doing that help their group function well.

- Model as needed. For example: "What have you noticed about Ha that she writes directly in her diary?" (her age, some family details, feelings toward her mother) "What are some things she writes that show you about her, but you have to think about and make an inference? For example, it says she decides to wake before dawn to touch the floor—I say this means she likes to be first, and so Ha is stubborn."

- After 10 minutes, ask students from several groups to share out one key insight from their chart. Address any significant misconceptions you overheard as students were working in their groups.

- Reinforce specific instances when you saw or heard students revisit the text or cite specific textual evidence. Remind students that in future lessons, they will add to these charts as they learn more about Ha.

Closing and Assessment

A. Debrief (5 minutes)

- Review the Things Close Readers Do Anchor Chart, and ask students what else they can add that close readers do. Guide students to add that when they answered questions that relied on their referring back to the text, they were also being close readers. Add two lines to the anchor chart:
  - Notice details
  - Answer questions based on the text
- Preview the homework.
- Review the learning targets. Students learned more about Ha's character from reading about something she cares about—the papaya tree and her relationship with her brothers—and paid attention to word choice as they continued to practice close reading.
- Ask students to complete an Exit Ticket in which they rank themselves on a scale of 1 to 5 for each of the targets, with 5 being total mastery and 1 being "I don't get it." For each rating they give themselves, ask students to justify their responses with evidence.
- Explain to students that in the next lesson, they will have an opportunity to "show what they know" about analyzing Ha's character (on the Mid-Unit Assessment). Let them know that there are no tricks to this assessment; it is very much like the thinking they have been practicing in Lessons 1–4.

B. Preview Unit 1 Recommended Texts List (5 minutes)

As time permits, share with students the **Unit 1 Recommended Texts list**. You might share some of the materials from the list with students (as an example of the types of texts featured on the list).

Homework

Read pages 10–21, from "TiTi Waves Goodbye" through "Two More Papayas," and complete **Quick Write 2: How is Ha's life affected by where and when she is living?**

Note: Students may refer to their Who Is Ha? Anchor Chart during the Mid-Unit Assessment in Lesson 5. Store the charts on a wall in the classroom if possible.

LESSON 5

Mid-Unit Assessment

Getting to Know a Character: Which Details in the Text Help Us Understand Ha?

Long-Term Targets Addressed (Based on ELA CCSS)

- I can analyze how specific dialogue or incidents in a plot propel the action, reveal aspects of a character, or provoke a decision. (RL.8.3)
- I can cite text-based evidence that provides the strongest support for my analysis of literary text. (RL.8.1)
- I can determine the meaning of words and phrases in literary text (figurative, connotative, and technical meanings). (RL.8.4)
- I can analyze the impact of word choice on meaning and tone (analogies or allusions). (RL.8.4)
- I can use evidence from literary texts to support analysis, reflection, and research. (W.8.9)
- I can effectively engage in discussions with diverse partners about eighth-grade topics, texts, and issues. (SL.8.1)

Supporting Learning Targets

- I can make inferences that deepen my understanding of *Inside Out & Back Again*.
- I can analyze how critical incidents in the novel reveal aspects of Ha's character.
- I can cite evidence from the text in my writing that supports my analysis.
- I can participate in discussions about the text with a peer, small group, and the whole class.

Ongoing Assessment

- Quick Write 2 (from homework)
- Mid-Unit Assessment: Getting to Know a Character: Which Details in the Text Help Us Understand Ha?

Agenda

1. Opening
    A. Engaging the Reader: Gallery Walk about Who Is Ha? (10 minutes)
2. Work Time
    A. Mid-Unit 1 Assessment: Getting to Know a Character: What Details in the Text Help Us Understand Ha? (30 minutes)
3. Closing and Assessment
    A. Debrief (2 minutes)
4. Homework
    A. Read pages 22–41 and keep adding details about Ha to your notes.

Teaching Notes

- In the opening of this lesson, students revisit the Who Is Ha? Anchor Charts they created during Lesson 4. This helps prepare them for the upcoming assessment, by both activating their background knowledge and seeing models of how their peers are inferring about Ha based on evidence from the text.

- In advance, post students' Who Is Ha? Anchor Charts around the room.

- Post learning targets on the whiteboard.

- Review Gallery Walk (see the Appendix).

- This is an "open book" assessment: students will need their texts and may use their journals, Quick Writes, and the anchor charts posted around the room.

- Consider the assessment data collected from this first assessment as a "baseline" for your students' capacity to use evidence from text to support their thinking (W.8.9).

- For homework, students do a first read of pages 22–41, which they address in more depth during Lesson 8.

Lesson Vocabulary

evidence (review); do not preview vocabulary from the text for the assessment

Materials

- Who Is Ha? Anchor Chart (from Lesson 4; student-created in small groups)
- Sticky notes (three per student)
- Markers (four different colors per group)
- *Inside Out & Back Again* (book; one per student)

- Quick Write model (from Lesson 3)

- Mid-Unit 1 Assessment: Getting to Know a Character: Which Details in the Text Help Us Understand Ha? (one per student)

- Mid-Unit 1 Assessment: Getting to Know a Character: Which Details in the Text Help Us Understand Ha? (Teacher Reference)

- 2-point rubric: writing from sources/short response (Teacher Reference to score students' assessments)

Opening

A. Engaging the Reader: Gallery Walk about Who Is Ha? (10 minutes)

Note: Post students' anchor charts around the classroom in advance.

- Show students the **Who Is Ha? Anchor Charts** that they created in their small groups during Lesson 4.

- Briefly review the Gallery Walk protocol. Inform students that the purpose is to see others' thinking. Distribute **sticky notes** to each student. Explain that they will look at the other charts and jot down on their sticky notes aspects of Ha's character and the *evidence* the other groups have provided. They will then get to add these sticky notes to their own small-group charts. Encourage group members to pair up and walk around with their partner to look at as many different charts as possible.

- Review class norms as needed to ensure that students circulate to look at one another's charts in a quiet and respectful manner.

- Begin the Gallery Walk: Give students 5 minutes to walk around, read other groups' charts, and jot their notes. Explain to them that this thinking will help prepare them for their upcoming assessment.

- Then ask students to gather with their own small group next to their own anchor chart. Ask students to share their sticky notes:

  - "Which new details did you gather about Ha and her situation?"

- Give each group **markers**, and encourage them to add information to their anchor chart. Specifically ask that each pair add one new piece of evidence from the text to their chart.

- As students work in their small groups, circulate to listen in and give support as needed. Praise students who are actively looking back in the novel for additional details. Remind them that close readers pay attention to details as they read and think about why those details are important. Commend students for finding specific evidence from the texts to support their thinking.

- Also listen for a few strong examples when students refer to specific details from the novel that reveal Ha's character.

Work Time

A. Mid-Unit 1 Assessment: Getting to Know a Character: What Details in the Text Help Us Understand Ha? (30 minutes)

- For the assessment, consider rearranging seats so students are not in their groups. Make sure students have the following materials:
  - Pen or pencil
  - *Inside Out & Back Again* book
  - **Quick Write model** (from Lesson 3)
- Distribute the Mid-Unit 1 Assessment: Getting to Know a Character: Which Details in the Text Help Us Understand Ha? Read the directions aloud as students read along silently.
- Reassure students that they have been practicing reading the novel and learning about Ha's character from the words and phrases the author uses. They will now start to use what they've learned as they do their own writing.
- Remind students of some of the reading and writing skills they have been learning that will help them on this assessment:
  - Read for the gist: What is your initial sense of what the text is mostly about?
  - Think about the questions.
  - Reread the text with the questions in mind. Look for details.
  - Write your answers, using specific evidence from the text to support your thinking.
- Give students 25 minutes to complete the assessment.
- Students who finish early may reread earlier portions of the novel, revisit "The Vietnam Wars" article, or read in their independent reading book for this unit.
- Collect assessments from students. Let them know that they will keep practicing close reading and citing evidence in lessons to come.

Meeting Students' Needs

For this assessment, provide appropriate accommodations (e.g., extra time) for ELL students and students with special needs.

Closing and Assessment

A. Debrief (2 minutes)

- Preview the homework with students.
- Review the assessment with the class. Ask students how they thought they did in terms of understanding Ha's character and connecting details from the book to what they noticed. Students can respond with a Fist-to-Five.

Homework

Complete a first reading of pages 22–41, from "Unknown Father" through "Promises." Keep noticing what the critical incidents and key details are helping us learn about Ha. Use your journal to record your notes.

Note: Review students' Quick Write 2. Identify a strong example to show (at the start of Lesson 6) as an exemplar of supporting ideas with evidence from text. Seek the student's permission in advance to share his or her work. Be prepared to highlight how the author of the model uses specific details to support his or her ideas and the way this student has woven evidence into the paragraph.

Review students' Mid-Unit Assessments. Provide specific feedback; time is allocated in Lesson 9 to share this feedback with students.

LESSON 6

Building Background Knowledge
Guided Practice to Learn about the History of Wars in Vietnam

Long-Term Targets Addressed (Based on ELA CCSS)

- I can determine the theme or central ideas of an informational text. (RI.8.2)
- I can use a variety of strategies to determine the meaning of unknown words or phrases. (L.8.4)
- I can effectively engage in discussions with diverse partners about eighth-grade topics, texts, and issues. (SL.8.1)

Supporting Learning Targets

- I can determine the central ideas in one section of the informational text "The Vietnam Wars."
- I can use context clues to determine word meanings.
- I can participate in discussions about the text with a peer, small group, and the whole class.

Ongoing Assessment

- Students' questions and notes for Section 1 of "The Vietnam Wars"

Agenda

1. Opening
   A. Sharing Exemplar: A Classmate's Quick Write 2 (5 minutes)
   B. Review Learning Targets: Distinguishing Informational Text from Historical Fiction (5 minutes)
2. Work Time
   A. Inferring Based on a Map and Previewing Informational Text: "The Vietnam Wars" (10 minutes)
   B. Read-Aloud and Guided Note-Taking: Section 1 of "The Vietnam Wars" (20 minutes)
3. Closing and Assessment
   A. Preview Homework and Read-Aloud (5 minutes)

---

4. Homework

    A. Reread section 1 of "The Vietnam Wars," complete Section 1 Note-Catcher, and read one new assigned section.

Teaching Notes

*   In advance, type up an exemplary student Quick Write 2 to share during Work Time. See the note at the end of Lesson 5 for details.

*   In this lesson, students do not work directly with pages 22–41 (which they have read for homework). Rather, students build background knowledge about Vietnam. Then, in Lesson 8, students return to discussing the novel in more detail.

*   In advance, have students reread "TiTi Waves Goodbye" (pages 10–11) and "Current News" (page 18). Be prepared to help students see connections between these poems and the informational text they will read in this lesson and in Lesson 7.

*   This lesson focuses on an informational text, which students will revisit throughout the unit. Carefully preview the Opening, which includes direct instruction regarding key distinctions—in terms of purpose and perspective—between informational text and literature. These distinctions are reinforced in future lessons as students continue to work with both types of text.

*   The article "The Vietnam Wars" is long and challenging. Be clear, for yourself and for your students, that there are two purposes for this reading:

    *   One purpose is to help students build basic background knowledge to assist in understanding the events in the novel. (Therefore, students do not need to understand every event in Vietnam's long and complicated history with various invaders.)

    *   The second purpose is for students to become better readers of complex informational text. In Lessons 6 and 7, students apply some key practices of close reading: reading along silently as a teacher reads aloud, rereading for gist, focusing on key vocabulary, and answering text-dependent questions. However, these lessons compress several close-reading practices into a single step.

*   Reinforce with students their work on "getting the gist" in Lessons 2–5, which may be needed more with this difficult text. Also, distinguish their initial and informal gist notes (which they jot by paragraph) from the written summary of the entire section, which they are asked to write later on their note-catcher (see Work Time).

*   Lessons 6 and 7 are designed as one arc. Lesson 6 provides direct instruction and guided practice with the first section of the text, which lays the foundation for students to work more independently (in small groups) during Lesson 7 with the middle three sections of the article.

*   In Lessons 9 and 10 (when students are further into the novel), they will do a more comprehensive close read of the final section of this same article. Give them more time for this section, because it addresses the key events that led to the fall of Saigon, which is most relevant to the novel and the focus of the module.

*   Do not inform students in advance that this piece addresses centuries of Vietnamese history; they will figure that out from the text. But throughout the lesson, consistently focus students on how

the details are helping them understand the main idea of the text and how that, in turn, helps them understand Ha's experiences.

- Questions and Notes: Section 1 note-catcher focuses on key vocabulary. Students are told the definitions of some concrete words that can be taught quickly to focus their attention on the more challenging academic vocabulary that they can figure out from context clues.

- If appropriate, collaborate with the social studies teacher, so students have additional time in social studies class to reread this text in greater detail or to go into the historical issues in greater depth.

- In advance, determine which section of the article (2, 3, or 4) to assign to each small group for homework. Note that students need to hear some of each section read aloud to do their homework more independently; allow time for this.

- This lesson involves the Think-Pair-Share protocol. Students may remain in the same pairs from previous lessons, or consider pairing students with new partners as needed.

- Review Think-Pair-Share (see the Appendix).

Lesson Vocabulary

central idea, key incidents, informational text, historical fiction, objective, perspective, context, annotate; honing, even, forged, crucible, pacified, string, gracious

Materials

- Document camera
- A student's exemplar Quick Write 2 (typed up in advance)
- Map of Asia (zoom out so students can see Vietnam and China)
- "The Vietnam Wars" article (one per student)
- "The Vietnam Wars" Questions and Notes: Section 1: "The Chinese Dragon" (one per student)

Opening

A. Sharing Exemplar: A Classmate's Quick Write 2 (5 minutes)

- Acknowledge that students are working hard to learn to analyze the text as they read, discuss, and write. Point out specific growth you are noticing that students are making with these skills.

- Using your **document camera** or other means of projection, show the class **a student's exemplar Quick Write 2** (from Lesson 4 homework) that is a strong example of supporting ideas with evidence from the text.

- Highlight how the author of the model uses specific details to support his or her ideas and the way the author weaves evidence into the paragraph.

- Encourage students to continue to cite and explain evidence in their own writing and during discussion.

EXPEDITIONARY
LEARNING

B. Review Learning Targets: Distinguishing Informational Text from Historical Fiction (5 minutes)

- Students should be seated in the small, heterogeneous numbered heads groups they have been meeting with so far in this unit.

- Invite students to share briefly, based on the Quick Writes they have written and additional details they noticed in their reading:

  - "What are some key details you noticed that helped you understand how Ha's life is affected by the time and place in which her story is set?"

- Call on a group member to share out one detail per group with the whole class. Listen for students to share such details as the following: "Ha's best friend, TiTi, and her family leave the country. Ha's father is missing in action and hasn't been heard from in 9 years. Her mother works two jobs to make ends meet. Food and gasoline are expensive. There's bad news about the communists being close to Saigon." Encourage students to add a few key details to their notes.

- Post learning targets for review, and read the first learning target aloud to students:

  - "I can determine the central ideas in one section of an informational text about the Vietnam War."

- Announce that today students will begin reading an informational text that will help them understand why there were bombs near Ha's home, why Americans were in Vietnam, and why communists were invading Saigon.

- Briefly distinguish *informational text* from literature, specifically *historical fiction*: *Informational text* is "factual information about real events"; *historical fiction*, like *Inside Out & Back Again*, is a "made-up/imagined story that is based on real events." Discuss the fact that authors of historical fiction usually do a lot of research to learn about the time and place they are writing about. And readers often get so interested in the events described in the novel that they then choose to read informational texts to help them better understand the time and place. The class will be doing that today.

- Emphasize that literature and informational texts typically have different purposes. Authors of informational text write to *inform* or teach the reader about a topic. This purpose means that informational text is usually written with a more straightforward, objective, "just the facts" perspective. Literature, on the other hand, is written to bring readers into a real or imagined world. Stories are often written from the perspective of a particular character: We see the world through that person's eyes.

- Discuss that informational text may have many *central ideas,* or important ideas. It is important to practice reading informational text closely to notice these ideas.

- For the next few days, students will not be reading or discussing the novel. Instead, their goal is to begin to build background knowledge that will help them understand why Ha's country is

---

TEACHER GUIDE · Grade 8 · Module 1 · Unit 1 · Lesson 6   **79**

experiencing war. Inform students that this text may begin to help answer some of the questions they generated during the very first lesson.

Work Time

A. Inferring Based on a Map and Previewing Informational Text: "The Vietnam Wars" (10 minutes)

- Display the **map of Asia** for students to view. Help students focus on South and North Vietnam. Ask students:
  - "What do you notice about these countries relative to the countries around them?"
- Listen for students to recognize that these countries are small and surrounded by much larger countries, specifically China.
- Ask students to think and then Turn-and-Talk with a partner about this question:
  - "Based on what you notice, what can you infer about the history of Vietnam and its relationship with the countries around it?"
- Invite volunteers to share out. Listen for students to infer that Vietnam may often have been invaded by larger countries. If students don't come to this conclusion yet, that is okay; the text will clarify this.
- Point out to students that their inferences are based on something they saw and something they already knew. And this inference is in effect a prediction: They will now get to read the text to see whether they were right.
- Distribute and display the article **"The Vietnam Wars."** Focus students on the title. Ask:
  - "How does the title help you understand the coming article?"
- Probe, asking specifically:
  - "Why do you think the title has the word 'Wars,' plural, rather than just 'War'?"
- Listen for students to infer that this article is about the history of war in Vietnam, not just the Vietnam War they may have heard about (which took place in the 1960s and 1970s).
- Focus students on the subtitle. Read it aloud as students read along silently: "By the time American troops arrived on their shores, the Vietnamese had already spent centuries honing a warrior tradition in a series of brutal wars." Ask students:
  - "What do you think the word *honing* means?"
- If needed, explain that the word *honing* means "perfecting or sharpening."
- Invite students to think and then Turn-and-Talk:
  - "In your own words, what does the subtitle of this article tell you about Vietnam?"
- Cold-call on a student to share with the class. Listen for students to state that the Vietnamese have been fighting wars for many centuries. Point out to students that the article's subtitle is one clear way the author signals his purpose and the main idea. They will read on to learn much more.
- Ask students to skim the article, just to get oriented to the text. Ask them to read and number the five subheadings (keep this brief).

EXPEDITIONARY
LEARNING

Meeting Students' Needs

- Heterogeneous grouping of students for regular discussion and reading exercises provides a collaborative and supportive structure for close reading complex texts. This also allows for more talk-time per student when processing and thinking require more support and collaboration. Consider pairing students within existing small groups for ease in flexing students from pairs to small groups, and vice versa.

- Some students may benefit from using a ruler or piece of paper to underline the lines as they are read aloud.

- Many students will benefit from seeing questions posted on the interactive whiteboard or via a document camera, but reveal questions one at a time to keep students focused on the question at hand.

- Some students may benefit from having access to "hint cards," small slips of paper or index cards that they turn over for hints about how/where to find the answers to text-dependent questions. For example, a hint card might say, "Check back in the third paragraph on page 7."

- Some students may benefit from receiving only Section 1 of the text for this specific lesson. This keeps them from being overwhelmed with the amount of text.

- Some students may benefit from having the Questions and Notes handout partially completed with sentence starters.

B. Read-Aloud and Guided Note-Taking: Section 1 of "The Vietnam Wars" (20 minutes)

- Note that as with other read-alouds in this unit, this is a "pure" read-aloud: Simply read slowly and fluently. Do not explain.

- Remind students that today they will focus on Section 1: "The Chinese Dragon, 208 B.C.–1428 A.D." Inform students that each paragraph includes quite a bit of information.

- Ask students to pair up. As they begin to dig into this challenging text, ask them to do the following:

  1. Read along silently as you hear Section 1 read aloud (one paragraph at a time).

  2. After each paragraph, reread to think, and jot notes about the gist: What is your initial sense of what this paragraph is mostly about?

  3. Talk with a peer: What did you jot down for the gist of each paragraph?

- For Section 1 of the text, follow these three steps:

  1. As students are talking with their peers, distribute **"The Vietnam Wars" Questions and Notes: Section 1: "The Chinese Dragon"** (one per student). Explain the *abbreviated* process they will follow with Section 1: They will use the Think-Pair-Share protocol as they reread, taking notes on vocabulary and other key questions.

  2. Circulate to listen in and support students as they work. Listen for patterns of confusion to determine which specific questions to address with the whole group.

3. When 5 minutes remain in Work Time, pause students and refocus the whole group. Remind students that they will reread this section for their homework, so it is okay if they are not quite finished. Explain that in addition to taking notes in their graphic organizer, students should feel free to *annotate,* or take notes on the text itself (they will learn more about annotating in future lessons). Check for understanding, focusing on specific questions you noted that were more difficult for students.

- Let students know that it is okay if they haven't had quite enough time to complete their note-catchers. This is part of their homework, including their more formal summary, and they will work more on summary writing later in this module. For now, they should do their best to write a sentence that says what this section is about.

- Remind students to hold on to their article "The Vietnam Wars," because they will return to this text over the coming week.

Closing and Assessment

A. Preview Homework and Read-Aloud (5 minutes)

- Inform students that their homework involves two parts: Everyone will reread Section 1 and complete their notes, then each group will *also* read one more section.

- Quickly assign each small group one of the following sections:
  - Section 2: "Everything Tends to Ruin, 1627–1941"
  - Section 3: "Life, Liberty, and Ho Chi Minh, 1941–1945"
  - Section 4: "The Fall of the French, 1945–1954"

- Explain that to help them with this difficult reading, you will read parts of each of these sections aloud as they read along silently.

- Be sure to read subtitles and dates. Read in a dramatic style that brings this complex history to life. But remember that this is a "pure" read-aloud: Read slowly and fluently, and do not stop to explain.

- Section 2: Read the first two paragraphs aloud as students read along silently, from "Everything Tends to Ruin, 1627–1941" to "In 26 years, Vietnam was a French colony."

- Section 3: Read the first long paragraph aloud as students read along silently, from "Life, Liberty, and Ho Chi Minh, 1941–1945" to " . . . their fugitive leader took the name that would plague a generation of generals in France and the United States: Ho Chi Minh."

- Section 4: Read the first two paragraphs aloud as students read along silently, from "The Fall of the French, 1945–1954" to "We will lose 10 men for every one you lose, but in the end it is you who will tire."

Homework

Reread Section 1 of the article "The Vietnam Wars" and complete your Section 1 note-catcher. Also, for your *new assigned section,* reread the few paragraphs you heard read aloud in class. (You may read the entire section if you choose, but focus on what you heard read aloud.)

LESSON 7

Building Background Knowledge

Small-Group Work to Learn More about the History of Wars in Vietnam

Long-Term Targets Addressed (Based on ELA CCSS)

- I can determine the central ideas of an informational text. (RI.8.2)
- I can use a variety of strategies to determine the meaning of unknown words or phrases. (L.8.4)
- I can effectively engage in discussions with diverse partners about eighth-grade topics, texts, and issues. (SL.8.1)

Supporting Learning Targets

- I can determine the central ideas in one section of the informational text "The Vietnam Wars."
- I can summarize a portion of an informational text about the Vietnam War.
- I can use context clues to determine word meanings.
- I can participate in discussions about the text with a peer, small group, and the whole class.

Ongoing Assessment

- Students' questions and notes for their assigned section of the text

Agenda

1. Opening
   A. Engaging the Reader: Reviewing Homework (8 minutes)
   B. Review Learning Targets (2 minutes)

---

2. Work Time

    A. Modified Jigsaw, Part I: Key Vocabulary and Questions (15 minutes)

    B. Modified Jigsaw, Part II: Sharing Our Summaries (15 minutes)

3. Closing and Assessment

    A. Debrief: Adding to Our Things Close Readers Do Anchor Chart (5 minutes)

4. Homework

    A. Reread section 4, "The Fall of the French"; complete the questions and notes; complete Quick Write 3.

Teaching Notes

- Lesson 7 continues the arc of instruction begun in Lesson 6. Students work more independently with Sections 2–4 of the same article, "The Vietnam Wars." (Note that the *final* section of the article, "Doc-Lap at Last," is addressed in Lessons 9 and 10.)

- Continue to remind yourself and students of the purpose of reading these middle sections of this dense informational text: to build basic background knowledge about the history of wars in Vietnam. Students do *not* need to understand every twist and turn in this long, complex history. Continue to focus them on the main idea, and encourage them to consider how this informational text is helping them understand the novel.

- If appropriate, collaborate with the social studies teacher so students have additional time in social studies class to reread this text in greater detail or to go into the historical issues in greater depth.

- This lesson involves a Jigsaw protocol, in which students build expertise about one portion of the text and then share that expertise with peers who read other portions. The note-catcher that students use is similar to the one they used as a whole class during Lesson 4.

- Work Time involves a modified Jigsaw: The sharing is done with the whole group as guided practice with teacher support. (Note that in Lesson 10, the Jigsaw structure is used again, but students are expected to share more independently.)

- There is a separate note-catcher for each section of the text. It is recommended that you give all students a full "packet" of all three note-catchers (since they will need all three during Work Time). At the beginning of Work Time, help each group focus on the one page for the single section of the text they are working on.

- The opening of this lesson includes a brief model on how to write a summary statement. Use students' summary writing about the section they read as baseline formative assessment data on their ability to summarize; consider including more guided practice for some groups if needed.

- Review: Cold-Call, Checking for Understanding, Jigsaw protocol (see the Appendix).

- Quick Write 3 (for homework).

EXPEDITIONARY
LEARNING

Lesson Vocabulary

- central idea, key incidents, informational text, historical fiction, context (review)
- Section 2: calling card, wary, misread, spurned, tends, ruin, pacify
- Section 3: tumult, time was ripe, swept, asserted
- Section 4: kindled, appealed, to no avail, committed, containing, backed

Materials

- "The Vietnam Wars" article (from Lesson 6)
- Sticky notes (five per student)
- "The Vietnam Wars" Questions and Notes: Sections 2, 3, or 4 (during the beginning of Work Time, each small group needs the note-catcher only for their own assigned section; during the latter part of Work Time, all students need all three note-catchers to take notes as their peers share)
- Things Close Readers Do Anchor Chart (begun in Lesson 2; added to in this lesson)
- Quick Write 3 (one per student; for homework)

Opening

A. Engaging the Reader: Reviewing Homework (8 minutes)

- Students should be seated in the small, heterogeneous numbered heads groups they have been meeting with so far in this unit.
- Ask students to get out their homework: **"The Vietnam Wars" Questions and Notes:** Section 1: "The Chinese Dragon" (one per student).
- Ask students to take 2 minutes to Turn-and-Talk with a peer about their notes. Listen in to gauge students' understanding.
- Refocus students as a whole group. Briefly model writing a summary statement for Section 1. Inform students that a strong summary is a brief statement about the most important information. Write: "The main idea of Section 1 is that the Vietnamese are warriors who have been fighting many different countries for more than 1,000 years."
- Ask students to check their own summary against this basic model.
- Then focus the whole group on the last question for Section 1:
  - "What seems to be the author's perspective toward the Vietnamese people? Which specific words or phrases led you to infer that perspective?"
- Cold-call on students to share out. Listen for them to have figured out that the author respects the Vietnamese people. If they do recognize this, probe by asking for specific words that led them to this inference. If students are struggling, model briefly. This might sound like: "I noticed a lot of

really positive words, such as 'warrior' and 'heroes' and 'momentous.' So I think the author respects the Vietnamese and how they fought for their country."

- Ask students to continue to focus on the author's word choice as they work in their groups.

B. Review Learning Targets (2 minutes)

- Post learning targets for review. Remind students that these are the same targets they worked with in Lesson 6. Ask for a volunteer to read the first learning target aloud to students.

- Remind students that today they will work collaboratively in groups on Sections 2, 3, and 4 of the article and share what they have learned with groups who read other sections.

- Remind them of the purpose for reading this informational text: It provides important background knowledge about the history of war in Vietnam, which will in turn help them understand the time and place that Ha describes in her diary. Also remind students that this history is very complex; they do not need to memorize every single name and date but should focus on the central ideas.

Meeting Students' Needs

Some students may benefit from having pictorial representations of the learning targets.

Work Time

A. Modified Jigsaw, Part I: Key Vocabulary and Questions (15 minutes)

- Inform students that now they will do work similar to what they did together for Section 1, but today, they will work in small groups.

- Briefly explain the Jigsaw protocol: Students in each group reread and summarize one section of the article, and they then share what they learned with peers in other groups who reread a different section.

- Remind students that their goal is to understand more about Vietnam so they can understand more about Ha and her family. They do not need to understand every detail in their section of the text.

- Give groups 2 minutes to reorient to their section, silently rereading. As students reread, circulate to distribute **"The Vietnam Wars" Questions and Notes** (for the specific section each group was assigned).

- Then ask groups to discuss the gist with their small group:

  - "What is the gist of this section? What was your initial sense of what it is mostly about?"

- Ask students to take 10 minutes to do the following:

  1. Read the questions on the Questions and Notes for your specific section.

  2. With a partner, reread your section of text with these questions in mind.

  3. Work with your partner to answer the questions.

- Then ask students to work in their small groups of four to prepare to share their brief summaries (which they wrote on the note-catchers).

EXPEDITIONARY
LEARNING

Meeting Students' Needs

- You may offer selected, shorter passages to specific groups based on each group's readiness. This provides an opportunity for students to read a complex text within the eighth-grade level span but differentiates the length of the text, not the complexity.

- Some students may benefit from a partially completed Questions and Notes organizer.

- Some students may benefit from paragraph frames.

- Many students will benefit from having a visible timer or stopwatch to help them pace themselves during these activities.

B. Modified Jigsaw, Part II: Sharing Our Summaries (15 minutes)

- Ask student groups to share with the class about the section they read.

- Allocate 5 minutes per section for sharing. Be clear that they are not sharing everything on their note-catcher: just the summary and specific evidence to help their peers understand that summary statement.

- Begin with the small groups that focused on Section 2:

  1. Call on a group member to share the summary of what his or her group read.

  2. Ask a different numbered group member to elaborate, citing specific evidence.

  3. Clarify as needed.

  4. Give students who did not read that section a moment to jot down the summary statement that was shared.

- Repeat with Section 3 and then Section 4 so the class hears the summary and evidence from each group.

- Ask students to hold on to their Questions and Notes (for all three sections) to support them as they reread and do a Quick Write for homework. Ask students to keep the article as well, because they will need it for their homework, and they will also read the last section in a future lesson.

Meeting Students' Needs

- It might benefit a specific small group for you to sit with them and read portions of the text aloud.

- Be strategic about the numbered head group members you call on during this lesson. Because students have read complex text fairly independently, you might consider calling on several of your stronger readers.

Closing and Assessment

A. Debrief: Adding to Our Things Close Readers Do Anchor Chart (5 minutes)

- Preview the homework. Remind students that this text is difficult and that they will revisit key passages in future lessons. Encourage them to persevere.

- Remind them also that the homework asks them to begin to connect this informational text to the novel. They read pages 22–41 of the novel a few days ago for homework and may want to revisit those pages as they write.

- Refer to the Things Close Readers Do Anchor Chart. Remind students that many aspects of close reading apply for both literature and informational text but that some aspects are more specific to the type of text. Emphasize that the reading practices they used today are some of the "things close readers do." They will continue to build their capacity with close reading throughout this unit and module. Ask students the following:

  - "Which new things did you do as close readers today?"

- Invite volunteers to share. Add their comments to the anchor chart. Listen specifically for students to notice new practices:

  - Pay attention to text structure: titles and headings (in informational text)

  - Consider the author's purpose/perspective

- If no student suggests these, remind them and add them to the anchor chart.

- Remind students that they have been practicing close analytical reading with both informational text and the novel and that in Lesson 8, they will return to the novel.

Homework

- Reread Section 4, "The Fall of the French." Use the questions on the note-catcher to help focus your reading.

- **Quick Write 3: What connections do you see between Ha's situation and the information you read in the article "The Vietnam Wars"?** How do the details in this informational text connect to Ha's circumstances? Be sure to include evidence from the novel and the article in your answer.

Meeting Students' Needs

Some students may benefit from having a paragraph frame for completing the Quick Writes.

LESSON 8

Development of the Plot

Impending Danger and Turmoil

Long-Term Targets Addressed (Based on ELA CCSS)

- I can analyze the development of a central idea throughout the text (including its relationship to the characters, setting, and plot). (RL.8.2)
- I can cite text-based evidence that provides the strongest support for my analysis of literary text. (RL.8.1)
- I can effectively engage in discussions with diverse partners about eighth-grade topics, texts, and issues. (SL.8.1)
- I can use a variety of strategies to determine the meaning of unknown words or phrases. (L.8.4)

Supporting Learning Targets

- I can make inferences to deepen my understanding of *Inside Out & Back Again*.
- I can cite evidence from the text to explain how the central idea develops over the course of the plot of *Inside Out & Back Again*.
- I can cite evidence from the text to analyze how various sections of the novel reveal aspects of Ha's character.
- I can participate in discussions about the text with a peer, small group, and the whole class.

Ongoing Assessment

- Quick Write 3 (from homework)
- Oral responses to text-dependent questions
- Double Arrow Graphic Organizer
- Exit Ticket

Agenda

1. Opening
   A. Engaging the Reader and Reviewing Learning Targets: Examining the Increasing Danger Right before the Fall of Saigon (5 minutes)

2. Work Time
   A. Rereading "TV News" and "Closed Too Soon," Using the Text to Understand the Crisis in Ha's Home (20 minutes)
   B. Rereading "Two More Papayas" and "Promises": What Matters to Ha? (15 minutes)

3. Closing and Assessment
   A. Debrief: Exit Ticket (5 minutes)

4. Homework
   A. Read pages 42–47 and complete Quick Write 4.

Teaching Notes

- In this lesson, students again focus on Ha's experience of and perspective about the events occurring around her—in this case, the impending fall of Saigon. Review pages 22–41 in the novel. Be prepared to help students bridge from "The Vietnam Wars" article they have been reading—which provides big-picture context about Vietnam—to the sense of escalating violence as described in the novel. The background knowledge students began to build in Lessons 6 and 7 prepares them to better understand Ha's experiences in this portion of the novel.

- Continue to help students distinguish between historical fiction (in this case, told from the subjective perspective of Ha) and informational text (in this case, told from the objective perspective of a journalist trying to present the ideas, opinions, and perspectives of different groups). (Review Lesson 6 Teaching Notes and Opening.) In this lesson, emphasize to students that Ha is a fictional character, experiencing and describing actual historical events from her particular subjective perspective. The events are described in her voice and through her eyes. She is not presenting an "objective" account of historical events.

- In Lessons 9 and 10, students will return to the informational text, focusing on Section 5 of the article "The Vietnam Wars" to continue to learn (from a more objective perspective) about this complex and multilayered conflict. It is important that students realize that many people, both within Vietnam and the United States, believe that the war was mishandled.

- In this lesson, students examine two poems about the escalating violence in Saigon and two poems about the papaya tree. The lesson is intentionally structured as one session so students can note patterns and contrasts. They write about two of these poems again for homework. Given your students' needs or school schedule, consider extending this lesson into a double session.

- This lesson includes a brief definition of the term *communism*. Students will return to this in more detail during Lesson 9. In advance: Build your own background knowledge about communism.

Consider collaborating with a social studies teacher to help students explore this complex historical concept in much more detail.

- Students also work with a complex quote from the text in this lesson (see Work Time). Key vocabulary words are defined for students because they are difficult to determine from the context. Do not worry, however, if students do not fully understand this quote during today's lesson; they will return to it during Lesson 9.

- Continue to reinforce how rereading helps students layer meaning; each time they revisit a poem, article excerpt, or specific quote, they can understand more of the nuance and significance.

- Throughout this lesson, reinforce the importance of effective collaboration (linked to SL.1). Name specific behaviors students are doing that are helping their groups think and learn together (e.g., paraphrasing peers' comments, inviting quieter students into the discussion).

- Review Numbered Heads Together (from Lesson 2).

Lesson Vocabulary

central idea, historical fiction, perspective, point of view, subjective, plot, stanza, symbolize; communists/communism, flaunt, blind conviction

Materials

- *Inside Out & Back Again* (book; one per student)
- Double Arrow Graphic Organizer (one per student)
- Lesson 8 text-dependent questions (one to display)
- Quick Write 4 (one per student; for homework)
- Half sheet of paper or index card (one per student)

Opening

A. Engaging the Reader and Reviewing Learning Targets: Examining the Increasing Danger Right before the Fall of Saigon (5 minutes)

- Students will be wondering about their Mid-Unit Assessments, of course! Share with them that you are looking over the answers and will return them soon.

- Remind students that for the past two lessons, they have been reading informational text about the history of wars in Vietnam. Last night, for homework, they completed Quick Write 3 to begin to connect this information back to the novel. Collect students' Quick Write 3 assignments.

- Be sure students have their texts *Inside Out & Back Again*. Invite students to pair up and briefly refresh their memory, skimming pages 22–41 of the novel:
  - "What has been going on in the story?"
  - "Which specific details do you notice that show signs of war?"

- Cold-call on a few students to share specific details their partner noticed that show the signs of war and increasing danger in Ha's country. As students share, remind them to help orient the class to which page and stanza they are referring to. Model as needed.

- Emphasize for students that one thing close readers do is cite textual evidence and that by orienting others to specific passages and portions of text, they can have more of a shared conversation about what they read. Remind them that when they write about a text, they need to tell readers where they found their evidence, so doing this in conversation is great practice.

- Post learning targets for review. Ask a student to read the first learning target aloud for the class:

  - "I can make inferences to deepen my understanding of *Inside Out & Back Again.*"

    - Students should recognize this target from many previous lessons.

- Ask a student to read the second learning target aloud for the class:

  - "I can cite evidence from the text to explain how the central idea develops over the course of the plot."

    - Ask students to recall that in previous lessons, they read to find the central idea of a text. Give students a moment to think, and then call on volunteers. (Ideally, students will refer to Lessons 6 and 7 and the article "The Vietnam Wars.")

    - Remind students that *Inside Out & Back Again* is historical fiction: a made-up story based on a real time and place in history. Today they are reading about historical events from Ha's particular *perspective,* or *point of view.* Ha's point of view is *subjective*: The events are described in her voice and through her eyes. She is telling us her experience, not just "the facts."

    - Focus on the word *plot*: Ask students to Turn-and-Talk briefly about what the word *plot* means. Cold-call on students for answers. Reinforce to students that the *plot* refers to "the events that make up a story: It is a word typically used when describing fiction."

- Cold-call on another student to read aloud the third learning target:

  - "I can cite evidence from the text to analyze how various sections of the novel reveal aspects of Ha's character."

    - Remind students that they have seen a similar target before. As they keep reading, they will learn more about Ha—the challenges she faces and how she grows as a character. They will continue to understand her more as they keep reading closely and paying attention to details in the text.

- Cold-call on another student to read the final target:

  - "I can participate in discussions about the text with a peer, small group, and the whole class."

    - Provide specific positive feedback for behaviors you have noticed in the last few lessons that are helping students meet this target (e.g., "I noticed that many of you are asking good specific questions of members of your small group," or "I heard so-and-so invite a quieter student into the discussion yesterday").

EXPEDITIONARY
LEARNING

Meeting Students' Needs

Many students will benefit from seeing questions posted on the interactive whiteboard or via a document camera, but reveal questions one at a time to keep students focused on the question at hand.

Work Time

A. Rereading "TV News" and "Closed Too Soon," Using the Text to Understand the Crisis in Ha's Home (20 minutes)

- Ask students to gather with their small, heterogeneous numbered heads groups. Ask them to reread and dig into two poems from their Lesson 5 homework to get a clearer picture of the increasing danger Ha is experiencing.

- Distribute the **Double Arrow Graphic Organizer** for students to record their thinking and take notes. Read aloud the directions on the graphic organizer. Ask students to work with the second (bottom) part of their graphic organizer first.

- Orient students to two poems in the text: "TV News" (pages 24–25) and "Closed Too Soon" (pages 38–40). Ask students to take 3 minutes to reread both poems silently, thinking about increasing conflict in Ha's country. Remind them that it is most important that they pay attention to details as they reread. It is okay if they want to begin to jot notes on the second, bottom arrow of their graphic organizer. After they read, they will talk with a peer and write more.

- Circulate and observe students reading, and support individual students as needed.

- Ask students to talk with one peer to share the notes they already jotted and to add to their graphic organizers. Remind them how talking about text with others helps them deepen their understanding of what they read.

- Encourage them to expand their conversation to their entire small group. Reinforce groups that are working well together, naming specific behaviors that are helping them collaborate effectively.

- After about 10 minutes, focus students as a whole group. Post the **Lesson 8 text-dependent questions** (with a document camera, on an interactive whiteboard, or on chart paper), and prepare to reveal them one at a time.

- Ask:

  - "What are some details from the text that describe the danger in Ha's country?"

- Call on specific group members to share details, and commend students for gathering specific evidence.

- Focus students on page 38. Ask:

  - "What does the title 'Closed Too Soon' mean? What is *closing*? Why does Ha say it is 'too soon'?"

- Again, call on a different numbered group member. (Note that this question is a basic check for understanding: Be sure students realize that Ha's school is closed early as a result of the escalating danger.)

- Ask students:

  - "Who are the *communists* Ha is referring to?"

- Students should be making connections to Section 4 in the article "The Vietnam Wars," which they read in Lessons 6 and 7. Clarify as needed, reminding students that at this time in Vietnam, the *communists* were "the people from the North led by Ho Chi Minh."

- Inform students that it is fine and even good if they have some questions about all this: The history is complicated. Define *communism* for students: "It is a system of government based on the idea that the community or state should hold the property, so everyone shares equally." Point out the word root *com,* which means "together."

- Remind students that they will continue to learn more about communism in Lessons 9 and 10, when they read the last section of "The Vietnam Wars" article. (They also can go much more in depth with this complicated concept in social studies.)

- Prompt students to turn to page 25. Focus them on one crucial sentence in the first stanza (clarify that a *stanza* is lines in a poem that are grouped together). Ask students to read along silently as you read aloud:

<blockquote>
Brother Quang says,

One cannot justify war

unless each side

flaunts its own

blind conviction.
</blockquote>

- Because these words are difficult to define from context, provide simple definitions (consider posting where all students can see):

  - *Flaunt* means "to show off." (Some students may have heard the phrase "When you've got it, flaunt it," which is typically used regarding physical traits.)

  - *Conviction* means "a strong belief or opinion." (Students may have heard the phrase "stand up for your *convictions*," which means to stand up for what you believe is right.)

- Reread the phrase from the text, emphasizing the defined terms. Then probe:

  - "Given these definitions, what do you think Brother Quang's statement means?"

    - Ask students to think and then talk with their groups about this question. Call on a group member to answer.

Note: The last text-dependent question requires inference and synthesis. Move through the other two questions fairly quickly to have enough time for this. Call on a different numbered heads group member to answer each question in turn.

- Probe deeper into the term *blind conviction* with students:
  - "If *conviction* is a strong belief or opinion, what might a *blind conviction* be?"
    - Ask students again to discuss with their small group. Call on a different numbered heads group member to answer. Listen for students to understand that *blind conviction* means "unquestioning belief in something." If students do not determine the figurative use of *blind* on their own, clarify: In this context, the word *blind* does not mean literally "without sight"; rather, it is a figurative word, meaning "unquestioning, so confident you have no doubt."
    - Ask students to think about how they might put Brother Quang's statement in their own words. Invite a volunteer to share. Listen for students to realize that Brother Quang is saying that both sides in war boast about how they believe in their own cause without a doubt: They are showing off how sure they are that they are right.
- Ask students to add any specific details to the bottom arrow based on their discussion or what they heard from other group members.

Meeting Students' Needs

- Graphic organizers provide the necessary scaffolding especially critical for learners with lower levels of language proficiency and/or learning, and they engage students more actively.
- For students who need additional support, provide a partially filled-in graphic organizer.
- When you're reviewing the graphic organizer, consider using a document camera to display the graphic organizer for students who struggle with auditory processing.

B. Rereading "Two More Papayas" and "Promises": What Matters to Ha? (15 minutes)

- Ask students to think about what is going on around Ha and what she cares about—specifically, the papaya tree. They need to reread "Two More Papayas" (page 21) and "Promises" (page 41) and complete the top arrow in the graphic organizer by citing details from the poems.
- Ask students to take 3 minutes to reread both of these short poems silently, thinking about the papaya tree and why the author chooses to spend so much time describing and referring to it. As they did earlier during Work Time, students can begin to jot down notes on their graphic organizer, but they will have time to talk with their group and write more after they read. Reinforce that reading, thinking, talking, and writing tend to go in a cycle: They all help us understand a text more deeply.
- Invite students to collaborate with a partner to share the notes they already jotted and to add to their graphic organizer. Reinforce pairs that are working well together, naming specific behaviors that are helping them collaborate effectively (this relates directly to SL.8.1).
- After about 10 minutes, focus students as a whole group. Ask the final text-dependent questions, one at a time. After each question, give students time to think. Then select specific group members to answer:

- "How is Ha's papaya tree doing? How do you know?"

- "Is the papaya tree healthy or not? What is your evidence?"

- Remind students that they have just closely read poems from two different parts of the novel: first about the events (plot) and then about the papaya tree. Ask students:

  - "What do you notice about how these two parts of the novel compare to each other? What is the relationship between the events in the novel and the papaya tree?"

    - Invite students to look at their notes and independently think about what they have described on both sides of the arrow. Then ask them to share their initial thoughts in small groups.

    - Circulate and listen in. Continue to probe, pushing students back into the text to support their thinking (e.g., "Which details do you notice in this poem 'TV News'? How does that compare to the specific words the author uses to describe the papaya tree?"). Listen for students to begin to make the connection that as Ha's society becomes more dangerous and deteriorates, the papaya tree flourishes and continues to grow and bear fruit. Notice any students who are starting to make this connection, and ask them if they would be willing to share their thinking with the group in a moment.

  - "What does the papaya tree symbolize for Ha? Read the last stanza of the poem 'Promises' for a clue."

    - If needed, remind students that they are making inferences based on the text. The text does not say directly, "The papaya tree is a symbol because. . . ."

    - Give students time to reread, think, and then talk in small groups. As groups discuss, circulate and listen for them to recognize that the papaya tree symbolizes hope. Do not give this away; instead, probe. (For example, consider asking: "Why does the papaya tree stand out in such a dangerous place? With danger all around, what feeling does the healthy papaya tree bring to Ha?")

- Ask for a thumbs-up when groups are ready to share their thinking. Invite a few students to share.

Meeting Students' Needs

Text-dependent questions can be answered only by referring explicitly back to the text being read. This encourages students to reread the text for further analysis and allows for a deeper understanding.

Closing and Assessment

A. Debrief: Exit Ticket (5 minutes)

- Ask students to take 2 minutes to answer the following questions on an **index card** or **half sheet of paper**:

  - "What are you learning about the importance of using specific evidence from the text to explain your thinking? How are you growing as a reader?"

EXPEDITIONARY
LEARNING

- Ask students to show with a Fist-to-Five how well they are doing with citing evidence from the text.
- As time permits, provide specific positive feedback to students based on observations of their work today: Give examples of comments you heard analyzing important events and reading closely to see how different parts of the novel are related to one another.
- Preview the students' homework.

Meeting Students' Needs

Consider having students who are struggling talk with their peers before they respond in writing to the questions.

Homework

Read pages 42–47 and complete **Quick Write 4: Ha's family faces a decision**.

Meeting Students' Needs

Some students may benefit from having paragraph frames as a scaffold for Quick Writes.

Note: Review students' Mid-Unit Assessments. Provide specific feedback; time is allocated in Lesson 9 to share this feedback with students.

Select an exemplary student response for the last question on the Mid-Unit Assessment. Type this paragraph (without the student's name) and prepare copies to share during Lesson 9. Be sure to approach the student in advance to seek permission to share his or her good work. Depending on your class culture, determine whether to share which student wrote the model paragraph.

LESSON 9

Building Background Knowledge

Vietnam as a "Battleground in a Larger Struggle"

Long-Term Targets Addressed (Based on ELA CCSS)

- I can determine the central idea of an informational text. (RI.8.2)
- I can use a variety of strategies to determine the meaning of unknown words or phrases. (L.8.4)
- I can analyze the impact of word choice on meaning and tone in informational text. (RI.8.4)
- I can effectively engage in discussions with diverse partners about eighth-grade topics, texts, and issues. (SL.8.1)

Supporting Learning Targets

- I can determine the central idea of two key paragraphs of "The Vietnam Wars."
- I can explain how Vietnam was a "battleground in a much larger struggle."
- I can use context clues to determine word meanings.
- I can participate in discussions about the text with a peer, small group, and the whole class.

Ongoing Assessment

- Quick Write 4 (from homework)
- Students' annotated texts

Agenda

1. Opening
   A. Review Results from Mid-Unit 1 Assessment and Review Learning Targets (10 minutes)

2. Work Time

    A. Reorienting to Informational Text and Read-Aloud of Section 5 of "The Vietnam Wars" (15 minutes)

    B. Guided Note-Taking on Two Key Paragraphs: Vietnam as a "Battleground for a Much Larger Struggle" (15 minutes)

3. Closing and Assessment

    A. Exit Ticket (5 minutes)

4. Homework

    A. Complete the questions and notes: "A Battleground for a Much Larger Struggle"; reread and annotate section 5, "Doc-Lap at Last."

Teaching Notes

- In advance: Select an exemplary student response for the last question on the Mid-Unit Assessment. Type this paragraph (without the student's name) and prepare copies to share during the opening of this lesson. Be sure to ask in advance to seek the student's permission to share his or her good work.

- Students revisit "The Vietnam Wars," which they worked with in Lessons 6 and 7; be sure students have their texts, or prepare new ones. Throughout the module, reinforce how important it is for students to keep track of their texts. Their annotations provide a record of their thinking and learning, and they will often revisit a text multiple times throughout a module.

- Continue to help students distinguish between historical fiction and informational text. (Review Lesson 6 Teaching Notes and Opening, and Lesson 8). Remind students that Ha is a fictional character, experiencing and describing actual historical events from her particular subjective perspective. By contrast, the article "The Vietnam Wars" presents a more "objective" account of historical events.

- This lesson homes in on one "big idea" regarding the conflict in Vietnam: how the country became a battleground in the broader struggle related to communism.

Lesson Vocabulary

central idea; *doc-lap,* battleground, communism, committed, contain, back (v.), fell, cringed, peace accord

Materials

- An anonymous model of an exemplary student response to the mid-unit writing prompt (one per student)

- "The Vietnam Wars" article (from Lesson 6; one per student)

- "The Vietnam Wars" Questions and Notes: "A Battleground for a Much Larger Struggle" (one per student)
- Half sheet of paper or index card (one per student)

Opening

A. Review Results from Mid-Unit 1 Assessment and Review Learning Targets (10 minutes)

- Students should be seated in their small, heterogeneous numbered heads groups for today's work. Collect students' homework (Quick Write 4) to review. Explain that they will work more with this homework during the next lesson.
- Share results with students from their Mid-Unit Assessment.
- Show and distribute an **anonymous model of an exemplary response**. Give students a few minutes to compare this model to their own response and think about how they might revise. (Consider allowing students to revise their work for credit, based on your classroom culture or specific school policies.)
- Briefly read the learning targets aloud, or ask a volunteer to do so. Inform students that for the next two days, they will return to the article "The Vietnam Wars" to help them build more background knowledge about the historical events that influence Ha and her family and their decision.
- Let them know that they will return to the second learning target in particular later in the lesson, after they are reoriented to the text.

Meeting Students' Needs

Providing models of expected work supports all learners, but especially challenged learners.

Work Time

A. Reorienting to Informational Text and Read-Aloud of Section 5 of "The Vietnam Wars" (15 minutes)

- Remind students that in Lesson 8 and for homework, they were focused on Ha's subjective perspective of the events around her. For the next few days, they will continue to build background knowledge about this historical era. Ask students to get out their **"The Vietnam Wars"** article (from Lesson 6) and/or redistribute it (one per student).
- Invite students to take 5 minutes to work with a peer to recall key ideas from Sections 1–4, which they have already read.
- Circulate and listen in to gauge how much students remember about the four key historical eras described in these first four sections, and note any patterns of confusion. Clarify as needed.
- Inform students that for the next two lessons, they will focus on Section 5, "Doc-Lap at Last." Ask students:
  - "What does *doc-lap* mean?"

EXPEDITIONARY
LEARNING

- Listen to see whether students recall the meaning from their previous reading of Sections 1–4. If they do not, encourage them to reread to see whether they can find and define this key term. If necessary, direct them to the section of the text where this answer can be found—the very last line of Section 3 ("Life, Liberty, and Ho Chi Minh")—and help students remember that *doc-lap* means "independence."

- Remind students that this article is challenging: It has lots of difficult words and lots of new information about a very complicated period of history. Orient students further to this key section of the text, Section 5 ("Doc-Lap at Last"). Cold-call on a student to answer this question:

  - "What are the relevant dates of this last section? How does that fit into the timeline of what we've read so far in the novel *Inside Out & Back Again*?"

- Listen for students to recognize that this informational text takes place in the same place and time as Ha's story, but slightly after what they have read so far in the novel.

- Inform them that, as they did with Section 1, they will first hear the text read aloud and will stop to think about each paragraph. Then, in the next lesson, they will reread using specific questions to guide their thinking.

- Read Section 5 aloud, one paragraph at a time, as students read along silently. Note that as with other read-alouds in this unit, this is a "pure" read-aloud: Simply read slowly and fluently, and do not stop to explain anything.

- After each paragraph, pause for a moment to give students time to think and jot a note about the gist in the margins:

  - "What is your initial sense of what this paragraph is mostly about?"

- Continue to reinforce this strategy of annotating text. It's a "thing close readers do" to help them focus, name key points, and keep a record that they can return to if they reread the text at a later point. It's okay if their initial sense of the gist is preliminary, tentative, incomplete, or even incorrect.

Meeting Students' Needs

Some students may benefit from having key sections prehighlighted in their texts. This will help them focus on small sections rather than scanning the whole text for answers.

B. Guided Note-Taking on Two Key Paragraphs: Vietnam as a "Battleground in a Much Larger Struggle" (15 minutes)

- Reread the second learning target: "I can explain how Vietnam was a 'battleground in a much larger struggle.'" Inform students that to help them meet that target, today they will focus on two key paragraphs: paragraph 1 of "Doc-Lap at Last," plus a paragraph from Section 4. (They will return to the rest of Section 5 during Lesson 10.)

- Distribute the **"The Vietnam Wars" Questions and Notes: "A Battleground in a Much Larger Struggle."** Direct students to this quote from the text (in Section 4, paragraph 3, which begins "By 1950 . . .").

- Ask students to pair up and use the Think-Pair-Share protocol to work through specific questions. Explain that they will have 10 minutes to think, reread, talk with their partner, and write notes. They will then return to the whole group. Remind them that these historical concepts are complicated; encourage them to persevere.

- Circulate to listen in and support students as they work. Listen for patterns of confusion to determine which specific questions to address as a whole group.

- When 5 minutes remain in Work Time, refocus the students as a whole group. Remind them that they will reread these paragraphs as part of their homework, so it is okay if they are not yet finished.

- Check for understanding, focusing on specific questions you noticed were more difficult for students.

- If time permits, ask a few students to share a summary of these two key paragraphs with the class. Encourage students to complete their notes and a summary statement as a part of their homework.

Meeting Students' Needs

For students who need additional support, you can provide a partially filled-in graphic organizer. For this lesson, consider adding some sentence starters to the notes section of the "The Vietnam Wars" Questions and Notes: "A Battleground in a Much Larger Struggle" document to provide more support for some students.

Closing and Assessment

A. Exit Ticket (5 minutes)

- Ask students to complete the following Exit Ticket on a **half sheet of paper or index card**:

  - "A lot of this history happened many years before Ha was even born. Why might it be important to have this background knowledge to help you understand the situation Ha and her family face?"

- Describe students' homework.

Meeting Students' Needs

Developing self-assessment and reflection supports all learners, but research shows it supports struggling learners most.

Homework

Complete "The Vietnam Wars" Questions and Notes: "A Battleground in a Much Larger Struggle"; and reread and annotate Section 5, "Doc-Lap at Last."

LESSON 10

Building Background Knowledge

The Impending Fall of Saigon

Long-Term Targets Addressed (Based on ELA CCSS)

- I can determine the central idea of an informational text. (RI.8.2)
- I can analyze the impact of word choice on meaning and tone in informational text. (RI.8.4)
- I can use a variety of strategies to determine the meaning of unknown words or phrases. (L.8.4)
- I can effectively engage in discussions with diverse partners about eighth-grade topics, texts, and issues. (SL.8.1)

Supporting Learning Targets

- I can determine the central idea of the section "Doc-Lap at Last" in the informational text "The Vietnam Wars."
- I can objectively summarize informational text.
- I can use context clues to determine word meanings.
- I can participate in discussions about the text with a peer, small group, and the whole class.

Ongoing Assessment

- Students' annotated texts
- Three Threes in a Row Note-Catcher

Agenda

1. Opening
   A. Share Annotations of "Doc-Lap at Last" and Review Learning Targets (5 minutes)

---

2. Work Time

    A. Reading for Key Details: Three Threes in a Row Note-Catcher (20 minutes)

    B. Determining the Central Ideas of "Doc-Lap at Last" (15 minutes)

3. Closing and Assessment

    A. Debrief: Returning to Brother Quang's Quote (5 minutes)

4. Homework

    A. Read pages 48–60 and complete Quick Write 5.

Teaching Notes

*   Students continue to work with Section 5 of "The Vietnam Wars." Be sure students have their texts. During Work Time, students carefully examine the photographs and associated captions that are part of Section 5. If you accessed the article via the Internet, ensure that students' texts include the photos. If this is not possible, search the Internet for the three iconic images shown in this article (a monk in flames, North Vietnamese tanks entering Saigon, and refugees loading onto a helicopter).

*   Review: Three Threes in a Row Note-Catcher (Work Time). Notice that for each row, the question in the left-hand column is intentionally a review from the previous lesson. Notice also that this is *not* a pass-the-paper activity—each student writes on his or her own note-catcher. They must listen, process, and summarize.

Lesson Vocabulary

central idea, objective summary, implications; *doc-lap,* cringe, peace accord; alienate, dissidents, condemn; operate, stealthily, under cover, pursue, elusive, alienate; columns (of soldiers), meeting little resistance, demoralized

Materials

*   "The Vietnam Wars" article (from Lesson 6; one per student)

*   Three Threes in a Row Note-Catcher (one per student)

*   "The Vietnam Wars" Questions and Notes, Section 5: "Doc-Lap at Last" (one per student)

*   Quick Write 5 (one per student; for homework)

Opening

A. Share Annotations of "Doc-Lap at Last" and Review Learning Targets (5 minutes)

*   Students should be seated in their small, heterogeneous numbered heads groups for today's work. Ask students to get out their **"The Vietnam Wars"** article.

- In preparation for today's thinking, invite students to Turn-and-Talk with a peer to share the annotations they made on each paragraph of Section 5, "Doc-Lap at Last." Reinforce with students the value of annotating text: It allows them to go back quickly to their jotted notes to remember what they already read.

- Post learning targets for students to review. Ask them to continue to work with this last section of the article today, which describes the same time period that Ha is writing about at this point in the novel. Read the target aloud:

  - "I can determine the central idea of the section 'Doc-Lap at Last' in the informational text 'The Vietnam Wars.'"

- Discuss with students the concept of a *central idea*. In addition, discuss the idea of an *objective summary*—a "just the facts" summary that focuses on the information the text provides rather than our personal reactions.

- Remind students that this informational text is long and complicated. Section 5 is the most relevant to understanding what Ha and her family are experiencing. Hence, students are focusing on this section for two lessons.

Work Time

A. Reading for Key Details: Three Threes in a Row Note-Catcher (20 minutes)

Note: This is not a pass-the-paper activity—each student writes on his or her own note-catcher. They must listen, process, and summarize.

- Focus students on the last section of the article "Doc-Lap at Last" that they reread for homework. Ask students to reread briefly, underlining key details that help them understand the central idea.

- Distribute the **Three Threes in a Row Note-Catcher** to students. Assign each group one row (three questions). (Depending on class size, more than one group may have the same set of three questions.)

- Give directions for Part 1:

  1. Your group answers just the three questions on your row.

  2. Take 10 minutes as a group to read your three questions, reread the text, and jot your answers.

- Directions for Part 2:

  1. Walk around the room to talk with students from other groups. Bring your notes and text with you.

  2. Ask each student to explain one and only one answer.

  3. Listen to each student's explanation and then summarize that answer in your own box.

  4. Record the name of the student who shared the information on the line in the question box.

  5. Repeat, moving on to another student, for an answer to another question. (Ask a different student for each answer so that you interact with six other students total.)

- Have students begin Part 1 in their small groups. Circulate to listen in and support as needed. Probe, pushing students to dig back into the text to find answers to each question.

- After 5 minutes, focus students as a whole group. Begin Part 2, inviting students to circulate. Give them about 7 minutes to do so. Then ask students to return to their seats and refocus as a whole group.

- Ask them to discuss what they think the central idea of Section 5 is. Invite numbered head 2s to share with the class. Ask students:

  - "What are the potential implications of this information on Ha's story?" (Briefly paraphrase to clarify the meaning of *implications*: "What might this mean for Ha and her family?")

Meeting Students' Needs

For students who struggle with following multiple-step directions, consider displaying these directions using a document camera or an interactive whiteboard. Or type these instructions for students to have in hand.

B. Determining the Central Ideas of "Doc-Lap at Last" (15 minutes)

- Restate specific student comments you overheard that indicate the degree to which students are developing a fairly clear understanding of the main idea of "Doc-Lap at Last." Remind them that this section is particularly important, given the events in the novel.

- Distribute **"The Vietnam Wars" Questions and Notes, Section 5: "Doc-Lap at Last."** Ask students to take 10 minutes to do the following:

  - Read the questions on their Questions and Notes for your specific section.

  - With your partner, reread your section of the text with these questions in mind.

  - Work with your partner to answer the questions.

- Refocus students on pages 60–67 of *Inside Out & Back Again*. Encourage them to skim these poems, looking carefully at the dates of Ha's diary entries. Ask:

  - "Where are we in Ha's story in relation to the dates we learned about by reading the last section of 'The Vietnam Wars'?"

- Listen for students to note the key date, April 30, 1975—the day Saigon fell.

- Collect the Three Threes in a Row Note-Catcher.

Meeting Students' Needs

For students who need additional support, you can provide a partially filled-in graphic organizer. For this lesson, consider adding some sentence starters to the notes section of the "The Vietnam Wars" Questions and Notes, Section 5: "Doc-Lap at Last" document.

Closing and Assessment

A. Debrief: Returning to Brother Quang's Quote (5 minutes)

- Remind students of the quote they read in a previous lesson, spoken by Brother Quang:

    One cannot justify war

    unless each side

    flaunts its own

    blind conviction.

- Ask students to think and then Turn-and-Talk with a peer:

    - "After reading this informational text, what new thinking do you have about what Brother Quang means?"

    - "What evidence does the text give for both sides of the conflict?"

- Invite a few students to share out. Listen for students to recognize that in a war, each side believes it is right. For example, the text says, "But the North refused to surrender" and "in the South, Communist rebels . . . laid mines and booby traps."

- Continue to emphasize the distinction between historical fiction and informational text: The news that "Saigon is gone" is news no one in Ha's community wants to hear. But people on each side of the conflict have different deeply held beliefs, or *convictions.*

- Preview the homework.

- Return students' Quick Write 4 homework. Encourage them to check their own understanding: Are they clear on the decision Ha's family is facing? What does Ha's family decide?

Meeting Students' Needs

Developing self-assessment and reflection supports all learners, but research shows it supports struggling learners most.

Homework

Read pages 48–60, through "Wet and Crying," and complete **Quick Write 5: How is Ha's mother being affected by the war?**

LESSON 11

Character Analysis

How Do Personal Possessions Reveal Aspects of Characters?

Long-Term Targets Addressed (Based on ELA CCSS)

- I can analyze how specific dialogue or incidents in a plot propel the action, reveal aspects of a character, or provoke a decision. (RL.8.3)
- I can cite text-based evidence that provides the strongest support for my analysis of literary text. (RL.8.1)
- I can effectively engage in discussions with diverse partners about eighth-grade topics, texts, and issues. (SL.8.1)

Supporting Learning Targets

- I can make inferences to deepen my understanding of *Inside Out & Back Again*.
- I can cite evidence from the poems "Choice" and "Left Behind" to explain how this incident reveals aspects of Ha and her family members.
- I can participate in discussions about the text with a peer, small group, and the whole class.

Ongoing Assessment

- Quick Write 5 (from homework)
- Students' annotated text
- Write-Pair-Share
- Jigsaw Recording Form

Agenda

1. Opening
   A. Engaging the Reader: How Do Possessions Reveal Something about a Person? (10 minutes)
   B. Review Learning Targets (2 minutes)

2. Work Time

    A. Jigsaw, Part I: Focus on Different Characters in "Left Behind" (20 minutes)

    B. Jigsaw, Part II: Small-Group Discussion: What Do Their Possessions Reveal about Ha and Her Family? (10 minutes)

3. Closing and Assessment

    A. Debrief (3 minutes)

4. Homework

    A. Complete Quick Write 6 and read independent reading book.

Teaching Notes

- This lesson uses a Jigsaw Recording Form structure that students were introduced to in Lesson 7. Students work in "expert groups" to draw inferences about characters based on those characters' possessions and then meet in their home groups of four to share what they learned. Note here that the second part of the Jigsaw takes place in small groups, not among the whole class.

- Preplan your home groups of four students. Students will move to expert groups based on the character that they choose to study more deeply.

- This lesson challenges students to infer about characters based on the symbolic significance of their possessions. The Opening makes this concept more concrete for students, but do not worry if students do not immediately grasp symbolism; it is an abstract concept that they will continue to work with as they analyze texts throughout the year.

- Encourage students if they are finding this challenging. Several scaffolds are in place to support students: a model and a recording form. They also get to write about their lingering questions as a part of their homework. Remind students that they will continue to develop inferring and drawing-conclusion skills throughout the module. Also, reinforce the real-world connections for students: Every day, we regularly come to conclusions or judgments about people based on what they have and how they describe those possessions. Throughout the lesson, remind students that often these judgments, or inferences, are correct, but sometimes they are not.

- Review the Jigsaw protocol (see the Appendix).

Lesson Vocabulary

evidence, incident, reveals, aspects, infer, symbol, symbolize; palm (of rice)

Materials

- *Inside Out & Back Again* (book; one per student)
- Jigsaw Recording Form (one per student)
- Quick Write 6 (one per student; for homework)

Opening

A. Engaging the Reader: How Do Possessions Reveal Something about a Person? (10 minutes)

- Ask students to sit with their small home groups (from the previous lessons). Welcome students and continue to give them specific positive feedback on ways you see them persevering as close readers.

- Inform them that today they will be closely reading a poem that will help them learn more about Ha's family members by describing the possessions that are important to them. Ask students:

  - "What object is so important to Ha that she writes about it more than any other object in her diary?"

- Listen for students to mention the papaya tree. Ask students:

  - "Why does she write about it so much?"

- Allow students to Turn-and-Talk to discuss this question; when pairs have an answer, they may signal with thumbs-up.

- Call on several students to respond. Ideally, students will say the papaya tree is important to Ha— she takes care of it, she has watched it grow from a seed, and she loves the papaya fruit.

- Instruct students to turn to page 55 and the poem "Choice." They will notice that this is the poem in which Ha describes the possessions she chooses to pack for her escape. Read the poem aloud for students to get the gist. Invite students to reread the poem silently, paying special attention to Ha's one item she chooses to pack in stanzas 2 through 4.

- After students have reread these stanzas, ask:

  - "What makes this doll so special?"

- Provide students with an opportunity to Turn-and-Talk before sharing with the class. Listen for students to notice that the doll is an important part of Ha's childhood. Connect back to the concept of symbolism, which students briefly discussed in an earlier lesson. The doll symbolizes childhood for Ha.

- Follow up with the question:

  - "What does Ha mean when she writes, 'I love her more for her scars'?"

- Again, invite students to Turn-and-Talk with a peer and share with the whole class.

- Back up to clarify one key vocabulary word in this poem that students may not understand from context: *palms* (stanza 1). Explain that in this context, a *palm* is describing an amount of rice: "a palm of rice is the amount of rice a person can hold in the palm of his or her hand." Explain to students that Ha gives us a glimpse into what is important to her and that today's work will show what is important to other members of her family.

B. Review Learning Targets (2 minutes)

- Post the learning targets for review. Read aloud the first learning target: "I can make inferences to deepen my understanding of *Inside Out & Back Again*."

- Remind students that they have practiced this target often. But in today's lesson, it will be more difficult: They will have to *infer* what certain objects mean to Ha or to other members of her family.

- Ask a volunteer to read the second target out loud:

  - "I can cite evidence from the poems 'Choice' and 'Left Behind' to explain how this incident reveals aspects of Ha and her family members."

    - Students should be familiar with this target from previous lessons. Ask students to Turn-and-Talk with a peer briefly about the words that seem most important in this target. Listen for students to mention the words *evidence, incident,* and *reveals aspects.* Clarify as needed.

- Remind students that they just worked as a class to analyze the poem "Choice" carefully to think more about what the papaya means to Ha. They will now do something similar with a small group to examine another poem to help them understand Ha's brothers and her mother as characters. Emphasize to students that as they continue reading the novel, it will be important to understand Ha's mother and brothers, because they are the main people with whom Ha interacts.

Work Time

A. Jigsaw, Part I: Focus on Different Characters in "Left Behind" (20 minutes)

- Inform students that today they will be creating a **Jigsaw Recording Form**, much the way they did with sections of the article "The Vietnam Wars." For this activity, they begin in their home groups of four. In their home group, each person chooses a different character on whom to focus. Students then leave their home group to join a new "expert group" (with other students who focused on the same character). Within that expert group, students discuss their specific character. Then, in Part II of the Jigsaw, students return to their original home group to share their learning.

- Distribute the Jigsaw Recording Form. In their home group, ask students to decide who will focus on which character in this poem: Brother Quang, Brother Vu, Brother Khoi, and Mother. (Point out that they can, of course, still pay attention to Ha, and that they can actually learn a lot about her from the way she describes her family and what matters to them.)

- Inform students that in a moment, they will reread the poem "Left Behind," with their character as a focus. Direct them to look at the top of the recording form and to read aloud the example about Ha. Remind students that they already discussed how important the papaya tree is to Ha, and here is what we can *infer,* or conclude, about Ha based on this prized possession. Focus students on pages 57–59, "Left Behind." They will need to locate the stanzas that refer to the character they are focusing on.

- Ask students to transition to sit with their expert group.

- Once they are settled into the expert group, ask students to reread the poem silently while focusing on their character.

- Then ask students in these expert groups to share details they noticed and work together to complete their graphic organizer. Be sure students know that in the next part of the lesson, they will be going back to their numbered heads small group and will need to be ready to explain what they talked about with their expert group.

- Circulate to support groups as needed. Commend students who are citing textual evidence and explaining their thinking. Probe to push students back into the text and to elaborate their inferences (e.g., "What do these items represent to the character? In what way are these items important? How do these items reflect the character's interests, values, and beliefs? What can you infer about this character's personality? What might these objects *symbolize*?").

- Encourage students if they are finding this challenging. The expert group arrangement and the model example on the Jigsaw Recording Form will scaffold this learning. Remind them that they will continue to develop inferring and drawing-conclusion skills throughout the module. Students will have an opportunity to write questions they still have as a part of their homework.

Meeting Students' Needs

For students who need additional support, you can assign them to a particular expert group (or character) and provide them with a partially filled-in Jigsaw Recording Form for their assigned character.

B. Jigsaw, Part II: Small-Group Discussion: What Do Their Possessions Reveal about Ha and Her Family? (10 minutes)

- Ask students to return to their home small group. Explain that they will be asked to share their expertise. Give directions:

  1. Choose someone in the group to be a timekeeper.

  2. Each person has 2 minutes to share the character he or she studied, the objects that are mentioned about that character, what the possessions say about the character, and how he or she knows this.

  3. Be sure to record the information your peers share on the Jigsaw Recording Form.

  4. If you have time, discuss the question at the bottom of your Jigsaw Recording Form.

Meeting Students' Needs

- Some students may benefit from being given sentence starters for sharing out with their home groups. For example, "My character was_____. He/she left behind _____. I infer these possessions tell us _____ about my character. The evidence I found to support my inference is _____."

- For students who struggle with following multiple-step directions, consider displaying these directions using a document camera or an interactive whiteboard. Another option is to type these instructions for students to have in hand.

Closing and Assessment

A. Debrief (3 minutes)

- Invite students to conclude their discussions and to refocus on today's learning targets. Explain that this was a very challenging thinking day in terms of making inferences based on textual evidence. Name specific behaviors you saw students doing that supported them in this work (e.g., citing specific lines, asking probing questions of their peers, and so forth).

- Invite a few groups to share out their insights related to the synthesis question:

  - "What can you learn about Ha from the way she describes her family members?"

- Frame the homework, including the Quick Write prompt. Review the word *symbol* as needed, reminding students about how they determined, in a previous lesson, that the papaya tree is a symbol of hope. This homework prompt is a challenge to them: What might the object *symbolize*? Be sure they notice the model paragraph about the papaya tree.

Meeting Students' Needs

Developing self-assessment and reflection supports all learners, but research shows it supports struggling learners most.

Homework

- Complete **Quick Write 6: The symbolic significance of what was "left behind."** Explain the more *symbolic* aspect of what the character you studied is forced to leave behind. Use specific evidence from your reading to support your thinking.

- Continue reading in your independent reading book for this unit.

Meeting Students' Needs

Some students may benefit from having paragraph frames as a scaffold for Quick Writes.

LESSON 12

Examining How Word Choice Contributes to Meaning and Tone

Close Reading of "Wet and Crying"

Long-Term Targets Addressed (Based on ELA CCSS)

- I can cite text-based evidence that provides the strongest support for my analysis of literary text. (RL.8.1)

- I can analyze the impact of word choice on meaning and tone. (RL.8.4)

- I can effectively engage in discussions with diverse partners about eighth-grade topics, texts, and issues. (SL.8.1)

Supporting Learning Targets

- I can make inferences to deepen my understanding of *Inside Out & Back Again*.

- I can explain how nuances in word meanings contribute to the overall tone of the poem.

- I can participate in discussions about the text with a peer, small group, and the whole class.

Ongoing Assessment

- Quick Write 6 (from homework)

- Write-Pair-Share Note-Catcher with text-dependent questions

Agenda

1. Opening
    A. Engaging the Reader and Reviewing Learning Targets (5 minutes)
2. Work Time
    A. Write-Pair-Share about "Wet and Crying" (10 minutes)
    B. Guided Practice: How Word Choice Contributes to Tone and Meaning (20 minutes)

3. Closing and Assessment

    A. Debrief and Discussion: What Happens to Hope? (10 minutes)

4. Homework

    A. Read pages 61–69 and complete Quick Write 7.

Teaching Notes

- Review: Write-Pair-Share protocol (see the Appendix).

- Choose strategic partnerships ahead of time. For this lesson, consider pairing up a few of your strongest students while you work directly with other students. On the other hand, heterogeneous pairs might be best. You know the composition of your class.

- This lesson introduces the Word Choice, Tone, and Meaning Note-Catcher, which serves as a scaffold toward the End-of-Unit Assessment. Students use this note-catcher to help them carefully analyze a single poem. In the next lesson, they will use this same note-catcher as they analyze a second poem as well as a new informational text.

- In advance: Review Work Time carefully for the explanation of the word *tone* as it relates to literary analysis. Students have been informally exposed to this concept in previous lessons, but this is the first lesson in which students work with a specific definition.

Lesson Vocabulary

symbol/symbolize, inferences, nuance, convey, tone; flecked, clusters

Materials

- *Inside Out & Back Again* (book; one per student)
- Write-Pair-Share Note-Catcher with text-dependent questions (one per student)
- Word Choice, Tone, and Meaning Note-Catcher (one per student)
- Document camera
- Things Close Readers Do Anchor Chart (begun in Lesson 2; added to in this lesson)—today's focus: how the author's word choice contributes to tone and meaning
- Quick Write 7 (one per student; for homework)

Opening

A. Engaging the Reader and Reviewing Learning Targets (5 minutes)

- Ask students to share with a peer their Quick Write 6 from their homework about Ha's family's possessions and what they might *symbolize*. Ask:
  - "What might the objects described in the poem represent for each person? What evidence supports your ideas?"

- Collect students' Quick Writes to gauge their ability to infer symbolism. Remind them that thinking about symbolism is challenging and that they will keep practicing throughout the year.

- Post learning targets for students to review. Focus students on the second target, and read it aloud:

  - "I can explain how *nuances* in word meanings contribute to the overall meaning of the poem."

- Have students think and then Turn-and-Talk about the word *nuance.* Students likely will need this word defined: "subtle differences in meaning." If needed, provide an example: The words *argue* and *bicker* both mean "to disagree," or the words *sprint* and *jog* both mean "to run," or the words *chuckle* and *snicker* both mean "to laugh," but each word in each pair has a slightly different meaning and feeling (or *tone*). *Argue,* for example, is strong; it means you are really into it with someone. *Bicker,* on the other hand, is like "light" arguing—something low-level and ongoing. Ask students to discuss the differences in the other words, and cold-call on pairs to respond.

- Inform students that today's work will be to examine how subtle nuances in the words in the poem "Wet and Crying" affect the *tone* (feeling) and the overall meaning of the text. As they look at how Ha's tone changes in the poem "Wet and Crying," they will come to understand more about how she is feeling about the events happening around her. Remind students that they will continue to make inferences and discuss their thinking with partners, small groups, and the class.

Meeting Students' Needs

- Reviewing academic vocabulary words benefits all students developing academic language.

- Some ELL students may be unfamiliar with more vocabulary words than are mentioned in this lesson. Check for comprehension of general words that most students would know.

Work Time

A. Write-Pair-Share about "Wet and Crying" (10 minutes)

- Be sure that students have their copies of *Inside Out & Back Again.* Ask students to arrange their seating to work in the pairs that you have defined.

- Remind students that they have been developing their skills with close reading throughout this unit. Today, they will have an opportunity to read closely on their own and with a peer.

- Ask them to reread the poem "Wet and Crying" on page 60, silently and independently. Remind students that this will refresh their memory and that they are reading for the gist of the poem.

- Invite students to talk with peers about the gist of the poem.

- Distribute the **Write-Pair-Share Note-Catcher**. Explain the Write-Pair-Share protocol with these basic directions:

  1. Listen to the text-dependent question.

  2. Think about your answer. Use the novel as a resource, and look for details from the text.

  3. Write your answer, making sure you refer to details from the text.

4. When given a signal, you will share your writing with your partner. (Pairs decide who will share first and who will listen.)

5. After both of you have shared, write down any new thinking.

6. Repeat with the next question; let the other partner share first.

- Each round/question will take 3 minutes.

- Begin. Circulate to observe students' work and provide support as needed.

- Model a sample response to one or both of the tone questions on the note-catcher. For example, invite students to share words or phrases in the fourth stanza that strike them as creating a powerful image. Listen for students to share such words as *chops, head falls,* or *silver blade slices.* Next, invite students to think about these images and describe the feeling the author is creating using these words. Give students time to talk with a peer, and then cold-call on several pairs to share such words as *deadly, cruel, final,* and so forth.

- After this Write-Pair-Share experience, ask for volunteers to share their thinking about this last question. Call on two or three students. Next, introduce the independent writing prompt.

Meeting Students' Needs

- Consider partnering ELL students who speak the same home language when discussion of complex content is required. This can allow students to have more meaningful discussions and clarify points in their native language.

- For students who struggle with following multiple-step directions, consider displaying these directions using a document camera or an interactive whiteboard. Another option is to type these instructions for students to have in hand.

- Some students may benefit from having key sections prehighlighted in their texts. This will help them focus on small sections rather than scanning the whole text for answers.

B. Guided Practice: How Word Choice Contributes to Tone and Meaning (20 minutes)

- Distribute and explain the **Word Choice, Tone, and Meaning Note-Catcher**, which students will use to record their thinking and discussion. Inform students that they will use this note-catcher with the poem and the audio text today. If possible, display the note-catcher on a **document camera** to orient students to the layout.

- On the note-catcher, read aloud the question in the left-hand column, Word Choice/Text Details:

  - "What are some specific *images, words,* and *phrases* the author uses that strike you emotionally and give you a feeling of the events described in the text?"

- Let students know that since this is their first time using this note-catcher, they will do some practice together.

- Focus students on the Practice row for stanza 4. Ask students to think independently about the question and to reread this stanza of the poem, focusing on the three words in italics: *chops, falls, slices.*

- Ask students to think and then talk with a peer about the middle column, Labeling the Feeling:

  - "What emotion or feeling does each of these words convey?"

- Be sure students understand that *convey* means "to communicate with or give the reader information."

- Listen for students to recognize that these three words have a violent feeling (which makes sense, since Ha's brother is using a knife).

- Ask students to add these feeling words' notes to the middle column.

- Then focus them on the right-hand column, Tone. Ask students whether they are familiar with the word *tone*. Many may know this word as it is used in other contexts. Distinguish that in this context, it is a noun (not a verb, like "to tone your muscles"). It is closely related to the general use of the word in everyday speech (e.g., many students have heard adults tell them, "Please speak in a respectful tone," or "Don't use that tone of voice with me!"). Point out that in the context of literary analysis, *tone* has a related but more precise meaning: "the feeling a text brings out in a reader, or the attitude an author has toward a subject." Inform students that they will work with this important concept in many lessons this year.

- Move students on to the task in the right-hand column:

  - "Based on the words and phrases you have selected, label the tone of the poem with one word."

- They can choose one of these words or use a new related word to describe the overall tone of stanza 4. Instruct them to, once again, think and write independently and then share with their partners and add to their notes.

- Do a quick go-round, asking one student from each group to share his or her best word to describe the tone. It is okay if several students use the same word; this will reinforce the patterns for students. (Plausible responses include "angry," "violent," and "harsh.")

- Then ask students to consider the "Meaning" question:

  - "How do those specific word choices and tone contribute to the meaning?"

- Paraphrase for students:

  - "In other words, how does the author's choice to use these words help us understand the point she is trying to make in this poem?"

- Invite students to Turn-and-Talk. Call on a group member to share out. Model if needed (e.g., "By using these violent words, the author creates a harsh tone that helps me understand how upset Ha is about the violence going on around her").

- Ask students to take about 5 minutes to work in pairs on the remaining rows of the note-catcher. (Let them know that they will discuss the question in the Meaning box as a whole group during the closing.)

- Listen in to gauge how well students are connecting the author's word choice with tone and then how tone contributes to meaning. Remind them they have been attending to word choice throughout this unit; this note-catcher just pushes them to be much more precise in their analysis of an author's craft.

- Refocus the whole group to check for overall understanding. Remind them that they will practice more with this note-catcher in the next lesson.

- Display the Things Close Readers Do Anchor Chart. Add the following:

  - Think about how the author's word choice contributes to tone and meaning.

Meeting Students' Needs

- To offer support for students who are struggling, consider adding additional scaffolds to the How Word Choice Contributes to Tone and Meaning Note-Catcher by adding additional examples, prompts, or sentence frames.

- To offer support for students in identifying the tone, consider providing a word bank of emotion words that could be used to describe literary tone (e.g., *cynical, hopeful, nostalgic, indignant, frantic, reserved, sarcastic, somber, sentimental,* and so forth). You may organize these words conceptually to help students understand less-familiar academic vocabulary. For example, group words that denote a positive or negative tone together. This will also push to expand students' vocabulary beyond typical words used to describe tone (e.g., *happy, sad, mad, excited*).

- To support ELL students, consider providing definitions of challenging vocabulary in the students' home language. Resources such as Google Translate and bilingual translation dictionaries can assist with one-word translations.

Closing and Assessment

A. Debrief and Discussion: What Happens to Hope? (10 minutes)

- Preview homework.

- Focus students on the specific question in the Meaning box of the Word Choice, Tone, and Meaning Note-Catcher:

  - "In the poem 'Wet and Crying,' what happens to hope?"

- Inform students that this will be their Quick Write prompt for homework. Because it is a challenging question, they will take a few minutes to discuss it as a class.

- Invite students to take 2 minutes on their own to think quietly or to write an initial response to this question.

- Then ask students to stand up, find a new partner, and take 2 minutes to share their thinking.

- Ask each pair to join another pair, so that they form groups of four. Invite them again to share their thinking. As students are sharing, find a student willing to share his or her response with the whole class; you can write the response on the document camera.

- Ask students to settle back into their seats. Focus them on the volunteer student's sample response. Read it aloud, or, if the student is willing, have him or her read it to the class. Highlight how the student author has used evidence in his or her writing.

- Talk with students about their interpretations of what happens to hope (fades, is destroyed, is forgotten). Point out how the author uses specific words (*cut, chops, head falls, slices, spill, clusters of eyes, wet and crying*) to develop a tone or feeling of death and destruction versus mere loss.

- Ask students to hold on to their note-catchers and journals to use as resources for their homework Quick Write.

Meeting Students' Needs

Conversation serves as "oral rehearsal" for writing and is a helpful scaffold for struggling writers.

Homework

Read pages 61–69, from "Sour Backs" through "Saigon Is Gone," and complete Quick Write 7: What happens to hope?

Meeting Students' Needs

Some students may benefit from having paragraph frames as a scaffold for Quick Writes.

LESSON 13

Comparing Meaning and Tone

The Fall of Saigon in Fiction and Informational Text

Long-Term Targets Addressed (Based on ELA CCSS)

- I can cite text-based evidence that provides the strongest support for my analysis of literary and informational text. (RL.8.1, RI.8.1)
- I can analyze the impact of word choice on meaning and tone. (RL.8.4, RI.8.4)
- I can effectively engage in discussions with diverse partners about eighth-grade topics, texts, and issues. (SL.8.1)

Supporting Learning Targets

- I can make inferences to deepen my understanding of *Inside Out & Back Again*.
- I can cite evidence from the poem "Saigon Is Gone" to explain the fall of Saigon and the emotional impact of this news on Ha and the other characters in the novel.
- I can analyze the word choices of two texts about the fall of Saigon and describe how that word choice contributes to the tone and meaning of each text.
- I can participate in discussions about the text with a peer, small group, and the whole class.

Ongoing Assessment

- Quick Write 7 (from homework)
- Word Choice, Tone, and Meaning Note-Catcher

Agenda

1. Opening
   A. Engaging the Reader and Reviewing Learning Targets: "Saigon Is Gone" (8 minutes)

---

2. Work Time

   A. Word Choice, Tone, and Meaning: "Saigon Is Gone" (10 minutes)

   B. Listening to a Read-Aloud of the Transcript of "Forgotten Ship" (15 minutes)

   C. Word Choice, Tone, and Meaning: "Forgotten Ship" (10 minutes)

3. Closing and Assessment

   A. Debrief (2 minutes)

4. Homework

   A. Reread and annotate the poem "Saigon Is Gone" and the transcript from "Forgotten Ship."

Teaching Notes

- In this lesson, continue to reinforce the distinction between historical fiction and informational text. (Review Lesson 6 Opening, plus other teaching notes throughout the unit.)

- The opening of this lesson includes reading the last two stanzas of "Saigon Is Gone" aloud, for dramatic effect. Prepare for this in advance.

- This lesson features a transcript of a radio broadcast titled, "Forgotten Ship: A Daring Rescue as Saigon Fell." The information is fairly intense, and there are multiple speakers. This lesson features the teacher reading aloud the transcript in dramatic fashion. Students are encouraged to follow along silently, and they will have the transcript to reread later as well.

- If students are familiar with a "readers' theater," consider assigning parts, or have students choose parts to read the transcript aloud either with the whole class or in small groups of six students.

- Students refer to the transcript during their End-of-Unit Assessment; be sure students hold on to their texts. Consider allowing ELL students to preview the transcript with you before this lesson. This will support their comprehension when listening to the read-aloud of the transcript during the lesson.

- This lesson is designed as scaffolding toward students' End-of-Unit Assessment (in Lesson 14). Therefore, students have some time to work with both texts with support, but they are not expected to have "fully analyzed" either text, which they work with further, independently, during the assessment itself.

- Display or distribute the Narrators Chart, which lists the narrators of the transcript as a reference for students (see Unit 1, Lesson 13, Supporting Materials).

Lesson Vocabulary

historical fiction, transcript, critical incident; communists, refugee, humanitarian, elite

Materials

- *Inside Out & Back Again* (book; one per student)

- Word Choice, Tone, and Meaning Note-Catcher (one per student and one to display)

- Transcript from "Forgotten Ship: A Daring Rescue as Saigon Fell" (one per student)
- Narrators Chart (one to display; consider also distributing to students)

Opening

A. Engaging the Reader and Reviewing Learning Targets: "Saigon Is Gone" (8 minutes)

- Welcome students and ask them to Turn-and-Talk with a partner:
  - "What happens to Ha and her family in the reading you did for homework?"
- Give them a minute to talk, and then probe:
  - "Which specific line in the novel helped you realize that everything has changed?"
- Build up the importance of this pivotal moment in the text. Say, "A pilot lands his helicopter on the ship and shouts . . ." Then read aloud from page 69:

> At noon today the Communists
>
> crashed their tanks
>
> through the gates
>
> of the presidential palace
>
> and planted on the roof
>
> a flag with one huge star.
>
> Then he adds
>
> what no one wants to hear:
>
> It's over;
>
> Saigon is gone.
>
> April 30
>
> Late afternoon

- Ask students:
  - "Based on what you read in 'The Vietnam Wars' article, why is the news that Saigon is gone something that no one wants to hear?"
- Invite students to Turn-and-Talk with a partner. Listen for them to realize that the events described in the poem are told from Ha's point of view: She lives in South Vietnam. The pilot on the ship is, in effect, reporting defeat.
- Probe:
  - "Is this really news that no one wants to hear?"
- Give students another moment to Turn-and-Talk. Cold-call on a student to share out. Again, emphasize the distinction between historical fiction and informational text. Listen for students to connect back to "The Vietnam Wars" article. They now should know that North Vietnamese pro-*communist* soldiers marched into Saigon to overtake the South Vietnamese army and unify the two countries.

- Challenge them to notice that in the poem "Saigon Is Gone," the phrase "no one" (as in "no one wants to hear") refers specifically to Ha, her family, and the other people on the ship: people from South Vietnam who are feeling the conflict. By contrast, the North Vietnamese soldiers *would* want to hear that Saigon is gone: That was their military objective.

- Remind students that this was a real event in history. They read about it in Section 5 of the article "The Vietnam Wars." Today they will listen to you read an article describing an event related to the fall of Saigon and will contrast the fictional and factual accounts of the event.

- Post learning targets for students to review. Read aloud the first learning target:

  - "I can cite evidence from the poem 'Saigon Is Gone' to explain the fall of Saigon and the emotional impact of this news on Ha and the other characters in the novel."

- Ask students to reread the poem and to learn more about this diary entry by listening to a related informational text. Specify that it is a transcript from a radio news piece. They will listen and also follow along with the *transcript*: "a typed version of what is being said."

- Invite students to Turn-and-Talk to a partner about what these learning targets mean for today's lesson. Ask students to show a thumbs-up if they understand the target, thumbs-sideways if they sort of get it, and thumbs-down if they are unclear. Answer any clarifying questions.

Work Time

A. Word Choice, Tone, and Meaning: "Saigon Is Gone" (10 minutes)

- Invite students to gather in the same groups from the day before. Ask them to get out their copies of **Inside Out & Back Again** and turn to page 67, "Saigon Is Gone." Distribute the **Word Choice, Tone, and Meaning Note-Catcher**. Students should recognize this from Lesson 12. Inform students that today they will use this note-catcher with both a poem and the transcript.

- Ask students to Turn-and-Talk with a peer to remind themselves about the purpose of each column of the note-catcher.

- Then ask them to follow the same process they did during the previous lesson:

  - Focus on the Word Choice/Text Details column:

    - "What are some specific *images*, *words*, and *phrases* the author uses that strike you emotionally and give you a feeling of the events described in the text?"

- Ask students to think about this question independently, reread the poem with the question in mind, and write their response using details from the text.

- Then, ask students to share their thinking with their partners and add notes based on what their partner says. Listen for students to notice such phrases as "whispers among adults," "escape," "dropping all the bombs," "helicopter circling," "people run and scream," "do not be frightened," "helicopter plunged," "the pilot . . . wet and shaking," "Communists crashed their tanks," and "It's over; Saigon is gone."

- Ask one or two paired groups to share words or phrases they selected, but keep this brief.

- Move students to the center column: Labeling the Feeling.

- Invite them to, once again, think and write independently and then share with their partners and add to their notes.

- Focus them on the right column, Tone. Give students time to think, talk, and write.

- Do a quick go-round, asking one person from each group to share his or her best word to describe the tone. Listen for such descriptors as *tense, upsetting, fearful, uncertain, anxious,* and *worried*.

- Inform them that they will return to the Meaning question at the end of the lesson.

Meeting Students' Needs

- Consider partnering ELL students who speak the same home language when discussion of complex content is required. This can allow students to have more meaningful discussions and clarify points in their native language.

- To offer support for students in identifying the tone, consider providing a word bank of emotion words that could be used to describe literary tone (e.g., *cynical, hopeful, nostalgic, indignant, frantic, reserved, sarcastic, somber, sentimental,* and so forth). You might organize these words conceptually to help students understand less-familiar academic vocabulary. For example, group words that denote a positive or negative tone together. This will also push to expand students' vocabulary beyond typical words used to describe tone (e.g., *happy, sad, mad, excited*).

B. Listening to a Read-Aloud of the Transcript of "Forgotten Ship" (15 minutes)

- Frame the connection between the poem and the upcoming transcript by asking the following question:

  - "What does the fact that Saigon is 'gone' mean for the people on board the ship?"

- Probe with the following questions as necessary:

  - "What has happened to Ha's home?"

  - "Can Ha and her family return to life as usual?"

- Cold-call on students to respond. Listen for students to recognize that the people on board the ship are trapped, because their enemy, the North Vietnamese Communists, have overtaken their home. Ha and her family cannot return home or live life as usual.

- Explain that the people on board the ship, and many other South Vietnamese people, are *refugees*. A *refugee* is "someone who has been forced to leave his or her country in order to escape war, persecution, or natural disaster." Ha and her family are refugees; this means they no longer have a home. Students will learn much more about refugees' experiences throughout the module.

- Remind the class that this novel is historical fiction: Events are described from Ha's perspective. She tells of how her family in South Vietnam escapes the communist takeover of Saigon. Other South Vietnamese people took different escape routes. The transcript will provide additional information about other families' daring story.

- Refer students to the Word Choice, Tone, and Meaning Note-Catcher. Direct them to the bottom half. Ask them to listen to you read aloud a radio transcript titled "Forgotten Ship: A Daring Rescue as Saigon Fell." While they are listening, they should follow along on the **transcript from "Forgotten Ship: A Daring Rescue as Saigon Fell."** (They will have time to reread and begin to complete their note-catcher later.)

- Reveal the **Narrators Chart** and explain to students that several narrators tell the story, and you have written their names and roles down on the chart to help students keep track. Give students about a minute to read over the names and roles on the Narrators Chart.

- Inform students that as they listen to the transcript, you will pause your reading from time to time for them to comment, clarify, and take notes about prominent descriptions and images. You will then begin reading aloud again while students listen to another part and take notes, and so on.

- Begin reading aloud: "Forgotten Ship: A Daring Rescue as Saigon Fell." Stop at, "The *Kirk*'s military mission that day was to shoot down any North Vietnamese jets that might try to stop U.S. Marine helicopters, as they evacuated people from Saigon. The North Vietnamese planes never came. But the *Kirk*'s mission was about to change, and suddenly."

- Explain to students that this ship had a military mission that changed to a *humanitarian* mission. Ask students:

  - "What do you think *humanitarian* means?" (Students should understand that the word means "to help other humans, to look out for others' welfare.")

- Before you begin reading the next section, inform students that they are going to hear about helicopters called *Hueys,* which are South Vietnamese helicopters escaping from the North Vietnamese communists.

- Begin reading aloud again and stop at, "The first two helicopters landed safely, but then there was no more room."

- Take a moment to let the events of what the students just listened to sink in. Ask students to Turn-and-Talk about what is happening. Be sure students understand that these helicopter pilots and people on board have taken a huge and desperate risk to escape. They literally flew out to sea, never to return. They would be shot down, would crash, or would be rescued by the U.S. Navy.

- Begin the final read-aloud portion, and stop at, "Then there was the helicopter that was too big to land."

- Give students a moment to think and to annotate their transcript.

- Cold-call on a few numbered heads group members to share their initial sense of what this portion of transcript is mostly about.

Meeting Students' Needs

- Consider allowing ELL students to preview the transcript with you before this lesson. This will help support their comprehension as they listen during this lesson.

- Some students may benefit from using a ruler or piece of paper to underline the lines in the transcript as they listen to the audio clip.

C. Word Choice, Tone, and Meaning: "Forgotten Ship" (10 minutes)

- Ask students to return to their Word Choice, Tone, and Meaning Note-Catcher: this time for the transcript "Forgotten Ship."

- Give students 2 minutes to reflect silently and write down prominent images that are described in this portion of the transcript, and invite students to share their notes with a peer.

- Then focus students on the bottom part of the note-catcher:

  - "How does the tone of the poem affect the meaning?"

  - "How does the tone of the transcript affect the meaning?"

  - "What does each author want you, the reader and listener, to understand?"

- As time permits, guide students to compare and contrast the tone of the two texts:

  - "Do you notice similarities between the tone of the transcript and the tone of the poem 'Saigon Is Gone'?"

  - "How is the tone of the two texts different?"

Meeting Students' Needs

Many students will benefit from seeing questions posted on the interactive whiteboard or via a document camera, but reveal questions one at a time to keep students focused on the question at hand.

Closing and Assessment

A. Debrief (2 minutes)

- Preview the homework with students. Explain that in the next lesson, they will get a chance to show what they know about how to use text details to determine tone. They will be able to use all of their work from today to support their writing. Ask them to be sure to bring their transcript of "Forgotten Ship" to class—they will need it for the assessment.

- Review the learning targets for today. Ask students to talk with a peer:

  - "How was your understanding of what Ha's family went through enhanced by listening to the transcript?"

- Collect students' note-catchers, because they will need them for the assessment in Lesson 14.

Homework

Prepare for the assessment: Reread and annotate the poem "Saigon Is Gone" and the transcript from "Forgotten Ship: A Daring Rescue as Saigon Fell."

LESSON 14

End-of-Unit Assessment

How Word Choice Contributes to Meaning and Tone in Literary and Informational Text

Long-Term Targets Addressed (Based on ELA CCSS)

- I can cite text-based evidence that provides the strongest support for my analysis of literary text. (RL.8.1, RI.8.1)
- I can analyze the impact of word choice on meaning and tone. (RL.8.4, RI.8.4)
- I can use evidence from informational texts to support analysis, reflection, and research. (W.8.9)

Supporting Learning Targets

- I can analyze how the word choice in both informational and literary texts affects the meaning and tone.
- I can cite evidence from text to support analysis of literary and informational text.

Ongoing Assessment

- End-of-Unit 1 Assessment

Agenda

1. Opening
   A. Review Learning Targets (2 minutes)
2. Work Time
   A. End-of-Unit 1 Assessment: Examining How Word Choice Contributes to Meaning and Tone in Literary and Informational Text (40 minutes)
3. Closing and Assessment
   A. Debrief (3 minutes)
4. Homework
   A. None.

Teaching Notes

During today's assessment, students independently formalize their thinking regarding the differences in tone between two pieces of writing having to do with the same subject. Use this not only as a summative assessment of the students' ability to write in response to literature (W.8.9) but also as a method to inform writing instruction for Unit 2 (which will focus much more extensively on the specific components of W.8.2).

After this lesson, hold on to the Things Close Readers Do Anchor Chart. In Unit 2, students will work with a resource that gives them even more details about close reading and will refer back to the chart they helped build.

Consider using the Expository Writing Evaluation Rubric (which can be found in Unit 1, Lesson 11, Supporting Materials) for assessing students' work. This could provide very useful formative assessment data to inform your more explicit and scaffolded writing instruction that unfolds throughout the second half of Unit 2.

Lesson Vocabulary

Do not preview vocabulary for today's assessment.

Materials

- *Inside Out & Back Again* (book; one per student)
- Transcript from "Forgotten Ship: A Daring Rescue as Saigon Fell" (from Lesson 13; one per student)
- Students' completed Word Choice, Tone, and Meaning Note-Catchers (collected at the end of Lesson 13)
- Lined paper for students' written responses to the assessment prompt
- End-of-Unit 1 Assessment: Examining How Word Choice Contributes to Meaning and Tone in Literary and Informational Text (one per student)
- End-of-Unit 1 Assessment: Examining How Word Choice Contributes to Meaning and Tone in Literary and Informational Text (Teacher Reference)
- Things Close Readers Do Anchor Chart (begun in Lesson 2)

Opening

A. Review Learning Targets (2 minutes)

- Remind students that the poem "Saigon Is Gone" is a part of the novel, which is *historical fiction*. The transcript "Forgotten Ship: A Daring Rescue as Saigon Fell" is an informational text, which is not fictional.
- Read aloud the target: "I can analyze how the word choice in both informational and literary texts affects the meaning and tone." Ask students to tell a partner what they have learned about *word choice* and *tone*.

- Inform them that in today's assessment, they will be doing this same thing. They have been practicing with the note-catchers, in discussions, and in their recent Quick Writes.

- Ask students to show a quick thumbs-up if they understand the targets, thumbs-sideways if they understand some aspects, and thumbs-down if they are unsure. Clarify as needed.

Work Time

A. End-of-Unit 1 Assessment: Examining How Word Choice Contributes to Meaning and Tone in Literary and Informational Text (40 minutes)

- Arrange student seating to allow for an assessment-conducive arrangement where students independently think, read, and write. Encourage students by explaining that you know they have been working very hard at reading closely and that today you want them to show what they have learned about word choice and tone in informational and fictional (or literary) texts.

- Ask students to gather their materials:

  - *Inside Out & Back Again*

  - **Transcript and annotations of "Forgotten Ship"**

  - **Word Choice, Tone, and Meaning Note-Catcher** (collected at the end of Lesson 13)

- Distribute the **End-of-Unit 1 Assessment: Examining How Word Choice Contributes to Meaning and Tone in Literary and Informational Text** and **lined paper**. Read the directions aloud as students read along silently. Address any clarifying questions.

- Invite students to begin. Circulate to observe, but do not offer support; this is the students' opportunity to apply independently the skills they have been learning.

- If students finish early, encourage them to reread some of their favorite poems from Part 1 of the novel or to continue reading their independent reading book for this unit.

- Collect the End-of-Unit Assessment.

Closing and Assessment

A. Debrief (3 minutes)

- Focus students on the Things Close Readers Do Anchor Chart that they helped create during this unit. Invite volunteers to read each bullet point aloud.

- Point out to students that they have practiced reading closely in the novel and have dealt with challenging informational text. Remind them that they are getting better and better at noticing details in a text and how these details contribute to the overall meaning and tone.

Homework

No homework.

UNIT OVERVIEW

Finding Home

Refugees

Case Study: Why Do People Flee Home?

In Unit 2, students will build their knowledge about refugees' search for a place to call home. They will read informational texts that convey the universal themes and experiences of refugees across various times and cultures. This study will draw students' attention to the challenges refugees face when they are fleeing and finding home. As students continue to move through the novel *Inside Out & Back Again,* they will focus on how particular incidents move the story forward and reveal aspects of Ha's character. Ha will be analyzed as a case study of a refugee who is faced with challenges that represent the universal refugee themes of fleeing and finding home. For their Mid-Unit Assessment, students will read an informational text and analyze one refugee's experience of finding home. Unit 2 culminates in a formal literary analysis essay in which students will explain the significance of the novel's title and how it relates to the universal refugee experience and the challenges Ha faces as a refugee.

Guiding Questions and Big Ideas

- How do critical incidents reveal character?
- Which common themes are universal to the refugee experience?
- *Critical incidents reveal a character's dynamic nature.*
- *Characters change over time in response to challenges.*

Mid-Unit 2 Assessment

Analyzing an Informational Text about a Refugee Experience

This assessment centers on ELA CCSS RI.8.1, RI.8.2, RI.8.3, RI.8.4, L.8.4.a, and W.8.9. In this on-demand assessment, students will read an unfamiliar informational text about a refugee experience (a speech by Til Gurung, a refugee from Bhutan) and then answer a range of literal and inferential text-dependent questions. The assessment will provide questions in the form of selected-response items, a graphic organizer, and short constructed-response items. Students will cite the strongest text-based evidence to support their answers.

End-of-Unit 2 Assessment

Analysis Essay: Explain the Significance of the Novel's Title and Its Relationship to Universal Refugee Experiences and Ha's Character

This assessment centers on ELA CCSS RL.8.1, RL.8.3, RL.8.4, RL.8.6, W.8.2.d, W.8.4, W.8.5, and W.8.9. For this writing assessment, students will explain aspects of Ha's character by responding to this specific prompt: "Consider the meaning of the novel's title, *Inside Out & Back Again*. How does this title relate to the universal refugee experience of fleeing and finding home, and in what ways is Ha's experience an example of this universal experience?" Students will choose the strongest evidence from the informational texts and the novel to construct an informational literary analysis essay.

Content Connections

This module is designed to address the CCS English Language Arts (ELA) standards. However, the module intentionally incorporates social studies and science content that many teachers may be teaching during other parts of the day. These intentional connections are described below.

Social Studies Connection

Social Studies Themes in Context

- Individual Development and Cultural Identity
    - Role of social, political, and cultural interactions in the development of identity
    - Personal identity as a function of an individual's culture, time, place, geography, interaction with groups, influences from institutions, and lived experiences
- Development, Movement, and Interaction of Cultures
    - Role of diversity within and among cultures

Central Texts

1. Thanhha Lai, *Inside Out & Back Again*. New York: HarperCollins, 2011.

2. Fox Butterfield, "Panic Rises in Saigon, but the Exits Are Few," *New York Times,* April 24, 1975.

3. Catherine Gevert, "Refugees: Who, Where, and Why," *Faces: People, Places and Cultures* 19, no. 1 (2002): 6–8.

4. Arthur Brice, "Children of War," *Scholastic,* March 1994.

5. Til Gurung, speech at Refugee Transitions' World of Difference Benefit Luncheon, San Francisco, November 3, 2010.

6. Ana Marie Fantino and Alice Colak, "Refugee Children in Canada: Searching for Identity." *Child Welfare* 80, no. 5 (2001): 587–596.

7. Research texts: See Unit 2, Lesson 19, for a complete list of texts students use in their short research project.

Unit-at-a-Glance Calendar

This unit is approximately 4 weeks, or 20 lessons, of instruction.

Lesson	Lesson Title	Long-Term Targets	Supporting Targets	Ongoing Assessment	Anchor Charts and Protocols
1	Collecting Details: The Challenges Ha Faces and Ha as a Dynamic Character	• I can cite text-based evidence that provides the strongest support for my analysis of literary text. (RL.8.1) • I can analyze how specific dialogue or incidents in a plot propel the action, reveal aspects of a character, or provoke a decision. (RL.8.3) • I can analyze the development of a theme or central idea throughout the text (including its relationship to the characters, setting, and plot). (RL.8.2)	• I can review and add to my strategies of things close readers do. • I can identify key details that help me understand Ha. • I can explain how key details in the novel reveal the challenges Ha faces and her dynamic character.	• Structured Notes • Think-Write-Pair-Share	• Numbered Heads protocol • Give One, Get One protocol • Think-Pair-Share protocol • Turn-and-Talk protocol • Who Is Ha? Anchor Chart • Things Close Readers Do Anchor Chart

| 2 | Rereading and Close Reading: Communism, "The Vietnam Wars," and "Last Respects" | • I can cite text-based evidence that provides the strongest support for my analysis of literary text. (RL.8.1)

• I can analyze how specific dialogue or incidents in a plot propel the action, reveal aspects of a character, or provoke a decision. (RL.8.3)

• I can analyze the development of a theme or central idea throughout the text (including its relationship to the characters, setting, and plot). (RL.8.2)

• I can analyze figurative language, word relationships, and nuances in word meanings. (L.8.5) | • I can explain how key details in the novel reveal the challenges Ha faces and her dynamic character.

• I can infer the symbolism in the poem "Last Respects." | • Structured notes for pages 83–90 (from homework)

• Who Is Ha? Anchor Chart

• Last Respects Note-Catcher | • Chalk Talk protocol

• Who Is Ha? Anchor Chart

• Turn-and-Talk protocol

• Think-Write-Pair-Share protocol

• Numbered Heads protocol |

| 3 | Building Background Knowledge: Fleeing Saigon as "Panic Rises" | • I can cite text-based evidence that provides the strongest support for an analysis of informational text. (RI.8.1)
• I can determine a theme or the central ideas of an informational text. (RI.8.2)
• I can analyze the connections and distinctions between individuals, ideas, or events in a text. (RI.8.3)
• I can use a variety of strategies to determine the meaning of unknown words or phrases. (L.8.4) | • I can identify the strongest evidence in the text "Panic Rises in Saigon, but the Exits Are Few" that helps me explain what challenges refugees from South Vietnam faced.
• I can use common Greek and Latin affixes (prefixes) and roots as clues to help me know what a word means.
• I can identify common themes that connect the universal refugee experience. | • Structured notes (for pages 91–111, from homework)
• Fleeing Home: What Challenges Did Ha's Family Face? Graphic Organizer
• Answers to text-dependent questions
• Prefixes Note-Catcher | • Think-Write-Pair-Share protocol
• Turn-and-Talk protocol
• Think-Pair-Share protocol |
| 4 | Building Background Knowledge, Predicting, and Focusing on Key | • I can cite text-based evidence that provides the strongest support for | • I can identify the strongest evidence in the text "Refugees: Who, Where, | • Structured notes (pages 135–157 from homework) | • Chalkboard Splash protocol
• Turn-and-Talk protocol |

	Vocabulary: "Refugees: Who, Where, and Why"	an analysis of informational text. (RI.8.1) • I can analyze the connections and distinctions between individuals, ideas, or events in a text. (RI.8.3) • I can use a variety of strategies to determine the meaning of unknown words or phrases. (L.8.4)	and Why" that helps me explain challenges refugees face when fleeing home. • I can identify the strongest evidence in the text "Refugees: Who, Where, and Why" that helps me explain challenges refugees face finding home. • I can use common Greek and Latin affixes (prefixes) and roots as clues to help me know what a word means.	• Prefixes Note-Catcher • Annotated article "Refugees: Who, Where, and Why"	• Partner Reading protocol
5	Building Background Knowledge and Summarizing: "Refugees: Who, Where, and Why," Part 2	• I can cite text-based evidence that provides the strongest support for an analysis of informational text. (RI.8.1)	• I can identify the strongest evidence in the article "Refugees: Who, Where, and Why" and the novel that helps me explain challenges	• Structured notes (for pages 135–157, from homework) • Annotated article "Refugees: Who, Where, Why" (from homework)	• Chalkboard Splash protocol • Fleeing Home Anchor Chart • Finding Home Anchor Chart

		• I can objectively summarize informational text. (RI.8.2) • I can analyze the connections and distinctions between individuals, ideas, or events in a text. (RI.8.3) • I can write informative/ explanatory texts that convey ideas and concepts using relevant information that is carefully selected and organized. (W.8.2)	refugees face when fleeing home. • I can identify the strongest evidence in the article "Refugees: Who, Where, and Why" and the novel that helps me explain challenges refugees face finding home. • I can write a paragraph that provides an objective summary of "Refugees: Who, Where, and Why." • I can identify universal themes that connect refugee experiences.	• Summary Writing Graphic Organizer • Fleeing Home and Finding Home Anchor Charts	
6	Building Background Knowledge: Challenges Bosnian Refugees Faced Fleeing and Finding Home	• I can cite text-based evidence that provides the strongest support for an analysis of informational text. (RI.8.1)	• I can determine a theme or the central idea of an informational text. (RI.8.2)	• Structured notes (pages 180–195 from homework) • Written summary of "Refugees: Who, Where,	• Think-Pair-Share protocol • Fleeing Home Anchor Chart

				and Why" (from homework)	• Finding Home Anchor Chart
		• I can analyze the connections and distinctions between individuals, ideas, or events in a text. (RI.8.3) • I can use a variety of strategies to determine the meaning of unknown words or phrases. (L.8.4)	• I can identify the strongest evidence in the text "Children of War" that helps me explain challenges refugees face when fleeing home. • I can identify the strongest evidence in the text "Children of War" that helps me explain challenges refugees face finding home. • I can identify common themes that connect the universal refugee experience.	• Summary Writing Graphic Organizer: "Children of War" • Evidence sort	• Fist-to-Five protocol
7	Mid-Unit Assessment: Analyzing an Informational Text about a Refugee Experience	• I can cite text-based evidence that provides the strongest support for an analysis of literary text. (RI.8.1)	• I can identify the strongest evidence in the speech by Til Gurung that helps me explain	• Mid-Unit 2 Assessment: Analyzing an Informational Text about a Refugee Experience	• None

		• I can objectively summarize informational text. (RI.8.2) • I can analyze the connections and distinctions between individuals, ideas, or events in a text. (RI.8.3) • I can determine the meaning of words and phrases in text (figurative, connotative, and technical meanings). (RI.8.4) • I can use a variety of strategies to determine the meaning of unknown words or phrases. (L.8.4) • I can use evidence from informational texts to support analysis, reflection, and research. (W.8.9)	why refugees leave their home. • I can identify the strongest evidence in the speech by Til Gurung that helps me explain challenges refugees face in their new country. • I can determine the meaning of unfamiliar words based on context clues. • I can cite evidence from the text to support analysis of an informational text.		

| 8 | Analyzing the Content of a Model Essay: "How Ha's Mother Is Turned 'Inside Out'" | • I can cite the textual evidence that most strongly supports an analysis of what the text says explicitly as well as inferences drawn from the text. (RI.8.1)

• I can evaluate the argument and specific claims in a text (assessing whether the reasoning is sound and the evidence is relevant and sufficient to support the claims). (RI.8.8)

• I can effectively engage in discussions with diverse partners about eighth-grade topics, texts, and issues. (SL.8.1) | • I can make connections between the universal refugee experiences of fleeing and finding home and the title of the novel *Inside Out & Back Again*.

• I can find the gist of a model essay.

• I can choose the strongest evidence to support my answers to questions about a model essay.

• I can evaluate the quality of evidence used to support the claims made in the model essay "How Ha's Mother Is Turned 'Inside Out.'" | • Structured notes (pages 196–212 from homework)

• Answers to questions about model essay | • Think-Pair-Share protocol

• Inside Out Anchor Chart

• Back Again Anchor Chart

• Fleeing Home Anchor Chart

• Finding Home Anchor Chart

• Numbered Heads protocol |
| 9 | Close Reading: Paragraph 1 of "Refugee and | • I can cite text-based evidence that provides the strongest | • I can find the gist of the first paragraph of "Refugee and | • Answers to text-dependent questions, Part A | • Give One, Get One protocol |

	Immigrant Children: A Comparison" (from "Refugee Children in Canada: Searching for Identity")	support for an analysis of literary text. (RI.8.1) • I can determine a theme or the central ideas of an informational text. (RI.8.2) • I can analyze the structure of a specific paragraph in a text (including the role of particular sentences in developing and refining a key concept). (RI.8.5) • I can read above-grade informational texts with scaffolding and support. (RI.8.10)	Immigrant Children: A Comparison." • I can analyze how specific words, phrases, and sentences help me understand how refugee and immigrant children are similar. • I can cite evidence to explain the similarities and differences between refugee children and immigrant children.		• Think-Pair-Share protocol • Inside Out Anchor Chart • Back Again Anchor Chart • Numbered Heads protocol • Similarities and Differences in How Refugees and Immigrants Adapt Anchor Chart • Mix and Mingle protocol
10	Analyzing the Significance of the Novel's Title: Connecting the Universal Refugee Experience to *Inside Out & Back Again*	• I can cite text-based evidence that provides the strongest support for my analysis of literary text. (RL.8.1)	• I can use the strongest evidence from the novel and from the informational text to support my	• "Refugee and Immigrant Children: A Comparison": Paragraph 1, Text-Dependent Questions, Part B	• Inside Out Anchor Chart • Back Again Anchor Chart

		• I can cite text-based evidence that provides the strongest support for an analysis of informational text. (RI.8.1) • I can read above-grade informational texts with scaffolding and support. (RI.8.10)	answers to questions. • I can make connections between evidence of the universal refugee experience and the title of the novel *Inside Out & Back Again.*		• Think-Pair-Share protocol • Jigsaw protocol
11	Close Reading: Paragraphs 2 and 3 of "Refugee and Immigrant Children: A Comparison" and Introducing the Grade 6–8 Expository Writing Evaluation Rubric	• I can cite text-based evidence that provides the strongest support for an analysis of literary text. (RI.8.1) • I can determine a theme or the central ideas of an informational text. (RI.8.2) • I can analyze the structure of a specific paragraph in a text (including the role of particular sentences in	• I can find the gist of paragraphs 2 and 3 of "Refugee and Immigrant Children: A Comparison." • I can analyze how specific words, phrases, and sentences help me understand what refugee and immigrant children need for successful adaptation.	• "Refugee and Immigrant Children: A Comparison": Paragraphs 2 and 3 Text-Dependent Questions, Part A	• Inside Out Anchor Chart • Back Again Anchor Chart • Think-Pair-Share protocol • Numbered Heads protocol

		developing and refining a key concept). (RI.8.5) • I can read above-grade informational texts with scaffolding and support. (RI.8.10)	• I can read a text closely in order to answer text-dependent questions.		
12	Analyzing the Significance of the Novel's Title: Connecting the Universal Refugee Experience to *Inside Out & Back Again,* Part 2	• I can cite text-based evidence that provides the strongest support for my analysis of literary text. (RL.8.1) • I can cite text-based evidence that provides the strongest support for an analysis of informational text. (RI.8.1) • I can read above-grade informational texts with scaffolding and support. (RI.8.10)	• I can use the strongest evidence from the novel and from the informational text to support my answers to questions. • I can make connections between evidence of the universal refugee experience and the title of the novel *Inside Out & Back Again.*	• "Refugee and Immigrant Children: A Comparison": Paragraphs 2 and 3 Text-Dependent Questions, Part B	• Jigsaw protocol • Inside Out Anchor Chart • Back Again Anchor Chart
13	Close Reading: Paragraph 4	• I can cite text-based evidence that provides the	• I can find the gist of paragraph 4 of "Refugee	• "Refugee and Immigrant Children: A Comparison":	• Numbered Heads protocol

	of "Refugee and Immigrant Children: A Comparison"	strongest support for an analysis of literary text. (RI.8.1) • I can determine a theme or the central ideas of an informational text. (RI.8.2) • I can analyze the structure of a specific paragraph in a text (including the role of particular sentences in developing and refining a key concept). (RI.8.5) • I can read above-grade informational texts with scaffolding and support. (RI.8.10)	and Immigrant Children: A Comparison." • I can analyze how specific words, phrases, and sentences help me understand what refugee and immigrant children need for successful adaptation. • I can read a text closely in order to answer text-dependent questions.	Paragraph 4 Text-Dependent Questions, Part A	• Think-Pair-Share protocol • Inside Out Anchor Chart • Back Again Anchor Chart
14	Analyzing the Significance of the Novel's Title: Connecting the Universal Refugee Experience to *Inside Out & Back Again*, Part 3	• I can cite text-based evidence that provides the strongest support for my analysis of literary text. (RL.8.1)	• I can use the strongest evidence from the novel and from the informational text to support my answers to questions.	• "Refugee and Immigrant Children: A Comparison": Paragraph 4 Text-Dependent Questions, Part B	• Jigsaw protocol • Inside Out Anchor Chart • Back Again Anchor Chart

		• I can cite text-based evidence that provides the strongest support for an analysis of informational text. (RI.8.1)			
		• I can read above-grade informational texts with scaffolding and support. (RI.8.10)	• I can make connections between evidence of the universal refugee experience and the title of the novel *Inside Out & Back Again*.		
15	Connecting the Universal Refugee Experience of Fleeing and Finding Home to the Title of the Novel *Inside Out & Back Again*	• I can cite text-based evidence that provides the strongest support for my analysis of literary text. (RL.8.1) • I can analyze how specific dialogue or incidents in a plot propel the action, reveal aspects of a character, or provoke a decision. (RL.8.3)	• I can make a claim about how the lives of refugees turn "inside out" when they flee home, using the strongest evidence I have collected from both the novel and informational text. • I can make a claim about how the lives of refugees	• Two Forming Evidence-Based Claims Graphic Organizers (one for Body Paragraph 1, "Inside Out," and one for Body Paragraph 2, "Back Again")	• Numbered Heads protocol • Think-Pair-Share protocol • Citing Books and Articles Anchor Chart • Inside Out Anchor Chart • Back Again Anchor Chart

		• I can cite text-based evidence that provides the strongest support for an analysis of informational text. (RI.8.1)	turn "back again" as they find a new home, using the strongest evidence I have collected from both the novel and informational text. • I can cite where I found my evidence.		
16	Planning the Introductory and Concluding Paragraphs of the End-of-Unit-Assessment Essay	• I can analyze how specific dialogue or incidents in a plot propel the action, reveal aspects of a character, or provoke a decision. (RL.8.3) • I can write informative/ explanatory texts that convey ideas and concepts using relevant information that is carefully selected and organized. (W.8.2) • I can produce clear and coherent writing that is	• I can plan effective introductory and concluding paragraphs for my analytical essay. • I can cite where I found my evidence.	• Forming Evidence-Based Claims Graphic Organizer (with a claim to answer the question: "Who is Ha before she flees home?") • Planning Your Essay Graphic Organizer (homework for Lessons 15 and 16)	• Numbered Heads protocol • Think-Pair-Share protocol • Who Is Ha? Anchor Chart • Citing Books and Articles Anchor Chart

		appropriate to the task, purpose, and audience. (W.8.4) • With support from peers and adults, I can use the writing process to ensure that the purpose and audience have been addressed. (W.8.5)			
17	End-of-Unit 2 Assessment, Part 1: First Draft of Analytical Essay	• I can cite text-based evidence that promotes the strongest support for my analysis of literary text. (RL.8.1) • I can analyze how specific dialogue or incidents in a plot propel the action, reveal aspects of a character, or provoke a decision. (RL.8.3) • I can cite text-based evidence that provides the	• I can write an essay explaining the universal refugee experience of turning "inside out" and "back again." • I can cite the strongest evidence from informational texts to support my claims about how refugees turn "inside out" and "back again."	End-of-Unit 2 Assessment, Part 1: First Draft of Analytical Essay	• Think-Pair-Share protocol • Who Is Ha? Anchor Chart • Inside Out Anchor Chart • Back Again Anchor Chart • Citing Books and Articles Anchor Chart

		strongest support for an analysis of informational text. (RI.8.1) • I can analyze full-length novels, short stories, poems, and other genres by authors who represent diverse world cultures. (RL.8.6) • I can write informative/ explanatory texts that convey ideas and concepts using relevant information that is carefully selected and organized. (W.8.2) • I can produce clear and coherent writing that is appropriate to the task, purpose, and audience (W.8.4) • I can use evidence from literary texts	• I can cite the strongest evidence from the novel *Inside Out & Back Again* to support my claims about who Ha is before she flees and how she is turned "inside out" and "back again." • I can cite where I found my evidence.		

	to support analysis, reflection, and research. (W.8.9)			
18	Introducing the Final Performance Task and Analyzing Statistics	• I can determine a theme or central idea of literary text. (RL.8.1) • I can analyze the connections and distinctions between individuals, ideas, or events in a text. (RI.8.3) • I can effectively engage in discussions with diverse partners about eighth-grade topics, texts, and issues. (SL.8.1)	• I can determine the factual details (specific to a time and place in history) that Thanhha Lai uses in the poems "Birthday" and "Saigon Is Gone." • I can analyze statistics about refugee experiences around the world in order to notice patterns.	• Specific Factual Details tickets • Chalk Talk participation and discussion	• Think-Pair-Share protocol • Numbered Heads protocol • Chalk Talk protocol
19	Launching Researching: Reading for Gist and Gathering Evidence Using the Research Guide	• I can conduct short research projects to answer a question. (W.8.7) • I can use evidence from informational	• I can find the gist of informational texts. • I can select the strongest evidence in an informational	• Research Guide	• Think-Pair-Share protocol • Numbered Heads protocol

		texts to support analysis, reflection, and research. (W.8.9) • I can express my own ideas clearly during discussions, and I can build on others' ideas during discussions. (SL.8.1)	text about who the refugees were, where they fled from, and why they had to flee.		
20	End-of-Unit 2 Assessment, Part 2: Final Draft of Analytical Essay	• I can write informative/ explanatory texts that convey ideas and concepts using relevant information that is carefully selected and organized. (W.8.2) • With support from peers and adults, I can use the writing process to ensure that the purpose and audience have been addressed. (W.8.5)	• I can use teacher feedback to revise my analytical essay to meet the expectations of the Grade 6–8 Expository Writing Evaluation Rubric.	• End-of-Unit 2 Assessment, Part 2: Final Draft of Analytical Essay	• Think-Pair-Share protocol • Citing Books and Articles Anchor Chart

		• I can use evidence from literary texts to support analysis, reflection, and research. (W.8.9)			

Finding Home

Refugees

Optional: Experts and Fieldwork

Experts

- Invite recent refugees to the United States who can speak about the experience of coming to a new country. This is an opportunity for students to understand Ha's experiences better.

- Seek out professionals or volunteers who support refugees in local centers. This is an opportunity for students to learn about the challenges and needs of refugees in their area and the local supports that attend to these needs.

Fieldwork

- Visit a local center that helps refugees acclimate to the United States.

- If a local museum has exhibits on Vietnam, consider taking students to help them learn more about where Ha comes from.

Optional: Extensions

- With Social Studies: Collaborate on a study of refugee issues in "finding home" in the local community or state.

Preparation and Materials

Students will be receiving many recording forms, graphic organizers, and texts throughout this module. It is suggested that students have a binder in which to collect these materials and refer back to them. Alternately, teachers who prefer to use notebooks or journals can use the recording forms and graphic organizers as a template to model for students to create these structures independently.

Reading Calendar

- Students read *Inside Out & Back Again* for homework for Lessons 1–10.

- Each night, they read some pages.

- Consider providing an *Inside Out & Back Again* reading calendar to help students, teachers, and families understand what is due and when.

Writer's Glossary

The Writer's Glossary includes academic words related to the writing process and products. These words come from the Grades 6–8 Expository Writing Evaluation Rubric. Student writing will be evaluated with this rubric through seventh and eighth grades. In Module 1 for both seventh and eighth grades, students are introduced to the rubric and its vocabulary. The purpose of the Writer's Glossary is to provide a place for students to reference these words throughout the rest of the year. Because there is not always enough information in the context of the rubric for students to infer a definition for themselves, the glossary defines all the words. It also includes space for students to add any other words that they do not know. Even though the definitions are in the glossary, you will need to go over them and give students examples so that they understand how these words are used in the rubric to refer to writing. As students progress through the rest of the year, they may encounter other academic words that relate directly to their writing or writing products. Feel free to create more pages for this glossary as more vocabulary about writing is encountered.

There are four pages in the Writer's Glossary: one page for each row of the expository writing rubric. Students use this glossary in Lessons 12–15. The full glossary is provided here for teachers who want to make a packet. The words related to a specific lesson are also provided in the Supporting Materials of Lessons 12–15, along with instructions for using the glossary page for that lesson.

Independent Reading and Reader's Response Letter

Some students, especially stronger readers, will finish *Inside Out & Back Again* early in the unit. They should be encouraged to complete independent reading related to the topic of the unit. See the Unit 2 Recommended Texts, which include texts at many levels. The daily lessons do not include time to check on students' independent reading, but consider how you might support students with this volume of reading. Included is a template for a Reader's Response letter, a format students can use to share their thinking about their reading with you or with other students. Some teachers create a binder of these letters, and then future students can look through them as they select books to read.

Reading Calendar

Inside Out & Back Again

This calendar shows what is due on each day. Teachers can modify this document to include dates instead of lessons.

Due at Lesson	Chapter Pages to Read	Gathering Textual Evidence
2	83–90	Take notes (in journals) using the Structured Notes Graphic Organizer. Focus on key details that reveal the challenges Ha is facing and her dynamic character, plus vocabulary that helps you understand her challenges and responses.
3	91–111	Take notes (in journals) using the Structured Notes Graphic Organizer. Focus on key details that reveal the challenges Ha is facing and her dynamic character, plus vocabulary that helps you understand her challenges and responses.

4	115–134	Take notes (in journal) using the Structured Notes Graphic Organizer. Focus on the strongest evidence that reveals how Ha is being turned "inside out" (the challenges Ha faces and her dynamic character), plus vocabulary that helps you understand her challenges and responses.
5	135–157	Take notes (in journal) using the Structured Notes Graphic Organizer. Focus on the strongest evidence that reveals how Ha is being turned "inside out" (the challenges Ha faces and her dynamic character), plus vocabulary that helps you understand her challenges and responses.
6	158–179	Take notes (in journal) using the Structured Notes Graphic Organizer. Focus on the strongest evidence that reveals how Ha is being turned "inside out" (the challenges Ha faces and her dynamic character), plus vocabulary that helps you understand her challenges and responses.
7	180–195	Take notes (in journal) using the Structured Notes Graphic Organizer. Focus on the strongest evidence that reveals how Ha is being turned "inside out and back again" (the challenges Ha faces and her dynamic character), plus vocabulary that helps you understand her challenges and responses.
8	196–212	Take notes (in journal) using the Structured Notes Graphic Organizer. Focus on the strongest evidence that reveals how Ha is being turned "inside out and back again" (the challenges Ha faces and her dynamic character), plus vocabulary that helps you understand her challenges and responses.
9	213–237	Take notes (in journal) using the Structured Notes Graphic Organizer. Focus on the strongest evidence that reveals how Ha is being turned "inside out and back again" (the challenges Ha faces and her dynamic character), plus vocabulary that helps you understand her challenges and responses.
10	238–247	Take notes (in journal) using the Structured Notes Graphic Organizer. Focus on the strongest evidence that reveals how Ha is being turned "inside out and back again" (the challenges Ha faces and her dynamic character), plus vocabulary that helps you understand her challenges and responses.
11	248–260	Take notes (in journal) using the Structured Notes Graphic Organizer. Focus on the strongest evidence that reveals how Ha is being turned "inside out" (the challenges Ha faces and her dynamic character), plus vocabulary that helps you understand her challenges and responses.

Writer's Glossary

This glossary includes academic words related to the writing process and products. The words for the four lessons here come from the Grades 6–8 Expository Writing Evaluation Rubric. Student writing will be evaluated with this rubric through seventh and eighth grades. In Module 1 of the seventh-grade materials, students were introduced to the rubric and its vocabulary. Feel free to create more pages for this glossary as more writing-related vocabulary is taught throughout the year.

Words from Grades 6–8 Expository Writing Evaluation Rubric

Writer's Glossary from Row 1 of the Expository Writing Rubric

Word/Phrase	Page	Definition
content	1	the ideas, facts, or opinions that are contained in a speech, piece of writing, film, program, etc.
extent	1, 2, 3, 4	expresses how true, large, important, or serious something is Ex: *The extent of his injuries was not clear immediately.*
conveys	1	to communicate or express something Ex: *The TV ad conveys the message that thin is beautiful.*
compelling	1	very interesting or exciting, so that you have to pay attention Ex: *The movie's story was compelling.*
task	1	a piece of work that must be done Ex: *I was given the task of building a fire.*
insightful	1	showing that you understand what a text, situation, or person is really like Ex: *Steve's comments about the story were insightful.*
comprehension	1	understanding Ex: *They don't have the least comprehension of what I'm trying to do.*
logically (opposite: illogically)	1, 3	seeming reasonable and sensible, ideas are in a clear order Ex: *He could logically present his argument for dessert to his mom.* Opposite: not reasonable, sensible, or clearly put together
Other new words you have encountered:		

Writer's Glossary from Row 2 of the Expository Writing Rubric

Word/Phrase	Page	Definition
command	2	control Ex: *John had command of his emotions and never had an angry outburst.*
relevant (opposite: irrelevant)	2	directly relating to the subject or problem being discussed or considered Ex: *Every detail in Sally's paper was relevant to the claim she made.* Opposite: not related to the subject being discussed
concrete details	2	definite and specific examples Ex: *Using quotes in an essay helps provide concrete details to support your claim.*
sustain	2	to make something continue to exist or happen for a period of time; to maintain something Ex: *A writer must sustain the main idea throughout an essay.*
varied (noun: variety)	2	consisting of or including many different kinds of things or people, especially in a way that seems interesting (variety: a selection of different things, or different ways of doing something) Ex: *Use varied details in your essay to support your claim.*
partially	2	not completely Ex: *If you only give one detail, you are only partially supporting your ideas.*
textual evidence	2	proof that comes from a written piece Ex: *Quotes from the novel count as textual evidence for your claim.*
consistently (opposite: inconsistently)	2, 3	the quality of always being the same, doing things in the same way throughout a piece of work Ex: *Jeff consistently used good vocabulary when he wrote.* Opposite: changing ideas, claims, or style in the middle of an essay.
minimal	2, 4	very small in degree or amount, especially the smallest degree or amount possible Ex: *If you use a minimal number of details, your essay will not prove your ideas completely.*

	2	a reason, argument, etc., that is based on what is reasonable or sensible
valid (opposite: invalid)		Ex: *The idea that South Sudan is a dangerous place is valid.*
		Opposite: something that is not logical or reasonable
Other new words you have encountered:		

Writer's Glossary from Row 3 of the Expository Writing Rubric

Word/Phrase	Page	Definition
coherent (opposite: incoherent)	3	when something, such as a piece of writing, is easy to understand because its parts are connected in a clear and reasonable way Opposite: when something is hard to understand or does not make sense
style	3	a particular way of doing, designing, or producing something
complex ideas	3	ideas consisting of many different parts
concept	3	an idea of how something is or should be done
precise	3	when information, such as details, is exact, clear, and correct
appropriate (opposite: inappropriate)	3	correct or suitable for a particular time, situation, or purpose Opposite: not correct or suitable for a particular time, situation, or purpose
transitions	3	words or phrases that help a writer connect one idea to another so a reader can follow the writer's thinking
unified	3	when things are connected, joined
enhance	3	to improve something
exhibit	3	to show clearly a particular quality, emotion, or ability
predominantly	3	mostly or mainly
Other new words you have encountered:		

Writer's Glossary from Row 4 of the Expository Writing Rubric

Word/Phrase	Page	Definition
conventions	4	formal agreements, especially between countries, about particular rules or behaviors Ex: *Standard English conventions ensure that anyone who speaks English can understand what is written in English.*
standard English grammar	4	rules for how the English language is spoken and written Ex: *In English grammar, the subject of a sentence usually comes before the verb.*
emerging	4	in an early state of development Ex: *A student who is an emerging writer is just beginning to learn how to write well.*
frequent	4	happening or doing something often Ex: *Frequent spelling mistakes make a writer's work hard to read and understand.*
hinder	4	to make it difficult for something to develop or succeed Ex: *Sentence fragments or run-on sentences hinder a reader's understanding of a piece of writing.*
Other new words you have encountered:		

Reader's Response Letter

Name: _____

Date: _____

Title of book: _____

Author of book: _____

Use the prompts below to write a three-paragraph reader's response letter about the independent reading book you just read. You can write it on this form or on a separate sheet of notebook paper. Remember that next year, students will look at your letter to decide whether to read this book.

EXPEDITIONARY
LEARNING

Dear eighth-grader,

For my independent reading book, I read _____ (title) by _____
(author). In this book (summarize here, including setting, plot, and character, but don't give away the end of
the book):

_____

_____

_____

This book is connected to *Inside Out & Back Again* and our study of the universal refugee experience
because . . .

_____

_____

_____

I would/would not recommend this book because . . .

_____

_____

_____

Sincerely,

(Name)

RECOMMENDED TEXTS

The following table includes texts with a range of Lexile text measures about refugees' transitions to America and the Vietnamese refugee experience.

It is imperative that students read a high volume of texts at their reading level to continue to build the academic vocabulary and fluency demanded by the CCSS.

Note that districts and schools should consider their own community standards when reviewing this list. Some texts in particular units or modules address emotionally difficult content.

Where possible, texts in languages other than English are also provided. Texts are categorized into three Lexile levels that correspond to Common Core bands: below-grade band, within band, and above band. Note, however, that Lexile measures are just one indicator of text complexity; teachers must use their professional judgment and consider qualitative factors as well. For more information, see the Appendix.

Common Core Band Level Text Difficulty Ranges:

- Grades 4–5: 740L–1010L
- Grades 6–8: 925L–1185L

Title	Author and Illustrator	Text Type	Lexile Measure
Lexile text measures in grades 4–5 band level (740L–1010L)			
Last Airlift: A Vietnamese Orphan's Rescue from War	Marsha Forchuk Skrypuch (author)	Informational	670
A Million Shades of Gray	Cynthia Kadohota (author)	Literature	700
Noodle Pie	Ruth Starke (author)	Informational	770
Goodbye, Vietnam	Gloria Whelan (author)	Literature	810
Shadow of the Dragon	Sherry Garland (author)	Literature	840
Echoes of the White Giraffe	Sook Nyul Choi (author)	Literature	870
The Lotus Seed	Sherry Garland (author)	Literature	880

Lexile text measures in grade 6 band level (925L–1070L)			
Escape from Saigon: How a Vietnam War Orphan Became an American Boy	Andrea Warren (author)	Biography	930
Hearts of Sorrow: Vietnamese-American Lives	James Freeman (author)	Informational	930
Vietnamese in America	Lori Coleman (author)	Informational	940
Refugees & Asylum Seekers	Dave Dalton (author)	Informational	940
Lexile text measures in grades 6–8 band level (925L–1185L)			
Migration and Refugees	Quang Nhuong Huynh (author)	Biography/Literature	1090
The Land I Lost: Adventures of a Boy in Vietnam	Quang Nhuong Huynh (author)	Biography/Literature	1090
When Heaven and Earth Changed Places: A Vietnamese Woman's Journey from War to Peace	Le Ly Hayslip with Jay Wurts (authors)	Historical Biography	1100
Refugees	Clarissa Aykroyd (author)	Informational	1150
Where the Ashes Are: The Odyssey of a Vietnamese Family	Qui Duc Nguyen (author)	Biography	NoLXL (YA)
Lexile text measures above band level (over 1185L)			
Strangers from a Different Shore: A History of Asian Americans	Ronald Takaki (author)	Informational	No LXL (AD)
Voices of Vietnamese Boat People: Nineteen Narratives of Escape and Survival	Mary Terrell Cargill and Jade Quang Huynh (editors)	Biography	NoLXL (AD)
The Vietnamese	Michelle Houle (author)	Informational	NoLXL (YA)
Weeping under This Same Moon	Jana Laiz (author)	Literature	NoLXL (YA)

LESSON 1

Collecting Details

The Challenges Ha Faces and Ha as a Dynamic Character

Long-Term Targets Addressed (Based on ELA CCSS)

- I can cite text-based evidence that provides the strongest support for my analysis of literary text. (RL.8.1)
- I can analyze how specific dialogue or incidents in a plot propel the action, reveal aspects of a character, or provoke a decision. (RL.8.3)
- I can analyze the development of a theme or central idea throughout the text (including its relationship to the characters, setting, and plot). (RL.8.2)

Supporting Learning Targets

- I can review and add to my strategies of things close readers do.
- I can identify key details that help me understand Ha.
- I can explain how key details in the novel reveal the challenges Ha faces and her dynamic character.

Ongoing Assessment

- Structured notes (classwork)
- Think-Write-Pair-Share

Agenda

1. Opening
   A. Engaging the Reader: Things Close Readers Do (10 minutes)
   B. Review Learning Targets: Introducing the Concept of a Dynamic Character (5 minutes)

---

2. Work Time

    A. Introduce and Model Structured Notes Graphic Organizer: Pages 73–78 (10 minutes)

    B. Independent Reading and Structured Notes: Focusing on Details from Pages 79–82 (15 minutes)

3. Closing and Assessment

    A. Debrief Learning Targets and Preview Homework (5 minutes)

4. Homework

    A. Complete first read of pages 83–90; take notes using Structured Notes Graphic Organizer.

Teaching Notes

- During this unit, students will continue to engage in small-group and partner discussions. Consider seating arrangements that will allow for these ongoing collaborative opportunities. Since students will use the small-group-created Who Is Ha? Anchor Charts as one support for writing the end-of-unit essay, you may wish to keep the student groups the same as in Unit 1.

- Continue to use the Numbered Heads strategy as a total participation strategy.

- The Opening welcomes students to Unit 2. Students will be wondering about their End-of-Unit 1 Assessments. Let them know you are working on the assessments and will return them soon. Lesson 5 includes time to return and review the assessments.

- Reading Homework: Unit 2 follows a different homework routine from that of Unit 1. In Unit 2, Lessons 1–10, students will read a portion of the novel and take notes in their journals using a Structured Notes Graphic Organizer. Students will collect key details and refine their note-taking to record the strongest evidence about the challenges Ha faces as she flees and finds home as well as how these challenges reveal her dynamic character. The structured notes are designed to scaffold to support the End-of-Unit 2 Assessment literary analysis essay. Each night, students will be given guiding questions to direct their note-taking. If students are not using journals, make copies of the structured notes in the Supporting Materials of this lesson when students are assigned structured notes for homework.

- Each night as students read for homework, they will gather key details from the novel to answer a note-taking question. Then at the opening of the next class, the emphasis is on selecting the strongest evidence from these details. Throughout the unit, students will be prompted to gather the strongest evidence more independently. Emphasize to students how important it is not just to notice details but also to begin to choose the best or strongest evidence to analyze literature. This relates to RL.1; review this standard in advance to notice how it increases in rigor from the seventh-grade version.

- The best close-reading work involves a balance of text-dependent questions and student-initiated responses (e.g., "notices and wonders," important points, clarifying or probing questions, gist notes). This lesson focuses on the new structured notes routine to support students with more open-ended independent work with a text. Future lessons in this unit also include specific text-dependent questions, which are powerful scaffolds to focus students on particularly challenging or important excerpts of the text.

- This lesson introduces the Odell Education resource Reading Closely: Guiding Questions handout. Students will refer to this document regularly as a way of understanding and connecting their learning targets. Preview the document in advance, thinking in particular about how it relates to the Things Close Readers Do Anchor Chart that students created during Unit 1.

- The Opening also introduces students to the concept of a dynamic character and includes a general example of how people are complicated and change over time. Consider replacing this generic example with a more specific one that would be relevant to your students.

- Review: Give One, Get One (see the Appendix).

- In advance: Post learning targets.

Lesson Vocabulary

key details, aspects, symbol/symbolize; rations, pouches, rounds, wedges, stranded

Materials

- *Inside Out & Back Again* (book; one per student)

- Things Close Readers Do Anchor Chart (from Unit 1)

- Reading Closely: Guiding Questions handout (one per student and one to display) (from Odell Education; also see odelleducation.com/resources)

- Highlighters (one per student)

- Document camera, overhead projector, or interactive whiteboard

- Student journals (one per student; begun in Unit 1, Lesson 2)

- Structured Notes Graphic Organizer (one to display)

- Structured Notes Graphic Organizer (Teacher Reference; see Supporting Materials)

Opening

A. Engaging the Reader: Things Close Readers Do (10 minutes)

- Welcome students, and signal the start of Unit 2. Inform them that for the next few weeks, they will continue to read the novel **Inside Out & Back Again**. They also will focus on Ha's character and how it changes over the course of the novel. Let students know you are reading their End-of-Unit 1 Assessments and will return them soon.

- Display the **Things Close Readers Do Anchor Chart**. Share with students that during Unit 1, they collected lots of great things close readers do.

- Inform students they will review these points in a modified Give One, Get One activity. Give directions:

  1. Work with a partner.

2. One student goes first. Choose one bullet/thing from the anchor chart to give to your partner, with an explanation or example of how this thing helps readers.

3. Then the second student goes. Choose a different bullet/thing to explain or give an example of how the thing helps readers.

• Pair up students. Give them about 5 minutes for this activity.

• Refocus the whole class and distribute the **Reading Closely: Guiding Questions handout**. Explain to students that this handout gives them even more information about many of the things close readers do. Point out that during Unit 1, students figured out a lot of these things on their own.

• Inform students that they are going to be looking for similarities between their Things Close Readers Do Anchor Chart and the Reading Closely: Guiding Questions handout.

• Orient students to the layout of the handout, and direct them to notice the three sections: Approaching Texts, Questioning Texts, and Analyzing Details.

• Invite them to look for aspects of the document that relate to what they have been learning and practicing as close readers. For example, direct students to the first section, Approaching Texts, and ask:

  • "What do you notice in this section that relates to the special type of novel we are reading?"

• Ideally, students will notice that the structure, language, and type of text is special in this novel because it is written in verse.

• Distribute **highlighters** and invite students to take about 3 minutes to work with a partner to highlight other items on the Reading Closely: Guiding Questions handout that relate to what they already know close readers do as well as to the text they are reading and the details they have been noticing.

• As the students work, circulate to listen in and provide support as needed. Be sure students are able to connect this new handout with what they've learned: the Things Close Readers Do Anchor Chart and their experience reading the text during Unit 1. For example, as students work, probe by asking them these sorts of questions about the Reading Closely: Guiding Questions handout:

  • "This handout mentions 'perspective.' Whose perspective are we reading in the novel? Who is writing the diary entries in the novel? How might the single perspective of Ha influence meaning?"

  • "This handout mentions 'language and structure.' How are the language and structure in these diary entries different from those of typical diary entries?"

  • "This handout emphasizes noticing and connecting details. What sorts of details have we collected while reading the novel? How do these details connect in terms of revealing Ha's character?"

• After about 3 minutes, refocus students as a whole group. Cold-call on student pairs to share similarities they noticed. Using the **document camera** (or **overhead**), highlight the related items on the Reading Closely: Guiding Questions handout. If time permits, invite student pairs to share the other characteristics they think will be important as they read the rest of the novel. Ask the students

---

TEACHER GUIDE • Grade 8 • Module 1 • Unit 2 • Lesson 1   **165**

to hold on to the Reading Closely: Guiding Questions handout, since it will be revisited throughout the module. It will help them continue to notice and name the many things close readers do that they will practice this year.

Meeting Students' Needs

Anchor charts provide a visual cue to students about what to do when you ask them to work independently. They also serve as note-catchers when the class is co-constructing ideas.

B. Review Learning Targets: Introducing the Concept of a Dynamic Character (5 minutes)

- Direct students' attention to the posted learning targets and remind them that they've just reviewed the strategies that close readers use and were able to read about more strategies on the Reading Closely: Guiding Questions handout. Cold-call on a student to read aloud the next learning target:

  - "I can identify key details that help me understand Ha."

- Share with them that just as they collected details throughout Unit 1, they will continue to collect these details as they read the novel in this unit.

- Remind students that they are looking for key details—those that are important or significant— about Ha's character. Emphasize that now that they are eighth-graders, they are learning how to find not just details, or many details, but the details that best support their analysis.

- Cold-call on another student to read aloud the last learning target:

  - "I can explain how key details in the novel reveal the challenges Ha faces and her dynamic character."

- Provide brief direct instruction on the concept of a dynamic character. Point out that just like real people, fictional characters sometimes have complicated personalities. Often characters are *dynamic,* which means they can "grow or change over time," like people in the real world. The students themselves have changed over time. Explain that they may have had a favorite toy or interest when they were younger, but now it's not as important to them. Share with students that they may not have intended to change their interests, but because of time and growing up, it just happened. So as students continue to read the novel, they will be noticing aspects of Ha's character or different sides of her personality.

- Invite students to paraphrase and apply this concept of a dynamic character. Think-Pair-Share:

  - "What is a dynamic character?"

  - "In which ways are *you* a dynamic character?"

- Invite students to make a prediction:

  - "How do you think Ha will grow and change? Why?"

Work Time

A. Introduce and Model Structured Notes Graphic Organizer: Pages 73–78 (10 minutes)

- Remind students that they have learned a lot about paying attention to every word and how and why this matters. Now they will do that again to help them become detectives and figure out everything they can about Ha. Share with students that as they begin Part 2 of the novel, they will be using a graphic organizer to collect the key details they notice about the different aspects of Ha's character. They will also be reading about challenges Ha faces as she and her family flee their home. Explain that since Ha is a dynamic character, these challenges will reveal more of her character but will also change her character. Invite students to get out their **student journal** in which they have been recording their notes.

- Display the **Structured Notes Graphic Organizer** on a document camera. Model for students how they will organize each page to collect notes. Refer to **Structured Notes Graphic Organizer (Teacher Reference).** Have students create four columns on a clean page of their journal:

  1. Label the far-left column "Key Detail." (Explain that this key detail may be a quote or a description of a scene.)

  2. Label the second column "Page."

  3. Label the third column "What challenges does Ha face fleeing home? How do the challenges reveal her dynamic character?"

  4. Label the far-right column "Vocabulary and Word Choice." Remind students that they have been looking closely at words and phrases to help them understand Ha. Now they will focus on words that help them understand what Ha is experiencing as she and her family flee Vietnam. Inform students that they will be keeping track of these sorts of words in their notes.

- Remind students that as they read the novel for homework, they will be collecting details and notes on this organizer. For each homework assignment, they should collect at least three details, although more than one detail could support the same character trait.

- Advise students that they will practice taking structured notes in class. Model for students what this structured note-taking will look like. Ask them to turn to page 73 in the novel and to read along silently as you read aloud.

- While you read the poem "S-l-o-w-l-y" on page 75, draw students' attention to the author's word choice. Ha writes that she *nibbles* on rice, but others *chew*. Remind students of the work they did in Unit 1 to analyze how word choice contributes to meaning and tone. Ask:

  - "What is the difference in meaning and tone between these two words? How are they similar?"

- Ideally, students will note that the nibbling Ha does reveals the small amount of food she has and her perception that others have enough food to actually chew it.

- Continue to read the next poem, "Rations." Explain that a *ration* is "a portion or an allowance of food or supplies." Read through page 78, to the end of the poem.

- On the document camera, think aloud to model for the class how to use the key details in what they read to help analyze Ha's character and the challenges she is facing. Say, "I notice that Ha is really suffering in these entries. She's very uncomfortable with either feeling thirsty, having to use the bathroom, or being hungry. I also notice that when Ha eats the hot, fresh rice, she thinks about the papaya." Ask:

- "Do you remember when we talked about the papaya as a *symbol*? What does the papaya *symbolize* to Ha?"

- Invite a student to share what the papaya symbolizes. Ideally, students will remember that the papaya is a symbol of hope. Say, "This makes me think that even though Ha is suffering, she wants to be hopeful. As soon as she experiences a small comfort, her mind goes right to the papaya . . . even though rice and papaya have nothing to do with each other, like she says."

- Model how to fill in the Structured Notes Graphic Organizer:

  1. In the far-left column (Key Detail), write, "The first hot bite of freshly cooked rice, plump and nutty, makes me imagine the taste of ripe papaya although one has nothing to do with the other."

  2. In the second column, write, "Page 78."

  3. In the third column, write, "Ha is suffering from thirst and hunger, but she wants to be hopeful. As soon as she experiences a small comfort, her mind goes right to the papaya . . . even though rice and papaya have nothing to do with each other, like she says."

  4. In the far-right column, write, "rations." Point out that Ha is focused on food. The word *rations* helps us understand what Ha is experiencing. Note that this word happens to be the title of the poem, but it doesn't have to be. This column is for adding words from the text that seem really important to capture what Ha is experiencing: She doesn't have enough food.

- Remind students that Ha is a character who is complicated, just like real people. She may change over the course of the novel.

- Ask students to Turn-and-Talk with a peer:

  - "What did you notice as I modeled this type of thinking for you?"

  - "What questions do you have about how to use this graphic organizer?"

- Call on a few volunteers to share with the class. Clarify as needed.

Meeting Students' Needs

- If students are not using a journal for notes, the Structured Notes Graphic Organizer in the Supporting Materials for this section may be provided for students' use.

- If no document camera is available, you may use an overhead transparency of the Structured Notes Graphic Organizer, draw a three-column Structured Notes Graphic Organizer on the chalkboard or whiteboard, or create a three-column Structured Notes Graphic Organizer to display on an interactive whiteboard.

- Hearing a complex text read slowly, fluently, and without interruption or explanation promotes fluency for students: They are hearing a strong reader read the text aloud with accuracy and expression and are simultaneously looking at and thinking about the words on the printed page. Be sure to set clear expectations that students read along silently as you read the text aloud.

- Providing models of expected work supports all learners, but especially challenged learners.

- When you're reviewing the graphic organizers or recording forms, consider using a document camera to display the document for students who struggle with auditory processing.

- For ELL students and other students needing additional supports, consider providing smaller chunks of text—sometimes just a few sentences—for a close read. Check in on students' thinking as they speak about their text.

- Use of protocols like Think-Pair-Share allows for total participation of students. It encourages critical thinking, collaboration, and social construction of knowledge. It also helps students practice their speaking and listening skills.

B. Independent Reading and Structured Notes: Focusing on Details from Pages 79–82 (15 minutes)

- Invite students to read pages 79–82 independently and silently in class while they keep their journals open to the Structured Notes page.

- When they finish reading, invite them to participate in a Think-Write-Pair-Share:

  - "Think about Ha's character and the section you just read. What is a key detail that helps you understand an aspect of Ha's dynamic character?"

- Cold-call on student pairs to share the page number, quote, and explanation, and record this information for the class to see. Students may respond with details such as these:

  - Ha doesn't want to be treated like a baby (page 80).

  - She's obsessed with food (page 81).

- Push students to dig deeper for details that are less obvious—for example, Ha comes to see the simple things of her old life as luxuries (page 82).

- Continue to emphasize focusing on vocabulary. Point out such words as *pouches, rounds,* and *wedges* (page 81), all of which students likely know or could figure out from context. Note how these words further demonstrate Ha's obsession with food.

- Be sure students notice the word *stranded*. Ask:

  - "What does it mean to be *stranded*?" Listen for students to realize it means "being stuck somewhere, often for a long time, with no help." This is a challenge Ha is facing.

Meeting Students' Needs

- Consider partnering ELL students who speak the same home language when discussion of complex content is required. This can enable students to have more meaningful discussions and clarify points in their native language.

- Research indicates that cold-calling improves student engagement and critical thinking. Prepare students for this strategy by discussing the purpose, giving appropriate think time, and indicating that you will use this strategy before you begin asking questions.

Closing and Assessment

A. Debrief Learning Targets and Preview Homework (5 minutes)

- Review the learning targets and remind students that rereading, looking for details, and explaining how those details reveal aspects of Ha's character are things they have been practicing and are among the things close readers do.

- Preview the homework. Inform students they will read pages 83–90 in the novel and will take notes on their Structured Notes Graphic Organizer (in their journals). Ask them to include at least three details from the reading in their notes. It is fine if several of the details show the same character trait.

Homework

Complete a first read of pages 83–90. Practice taking Structured Notes (in your journal) using the same graphic organizer you used during class. Focus on key details that reveal the challenges Ha is facing and her dynamic character, plus new or important vocabulary that helps you understand the specific challenges she faces as she flees Vietnam (for example, such words as *rations* that we talked about in class).

Meeting Students' Needs

- Vocabulary can be a source of difficulty for struggling readers. Provide a brief list with definitions of the challenging vocabulary words from the reading homework. Do this only for students who need this support.

- Most important is to provide words that cannot be easily determined from context. There are few of these in the novel. On page 83, for example, the word *stews* (soaks in heat) might be appropriate.

LESSON 2

Rereading and Close Reading

Communism, "The Vietnam Wars," and "Last Respects"

Long-Term Targets Addressed (Based on ELA CCSS)

*   I can cite text-based evidence that provides the strongest support for my analysis of literary text. (RL.8.1)
*   I can analyze how specific dialogue or incidents in a plot propel the action, reveal aspects of a character, or provoke a decision. (RL.8.3)
*   I can analyze the development of a theme or central idea throughout the text (including its relationship to the characters, setting, and plot). (RL.8.2)
*   I can analyze figurative language, word relationships, and nuances in word meanings. (L.8.5)

Supporting Learning Targets

*   I can explain how key details in the novel reveal the challenges Ha faces and her dynamic character.
*   I can infer the meaning of symbolism in the poem "Last Respects."

Ongoing Assessment

*   Structured notes for pages 83–90 (from homework)
*   Who Is Ha? Anchor Chart
*   "Last Respects" Note-Catcher

Agenda

1. Opening
    A. Engaging the Reader: Establish Opening Routine (10 minutes)
    B. Review Learning Targets (3 minutes)

---

2. Work Time

    A. Rereading Section 5 of "The Vietnam Wars": Communism (10 minutes)

    B. Rereading and Structured Notes: Learning about Ha's Dynamic Character from the Poem "Last Respects" (20 minutes)

3. Closing and Assessment

    A. Debrief Learning Targets (2 minutes)

4. Homework

    A. Read pages 91–111; take notes using the Structured Notes Graphic Organizer.

Teaching Notes

- This lesson introduces a new opening 10- to 15-minute routine that students will follow throughout Unit 2, which allows them to work with the portion of the novel they read for homework. Students share their structured notes homework and are encouraged to add to their notes based on this discussion. Given this routine, it is important that students do their homework and not rely on getting notes from their peers. Circulate to listen in and look at students' notes to gauge their independent work.

- Across lessons, the opening sections involve a variety of structures and prompts. The predictability of the routine creates accountability and efficiencies; the variety promotes engagement.

- Groups continue to add to their small-group Who Is Ha? Anchor Charts (created during Unit 1).

- In advance: Prepare for the Chalk Talk. Post the Who Is Ha? Anchor Charts around the room. Alongside each group's chart, also post two fresh pieces of chart paper. At the top of each new sheet, write the focus question: "What have you learned about Ha's dynamic character?"

- The best close-reading work involves a balance of text-dependent questions and student-initiated responses (e.g., notices and wonders, important points, clarifying or probing questions, gist notes). The previous lesson focused on the new structured notes routine to support students with more open-ended independent work with a text. This lesson and future lessons in this unit also include specific text-dependent questions, which are powerful scaffolds to focus students on particularly challenging or important excerpts of the text.

- During Work Time, students revisit the last section of the informational text "The Vietnam Wars," which they read in Unit 1 (Lessons 6, 7, 9, and 10). Help students notice how their knowledge has grown from Unit 1: Likely, much more of this text will make sense to them at this point. Emphasize also the value of rereading to deepen their understanding.

- Reread Unit 1, Lesson 10, to refresh your memory about how students have already worked with the excerpt that they will reread today. Today, students revisit this text specifically to understand more about the communists and why Ha is so scared.

- This lesson informally introduces the word *totalitarian,* which is more explicitly taught in Lesson 3. Be prepared to provide a layman's definition of this complex term: "a system of government in which the state holds total authority over the society and tries to control its citizens." Through your informal discussion with students across Lessons 2 and 3, help them notice why Ha might be so afraid; even though she is a child, she has a sense that the communists are trying to control her family.

- Continue to help students connect the work they are doing as readers to their Things Close Readers Do Anchor Chart (from Unit 1) and the Reading Closely: Guiding Questions handout (from Lesson 1).

- Review: Chalk Talk, Think-Write-Pair-Share (see the Appendix).

Lesson Vocabulary

infer, symbolism; communism, totalitarianism, last respects, formal, regret

Materials

- *Inside Out & Back Again* (book; one per student)
- Who Is Ha? Anchor Charts (begun in Unit 1, Lesson 4)
- Chart paper (two per group)
- Markers (one per student)
- "The Vietnam Wars" text (from Unit 1, Lesson 6; one per student)
- "Last Respects" Note-Catcher (one per student)
- Document camera

Opening

A. Engaging the Reader: Establish Opening Routine (10 minutes)

- Students should be sitting with their small groups and should each have their novel **Inside Out & Back Again**.

- Post the **Who Is Ha? Anchor Charts** around the room. Alongside each group's chart, also post two fresh pieces of **chart paper** with the focus question:
  - "What have you learned about Ha's dynamic character?"

- Inform students that at the start of class each day in this unit, they will use different ways to share and discuss the portion of the novel they read for homework. They will use the structured notes they took from the reading homework for this sharing and discussion time. Reinforce the importance of taking good notes so they are prepared for discussions. Also emphasize that writing and talking about what they read are both good ways to deepen their understanding of a text. These discussions matter!

- For the opening routine today, inform students that they will participate in a *silent* discussion called a Chalk Talk. Describe the basic process to students:
  - Small groups gather around their chart paper, marker in hand.

- The teacher poses a question to the groups (in this case, the question is written on the chart paper).

- Students write their thinking and responses to the question on the chart paper.

- After this silent thinking and writing time, students read what their peers have written and think about central ideas and patterns.

- Focus students on their Who Is Ha? Anchor Charts posted around the room. Point out the two new pieces of chart paper next to each. Inform students that in a moment they will write on these blank charts to get as much information out as possible. Point out that two new pieces of paper will allow everyone in the group plenty of space to write all of their great details.

- Read the focus question on top of the two new charts:

  - "What have you learned about Ha's dynamic character?"

- Distribute **markers**. Remind students that Chalk Talk is a silent activity. Give students about 3 minutes in their small groups to add their thinking to these two charts, silently, while referring to their structured notes.

- After 3 minutes, refocus students. Ask them to stay in their groups and silently read the details posted by the other members of their group. Invite them to consider the following:

  - "What do you notice?"

  - "What is the strongest evidence? Why?"

- After students have spent about 1 minute silently reading, invite them to talk in their small groups. Provide positive feedback about how students are weighing which specific details help them best understand how Ha is changing.

- Invite students to look back at their group's original Who Is Ha? Anchor Chart. Ask:

  - "Is there anything you want to add to your original Who Is Ha? Anchor Chart?"

- Give students a minute to add to their original anchor chart: They may notice that even though Ha is changing, some aspects of her character remain the same (e.g., she is stubborn).

Meeting Students' Needs

- Anchor charts provide a visual cue to students about what to do when you ask them to work independently. They also serve as note-catchers when the class is co-constructing ideas.

- Use of protocols like Chalk Talk allows for total student participation. It encourages critical thinking, collaboration, and social construction of knowledge. It also helps students practice their speaking and listening skills.

B. Review Learning Targets (3 minutes)

- Direct students' attention to the posted learning targets. Point out that the first target is the same target from the previous lesson. Cold-call on two students to share a key detail that their group discussed during the Chalk Talk.

- Focus students on the second target:

  - "I can infer the symbolism in the poem 'Last Respects.'"

- Explain that sometimes an author creates layers of meaning. For example, the author creates layers of meaning with the symbol of the papaya. Remind students of the work they did during Unit 1, including the model Quick Write you shared with them: The papaya is Ha's favorite fruit, but its deeper meaning is that it is a symbol of hope. *Symbolism* is when "an author uses an object to represent something else." Explain that "usually readers will need to *infer,* or use clues from the text and their understanding, to understand the symbolism and the deeper meaning of the story."

- Invite students to Turn-and-Talk:

  - "How would you define *symbolism* in your own words?"

- Share with students that to reach this target, today they will reread a short excerpt of informational text as well as one poem from the novel.

Meeting Students' Needs

Posting learning targets enables students to refer to them throughout the lesson to check their understanding. They also provide a reminder to students and teachers about the intended learning behind a given lesson or activity.

Work Time

A. Rereading Section 5 of "The Vietnam Wars": Communism (10 minutes)

- Ask students to take out take out their **"The Vietnam Wars"** text (from Unit 1) and reread the last section.

- Have students Turn-and-Talk with a peer:

  - "Based on what you have read in the novel and what you have reread in the article, how does this part of the article relate to Ha's situation? Why did Ha's family flee their home?"

- Listen for students to understand that Ha and her family fled their home country of South Vietnam because of the communist takeover.

- Direct students to look at the photograph showing a flag with a star and the caption next to it. Ask:

  - "What is this photograph showing?"

- Make sure students understand that this photograph shows the conquering communists, the Viet Cong, rolling into South Vietnam.

- Help students notice the intensity of the photograph, which conveys some sense of the totalitarian nature of North Vietnamese communism. Ask:

  - "Why might the author have chosen to include this photograph?" The photograph shows the military might of the communists and the helpless people on the streets.

- "What do you notice about the flag? What does a flag symbolize?" Draw particular attention to the high-waving, colorful, proud flag in the picture. Ideally, students will understand that a flag is a symbol that represents a country or a group of people. It often symbolizes the values and beliefs of the people it represents. The prominent flag in the photograph reveals the defeat of South Vietnam.

Meeting Students' Needs

- Remind students that they have read this text before, in Unit 1. For ELL students and other students needing additional support, consider providing smaller chunks of text—sometimes just a few sentences—for a close read. You can also provide chunks of text for them on separate sheets of paper or notecards. This makes the reading of complex texts more manageable and allows them to focus on one small section at a time.

- Check in on students' thinking as they speak about their text.

B. Rereading and Structured Notes: Learning about Ha's Dynamic Character from the Poem "Last Respects" (20 minutes)

- Direct students to the poem "Last Respects" on pages 85 and 86. Read aloud the title and ask students:

  - "What does the term *last respects* mean? When is this term used?"

- Ideally, students will understand that this term refers to "the honor and recognition given to an individual upon death." If students do not know what this phrase means, define it for them.

- Inform students that in a moment, they will each reread this poem (from last night's homework) silently. Set a purpose for reading: "As you reread this poem, pay attention to words and phrases that relate to the title, 'Last Respects.'" Then invite students to reread this poem silently.

- While they reread, distribute the **"Last Respects" Note-Catcher**.

- Orient students to the note-catcher. Focus them on Part A. Explain to them that it looks very similar to the Structured Notes Graphic Organizer they are using to collect notes from the novel:

  1. In the far-left column, they will be noting key details in the poem that are related to the phrase "last respects"—specifically, details that relate to death and dying.

  2. In the second column, students will record the page number and stanza to reference the images they note.

  3. In the third column, they will answer the question, "How are these key details related to death and dying?"

  4. The far-right column should be labeled "Vocabulary." This column will focus on words and phrases that help students understand the poem.

- If necessary, share these examples to get them started: "The *formal* lowering" of the flag is a ceremonial and official symbol of defeat, and the line "South Vietnam no longer exists" shows the death or defeat of Ha's country.

- Remind students of the photograph they looked at earlier in the lesson and ask:
  - "How does the image of the flag Ha describes compare with the image of the flag in the photograph?"

- Remind students of the Reading Closely for Details document (from Lesson 1). Point out that one thing close readers do is begin to connect details. Give students a few minutes to think on their own, and write:
  - "Which details do you notice in the poem that relate to death and dying?"

- Then invite students to participate in a Think-Write-Pair-Share, in which they pair up, share their thinking, and add to their "Last Respects" Note-Catcher.

- Next, focus students on Part B of the "Last Respects" Note-Catcher. Inform them that this part of the note-catcher involves inferring. They need to use clues from the poem and what they know about Ha to answer the questions. Invite pairs to answer the text-dependent questions.

- Circulate while the class is working and probe as needed with questions such as these:
  - "Look at the poem 'Sssshhhhhhh' on page 46. In the fourth stanza, what does Brother Khoi say about his chick? What do you think about his decision to throw it overboard now?"
  - "Look at the poem 'Choice' on pages 55 and 56. What is Ha's choice?"

- Be sure students realize that Ha throws the doll overboard. Ask:
  - "How does Ha describe the doll she chooses to bring with her? What does Ha love most about this doll? Why is it special to her? What do you think about her decision to throw the doll overboard now?"

- Debrief the details from Part A of the note-catcher using the Numbered Heads protocol. Begin by asking each group to share one image or detail from the poem that relates to death or dying; call on number 2s to share these details. Using a **document camera**, display Part A of the note-catcher. Point out to students that it looks just like the Structured Notes Graphic Organizer that they are using to take notes for homework. Using the document camera, model taking notes and invite students to add these notes to their own notes in Part A of the note-catcher.

- Reinforce with students that this poem provides key details that will help them learn about the challenges Ha is facing and how her character is changing. Direct students' attention next to Questions 1 and 2 in Part B of the note-catcher.

- Call on number 4s in each group to share why these objects are important to Ha and her brother. Record the key detail in the first column and the page number (86) in the second column: "Ha wraps her doll and Brother Khoi's dead chick in her mother's white handkerchief and throws it overboard."

- Focus on the next question, which asks for the best evidence to support their answer to Question 2. Ask number 1s to share their groups' thinking.

- Finally, ask students to think about this scene:
  - "Is this simply throwing a bundle of special objects overboard, or does it represent something else symbolically for the characters?"

- Invite number 3s to share their groups' thinking.

Meeting Students' Needs

- Graphic organizers and recording forms engage students more actively and provide scaffolding that is especially critical for learners with lower levels of language proficiency and/or learning.

- Use of such protocols as Think-Write-Pair-Share allows for total student participation. It encourages critical thinking, collaboration, and social construction of knowledge. It also helps students practice their speaking and listening skills.

- Some students may benefit from having access to "hint cards," small slips of paper or index cards that they turn over for hints about how/where to find the answers to text-dependent questions. For example, a hint card might say, "Check back in the first stanza."

Closing and Assessment

A. Debrief Learning Targets (2 minutes)

- Provide specific positive feedback based on comments you heard students making that showed evidence of close reading for details and inferring. (For example: "I heard Keisha and Jesse having a great conversation about what the doll means to Ha; they inferred that by choosing to throw the doll overboard, she is ready to let go not just of the doll but of her childhood.")

- Share with students that they have been learning about Ha's character throughout Part 1 of the novel, and Ha is beginning another part of her life as a refugee. They will be learning more about her dynamic character as she faces more challenges.

Meeting Students' Needs

Providing specific and focused feedback helps students set concrete goals for reaching learning targets.

Homework

Complete a first read of pages 91–111. Take notes (in your journals) using the Structured Notes Graphic Organizer. Focus on key details that reveal the challenges Ha is facing and her dynamic character, plus vocabulary that helps you understand her challenges and responses.

Meeting Students' Needs

- Vocabulary can be a source of difficulty for struggling readers. Provide a brief list with definitions of challenging vocabulary words from the reading homework. This should be done only for students who need it.

- Most important is to provide words that cannot easily be determined from context. There are a few of these in the novel. On pages 91–111, these words may include the following: *composure* (calm state of mind), *tangible* (touchable), *remnant* (fragment, small piece), and *sponsor* (a person who is responsible for another person).

LESSON 3

Building Background Knowledge

Fleeing Saigon as "Panic Rises"

Long-Term Targets Addressed (Based on ELA CCSS)

- I can cite text-based evidence that provides the strongest support for an analysis of informational text. (RI.8.1)
- I can determine a theme or the central ideas of an informational text. (RI.8.2)
- I can analyze the connections and distinctions between individuals, ideas, or events in a text. (RI.8.3)
- I can use a variety of strategies to determine the meaning of unknown words or phrases. (L.8.4)

Supporting Learning Targets

- I can identify the strongest evidence in the text "Panic Rises in Saigon, but the Exits Are Few" that helps me explain what challenges refugees from South Vietnam faced.
- I can use common Greek and Latin affixes (prefixes) and roots as clues to help me know what a word means.
- I can identify common themes that connect the universal refugee experience.

Ongoing Assessment

- Structured notes (for pages 91–111, from homework)
- Fleeing Home: What Challenges Does Ha's Family Face? Graphic Organizer
- Answers to text-dependent questions
- Prefixes Note-Catcher

Agenda

1. Opening
   A. Engaging the Reader: What Challenges Does Ha's Family Face? (10 minutes)
   B. Review Learning Targets (2 minutes)

2. Work Time

    A. Teacher Read-Aloud: "Panic Rises in Saigon, but the Exits Are Few" (5 minutes)

    B. Answering Text-Dependent Questions for "Panic Rises in Saigon, but the Exits Are Few" (15 minutes)

    C. Guided Practice: Vocabulary to Deepen Understanding (10 minutes)

3. Closing and Assessment

    A. Debrief Learning Targets and Preview Homework (3 minutes)

4. Homework

    A. Finish answering text-dependent questions.

    B. Read pages 115–134; take notes using the Structured Notes Graphic Organizer.

Teaching Notes

- Lessons 3–6 will focus on informational texts that help students explore the refugee experience in preparation for the Mid-Unit Assessment. Students are at a logical point in the novel (as Ha travels to America) to read informational texts to build more knowledge about the world—specifically, to broaden their understanding of common refugee experiences.

- Although Lessons 3–6 will emphasize informational texts, students will continue to read the novel for homework.

- The opening activity each day allows for group discussion, including a focus on key vocabulary or critical passages that help reveal aspects of the challenges Ha faces (i.e., the conflict in the novel) and Ha's character as a sort of case study of the more universal refugee experience.

- Students will discuss how Ha's life is being turned "inside out." This will help them understand the meaning of the novel's title, which students will write about as part of their End-of-Unit essay. The focus of students' structured notes (for homework) will change as they begin to find evidence of how Ha's life is being turned "inside out."

- Do not define the phrase "inside out" for students. Let them gradually come to an understanding of this phrase across Lessons 3–6 as they read, think, talk, and write about some common central ideas in the universal experience of refugees all over the world.

- In this lesson, students return to the informational text from Unit 1, Lesson 1: "Panic Rises in Saigon, but the Exits Are Few." In Unit 1, they read selected quotes from the full text to build some basic background knowledge and to pique their interest about the topic of the module. In this lesson, they read the entire text to deepen their understanding of the challenges faced by Vietnamese refugees as Saigon fell.

- Emphasize for students the interplay between the novel and the informational texts (this interplay relates directly to CCSS Shifts 1 and 2). Help them notice how, across the module, their understanding of a topic is growing. Students should be noticing the value of rereading a text once they know more about a topic. Throughout Unit 1 (by reading both the novel and informational texts), students built a great deal of background knowledge about the fall of Saigon. They now can use this knowledge to analyze the article more fully and make richer connections back to the novel.

- In the Opening, students are asked to think about the relationship between informational text and historical fiction, which was emphasized throughout Unit 1. Review Unit 1, Lesson 6, in advance to determine which connections to make for students here.

- In advance: Create the model graphic organizer Fleeing Home: What Challenges Does Ha's Family Face? (see model in Supporting Materials) on your interactive whiteboard, chart paper, or document camera. This should look like the graphic organizer that students will complete.

- This lesson includes explicit instructions related to CCSS L.8.4. Emphasize with students the value of learning prefixes, suffixes, and word roots/families as a powerful strategy to build their vocabulary as they read increasingly complex texts.

- In this lesson, through embedded vocabulary instruction, students learn new prefixes (*uni, in,* and *e*) and two new roots: *migrare* (Latin for "to move from one place to another") and *vac* (Latin for "to empty"). In Lessons 3 and 4, students complete a Prefixes Note-Catcher listing some common prefixes from readings. Encourage students to hold on to this Prefixes Note-Catcher, which they can continue to add to throughout the year. Some future lessons in this unit continue to point students to prefixes they might add.

- Post learning targets.

Lesson Vocabulary

informational text, common themes, cause, motivate/motivation; flee, inexorable, stringent, emigration/immigration/migrate/migration, evacuees (n.)/evacuate (v.), totalitarian

Materials

- *Inside Out & Back Again* (book; one per student)
- Fleeing Home: What Challenges Does Ha's Family Face? Graphic Organizer (one per student)
- Document camera
- "Panic Rises in Saigon, but the Exits Are Few" (one per student)
- Text-dependent questions for "Panic Rises in Saigon, but Exits Are Few" (one per student)
- Prefixes Note-Catcher (one per student)

Opening

A. Engaging the Reader: What Challenges Does Ha's Family Face? (10 minutes)

- Students should be in their small groups, and each should have the novel *Inside Out & Back Again*.
- Assign them to work with their odd- or even-numbered partner (i.e., in each small group, numbers 1 and 3 work together and numbers 2 and 4 work together). Explain that the students are becoming

increasingly independent with the novel. They will spend some time each day sharing with each other about the novel. In the next few lessons, they also will have time to read informational texts about other refugees' experiences to help them put what they are learning about Ha in a larger context.

- Ask students to think and then talk with their partner about the title of the novel *Inside Out & Back Again*. Ask:

  - "How is Ha's life being turned 'inside out'?"

- There is no need to clarify at this point: Advise students that they will keep thinking more about what "inside out" means over the coming lessons.

- Display and distribute the **Fleeing Home: What Challenges Does Ha's Family Face? Graphic Organizer** (on a **document camera**). Inform students that to help them identify common central ideas among refugee experiences, they will read several informational texts during the next few lessons and use graphic organizers to take notes. Today, they will first think about the questions on this graphic organizer as they relate to Ha and her family, based on evidence from the novel. Then they will complete a similar graphic organizer on Vietnamese refugees based on an informational article. This investigation will give students a better understanding of Ha's family's motivation, or reason, for leaving Vietnam.

- Read the graphic organizer prompt aloud. Ask:

  - "What do you think the word *flee* means?"

- Give students a moment to think and then talk with a peer. Invite volunteers to respond. Listen for students to say "run away" or "escape." Point out that *flee* has the same root as *fly* and *flight. Flee* implies great haste; usually when people flee, it is to escape immediate danger. *Escape,* by contrast, has a wider variety of meanings and often takes longer (e.g., escaping from prison or escaping from a boring job).

- Invite students to Think-Pair-Share with their odd- or even-numbered partner in response to the graphic organizer prompt:

  - "Which poems might have the strongest evidence to help you answer the question about the challenges they face?"

- Give students a few minutes to go back to the text, skimming for which poems they think are most relevant.

- Refocus students as a whole group. Probe and make a list on the board (with poem titles and page numbers) to be sure all students have identified some poems that provide particularly strong evidence to answer the question about challenges Ha's family faces (it's great if students have identified other poems as well):

  - "Choice" (page 55)

  - "Wet and Crying" (page 60)

  - "One Mat Each" (page 63)

  - "Should We" (pages 44 and 45)

  - "S-l-o-w-l-y" (page 75)

- Inform students that now that they have identified some poems, you would like them to choose just one or two to find some specific evidence they think is particularly strong. Give pairs a few minutes to work. Ask:

  - "After the family flees Vietnam, what specific challenges does the family face?"

- Possible answers include "not enough food on the ship," "not enough water," "going to the bathroom," "ship troubles," "living in a tent city," and so forth.

- Then refocus students as a whole group and probe again:

  - "In the poem 'Should We,' what does the family fear for Ha's brothers?"

- Encourage students to think about the mental and emotional effects of a communist takeover—for example, the fear of Brother Quang's being brainwashed and Brother Khoi's being interrogated to reveal private family conversations.

- Ask students:

  - "Why might the communists want to probe family secrets?"

- Help them understand the nature of totalitarianism and the government's desire to have a great deal of control over its citizens. Reinforce with students that this novel is told from Ha's perspective, so we are seeing the fears of communism through her eyes.

- Model completing the graphic organizer, citing the strongest details from the text that show challenges the family faces as they flee. Emphasize to students that since they are eighth-graders, it is not enough just to "cite evidence"—they should be pushing themselves to select the best details to support their analysis of the text.

- Share an example from a student pair who are doing this well, or model as needed. A good example would be "The refugees do not have enough good food on the ship." Text-based evidence comes from the poem "S-l-o-w-l-y": "Hard and moldy, yet chewy and sweet/inside./I chew each grain/slowly" (75).

- As time permits, repeat with one more detail and explanation. Another strong example is "having to leave things they love behind, including the papaya tree." Text-based evidence comes from the poem "Wet and Crying": "Brother Vu chops;/the head falls;/a silver blade slices./Black seeds spill like clusters of eyes, wet and crying" (60).

- Have students Turn-and-Talk briefly to discuss. Call on a new voice to share his or her thinking.

B. Review Learning Targets (2 minutes)

- Post learning targets for review. Read aloud the first two learning targets:

  - "I can identify the strongest evidence in the text **'Panic Rises in Saigon, but the Exits Are Few'** that helps me explain what challenges refugees from South Vietnam faced."

  - "I can use common Greek and Latin affixes (prefixes) and roots as clues to help me know what a word means."

- Explain that today students will focus on informational text to help them better understand Ha's experience leaving Vietnam. Sometimes informational texts include vocabulary that readers have to figure out to build knowledge on the subject. Emphasize that paying attention to the parts of words (prefixes, roots, and suffixes) is a powerful strategy for figuring out unfamiliar vocabulary.

- Ask for student volunteers to explain the difference between *informational text* and *fiction* (historical fiction in particular). Listen for mention of "a purpose to inform, real events, objective, straightforward," and a "just-the-facts" perspective versus "to entertain, written from the perspective of a particular character, and so forth." Point out to students that they talked a lot about this difference in Unit 1.

- Read the third learning target aloud:

  - "I can identify common themes that connect the universal refugee experience."

- Discuss *common themes* with students—"ideas or experiences that are universal." Ask:

  - "Does anyone know what *universal* means?"

- Call on volunteer(s) to help with the definition: "applies to everyone or all members of a group; general." The prefix *uni* comes from the Latin *unus* and means "one" or "single." Explain that so far, the informational texts they've been reading were chosen specifically to build knowledge about Vietnam, but this is the first of several informational texts they will be reading about the refugee experience.

Work Time

A. Teacher Read-Aloud: "Panic Rises in Saigon, but the Exits Are Few" (5 minutes)

- Remind students of the quote strips they read during the first day of this module. (They used the quotes, along with the Gallery Walk pictures, in Unit 1, Lesson 1, to try to predict what the unit was going to be about.) Inform them that they now get to read the full article "Panic Rises in Saigon, but the Exits Are Few" by Fox Butterfield. They will be reading for two reasons: to connect the events of the article with the novel and to understand the refugee experience better.

- Display the question:

  - "What challenges did the South Vietnamese face?"

- Ask students to follow along silently while you read aloud as a model of strong reading. Explain that students will have an opportunity to read this text on their own, too. Conduct a true read-aloud—read fluently, naturally, and with feeling, but do not pause to explain or go over vocabulary.

Meeting Students' Needs

Hearing a complex text read slowly, fluently, and without interruption or explanation promotes fluency for students. They are hearing a strong reader read the text aloud with accuracy and expression and are simultaneously looking at and thinking about the words on the printed page. Be sure to set clear expectations that students read along silently as you read the text aloud.

B. Answering Text-Dependent Questions for "Panic Rises in Saigon, but the Exits Are Few"
(15 minutes)

- Pair students of mixed abilities together. Distribute the **Text-Dependent Questions for "Panic Rises in Saigon, but the Exits Are Few"** handout. Explain that they should read through the article silently and then work with their partner to annotate the text by underlining the evidence they find that helps them answer several questions.

- Direct students to look at the graphic organizer on the page, and point out that it is very similar to the one they completed about Ha. Ask students to read silently the next two questions before they begin rereading to look for evidence.

- As students are working, circulate and notice students who have answered the questions with strong evidence from the text(s). Listen and look for such details as, "The South Vietnamese couldn't get visas to get out," "The South Vietnamese feared for their lives because three civilians had already been killed by a grenade in the food market," and "They were afraid of the advancing North Vietnamese."

- Ask for a thumbs-up when groups are ready to share their answers. Invite a few students to share their responses to the questions. Clarify as needed.

Note: As students read, post these words on the board: inexorable, stringent, emigration, evacuees.

Meeting Students' Needs

- Mixed-ability grouping of students for regular discussion and close-reading exercises provides a collaborative and supportive structure for reading complex texts. Determine these groups ahead of time.

- Text-dependent questions can be answered only by referring back to the text being read. This encourages students to reread the text for further analysis and allows for a deeper understanding.

- Some students may benefit from having access to "hint cards," small slips of paper or index cards that they turn over for hints about how/where to find the answers to text-dependent questions. For example, a hint card might say, "Check back in the third paragraph."

C. Guided Practice: Vocabulary to Deepen Understanding (10 minutes)

- Refocus students as a whole group. Distribute the **Prefixes Note-Catcher**. Inform students that they will focus on several important words in the article that will help them think about what it was like for real people trying to leave Saigon, just as Ha is. Explain that they will complete the note-catcher as the class discusses the words. The first prefix comes from the word *universal,* which was discussed as part of the third learning target. Ask:

  - "Who remembers what the prefix *uni* means?"

- Cold-call on a student to provide the definition: "single or one." Ask:

  - "Who can give us a word that starts with *uni*?"

- Invite students to share their ideas. Encourage students to write these words in the note-catcher. Expect them to mention "universal" but also such possible answers as "university," "unique," "uniform," and so forth.

- Direct students' attention to the board and ask them to circle the four words in their text: *inexorable, stringent, emigration, evacuees.*

- Focus them on the word *inexorable.* Ask for a student volunteer to read the sentence. Then ask:

  - "After reading the sentence, what do you think the word *inexorable* means?"

- Give students a moment to think and then talk with a peer.

- Call on student volunteers, listening for such answers as "unstoppable." Students may get close and say "inevitable." Tell them it means "impossible to stop, or relentless." Point out the prefix *in*, which means "not." Ask students to write the meaning of the prefix in their note-catchers. Students may recognize that *ex* has something to do with leaving, "out of," or "from." Ask:

  - "How does an *inexorable advance* of communists add to the feeling of panic?"

- Call on student volunteers, listening for such answers as, "They can't stop the communists, so now they have to get out of the country," or "The communists can't be stopped, so they have to flee." Pause to give students time to write the meaning of the word *inexorable* in their note-catchers.

- Next, focus students on the phrase *stringent emigration laws.* Ask:

  - "Based on context clues, what you think *stringent* means?"

- Give students a moment to think and then talk with a peer.

- Call on a new voice in the room. Listen for "strict." Give students that synonym if they cannot come up with it themselves.

- Next, focus students on the word *emigration.* Ask:

  - "How many of you actually read this as "stringent *im*migration laws?" Pause for show of hands.

- Ask:

  - "Which word can be found in the word *emigration*?"

- Cold-call on a student to answer. Listen for the response "migration," and guide students as needed. Ask:

  - "So what does *migration* or *migrate* mean?"

- Cold-call on a student to answer "to move" or something similar. Ask:

  - "So, what is the prefix added to that word?" If necessary, remind students that *pre* means "before" (e.g., pregame show): A *prefix* is "something that goes in front of a word root to signal meaning."

- Cold-call on a student to answer that the prefix is *e.* Ask:

  - "What do you think that prefix *e* might mean?"

- Ask for student volunteers to answer "out." If no student provides the answer, give them the definition:

  - "When we use the prefix *e,* which means 'out,' with the root *migrate,* we come up with a word that specifically means 'moving out.' People were moving out. And when we look at the phrase,

---

it turns out that South Vietnam had strict laws about 'moving out.'" Ask students to add the prefix and the word *emigration* to their note-catchers.

- Ask:
  - "Why might Vietnam have had strict rules about people leaving the country?"
- Point out that the answer to this question is not found directly in the text but that students may be able to make an inference. Give students time to think and then talk with a peer.
- Cold-call on a student to share out. Guide the class to understand that the communist government may not have wanted to lose citizens who had valuable skills. This relates to the *totalitarian* nature of communism: The government wanted "total" control.
- Direct the students' attention to another word near the end of the article, *evacuees.* Ask:
  - "Which part of speech is this word? A verb, or noun, or what?"
- Call on a student volunteer who should be able to tell you it's a noun. Confirm that *evacuee* is a noun.
- Point out that this word also has the prefix *e.* Ask:
  - "We've just talked about this prefix *e,* which means 'out.' But now we have a different root. What is the root you can find in the word *evacuees?*"
- Students should answer "vac." Then ask:
  - "Where have you seen that root before? What other words contain *vac* as a root?"
- Ask students to think and then talk with a peer.
- Look for a variety of words, such as *vacation, vacuum,* and *vacate.* Ask:
  - "What do you think the root *vac* might mean?"
- Call on student volunteers, who might answer "empty." If no student volunteers the correct meaning, tell them:
  - "Now we have this prefix *e,* which means 'out,' and this root *vac,* which means 'empty.' What do you think *evacuees* are doing?"
- Listen for such responses as, "They are emptying out." Ask for a student to clarify—as a noun, is this a person, place, or thing that is "emptying out"? Briefly explain that *evacuees* in this case are emptying out of Vietnam. This is a word that is sometimes used as refugees escape dangerous areas. Have students add the definition of *evacuees* to their note-catchers.
- Ask:
  - "Who can give us a word that you know that starts with *in?*"
- Ask students to share their ideas and invite the class to write those words in their note-catchers. Possible answers include "indivisible" (from the Pledge of Allegiance), "invisible," "indecisive," and so forth.
- Ask:
  - "Who can give us a word that you know that starts with the prefix *e?*
- Ask students to share their ideas and invite the class to write those words in their note-catchers. Possible answers include "evaporate," "evade," "elevate," and so forth.

Meeting Students' Needs

- Encourage students to use word-attack strategies, identifying prefixes, root words, suffixes, cognates, and context.

- To support ELL students, consider providing definitions of challenging vocabulary in the students' home language. Resources such as Google Translate and bilingual translation dictionaries can assist with one-word translations.

- ELL students may be unfamiliar with more vocabulary words than are mentioned in this lesson. Check for comprehension of general words that most students would know.

- For students who struggle to read complex texts, consider previewing the following vocabulary words from this text: *inexorable, stringent, emigration, immigration, migrate, migration,* and *evacuees.* If you choose to select additional words to preview, focus on words whose meaning may be difficult to determine using context clues from the text. It is important for students to practice using context clues to determine word meaning so that they become more proficient readers.

- It will be helpful to keep track of prefixes and suffixes learned, both for students and teachers. For more information on working with affixes, consider such sites as the Online Etymology Dictionary at etymonline.com and the American Heritage Dictionary at ahdictionary.com.

Closing and Assessment

A. Debrief Learning Targets and Preview Homework (3 minutes)

- Refocus students on the last two learning targets:

    - "I can use common Greek and Latin affixes (prefixes) and roots as clues to help me know what a word means."

    - "I can identify common themes that connect refugee experiences."

- Ask students to Think-Pair-Share:

    - "How are these two targets related? In other words, how did figuring out specific words and phrases help you identify common themes that connect refugee experiences?"

- Invite students to share out as time permits. Continue to emphasize that using word roots is a powerful strategy to figure out words in a particular text and also to learn words they may encounter in many other texts.

- Preview the homework. Explain to students that in this next section of the novel, Ha and her family arrive in the United States. Ask students to look for evidence to answer the question, "How is Ha's life being turned 'inside out'?" Have students add this question to the third column in their structured notes.

Meeting Students' Needs

- Checking in with learning targets helps students self-assess their learning. This research-based strategy supports struggling learners the most.
- Encourage ELL students to use word-attack strategies, identifying prefixes, root words, suffixes, cognates, and context.

Homework

- Finish your answers to the text-dependent questions if you did not do so in class.
- Complete a first read of pages 115–134. Take notes (in your journal) using the Structured Notes Graphic Organizer. Focus on the strongest evidence that reveals how Ha is being turned "inside out," plus vocabulary that helps you understand her challenges and responses.

Meeting Students' Needs

- Vocabulary can be a source of difficulty for struggling readers. Provide a brief list with definitions of the challenging vocabulary words from the reading homework. Do this only for those students who need this support.
- Most important is to provide words that cannot be easily determined from context. There are a few of these in the novel. On pages 115–134, these words include *giddy* (excited, extremely happy), *contorted* (twisted), *recoils* (springs back), *goodwill* (kindness, generosity), *lotus-pod* (the large, round, center part of a flower native to Asia), *monsoon* (downpour), and *anchors down* (holds down).

LESSON 4

Building Background Knowledge, Predicting, and Focusing on Key Vocabulary

"Refugees: Who, Where, and Why"

Long-Term Targets Addressed (Based on ELA CCSS)

- I can cite text-based evidence that provides the strongest support for an analysis of informational text. (RI.8.1)
- I can analyze the connections and distinctions between individuals, ideas, or events in a text. (RI.8.3)
- I can use a variety of strategies to determine the meaning of unknown words or phrases. (L.8.4)

Supporting Learning Targets

- I can identify the strongest evidence in the text "Refugees: Who, Where, and Why" that helps me explain challenges refugees face when fleeing home.
- I can identify the strongest evidence in the text "Refugees: Who, Where, and Why" that helps me explain challenges refugees face finding home.
- I can use common Greek and Latin affixes (prefixes) and roots as clues to help me know what a word means.

Ongoing Assessment

- Structured notes (pages 135–157 from homework)
- Prefixes note-catcher
- Annotated article "Refugees: Who, Where, and Why"

Agenda

1. Opening
   A. Engaging the Reader: Chalkboard Splash (8 minutes)
   B. Review Learning Targets (2 minutes)

---

2. Work Time

    A. Prediction and Read-Aloud of "Refugees: Who, Where, and Why" (13 minutes)

    B. Vocabulary in Context: Prefixes and Root Words (10 minutes)

    C. Partner Reading: Reread "Refugees: Who, Where, and Why" (10 minutes)

3. Closing and Assessment

    A. Debrief Learning Targets and Preview Homework (2 minutes)

4. Homework

    A. Read pages 135–157; take notes using the Structured Notes Graphic Organizer.

    B. Reread and annotate the article "Refugees: Who, Where, and Why."

Teaching Notes

- In this lesson, students first make a basic prediction and then read the informational text "Refugees: Who, Where, and Why" silently as the teacher reads aloud. Do not worry if students do not understand everything at this point. Encourage them to persist. Their understanding will grow as they consider key vocabulary and reread this text across Lessons 4 and 5. Note, too, that students read the statistics at the end of the article much later in the unit, when they launch a short research project about refugees. It is great if students notice the statistics in Lessons 4 and 5, but do not feel a need to thoroughly address these bullet points yet.

- Students focus on specific vocabulary words in this lesson. These strong academic words are central to students' conceptual understanding and offer an opportunity to teach several new prefixes. Students work with most of these words during Work Time. Note that the word *asylum* is held for students to think about later, during their partner reading.

- In this lesson, students practice a new, basic structure of partner reading (see Work Time). This structure is particularly useful to ensure that all students are actively engaged as readers with a challenging text. Paired reading in effect has students share the load of everything reading demands; the person reading aloud is focusing more on decoding and fluency, and the person listening is focusing more on comprehension. It is crucial that students take turns with both roles to continue to develop their full range of literacy skills.

- Review the Numbered Heads protocol.

- Post learning targets, prompt for "engaging the reader," vocabulary words (but not definitions): *overburdened* (Section 3), *malnourished* (Section 3), *overcrowded* (Section 3), *repatriation* (Section 4), *resettle* (Section 4), and *devastation* (Section 6).

Lesson Vocabulary

plight, universal experiences, prediction; asylum, overburdened, malnourished, overcrowded, repatriation, resettle/resettlement, devastation

---

Materials

- *Inside Out & Back Again* (book; one per student)
- Blank sentence strips—tagboard strips, 24-by-3 in. (one per student)
- Markers (one per student)
- "Refugees: Who, Where, and Why" (one per student)
- Document camera
- Prefixes Note-Catcher (from Lesson 3; see Supporting Materials for Teacher Reference related to this lesson's Work Time)

Opening

A. Engaging the Reader: Chalkboard Splash (8 minutes)

- Students should be sitting in their small groups, and each should have the novel *Inside Out & Back Again*.
- Remind them that you specifically asked them to pay attention to how Ha is turned "inside out." Invite them to work with a partner:
  - "What is the strongest evidence that shows how Ha is turned 'inside out' as her family settles in in Alabama?"
- As students talk in their pairs, distribute a **blank sentence strip** and a **marker** to each student. Ask students to write their strongest evidence (a direct quote, including the page number) on their strip. Then ask them to place their strip on the wall for a Chalkboard Splash.
- Invite students to line up and walk by the board in an organized manner to look at all of the "splashes" of detail and think about one they want to add to their notes.
- As students return to their seats, encourage them to write down in their journal at least one new strong piece of evidence they noticed and why they chose it.

B. Review Learning Targets (2 minutes)

- Read aloud the first two learning targets:
  - "I can identify the strongest evidence in the text 'Refugees: Who, Where, and Why' that helps me explain challenges refugees face when fleeing home."
  - "I can identify the strongest evidence in the text 'Refugees: Who, Where, and Why' that helps me explain challenges refugees face finding home."
- Ask:
  - "What do you notice about the difference between the two?" Students should notice that one focuses on "fleeing" home and the other on "finding" home.
- Point students to the third target, which they should recognize from the previous lesson. Invite them to Turn-and-Talk:
  - "What do you remember about the words, word roots, and prefixes we learned yesterday?"

- Emphasize that paying attention to prefixes and word roots is a powerful way to figure out and learn a lot of hard words quickly and that the more words students learn, the better readers they will become. Today they will continue to focus on words that are important for understanding what refugees experience as they flee home and find home.

Meeting Students' Needs

Posting learning targets enables students to refer to them throughout the lesson to check their understanding. They also remind students about the intended learning behind a lesson or activity.

Work Time

A. Prediction and Read-Aloud of "Refugees: Who, Where, and Why" (13 minutes)

- Inform students that for the next few days, they will be reading an informational text that explains the *plight,* or "difficulties," of refugees across the world and in different time periods. Explain that each refugee experience is unique, but many refugees share some commonalities or *universal experiences.* Review with students (from Lesson 3) the following:

  - "What does *universal* mean in the term *universal experiences*?" Be sure students understand that *universal* refers to "across the world and across time."

- Distribute the text **"Refugees: Who, Where, and Why."** Focus students on the title and invite them to take 1 or 2 minutes to make a *prediction* based on everything they have been learning about Ha and why many South Vietnamese people fled during the fall of Saigon. Ask students to jot notes on the top of their text in response to these questions:

  - "Who are refugees?"

  - "Where might refugees be from?"

  - "Why might someone become a refugee?"

- Inform students that in a moment, you will read the text aloud as they follow along silently. They will then have time to reread the text with a peer. Set a purpose for them: As you read aloud, they should look for evidence that confirms their prediction or that surprises them.

- Before reading aloud, display the article using the **document camera**. Remind students that it is often helpful to chunk long and complex text; they did something similar with "The Vietnam Wars" text. Have the students draw lines to divide the text into the following sections:

Section 1: Paragraphs 1 and 2, beginning with "Attila the Hun" and ending with "teachers, accountants, and doctors"

Section 2: Paragraphs 3 and 4, beginning with "Refugees are protected" and ending with "Africa and Europe"

Section 3: Paragraphs 5–7, beginning with "Many countries are hosts" and ending with "the basic needs of refugees"

Section 4: Paragraphs 8–10, beginning with "Most refugees hope to return" and ending with "refugees were offered resettlement"

Section 5: Paragraphs 11–15, beginning with "People become refugees" and ending with "in search of food and water"

Section 6: Final paragraph of the main article, beginning with "Since early times" and ending with "one we can all achieve"

- Ask students to code the text as you read:

  1. Underline evidence that confirms your prediction.

  2. Put a *!!* mark by anything that surprises you.

- Read aloud as students read silently. This should be a true read-aloud; read fluently, naturally, and with feeling, but do not pause to explain or go over vocabulary. Vocabulary instruction will come next.

- Invite students to Turn-and-Talk:

  - "What is the strongest evidence in the article that confirmed your prediction?"

  - "Which details in the text most surprised you? Why?"

- As time permits, cold-call on a few students to share out to gauge students' initial understanding of the text. But do not spend too much time probing or clarifying; students' understanding will grow across the next two lessons as they consider key vocabulary and reread this text. Let them struggle a bit! (Remember, too, that students will examine the statistics much more closely later in the unit.)

Meeting Students' Needs

- For ELL students or other students who struggle with language, provide them with a completed Prefix Note-Catcher as well as a glossary of other key words.

- Encourage ELL students to use word-attack strategies, identifying prefixes, root words, suffixes, cognates, and context.

- Hearing a complex text read slowly, fluently, and without interruption or explanation promotes fluency for students. They are hearing a strong reader read the text aloud with accuracy and expression and are simultaneously looking at and thinking about the words on the printed page. Be sure to set clear expectations that students read along silently as you read the text aloud.

B. Vocabulary in Context: Prefixes and Root Words (10 minutes)

- Ask students to take out their Prefixes Note-Catcher from Lesson 3. Display a copy on the document camera or overhead (for modeling). Ask them to focus on several important words in the article that will help them think about what it was like for real people trying to flee and find home. They will complete the note-catcher as the class discusses the words.

- Point students to the board and ask them to circle these six words in their text: *overburdened* (Section 3), *malnourished* (Section 3), *overcrowded* (Section 3), *repatriation* (Section 4), *resettlement* (Section 4), and *devastation* (Section 6).

- Focus them on the word *overburdened*. Read aloud the sentence: "A hospital and several clinics provide health care, but these are *overburdened* with many patients." Ask:

  - "After reading the sentence, what do you think the word *overburdened* means?"

- Give students a moment to think and then talk with a peer.

- Call on student volunteers, listening for such answers as "too crowded," "pushed beyond their limits," or "maxed out." Tell them it means "overloaded" or "too much to deal with."

- Read aloud the sentence: "Schooling is provided for children, but classes are very *overcrowded*." Ask:

  - "What do you think the word *overcrowded* means?"

- Give students a moment to think and then talk with a peer.

- Call on a numbered heads group member to answer. Be sure students understand that *overcrowded* means "too crowded" or "beyond filled to capacity."

- Focus students on their Prefix Note-Catcher. Instruct them to add the prefix *over* and the words *overburdened* and *overcrowded*. Ask:

  - "What does the prefix *over* mean?"

- Clarify as needed, and ask students to write "too" next to this prefix in their note-catcher.

- Next, focus students on the word *malnourished*. Read: "Most refugees are sick and *malnourished* when they arrive." Ask:

  - "Cover up the prefix *mal*. What does the word *nourished* mean?"

- Give students a moment to think and then talk with a peer.

- Call on a numbered heads group member to answer. Be sure students understand that *nourished* means "well fed, having enough nutrition."

- Ask:

  - "So, what do you think *malnourished* means?"

- Give students a moment to think and then talk with a peer.

- Call on a numbered heads group member to answer. Clarify as needed. Be sure students understand that people who are *malnourished* are "underfed and/or have improper nutrition." Point out that the prefix *mal* can mean "bad." Students may be familiar with words like *malady* (sickness), *malice* (evil), or *malpractice* (when a professional does something wrong or illegal). Direct students to write the meaning of the prefix on their Prefix Note-Catcher.

- Help students make a connection to Ha and the poems they most recently read about her on the boat:

  - "What do you remember about the food Ha has on the boat? Do you think she is malnourished when she arrives in the United States?"

- Next, focus students on the word *repatriation*. Read: "Most refugees hope to return to their homes. As conflicts are resolved, many refugees undergo *repatriation*." Point out that this word also is defined for them at the end of the text. Ask:

  - "Cover up the prefix *re*. What do you think *patriation* means? Does this word part remind you of another word you might know?"

- Give students a moment to think and then talk with a peer.

- Call on a numbered heads group member to answer. Students may connect this word part to *patriot* or *patriotic*. Explain that *patria* means "native land or homeland." Ask:

  - "In your own words, how would you define *repatriation*?"

- Give students time to think and talk.

- Call on a numbered heads group member to answer. Be sure students understand that *re* means "again." Direct students to the Prefix Note-Catcher and have them write the prefix, its meaning, and the word *repatriation*. Ask:

  - "What is the difference between *repatriation* and *resettlement*?"

- Be sure students realize that *repatriation* involves returning to one's original home once it is safe to do so, while *resettlement* involves settling in a new country—making a new home.

- Next, focus students on the word *devastation*. Read: "Since early times, large groups of people have been forced to leave their homelands because of persecution and the *devastation* of their lands." Ask:

  - "Based on context clues, what do you think the word *devastation* means?"

  - "Does this word remind you of another word you might know?"

- Give students a moment to think and then talk with a peer.

- Invite a volunteer to respond. Students may connect this word to *devastate* or *destroy*. Explain that in this case, *devastation* refers to "the removal or taking away of land through damage or destruction." The prefix *de* means "the opposite of," "removal," or "a taking away." Direct students to write the meaning of the prefix in their note-catcher.

C. Partner Reading: Reread "Refugees: Who, Where, and Why" (10 minutes)

- Inform students that for the remainder of class, they are going to work with a partner to reread this article more carefully. It is fine if they do not finish; they will be working with this text again in the next lesson.

- Pair students of mixed abilities to work together. Ask them to use the Partner Reading protocol to annotate the sections of the text. Briefly explain the process:

  1. Decide who is Partner A and who is Partner B.

  2. Partner A, read the first two paragraphs out loud.

  3. Partner B, state the gist of that section.

  4. Together, briefly discuss to refine the gist: Make sure your gist makes sense, add information your partner has that you think is important, and so forth.

  5. On your own, annotate your text: Write down the gist of that section in the margins.

  6. Switch roles and move on to the next two paragraphs.

  7. Follow the same process, reading every two paragraphs, sharing the gist and annotating the text, and then switching roles, until you finish reading the article.

- Ask students to circle the word *asylum* (in Paragraph 3). Challenge them to try to figure out this word as they read with their partners.

- Invite students to begin reading, reminding them to use their "six-inch voices" to keep noise to a minimum. Say, "Six-inch voices can only be heard from six inches away." Explain to students that they will be using this annotated text to write a summary in the next lesson.

Meeting Students' Needs

- Weaker readers, who are usually dysfluent, may not be able to read this text aloud. As an alternative, let students choose who reads aloud; read aloud the article to all with students following, and then have them read it silently; or use a combination of both.

- Inform the students that if one student does not want to read, it is okay if the other student does all the reading, or they may choose the silent-read option. Present all the options and use your own judgment.

Closing and Assessment

A. Debrief Learning Targets and Preview Homework (2 minutes)

- Review the learning targets with students. Ask:
  - "How are these targets related? In other words, how did figuring out specific words and phrases help you meet the first two targets?"
- Invite students to share out as time permits. Help them notice that many of the words related to refugees' experiences have to do with:
  - Too much (e.g., too crowded).
  - Negative experiences (e.g., malnutrition).
  - Moving to and from (going back to one's home country or settling again in a new country).
- Continue to emphasize that using prefixes and word roots is a powerful strategy to figure out the meanings of words in a particular text and also to learn words they may encounter in many other texts.
- Preview the homework and note-taking assignment. Be sure students notice that this homework has two parts.

Meeting Students' Needs

Checking in with learning targets helps students self-assess their learning. This research-based strategy supports struggling learners most.

Homework

- Complete a first read of pages 135–157. Take notes (in your journals) using the Structured Notes Graphic Organizer. Focus on the strongest evidence that reveals how Ha is being turned "inside out," plus vocabulary that helps you understand her challenges and responses.

- Continue rereading the article "Refugees: Who, Where, and Why" and annotating for the gist of each section.

Note: Be prepared to return students' End-of-Unit 1 Assessments in Lesson 5 if you have not already done so.

Meeting Students' Needs

- Vocabulary can be a source of difficulty for struggling readers. Provide a brief list with definitions of the challenging vocabulary words from the reading homework. This should be done only for students who need it.

- Most important is to provide words that cannot be easily determined from context. There are a few of these in the novel. On pages 135–157, these words might include *diacritical mark* (accent mark) and *lacquer* (polish, gloss).

LESSON 5

Building Background Knowledge and Summarizing

"Refugees: Who, Where, and Why," Part 2

Long-Term Targets Addressed (Based on ELA CCSS)

- I can cite text-based evidence that provides the strongest support for an analysis of informational text. (RI.8.1)
- I can objectively summarize informational text. (RI.8.2)
- I can analyze the connections and distinctions between individuals, ideas, or events in a text. (RI.8.3)
- I can write informative/explanatory texts that convey ideas and concepts using relevant information that is carefully selected and organized. (W.8.2)

Supporting Learning Targets

- I can identify the strongest evidence in the article "Refugees: Who, Where, and Why" and the novel that helps me explain challenges refugees face when fleeing home.
- I can identify the strongest evidence in the article "Refugees: Who, Where, and Why" and the novel that helps me explain challenges refugees face finding home.
- I can write a paragraph that provides an objective summary of "Refugees: Who, Where, and Why."
- I can identify universal themes that connect refugee experiences.

Ongoing Assessment

- Structured notes (for pages 135–157, from homework)
- Annotated article "Refugees: Who, Where, and Why" (from homework)
- Summary Writing Graphic Organizer
- Fleeing Home and Finding Home Anchor Charts

Agenda

1. Opening
   A. Engaging the Reader: Chalkboard Splash of Evidence about "Inside" and "Outside" (8 minutes)
   B. Review Learning Targets (2 minutes)
2. Work Time
   A. Finding Evidence from Text: Introducing the Fleeing Home and Finding Home Anchor Charts (10 minutes)
   B. Summarizing: Capturing the Essence of the Text (23 minutes)
3. Closing and Assessment
   A. Debrief Learning Targets and Preview Homework (2 minutes)
4. Homework
   A. Use the Summary Writing Graphic Organizer to write about the article "Refugees: Who, Where, and Why"
   B. Read pages 158–179 of *Inside Out & Back Again*; take notes using the Structured Notes Graphic Organizer.

Teaching Notes

- Students continue to work with the informational text "Refugees: Who, Where, and Why" to understand universal aspects of refugees' experiences around the world and throughout history.

- Even as students begin to recognize patterns, continue to emphasize that each individual's experience is unique. There is no singular "refugee experience." Even within one country, refugees' experiences vary widely. Use sensitivity with this topic, particularly because there are likely to be students in many classrooms who are themselves refugees.

- Across the unit, students will help create two class anchor charts: Fleeing Home and Finding Home. These anchor charts build directly on the graphic organizer completed during Lesson 3 about why Ha's family flees. The two anchor charts help students begin to see patterns and common themes across the novel and the informational texts and across countries and refugees' experiences.

- Students will draw on this knowledge for their End-of-Unit 2 essay as well as their final performance task (a research-based narrative) in Unit 3. Be sure to hold on to these anchor charts.

- In this lesson, students are introduced to both anchor charts to help them understand the arc of the universal refugee experience. However, today they begin to fill in only the Fleeing Home Anchor Chart based on evidence from "Refugees: Who, Where, and Why" as well as their structured notes from reading the novel.

- At the end of this lesson, students begin to summarize the article "Refugees: Who, Where, and Why." But be clear with students that they are not finished with this text—they will return to it during their research later in this unit (Lessons 17 and 18), including a more careful examination of the statistics at the end of the article.

- Be prepared to return students' End-of-Unit 1 Assessments if you have not already done so. Note patterns of strength; be prepared during the lesson opening to share things many students did well.
- Review: Chalkboard Splash (see the Appendix).
- Post learning targets, prompt for "engaging the reader."

Lesson Vocabulary

universal experience, summary, controlling idea, key details, clincher

Materials

- *Inside Out & Back Again* (book; one per student)
- Blank sentence strips—tagboard strips, each 24-by-3 in. (four per student)
- "Refugees: Who, Where, and Why" (from Lesson 4; students' annotated copies)
- Fleeing Home Anchor Chart (new; teacher-created)
- Finding Home Anchor Chart (new; teacher-created)
- Summary Writing Graphic Organizer (one per student)
- Document camera

Opening

A. Engaging the Reader: Chalkboard Splash of Evidence about "Inside" and "Outside" (8 minutes)

- Students should be sitting with their small groups and have their copies of *Inside Out & Back Again*. Explain to the class that Ha and her family are facing many challenges as they try to make a new home for themselves in Alabama. Ha writes a lot of poems that describe how her life feels like it's being turned "inside out," and today students are going to focus on two of these poems from last night's homework. (They will return to the second part of their homework later in the lesson.)
- Invite them to take a few minutes to silently reread "Loud Outside" on pages 145 and 146 and "Quiet Inside" on pages 149 and 150. Distribute four blank **sentence strips** to each student.
- On the whiteboard, create a T-chart with one side labeled "Inside Challenges" and the other side labeled "Outside Challenges."
- Refocus students as a whole group and explain that they are going to do a Chalkboard Splash with the strongest evidence from these two poems. Ask students to think about these questions:
  - "What is the strongest evidence from the text that describes some of the challenges Ha and her family are facing 'inside'?"
  - "What is the strongest evidence from the text that describes some of the challenges Ha and her family are facing 'outside'?"

- Ask students to use details from the two poems they just reread to write down two pieces of the strongest evidence for each question. Give students 3 to 4 minutes to work. Circulate to listen in and gauge how well students are grasping this central metaphor in the novel. Probe, but do not worry if students are still not entirely clear; this will remain a focus throughout the unit.

- Invite students to place their strongest evidence on the T-chart and have them add to their structured notes. Give specific positive praise for comments you hear students making that indicate they are actively choosing the "strongest" evidence (e.g., "I heard so-and-so say that she thought this line in the poem really showed it best, because . . .").

- Return students' End-of-Unit 1 Assessments if you have not already done so. Give specific positive praise for patterns you noticed in students' work.

B. Review Learning Targets (2 minutes)

- Focus the class on the learning targets. Point out that the second and third targets are identical to those from the previous lesson.

- Focus students on the first target and invite a volunteer to read it aloud:

  - "I can write a paragraph that provides an objective summary of 'Refugees: Who, Where, and Why.'"

- Explain that students will use their annotated notes to write a summary of the article. Ask for student volunteers to answer the question:

  - "What does it mean to *summarize*?" Be sure students understand that to *summarize* means "to give the short version of something. A good summary includes the main idea and the important details."

- Read aloud the last learning target:

  - "I can identify universal themes that connect refugee experiences."

- Share with students that today they will use the article and the novel to learn about some universal experiences or common themes among refugees. They will use the strongest evidence from both texts to do this.

Meeting Students' Needs

Learning targets are a research-based strategy that helps all students, but especially challenged learners.

Work Time

A. Finding Evidence from Text: Introducing the Fleeing Home and Finding Home Anchor Charts (10 minutes)

- Remind students that in the past few lessons, they have begun thinking more about the universal refugee experience. Today, they will start two new anchor charts that will help them capture that thinking as they continue to read the novel and additional informational texts.

- For now, they are now going to think about how this universal refugee experience applies to Ha. When Ha and her family flee their home, they become refugees. When they flee, they face challenges. Now Ha and her family are in Alabama, and they are trying to find a new home there, which also is challenging.

- Post the new **Fleeing Home Anchor Chart** and the **Finding Home Anchor Chart** (see blank examples in the Supporting Materials). Explain that students will be collecting the strongest evidence from the informational texts and the novel that answers the questions, "What challenges do refugees face when fleeing home?" (on the Fleeing Home Anchor Chart) and "What challenges do refugees face finding home?" (on the Finding Home Anchor Chart).

- Explain that in the novel, Ha experiences challenges fleeing home, and now that she is in Alabama trying to make a new home, she is facing new challenges. This pattern of fleeing and finding home is something students will consider further as they read more of the novel and informational texts.

- Share with students that in today's lesson, they will think mostly about the "fleeing home" part of the refugee experience. Invite them to discuss these questions with their small groups:

    - "According to the article 'Refugees: Who, Where, and Why,' what challenges do refugees face when fleeing home? What is the strongest evidence from the article to support this?"

- Invite a numbered heads group member from each group to respond, and remind students they must share evidence from the text to support their answer. Record the answers on the anchor chart.

- Next, invite students to review their structured notes from reading homework to answer the same questions on the new Fleeing Home Anchor Chart. Remind students that they are looking for the strongest evidence of the challenges Ha faces when fleeing home at this point. They must have specific evidence from the text to support what they say.

- Once groups have discussed the question, call on group members to respond and add the answers to the new Fleeing Home Anchor Chart.

- Explain to students that they will continue to add to the Fleeing Home Anchor Chart, and they will also begin to add to the Finding Home Anchor Chart.

Meeting Students' Needs

Anchor charts provide a visual cue to students about what to do when you ask them to work independently. They also serve as note-catchers when the class is co-constructing ideas.

B. Summarizing: Capturing the Essence of the Text (23 minutes)

Note: Many eighth-graders may have been taught one or more techniques for composing a topic sentence. Reinforce and build on this previous learning.

- Ask students to work with the same partner they worked with during Lesson 4 for the paired reading. (It is fine for students to work with a new person if their partner is absent.)

- Invite students to pull out their annotated **"Refugees: Who, Where, and Why"** article (homework from Lesson 4). Remind them that they have already heard this text read aloud, thought about some key vocabulary, and then reread with a partner to annotate for the gist of each section. Invite student pairs to review the annotations they made in the margins of the article and discuss:

  - "What was your initial sense of what this article is mostly about?"

- Ask them to jot this initial gist statement about the full article at the top of the article, near their notes about the title.

- Distribute the **Summary Writing Graphic Organizer**, display it on a **document camera**, and orient students to it. Read the top portion and move on to draw students' attention to the phrase *controlling idea*. Explain that the *controlling idea* is "a sentence that makes the reader want to know more about what you have to say." A good topic sentence has a clear controlling idea that makes the reader ask a question in his or her mind.

- Model for students: "For example, 'Throughout the world, refugees have fled their homes for many reasons.' This makes me ask the question in my mind, 'What are the reasons refugees flee their homes?'"

- Ask student pairs to take a few minutes to do the following:

  - Review your gist note at the top of the article.

  - Work together to craft a topic sentence that will make the reader want to know more and ask a question in his or her mind.

- Circulate to support students by asking:

  - "What question does this make you think of when you read your own sentence?"

- Invite student pairs to share their sentences with the class.

- Refocus students on the Summary Writing Graphic Organizer, specifically the key details. Explain that the key details will be the most important points of the article. Remind students that by chunking the article and annotating with their partner (in Lesson 4), they have already taken a big step toward identifying the key details.

- Ask student pairs to take about 5 minutes to do the following:

  1. Review your annotations for each section of the article.

  2. Work together to write well-crafted sentences in the graphic organizer.

- Circulate to support students by asking:

  - "What seems most important from this section of the article? Why?"

  - "If someone hadn't read this article, what would they most need to know?"

- As you circulate, look for pairs who are creating strong sentences. When most students are finished, refocus the class as a whole and invite a few of these pairs to share their sentences. Identify specifically for the class what makes these strong examples.

- Finally, draw students' attention to the bottom of the graphic organizer. Explain that the last sentence of the summary paragraph is sometimes called a *clincher,* a memorable statement that leaves the reader with something to think about.

- Model briefly: "For example, 'Refugees are everyday people who rely on other everyday people for their survival.'"

- Invite student pairs to collaborate on a clincher for their summary paragraph. Circulate and support students by asking:

  - "What do you want your reader to leave thinking about based on this sentence?"

- Ask for volunteers to share clincher statements, and provide time for students to revise what they have.

- Inform students that as part of their homework, each student will use this Summary Writing Graphic Organizer to write an individual summary paragraph.

Meeting Students' Needs

- Graphic organizers and recording forms engage students more actively and provide the scaffolding that is especially critical for learners with lower levels of language proficiency and/ or learning. For students who need additional support, you may want to provide a partially filled-in graphic organizer.

- When you're reviewing the graphic organizers or recording forms, consider using a document camera to display the document for students who struggle with auditory processing.

Closing and Assessment

A. Debrief Learning Targets and Preview Homework (2 minutes)

- Review the learning targets. Invite student volunteers to define *summarize, controlling idea, key details,* and *clincher.*

- Preview homework. Be sure students note that this is a two-part homework assignment.

Meeting Students' Needs

Checking in with learning targets helps students self-assess their learning. This research-based strategy supports struggling learners most.

Homework

- Use the Summary Writing Graphic Organizer to write a summary paragraph about the article "Refugees: Who, Where, and Why."

- Complete a first read of pages 158–179 of *Inside Out & Back Again.* Take notes (in your journal) using the Structured Notes Graphic Organizer. Focus on the strongest evidence that reveals how Ha is being turned "inside out," plus vocabulary that helps you understand her challenges and responses.

Meeting Students' Needs

- Vocabulary can be a source of difficulty for struggling readers. Provide a brief list with definitions of the challenging vocabulary words from the reading homework. Do this only for students who need this support.

- Most important is to provide words that cannot be easily determined from context. There are a few of these in the novel. On pages 158–179, these words might include *endures* (tolerates), *hogwash* (nonsense), *solitude* (privacy), and *yearning* (longing and desire).

LESSON 6

Building Background Knowledge

Challenges Bosnian Refugees Faced Fleeing and Finding Home

Long-Term Targets Addressed (Based on ELA CCSS)

- I can cite text-based evidence that provides the strongest support for an analysis of informational text. (RI.8.1)
- I can determine a theme or the central idea of an informational text. (RI.8.2)
- I can analyze the connections and distinctions between individuals, ideas, or events in a text. (RI.8.3)
- I can use a variety of strategies to determine the meaning of unknown words or phrases. (L.8.4)

Supporting Learning Targets

- I can identify the strongest evidence in the text "Children of War" that helps me explain what challenges refugees face when fleeing home.
- I can identify the strongest evidence in the text "Children of War" that helps me explain challenges refugees face finding home.
- I can identify common themes that connect the universal refugee experience.

Ongoing Assessment

- Structured notes (pages 180–195 from homework)
- Written summary of "Refugees: Who, Where, and Why" (from homework)
- Summary Writing Graphic Organizer: "Children of War"
- Evidence sort

Agenda

1. Opening
    A. Engaging the Reader: Think-Pair-Share "Inside Out" (5 minutes)
    B. Review Learning Targets (2 minutes)

---

2. Work Time

    A. Independent Read: "Children of War" (10 minutes)

    B. Fleeing and Finding Home Anchor Charts (8 minutes)

    C. Rereading: Preparing to Summarize (10 minutes)

3. Closing and Assessment

    A. Evidence Sort and Preview Homework (10 minutes)

4. Homework

    A. Use the Summary Writing Graphic Organizer to write a summary paragraph.

    B. Read pages 180–195; take notes using the Structured Notes Graphic Organizer.

Teaching Notes

- In this lesson, students read an interview with four refugees and answer questions similar to those they answered in Lessons 3–5. This text is somewhat simpler than other texts students have read, particularly because the speakers in the interview are children. Therefore, this text (and this lesson) is used primarily to help students identify how specific refugees' stories fit the more general patterns identified in "Refugees: Who, Where, and Why." This easier text also was chosen so students can practice summary writing more independently (during Work Time and leading into their homework).

- This text is used in part to help reinforce the point that even though there are "universal" aspects of refugees' experiences, each refugee has his or her own unique story to tell. Experiences across groups, even for groups from the same country, can vary widely.

- Many classes may have students who are themselves refugees. Handle this topic sensitively, being sure not to stereotype or generalize. If your classroom culture is safe enough, and your students are willing, consider asking any students who are refugees to be "resident experts" on this topic. Honor their experiences.

- Students continue to complete the Fleeing Home and Finding Home Anchor Charts during this lesson.

- Students annotate the article for evidence to answer the questions and then debrief as a group. This will give you a chance to monitor student progress, provide needed support immediately, and plan for differentiation to meet the needs of students who are still struggling with finding strong textual evidence.

- At the start of Work Time, before students begin reading independently, collect their homework summaries of "Refugees: Who, Where, and Why." As students read, do a spot-check of these summaries to look for patterns to inform instruction. Then, later during Work Time, briefly name specific patterns of strength and one or two focus areas for improvement. Consider identifying a strong example to share with the class. Students will have a chance to apply that feedback immediately during their group work, which includes time to talk together to plan a summary of "Children of War."

- Before students read independently, give them a few key bits of background information about the text they will read. Do not explain more: This is an opportunity for students to view the text as the experts and build their own knowledge of the world through their independent reading.

- The closing of this lesson includes an "evidence sort" activity. Prepare in advance: Cut sentence strips and quote cards for each group. Clip them together, or put them in envelopes.
- Post: learning targets, Fleeing Home Anchor Chart, Finding Home Anchor Chart.

Lesson Vocabulary

commonalities, common themes, discriminated against, targeted, summary, summarize, unique; Muslim, ethnic

Materials

- *Inside Out & Back Again* (book; one per student)
- "Children of War" (one per student)
- Fleeing Home and Finding Home Anchor Charts (created in Lesson 5; post around the room where students can see the charts)
- Summary Writing Graphic Organizer: "Children of War" (one per student)
- Document camera
- Sentence Strips: Claims from "Refugees: Who, Where, and Why" (one set per group)
- Quote Cards: Evidence from "Children of War" (one set per group)
- Extension question (optional)

Opening

A. Engaging the Reader: Think-Pair-Share "Inside Out" (5 minutes)

- Students should be sitting in their numbered heads groups. They will work with their odd- or even-numbered partner. Invite students to review their structured notes silently for a minute. Be sure to collect the students' written homework summaries (see Teaching Notes).
- Ask students to refer to their structured notes and Think-Pair-Share:
  - "Is Ha's life still 'inside out'? What is the strongest evidence from your reading last night?"
- Explain that there is not only one correct answer to this question; students are simply stating their opinions and providing evidence they think best illustrates this idea of being turned "inside out."
- Cold-call on students to share their thinking with the whole group. Listen for them to identify examples of how Ha's life is not settled. Possible answers include, "Someone throws eggs at their house," "The neighbors won't talk to them," "She still has a lot of wishes that aren't coming true," and "Kids are still picking on her at school with 'ha, ha, ha.'"
- Note that some students may argue that Ha's life is no longer "inside out": She is beginning to "find home." She now has a tutor to teach her English.

Meeting Students' Needs

Consider partnering ELL students who speak the same home language when discussion of complex content is required. This can allow students to have more meaningful discussions and clarify points in their native language.

B. Review Learning Targets (2 minutes)

- Focus the class on the learning targets, and point out that they are very similar to yesterday's targets. Ask:

  - "What is different about the first target today compared to those of the last few lessons?"

- Listen for students to notice that they are still doing the same kind of thinking, just with a different text.

- Be sure to emphasize that every individual refugee's experience is unique but that there are some predictable or common patterns for anyone who moves to a new place.

- Continue to emphasize the rigor of not only finding evidence but thinking about the strongest evidence: Which details best support your thinking, and why?

- Focus most on the third learning target. Cold-call on a student to read it aloud:

  - "I can identify common themes that connect the universal refugee experience."

- Point out to students that they are reading a variety of texts that will help them begin to notice patterns and themes. They have read the novel, of course, and in Lesson 3 they revisited "Panic Rises in Saigon, but the Exits Are Few," which they first encountered in Unit 1. They also read "Refugees: Who, Where, and Why" in Lessons 4 and 5. As they read today, they should notice how refugee experiences align to and expand upon some patterns they have identified.

Meeting Students' Needs

Posting learning targets enables students to refer to them throughout the lesson to check their understanding. This also provides a reminder to students and teachers about the intended learning behind a given lesson or activity.

Work Time

A. Independent Read: "Children of War" (10 minutes)

- Distribute the text **"Children of War."** Remind students of how they have been learning about approaching texts. Invite students to scan the text briefly to notice how this informational text is different from the text they read for the previous lesson. (Students should be able to identify that it is an interview.) Ask:

  - "In which year was this article written?"

- Do not give too much background on the text, but inform students that because they may not know the history of the war in Bosnia, you want to give them several key points that will help them understand the interviews:

  - This text is about refugees from the war in Bosnia in the 1990s.

  - A statistic from "Refugees: Who, Where, and Why" that supports our understanding of this text reads: "1990s . . . War in the Balkans forces thousands to leave their homes as Yugoslavia breaks apart."

  - There is a key vocabulary word they may have heard, but you want to be sure they understand: *Muslim*. Define *Muslim* for students as "a follower of the religion of Islam." Explain that there are Muslims in many countries, and sometimes they have been *discriminated* against or *targeted* because of their religion.

  - Another key vocabulary word is the word *ethnic*. Review this term, which is used in "Refugees: Who, Where, and Why." Ask students:

    - "What is an *ethnic* group?"

- Listen for them to say something about large groups with common characteristics. Clarify and provide a specific definition: *Ethnic* is "an adjective used to describe large groups of people with common religious, tribal, cultural, racial, or national origins."

- Inform students that because this text is relatively easy, they will be reading it silently on their own. Set their purpose for reading. As they read, they should underline the strongest evidence they find in the text to answer the following questions, posted on the board:

  - "What challenges did the Bosnian refugees face as they fled home?"

  - "What challenges did they face in the United States?"

- As students read silently, do a spot-check of these summaries to look for patterns to inform instruction. Consider identifying a strong example to share with the class later during Work Time, as time permits. Then circulate, encouraging students to annotate the text.

Meeting Students' Needs

- To support ELL students, consider providing definitions of challenging vocabulary in students' home language. Resources such as Google Translate and bilingual translation dictionaries can assist with one-word translations.

- ELL students may be unfamiliar with more vocabulary words than are mentioned in this lesson. Check for comprehension of general words that most students would know.

- Consider partnering ELL students who speak the same home language when discussion of complex content is required. This can enable students to have more meaningful discussions and clarify points in their native language.

- For students who struggle with reading grade-level text, consider chunking the text for them onto separate sheets of paper. This makes reading complex texts more manageable and allows them to focus on one small section at a time.

B. Fleeing and Finding Home Anchor Charts (8 minutes)

- Post the **Fleeing Home** and **Finding Home Anchor Charts**. Focus students as a whole group as they continue to work with their partner.

- Ask students to Think-Pair-Share about the evidence they underlined as they read:

  - "After reading this article, what other reason can we add for challenges refugees face when fleeing home? What is the strongest evidence from the article to support this?"

- Cold-call on students for answers to complete the top part of the anchor chart. Consider having the class use thumbs-up or thumbs-down to indicate whether reasons and evidence are strong enough for the anchor chart. Possible answers include lack of food, extremely unsafe conditions, or others, with appropriate quotes from the text ("we were walking on this bridge over the river and the Serbs started shooting," "or risk getting shot," "they tried to kill me because of my religion").

- Ask students to Think-Pair-Share:

  - "What challenges do refugees face finding home? What is the strongest evidence to support your answer?"

Meeting Students' Needs

- Anchor charts serve as note-catchers when the class is co-constructing ideas.

- Cold-call on students for answers to complete the top part of the anchor chart. Consider having the class use thumbs-up/thumbs-down to indicate whether reasons and evidence are strong enough for the anchor chart. Possible answers include life not being as good in the new country, worrying about friends and family left behind, or others, with appropriate evidence from the text ("It's not as good as it was in Bosnia," "I want to get my family here," "without friends").

- Give students specific positive praise for ways in which you noticed them citing evidence from this text and the novel. Note in particular whether you heard students beginning to approach the actual eighth-grade standard, which requires them to cite not just any evidence but the strongest evidence to support their analysis.

C. Rereading: Preparing to Summarize (10 minutes)

- Inform students that they will now reread the article on their own and begin the **Summary Writing Graphic Organizer: "Children of War."** Explain that this graphic organizer is just like the one they did for "Refugees: Who, Where, and Why."

- Cold-call on a student to explain what it means to *summarize,* such as "write a brief description of the main points." Include any necessary teaching points from the review of student homework, such as review of key details, controlling idea, and so forth. Consider sharing a strong example on the **document camera** if time allows. Explain that after individual work time, they will have an opportunity to share and discuss with their classmates.

- Circulate and monitor students as they answer the questions, providing support where needed.

- Invite students to pair up to share their answers. Refocus the group, and invite some volunteers to share their answers with the whole class.

Meeting Students' Needs

- Text-dependent questions can be answered only by referring explicitly to the text being read. This encourages students to reread the text for further analysis and allows for a deeper understanding.

- Some students may benefit from having access to "hint cards," small slips of paper or index cards that they turn over for hints about how/where to find the answers to text-dependent questions. For example, a hint card might say, "Check back in the third paragraph."

Closing and Assessment

A. Evidence Sort and Preview Homework (10 minutes)

- Students should work with their numbered heads groups. Distribute the **Sentence Strips: Claims from "Refugees: Who, Where, and Why"** and the **Quote Cards: Evidence from "Children of War"** (one set per group).

- Explain the activity: "In the past few lessons, you have been identifying evidence to support your thinking on the common themes that connect the universal refugee experience. Today, after reading about actual refugee experiences, you are going to think about how those experiences relate to the article 'Refugees: Who, Where, and Why.'"

- Remind the class that although some aspects of the refugee experience are universal, each refugee experience is also *unique*—one of a kind. Remind students that the prefix *uni* means "one"—in some ways, all refugees share one experience, but it is equally true that each refugee has his or her own "one" experience. The four teens who are interviewed in the article have things in common and experiences that are unique to them—this is even true for the two teens who are brother and sister. However, these unique experiences can still be categorized under those more universal themes.

- Give directions:

  1. Find and read the three sentence strips (from "Refugees: Who, Where, and Why") aloud as a group.

  2. Read each quote card (from the four Bosnian teens).

  3. Discuss which sentence each quote goes with and why.

  Note: Many of the quotes could be matched with more than one sentence strip. There is not always one "right" answer. Your job is to provide reasons for why you think a specific quote is especially strong evidence for a certain sentence strip.

- Check that students understand the process, and then invite them to begin. Circulate and listen in. Provide support as needed without providing answers. Ask probing questions, such as these:

- "Why did you match that piece of evidence with that part of the refugees' article?"
- "Explain your thinking."
- "Say more."

- When you hear students providing reasons or details, give specific praise, such as, "I like how you explained your thinking as to why this quote belonged here."

- When all groups have their evidence sorted, call on a group member to share one quote card and the matching sentence strip he or she matched it with and then explain his or her reasons.

- If time permits, review the third learning target:

  - "I can identify common themes that connect the universal refugee experience."

- Ask students to self-evaluate using Fist-to-Five.

Meeting Students' Needs

For students who finish early, consider distributing the Extension Question (optional).

Homework

- Use the Summary Writing Graphic Organizer to write a summary paragraph of the article "Children of War."

- Complete a first read of pages 180–195. Take notes (in your journal) using the Structured Notes Graphic Organizer. Focus on the strongest evidence that reveals how Ha is being turned "inside out" (the challenges Ha faces and her dynamic character), plus vocabulary that helps you understand her challenges and responses.

Meeting Students' Needs

- Vocabulary can be a source of difficulty for readers who struggle. Provide a brief list with definitions of the challenging vocabulary words from the reading homework. This should be done only for students who need this support.

- Most important is to provide words that cannot be easily determined from context. There are a few of these in the novel. On pages 180–195, these words might include *firm* (tighten) and *relieved* (free from fear or worry).

LESSON 7

Mid-Unit Assessment

Analyzing an Informational Text about a Refugee Experience

Long-Term Targets Addressed (Based on ELA CCSS)

- I can cite text-based evidence that provides the strongest support for an analysis of literary text. (RI.8.1)
- I can objectively summarize informational text. (RI.8.2)
- I can analyze the connections and distinctions between individuals, ideas, or events in a text. (RI.8.3)
- I can determine the meaning of words and phrases in text (figurative, connotative, and technical meanings). (RI.8.4)
- I can use a variety of strategies to determine the meaning of unknown words or phrases. (L.8.4)
- I can use evidence from informational texts to support analysis, reflection, and research. (W.8.9)

Supporting Learning Targets

- I can identify the strongest evidence in the speech by Til Gurung that helps me explain why refugees leave their home.
- I can identify the strongest evidence in the speech by Til Gurung that helps me explain challenges refugees face in their new country.
- I can determine the meaning of unfamiliar words based on context clues.
- I can cite evidence from the text to support analysis of an informational text.

Ongoing Assessment

- Mid-Unit 2 Assessment: Analyzing an Informational Text about a Refugee Experience

Agenda

1. Opening
   A. Review Learning Targets (2 minutes)

---

2. Work Time

    A. Mid-Unit Assessment: Analyzing an Informational Text about a Refugee Experience (40 minutes)

3. Closing and Assessment

    A. Debrief (3 minutes)

4. Homework

    A. Read pages 196–212; take notes using the Structured Notes Graphic Organizer.

Teaching Notes

- During today's assessment, students independently read an unfamiliar informational text about a refugee experience and answer literal and inferential text-dependent questions as well as questions that assess students' ability to determine word meaning based on context clues (L.8.4). Students also answer three constructed-response questions that require evidence from the text to support their answers. The last one is similar to the Quick Writes with which students are already familiar (W.8.9).

- Consider using the 2-point rubric to assess students' short constructed responses on this assessment. (See Unit 1, Lesson 5, Supporting Materials.)

- Post: learning targets.

Lesson Vocabulary

Do not preview vocabulary for today's assessment.

Materials

- Til Gurung's speech from the Refugee Transitions' "World of Difference Benefit Luncheon" for Mid-Unit 2 Assessment (one per student)

- Mid-Unit 2 Assessment: Analyzing an Informational Text about a Refugee Experience (one per student)

- Mid-Unit 2 Assessment: Analyzing an Informational Text about a Refugee Experience (Teacher Reference)

- Extension question (optional)

- Extension question (Teacher Reference)

- Optional: 2-point rubric (from Unit 1, Lesson 5; see Teaching Notes)

Opening

A. Review Learning Targets (2 minutes)

- Read aloud the first two learning targets.

- Remind students that these learning targets should be familiar to them, since they have been practicing these skills over the past several lessons.

Work Time

A. Mid-Unit Assessment: Analyzing an Informational Text about a Refugee Experience (40 minutes)

- Remind students that they have been reading informational texts on different refugee experiences. They have been collecting details from each text to help them understand why refugees flee home, the challenges they face in their new home, and some common themes among different refugee experiences. Share with students that they will show that they know how to do this type of analysis on their own in this assessment.

- Arrange seating to allow for an assessment-conducive setup where students independently think, read, and write. Encourage students by telling them that they have been working hard at reading closely, and today you want them to show what they have learned about word choice and tone in informational and fiction text.

- Distribute **Til Gurung's speech from the Refugee Transitions' "World of Difference Benefit Luncheon"** and the **Mid-Unit 2 Assessment: Analyzing an Informational Text about a Refugee Experience**. Read the directions aloud.

- Address any clarifying questions. Invite students to begin. Circulate to observe but not support; this is students' opportunity to independently apply the skills they have been learning.

- If students finish early, encourage them to complete the **extension question** for extra credit.

- Collect the assessment.

Meeting Students' Needs

- On-demand assessments give the teacher valuable information about skills that students have mastered or those that still need to be developed.

- ELL students and others may benefit from having extended time, a bilingual glossary or dictionary, and a separate testing location.

Closing and Assessment

A. Debrief (3 minutes)

- Talk with students about the work they have done in this first unit, reading closely in the novel and with challenging informational text. Remind them that they are getting better at collecting details and evidence from texts.

Homework

Complete a first read of pages 196–212. Take notes (in your journal) using the Structured Notes Graphic Organizer. Focus on the strongest evidence that reveals how Ha is being turned "inside out"

(the challenges Ha faces and her dynamic character), plus vocabulary that helps you understand her challenges and responses.

Meeting Students' Needs

- Vocabulary can be a source of difficulty for readers who struggle. Provide a brief list with definitions of the challenging vocabulary words from the reading homework. Do this only for students who need this support.

- Most important is to provide words that cannot be easily determined from context. There are a few of these in the novel. On pages 196–212, these words might include *echoes* (repeats), *strained* (tense), and *hoists* (lifts).

LESSON 8

Analyzing the Content of a Model Essay

"How Ha's Mother Is Turned 'Inside Out'"

Long-Term Targets Addressed (Based on ELA CCSS)

- I can cite the textual evidence that most strongly supports an analysis of what the text says explicitly as well as inferences drawn from the text. (RI.8.1)
- I can evaluate the argument and specific claims in a text (assessing whether the reasoning is sound and the evidence is relevant and sufficient to support the claims). (RI.8.8)
- I can effectively engage in discussions with diverse partners about eighth-grade topics, texts, and issues. (SL.8.1)

Supporting Learning Targets

- I can make connections between the universal refugee experiences of fleeing and finding home and the title of the novel *Inside Out & Back Again*.
- I can find the gist of a model essay.
- I can choose the strongest evidence to support my answers to questions about a model essay.
- I can evaluate the quality of evidence used to support the claims made in the model essay "How Ha's Mother Is Turned 'Inside Out'"

Ongoing Assessment

- Structured notes (pages 196–212 from homework)
- Answers to questions about model essay

Agenda

1. Opening
   A. Introducing the Assessment Prompt (7 minutes)

2. Work Time

    A. Transitioning from the Physical Fleeing and Finding Home to the Emotional "Inside Out" and "Back Again" (8 minutes)

    B. Reading the Model Essay for Gist: "How Ha's Mother Is Turned 'Inside Out'" (10 minutes)

    C. Analyzing the Content of the Model Essay: Answering Text-Dependent Questions (15 minutes)

3. Closing and Assessment

    A. Whole-Group Sharing Answers to Two of the Text-Dependent Questions (5 minutes)

4. Homework

    A. Read pages 213–234; take notes using the Structured Notes Graphic Organizer.

Teaching Notes

- In this lesson, students are introduced to the End-of-Unit Assessment prompt. From the assessment prompt, they then begin to transition from the idea of how refugees flee and find a new home to a focus on the more psychological and emotional aspects of being turned "inside out."

- To reflect the transition in thinking from physical to emotional aspects of the universal experience of refugees, students work as a class to transfer the details collected on the Fleeing Home and Finding Home Anchor Charts onto two new anchor charts: Inside Out and Back Again. This activity helps students begin to focus on the figurative language in the title of the novel.

- Students spend much of this lesson reading and analyzing a model essay: "How Ha's Mother Is Turned 'Inside Out.'" This essay is similar in structure to part of the essay students will write about Ha (although the model focuses only on the "inside out" aspect of the novel's title, since students have not yet finished the book). Because the model is about Ha's mother, it gives students an opportunity to consider her character more closely while they also learn about the structure of the essay they eventually will write about Ha. Students "read like readers" for gist and then dig deeper into the content of the essay by answering text-dependent questions. Their analysis of the model essay aligns with RI.8.8.

- In advance: Review the model essay with a focus on the content of the essay.

- Post: learning targets, anchor charts.

Lesson Vocabulary

universal

Materials

- *Inside Out & Back Again* (book; one per student)

- End-of-Unit 2 Assessment prompt (one per student and one for display)

- Prefixes Note-Catcher (from Lesson 3)

- Inside Out Anchor Chart and Back Again Anchor Chart (both new; teacher-created; see example in Supporting Materials)
- Fleeing Home and Finding Home Anchor Charts (created in Lesson 5; post around the room where students can see the charts)
- Model essay: "How Ha's Mother Is Turned 'Inside Out'" (one per student and one for display)
- Questions about the model essay (one per student and one for display)
- Questions about the model essay (Teacher Reference)

Opening

A. Introducing the Assessment Prompt (7 minutes)

- Display and distribute the **End-of-Unit 2 Assessment prompt**, and invite students to read it aloud with you:
  - "Consider the meaning of the novel's title, *Inside Out & Back Again*. How does this title relate to the universal refugee experience of fleeing and finding home, and in what ways is Ha's experience an example of this universal experience?"
- Inform students that their End-of-Unit Assessment will be an essay in which they respond to this question by finding the strongest evidence to connect the experiences of the character Ha in the novel *Inside Out & Back Again* with the experiences of real-life refugees in informational texts.
- Explain to the class that any time they write in response to a prompt, it is important that they take time to understand fully what the prompt is asking. This is similar to what students have been doing with learning targets almost every day.
- Circle the word *universal,* which has been a focus throughout the unit. Underline the word part *univers.* Ask students to Think-Pair-Share:
  - "How does the word *universal* relate to the word *universe*?"
  - "What does the prefix *uni* mean?"
- Students should remember this type of thinking from Lesson 6. Reinforce that *universal* means "common to all people in a particular group," so the *universal refugee experience* means "experiences common to all refugees around the world," of which Ha is one.
- Be sure that students have written the prefix *uni* on their **Prefixes Note-Catcher**.
- Underline the phrases *Inside Out* and *Back Again.* Ask:
  - "What do you think it means to turn 'inside out,' as the title of the novel suggests?"
- Listen for: "Turning inside out is everything changing and things becoming challenging—feeling very confused and uncertain." Then ask:
  - "What does it mean to turn 'back again,' as the title of the novel suggests?"
- Listen for: "Everything settling down and going back to normal. Feeling more comfortable and less confused." These are concepts students have worked with informally in previous lessons. At this point, be sure all students understand the figurative language in the novel's title, as this will be crucial for their success on the End-of-Unit Assessment.

Meeting Students' Needs

- Posting learning targets enables students to refer to them throughout the lesson to check their understanding. They also provide a reminder to students and teachers about the intended learning behind a given lesson or activity.
- Discussing and clarifying the language of learning targets help build academic vocabulary.

Work Time

A. Transitioning from the Physical Fleeing and Finding Home to the Emotional "Inside Out" and "Back Again" (8 minutes)

- Be sure students have their texts *Inside Out & Back Again*. Invite students to read the first learning target with you:
  - "I can make connections between the universal refugee experiences of fleeing and finding home and the title of the novel *Inside Out & Back Again*."
- Inform students that they are going to connect refugees' universal experience of fleeing and finding home (leaving a country and going somewhere new) to the universal emotional experience of being turned "inside out" and then coming "back again" just as Ha does in the novel.
- Clarify with a concrete example to show how physically fleeing home is related to but not the same as being turned inside out, and how physically finding a new home is related to but not the same as coming back again. Say: "When Ha is in Alabama, she is no longer fleeing home—she is beginning to find home. However, she is still turning inside out because she doesn't understand anything, and the other children are mean to her when she first starts school. She only really turns back again when she begins to settle in by making friends and understanding the language."
- Display the two new **Inside Out** and **Back Again Anchor Charts** (see Supporting Materials for a model). Inform students that they are going to start thinking about how the strongest evidence they have recorded on the **Fleeing Home** and **Finding Home Anchor Charts** connects with the title of the novel *Inside Out & Back Again*. Point out that the top half of each of the Inside Out and Back Again Anchor Charts is for details from the novel. The bottom half is for evidence from informational texts.
- Emphasize that not all of the evidence they gathered before (about refugees fleeing and finding home) will be relevant to the emotional aspect. That is fine. As a class, review some of the key details on the Fleeing Home and Finding Home Anchor Charts, and consider whether and how these relate to the more emotional experience of turning "inside out" or "back again":
  - "Is this evidence about 'turning inside out'? Or 'turning back again'? Why do you think that?"
- Listen for students to explain that things involving emotional turmoil are about turning "inside out" and that things related to settling in and becoming more comfortable are about turning "back again." Ask:
  - "Is it evidence from the novel? Or from an informational text? So should it go on the top or bottom of the anchor chart?"
- Move the most relevant evidence onto either the Inside Out Anchor Chart or the Back Again Anchor Chart.

TEACHER GUIDE · Grade 8 · Module 1 · Unit 2 · Lesson 8   **223**

> ## Meeting Students' Needs
>
> - Learning targets are a research-based strategy that helps all students, but they help challenged learners the most.
> - Posting learning targets enables students to refer to them throughout the lesson to check their understanding. They also provide a reminder to students and teachers about the intended learning behind a given lesson or activity.
> - Anchor charts serve as note-catchers when the class is co-constructing ideas.

B. Reading the Model Essay for Gist: "How Ha's Mother Is Turned 'Inside Out'" (10 minutes)

- Inform students that to prepare them to write their End-of-Unit Assessment literary analysis essay, they will study a model essay. They will first read it "like a reader," thinking about the content: What is the author trying to communicate? In a future lesson, they will reread it "like a writer," thinking about how the author actually writes it.

- Invite the class to read the second learning target with you:
  - "I can find the gist of a model essay."

- Invite students to get into numbered heads groups. Pair up student numbers 1 and 2 and numbers 3 and 4.

- Display and distribute the **model essay: "How Ha's Mother Is Turned 'Inside Out.'"** Advise students that this model essay responds to a prompt that is *similar* to (but not exactly the same as) the prompt they have as their End-of-Unit Assessment. But it focuses only on the "inside out" part, since students are still reading the novel. And this model essay is about a member of Ha's family: Ha's mother.

- Read the prompt and the model essay aloud, and invite students to follow along silently.

- Ask students to Think-Pair-Share:
  - "What do you notice?"
  - "What do you wonder?"

- Invite students to consider the gist of the first paragraph. Ask them to Think-Pair-Share:
  - "So what is your initial sense of what this first paragraph is mostly about?"

- Listen for: "It introduces the idea of refugees turning inside out and back again as they flee and find home, and it introduces the idea that Ha's mother turns inside out when she has to flee Vietnam with her family."

- Model annotating the gist in the margin. Invite students to do the same with their essays.

- Invite pairs to read the rest of the essay, annotating the gist of each paragraph. Circulate to support students in rereading the essay for the gist. Ask:
  - "So what is your initial sense of what this paragraph is mostly about?"

- Invite students to get back into their groups to share their gist ideas for each paragraph.

Meeting Students' Needs

Reviewing academic vocabulary words benefits all students developing academic language. Consider allowing students to grapple with a complex text before explicit teaching of vocabulary. After students have read for gist, they can identify challenging vocabulary for themselves. Teachers can address student-selected vocabulary as well as predetermined vocabulary upon subsequent encounters with the text. However, in some cases and with some students, preteaching selected vocabulary may be necessary.

C. Analyzing the Content of the Model Essay: Answering Text-Dependent Questions (15 minutes)

- Invite students to read the third learning target with you:
  - "I can choose the strongest evidence to support my answers to questions about a model essay."
- Pair up students in their numbered heads groups—odd numbers together and even numbers together.
- Display **questions about the model essay**. Draw the students' attention to the questions that say they must provide evidence to answer them. Remind students that this means they must find details in the essay to support their answers.
- Ask students to begin. Circulate to support students in rereading the text to answer the questions.
- Remind students that they will return to this model essay several more times in future lessons. Be sure they file it away.

Meeting Students' Needs

- Text-dependent questions can be answered only by referring explicitly to the text being read. This encourages students to reread the text for further analysis and allows for a deeper understanding.

- Some students may benefit from having access to "hint cards," small slips of paper or index cards that they turn over for hints about how/where to find the answers to text-dependent questions. For example, a hint card might say, "Check back in the third paragraph."

- For ELL students, consider providing extended time for tasks and answering questions in class discussions. ELL students receive extended time as an accommodation on some assessments.

Closing and Assessment

A. Whole-Group Sharing Answers to Two of the Text-Dependent Questions (5 minutes)

- Call on pairs to share answers to the first two questions with the class. (Refer to the **questions about the model essay [Teacher Reference]** in the Supporting Materials to guide students toward the appropriate answers.)

TEACHER GUIDE · Grade 8 · Module 1 · Unit 2 · Lesson 8   **225**

- Invite the class to read aloud the fourth and final learning target with you:

  - "I can evaluate the quality of evidence used to support the claims made in the model essay 'How Ha's Mother Is Turned Inside Out.'"

- Invite students to Think-Pair-Share:

  - "Look at Question 2. Does the writer support his or her claim with relevant and complete evidence?"

- Listen for students to cite specific evidence to justify their analysis of the model essay.

Homework

Complete a first read of pages 213–234. Take notes (in your journal) using the Structured Notes Graphic Organizer. Focus on the strongest evidence that reveals how Ha is a dynamic character who is growing and changing over time.

Meeting Students' Needs

- Vocabulary can be a source of difficulty for readers who struggle. Provide a brief list with definitions of the challenging vocabulary words from the reading homework. This should be done only for students who need it.

- Most important is to provide words that cannot easily be determined from context. There are a few of these in the novel. On pages 213–234, these words might include *shoulder the world* (carry a lot of worries), *superstitious* (believes that things happen because of the supernatural), *writhes* (squirming, twisting, and turning), *compromise* (reach an agreement by adjusting), and *incense* (a spice that, when burned, releases a perfume smell).

LESSON 9

Close Reading

Paragraph 1 of "Refugee and Immigrant Children: A Comparison" (from "Refugee Children in Canada: Searching for Identity")

Long-Term Targets Addressed (Based on ELA CCSS)

- I can cite text-based evidence that provides the strongest support for an analysis of literary text. (RI.8.1)
- I can determine a theme or the central ideas of an informational text. (RI.8.2)
- I can analyze the structure of a specific paragraph in a text (including the role of particular sentences in developing and refining a key concept). (RI.8.5)
- I can read above-grade informational texts with scaffolding and support. (RI.8.10)

Supporting Learning Targets

- I can find the gist of the first paragraph of "Refugee and Immigrant Children: A Comparison."
- I can analyze how specific words, phrases, and sentences help me understand how refugee and immigrant children are similar.
- I can cite evidence to explain the similarities and differences between refugee children and immigrant children.

Ongoing Assessment

- Answers to text-dependent questions, Part A

Agenda

1. Opening
    A. Engaging the Reader: Give One, Get One about Pages 213–234 of *Inside Out & Back Again* (5 minutes)
    B. Unpacking Learning Targets (2 minutes)
2. Work Time
    A. Vocabulary and Predictions before Reading: Venn Diagram to Compare Refugees and Immigrants (8 minutes)
    B. Reading Aloud and Rereading for Gist: Paragraph 1 of "Refugee and Immigrant Children: A Comparison" (10 minutes)
    C. Rereading and Text-Dependent Questions (15 minutes)
3. Closing and Assessment
    A. Mix and Mingle: A Similarity in How Refugees and Immigrants Adapt (5 minutes)
4. Homework
    A. Complete the homework question at the bottom of "Refugee and Immigrant Children: A Comparison" Paragraph 1.
    B. Read pages 238–247; take notes using the Structured Notes Graphic Organizer.

Teaching Notes

*   This lesson introduces students to one section of the article "Refugee Children in Canada: Searching for Identity." The section, "Refugee and Immigrant Children: A Comparison," describes the similarities in the adaptation process of refugees and immigrants. This full article is complex, but students read only this specific section, which compares refugees and immigrants. This section of the text was chosen because it best aligns with Ha's experiences in the novel.

*   Across the next six lessons, students will work closely with the four paragraphs in "Refugee and Immigrant Children: A Comparison." The text is divided into three chunks: Paragraph 1, Paragraphs 2–3, and Paragraph 4. Students spend 2 days with each chunk:
    *   On the first of each 2-day cycle, they read closely just to understand the complex text. For homework, they think and write about one key sentence or phrase.
    *   On the second day of each 2-day cycle, they revisit the text, answering additional text-dependent questions and applying the concepts to specific poems in the novel.

*   In advance: Review the first paragraph of the "Refugee and Immigrant Children: A Comparison" section as well as the note-catchers in Lessons 9 and 10.

*   Remind students of their strong work with "The Vietnam Wars" text in Unit 1. This text is even more challenging, but many of the strategies they used to make sense of the Unit 1 text will serve them well here. Remind students that close reading is a challenge. They can all do it by working at it, and they will rise to the challenge.

Lesson Vocabulary

refugee, refuge, immigrant, significant, disruptive, interrupt, sense of identity, generational gap, cultural gap

Materials

- *Inside Out & Back Again* (book; one per student)
- Inside Out Anchor Chart and Back Again Anchor Chart (begun in Lesson 8)
- "Refugee and Immigrant Children: A Comparison" section from the full article "Refugee Children in Canada: Searching for Identity" (one per student)
- Prefixes Note-Catcher (begun in Lesson 3)
- Similarities and Differences in How Refugees and Immigrants Adapt Anchor Chart (new; co-created with students during Work Time; see Supporting Materials)
- "Refugee and Immigrant Children: A Comparison": Paragraph 1, Text-Dependent Questions, Part A (one per student and one to display)
- Homework question (one per student)

Opening

A. Engaging the Reader: Give One, Get One about Pages 213–234 of *Inside Out & Back Again* (5 minutes)

- Inform students that they are going to do a simple interactive activity to share some of their learning from their homework reading.
- Talk about the Give One, Get One protocol. Ask students to circulate until you give the signal (music or a hand signal), about 15 seconds later. When you give the signal, each student turns to the student closest to him or her and shares one piece of evidence he or she recorded on the Structured Notes Graphic Organizer from reading pages 213–234 that reveals an aspect of Ha's dynamic character. Each student gives one piece of evidence and receives one piece of evidence from the peer he or she is speaking to. Repeat this three times.
- Cold-call on a few students to share their evidence with the whole group. Invite students to suggest which anchor chart to record the evidence on—**Inside Out** or **Back Again**. Confirm whether the rest of the group agrees, and record the evidence on the appropriate anchor chart.

Note: If this Give One, Get One activity is not appropriate for your group, consider doing the same thing, but with an inner circle and outer circle. Divide the group in half—one half makes an inner circle, facing out, and the other half makes a circle around them, facing in. Students facing each other give one and get one, before the inner group moves one step to the left. Students then give one and get one with the next person.

Meeting Students' Needs

- Use of such protocols as Give One, Get One allows for total student participation. It encourages critical thinking, collaboration, and social construction of knowledge. It also helps students practice their speaking and listening skills.

- Learning targets are a research-based strategy that helps all students, but it helps challenged learners the most.

- Posting learning targets enables students to refer to them throughout the lesson to check their understanding. The learning targets also provide a reminder to students and teachers about the intended learning behind a given lesson or activity.

B. Unpacking Learning Targets (2 minutes)

- Post the learning targets for students, and invite them to read along silently as you read aloud:

  - "I can find the gist of the first paragraph of **'Refugee and Immigrant Children: A Comparison.'"**

  - "I can analyze how specific words, phrases, and sentences help me understand how refugee and immigrant children are similar."

  - "I can cite evidence to explain the similarities and differences between refugee children and immigrant children."

- Inform students that today they will be reading part of an informational text that will help them meet these targets. Ask the class to Think-Pair-Share:

  - "How might reading an informational text help us understand Ha?"

- Listen for: "By reading this text, we are building knowledge about the universal refugee experience of turning 'inside out' and 'back again.' This is what Ha is going through."

- Remind students that this information will help them learn about the world, and it will be important when they write their End-of-Unit Assessment essay: Ha is just one unique (fictional) example of the more universal refugee experience.

Work Time

A. Vocabulary and Predictions before Reading: Venn Diagram to Compare Refugees and Immigrants (8 minutes)

- Distribute and focus students on the "Refugee and Immigrant Children: A Comparison" section from the full article **"Refugee Children in Canada: Searching for Identity."**

- Explain that this is one section from an article about refugee children who have fled their home country and then come to Canada to make a new home. It is a complex piece of text, so they are going to look at only a small section of it. Today they will dig into a single paragraph. In Lesson 10, they will think more about how the important concepts in this paragraph apply to Ha.

- Point out the word *refugee,* and ask students:
  - "We have been talking about refugees for a few weeks now. What is a *refugee*?"
  - "What is a *refuge*?"
- Some students may know that a *refuge* is "a place of safety." Clarify if needed. Ask:
  - "So how are these two words related to each other?"
- Cold-call or ask for volunteers to share their responses. Listen for: "a *refugee* is 'someone who flees his or her home to go to a place that is safe.'"
- Focus on the word *immigrant.* Briefly review the work students did in Lesson 3, when they studied a word that sounds very similar, *emigrate.* Ask for a volunteer to remind the class:
  - "What did we learn the word *emigrate* means?"
- Listen for the response: "to move out." Cold-call on a student to answer:
  - "Which word root do you see in both words? What does *migrant* mean?"
- Listen for a response such as: "someone who moves." Cold-call on a student to answer:
  - "So, what is the prefix added to that word?"
- Listen for: "*im.*" Probe:
  - "What might the prefix *im* mean?"
- Invite volunteers to respond; listen for someone to say: "not." Tell them the answer if needed: "That means, when we put that prefix *im,* which means 'not,' with that root, *migrant,* we come up with a word that specifically means 'someone who is not moving.'"
- Clarify that an *immigrant* is "someone who has chosen to move to a new country, but this person then settles where he or she has moved—and doesn't move again." Encourage students to add the prefix *im* to their **Prefixes Note-Catcher**.
- Paraphrase to clarify for all by saying something like: "So both immigrants and refugees move to another place, but they move for different reasons." Ask:
  - "So what is the difference between a *refugee* and an *immigrant*?"
- Listen for: "A *refugee* is someone who has been forced to move—to flee. But an *immigrant* has chosen to move." Then ask:
  - "So is Ha a refugee or an immigrant? How do you know?"
- Students should easily recognize that Ha is a refugee: She flees her home quickly because of impending danger.
- Invite students to get into numbered heads groups, with odd numbers pairing up and even numbers pairing up.
- Post questions one at a time. Invite students to Think-Pair-Share and record their suggested answers on the **Similarities and Differences in How Refugees and Immigrants Adapt Anchor Chart**:
  - "So what common challenges do you think refugees and immigrants both face?"
  - "Which challenges are unique to refugees?"
  - "Which challenges are unique to immigrants?"

B. Reading Aloud and Rereading for Gist: Paragraph 1 of "Refugee and Immigrant Children: A Comparison" (10 minutes)

- Display the first paragraph of the section "Refugee and Immigrant Children: A Comparison."

- Remind students that when text is really challenging, it is often helpful to chunk it into smaller sections. Today, they will hear you read just one paragraph of this section of the text, and then they will have time to think, talk, and annotate for gist.

- Read aloud only paragraph 1 in this section as students read silently.

- Then ask students to reread the paragraph on their own. Emphasize how important it is to reread with a text this challenging. It is fine if it still seems difficult.

- Ask students to Think-Pair-Share:

  - "So what is your initial sense of what this paragraph is mostly about?"

- Invite students to annotate the first paragraph for the gist based on their discussion with their partner.

- Invite volunteers to share their gist with the whole group. Listen for: "There are similarities in the challenges immigrant children and refugee children face in a new country."

Meeting Students' Needs

- Hearing a complex text read slowly, fluently, and without interruption or explanation promotes fluency for students: They are hearing a strong reader read the text aloud with accuracy and expression, and they are simultaneously looking at and thinking about the words on the printed page. Be sure to set clear expectations that students read along silently as you read the text aloud.

- To support ELL learners, consider providing definitions of challenging vocabulary in students' home language. Resources such as Google Translate and bilingual translation dictionaries can assist with one-word translations.

- Asking students to identify challenging vocabulary helps them monitor their understanding of a complex text.

C. Rereading and Text-Dependent Questions (15 minutes)

- Refocus the group. Display and distribute the **"Refugee and Immigrant Children: A Comparison" Paragraph 1, Text-Dependent Questions, Part A**.

- Reread just the first sentence of paragraph 1: "Refugee and immigrant children in Canada have significant similarities."

- Focus on the first text-dependent question:

  1. Invite students to read the question with you.

  2. Direct their attention to the part of the text that the vocabulary was taken from so they can read it in context.

---

3. Invite pairs to discuss what they think the answer might be.

4. Invite pairs to record their ideas on their note-catcher.

5. Select a student to share his or her answer with the whole group and clarify what it means where necessary.

6. Invite students to revise their notes if they are incorrect.

- Reread the second sentence of paragraph 1: "Both groups must deal with migration, which represents a disruptive loss to one's life."

- Invite students to Think-Pair-Share:

  - "We talked about *migration* earlier in relation to the word *immigrants*. What does *migration* mean?"

  - "Let's look at the *disruptive losses* part. So what does *disruptive* mean?"

- Listen for: "When something is *disruptive,* it 'stops things from happening.'" Point out to students that the word *disrupt* has a similar root as the word *interrupt*: *Rupt* means "to break."

- Focus students on the longest sentence in the paragraph. Reread this sentence as students read along silently: "Both refugee and immigrant children may encounter society's discrimination and racism, and both have to accomplish the central task of childhood and adolescence—developing a sense of identity—while trying to bridge generational and cultural gaps."

- Focus on the remaining text-dependent questions:

  1. Invite students to read the question with you.

  2. Direct their attention to the appropriate part of the text.

  3. Invite pairs to discuss what they think the answer might be.

  4. Invite pairs to record their ideas on their note-catcher.

  5. Select a student to share his or her answer with the whole group and clarify what it means where necessary.

  6. Invite students to revise their notes where they are incorrect.

  7. Move on to the next question.

Meeting Students' Needs

Text-dependent questions can be answered only by referring explicitly to the text being read. This encourages students to reread the text for further analysis and allows for a deeper understanding.

Closing and Assessment

A. Mix and Mingle: A Similarity in How Refugees and Immigrants Adapt (5 minutes)

- Ask students to skim the paragraph and underline every time the word *both* appears. Point out that the author uses this word five times in the paragraph. The author is choosing words carefully to signal to readers that there are five main similarities between how refugees and immigrants adapt.

- Ask students to take a few minutes to reread and think about one similarity in how refugees and immigrants adapt that they think is the most important and why.

- Mix and Mingle:

  - Invite students to move around the room for 15 seconds.

  - Use a signal (music or a hand signal) to get students to stop and share what they consider to be the most important similarity between how refugees and immigrants adapt with the student closest to them. Remind students to justify why they think that is the most important similarity.

  - Repeat until students have shared their similarity three times.

- Distribute the homework question.

Homework

- We discussed what *disruptive loss* means in this lesson. Complete the homework question at the very bottom of "Refugee and Immigrant Children: A Comparison" Paragraph 1, Text-Dependent Questions.

- Complete a first read of pages 238–247. Take notes (in your journals) using the Structured Notes Graphic Organizer. Focus on key details and the strongest evidence that reveal the challenges Ha is facing and her dynamic character, plus new or important vocabulary that helps you understand the specific challenges she faces as a refugee.

Meeting Students' Needs

- Vocabulary can be a source of difficulty for readers who struggle. Provide a brief list with definitions of the challenging vocabulary words from the reading homework. Do this only for students who need it.

- Most important is to provide words that cannot be easily determined from context. There are a few of these in the novel. On pages 238–247, these words might include *consulted* (seek information or advice), *monastery* (a place where monks, people who take religious vows, live), and *whim* (a sudden change of mind).

Analyzing the Significance of the Novel's Title

Connecting the Universal Refugee Experience to *Inside Out & Back Again*

Long-Term Targets Addressed (Based on ELA CCSS)

- I can cite text-based evidence that provides the strongest support for my analysis of literary text. (RL.8.1)
- I can cite text-based evidence that provides the strongest support for an analysis of informational text. (RI.8.1)
- I can read above-grade informational texts with scaffolding and support. (RI.8.10)

Supporting Learning Targets

- I can use the strongest evidence from the novel and from the informational text to support my answers to questions.
- I can make connections between evidence of the universal refugee experience and the title of the novel *Inside Out & Back Again*.

Ongoing Assessment

- "Refugee and Immigrant Children: A Comparison": Paragraph 1, Text-Dependent Questions, Part B

Agenda

1. Opening
   A. Engaging the Reader: Pages 237–247 of *Inside Out & Back Again* (5 minutes)
   B. Unpacking Learning Targets (2 minutes)

---

2. Work Time

    A. Jigsaw Part 1: Pairs Reread the First Paragraph of "Refugee and Immigrant Children: A Comparison" and Connect to a Poem from the Novel with Text-Dependent Questions (20 minutes)

    B. Jigsaw Part 2: Group Discussion to Determine Whether the Issues Are "Inside Out" or "Back Again" (13 minutes)

3. Closing and Assessment

    A. Adding to the Inside Out and Back Again Anchor Charts (5 minutes)

4. Homework

    A. Read pages 248–260; take notes using the Structured Notes Graphic Organizer.

Teaching Notes

- In this lesson, students continue to work with paragraph 1 of the section "Refugee and Immigrant Children: A Comparison" in the informational text "Refugee Children in Canada: Searching for Identity." They reread and answer additional text-dependent questions that relate directly to poems in the novel.

- Students participate in a Jigsaw activity, in which they work in pairs on different poems from the novel to connect real-life refugees' experiences to Ha's experiences. They find details in the poems that show evidence of the issues discussed in paragraph 1 of the "Refugee and Immigrant Children: A Comparison" section of the informational text.

- For the second part of the Jigsaw, students get back into numbered heads groups to share the learning from their poems and work together to determine whether the details they have collected from paragraph 1 and their poem best support the idea of turning "inside out" or coming "back again."

- The Jigsaw structure is abbreviated but similar to that of Unit 1, Lessons 7 and 11. In advance: To refresh your memory, review these lessons and the Jigsaw protocol (see the Appendix).

- Post: learning targets, directions for Jigsaw Part 1 (see Work Time), homework question.

Lesson Vocabulary

strongest evidence, dependency reversal, discrimination, racism

"Rainbow": lacquer, barrettes

"Loud Outside": pluck

"More Is Not Better": stalking

Materials

- *Inside Out & Back Again* (book; one per student)
- Sticky notes (three per student)
- Inside Out and Back Again Anchor Charts (begun in Lesson 8)
- "Refugee and Immigrant Children: A Comparison" (from Lesson 9)

- Document camera
- "Refugee and Immigrant Children: A Comparison": Paragraph 1, Text-Dependent Questions, Part B (one per student and one for display)

Opening

A. Engaging the Reader: Pages 237–247 of *Inside Out & Back Again* (5 minutes)

- Ensure that students have their copies of *Inside Out & Back Again*. Give students **sticky notes**. Invite them to record the strongest pieces of evidence that they found from pages 237–247 that reveal an aspect of Ha's dynamic character.

- Ask:
    - "How is Ha changing?"
    - "Where do your details best fit?"
    - "Do they show Ha turning 'inside out' or coming 'back again'?"

- Invite students to put their sticky note on either the **Inside Out Anchor Chart** or the **Back Again Anchor Chart**, based on which chart their evidence is most relevant to.

- Review three of the sticky notes with the whole group and invite discussion of why they show strong evidence revealing an aspect of Ha's dynamic character. Invite the whole group to determine whether the three chosen sticky notes have been put on the appropriate anchor charts.

B. Unpacking Learning Targets (2 minutes)

- Post the learning targets, and read them aloud as students follow along silently:
    - "I can use the strongest evidence from the novel and from the informational text to support my answers to questions."
    - "I can make connections from the universal refugee experience to the title of the novel *Inside Out & Back Again*."

- Invite students to Think-Pair-Share:
    - "What does the *strongest evidence* mean?"

- Continue to emphasize that now that they are eighth-graders, they are really being challenged to think about which evidence best proves their point. This is what they will have to do in college and in a broad range of career fields, from law, to auto mechanics, to social work.

Meeting Students' Needs

- Posting learning targets enables students to refer to them throughout the lesson to check their understanding. The learning targets also provide a reminder to students and teachers about the intended learning behind a given lesson or activity.

- Discussing and clarifying the language of learning targets help build academic vocabulary.

Work Time

A. Jigsaw Part 1: Pairs Reread the First Paragraph of "Refugee and Immigrant Children: A Comparison" and Connect to a Poem from the Novel with Text-Dependent Questions (20 minutes)

- Be sure students have their article "Refugee Children in Canada: Searching for Identity." Using a **document camera**, display paragraph 1 of the section **"Refugee and Immigrant Children: A Comparison."** Remind students that they began to look closely at this same paragraph of the text in the previous lesson. Emphasize how important and valuable it is to reread challenging text.

- Focus students on the second sentence in paragraph 1: "Both groups must deal with migration, which represents a disruptive loss to one's life."

- Remind students of the homework question:

  - "What does it mean to have a disruptive loss to one's life? What disruptive loss does Ha face in the novel *Inside Out & Back Again*?"

- Ask students to pair up to share their answers with a peer.

- Then ask for volunteers to share their answers with the whole group.

- Explain that today students will continue to build on this idea of the "disruptive loss" faced by refugees and immigrants.

- Display and distribute **"Refugee and Immigrant Children: A Comparison": Paragraph 1, Text-Dependent Questions, Part B**. Advise students that in this lesson they are going to use these questions and make notes to dig deeper into paragraph 1 of "Refugee and Immigrant Children: A Comparison" to understand it better. They are going to relate some of the challenges faced by the real-life refugee and immigrant children to Ha's experiences when she arrives in Alabama.

- Inform students that they will work in pairs for an activity called a Jigsaw. Each pair will be assigned one poem from the novel to connect to the real-life refugee experiences in "Refugee and Immigrant Children: A Comparison."

- Focus students on the question sheet. Point out the two columns in which students are to record answers. Make it clear that one column is for answers from the informational text, and the other is for details from their assigned poem.

- Pair students with a peer from a different numbered heads group. Assign each pair *one* of the following poems:

  - "Rainbow" (page 142)

  - "Loud Outside" (page 145)

  - "More Is Not Better" (page 168)

- As far as possible, ensure that at least one student in each numbered heads group is working on each of the poems, so that when they come back into their groups, they will have a range of poems to discuss.

- Post these directions:
  1. Reread the first paragraph of "Refugee and Immigrant Children: A Comparison."
  2. Think about the questions.
  3. Discuss your thinking with your partner.
  4. Then write down your thinking in the center column.
  5. On your own, reread your pair's assigned poem.
  6. With your partner, discuss your thinking about the key details in the poem.
  7. Then write down your thinking in the right-hand column.

- Ask students to ignore the synthesis questions at the bottom of the question sheet for now; they will return to this in the second part of the Jigsaw.

- Circulate to assist students in rereading the first paragraph of the informational text, reading the poem they have been assigned, and identifying details from the poem that are evidence of similar challenges to those faced by the refugees and immigrants.

- This vocabulary from the poems may need to be discussed:
  - "Rainbow": lacquer, barrettes
  - "Loud Outside": pluck
  - "More Is Not Better": stalking

    Pluck and *stalking* are words that students can probably figure out from the context. They may need to be told what *lacquer* and *barrettes* mean.

- As students work, ask probing questions as needed:
  - "What challenges do refugee and immigrant children face?"
  - "What evidence of those challenges can you find experienced by Ha in your poem?"
  - "What is the strongest evidence of those challenges that you can find in your poem?"

Meeting Students' Needs

- ELL students may be unfamiliar with more vocabulary words than are mentioned in this lesson. Check for comprehension of general words (e.g., law, peace, and so forth) that most students would know.

- Consider partnering ELL students who speak the same home language when discussion of complex content is required. This allows students to have more meaningful discussions and to clarify points in their native language.

- For students who struggle to read complex texts, consider previewing these vocabulary words from the text: *represents, endure, adolescents, interpreters,* and *encounter.* If you select additional words to preview, focus on those whose meaning may be difficult to determine using context clues from the text. It is important for students to practice using context clues to determine word meaning so that they become more proficient readers.

- Reviewing academic vocabulary words benefits all students developing academic language. Consider allowing students to grapple with a complex text before explicit teaching of vocabulary. After students have read for gist, they can identify challenging vocabulary for themselves. Teachers can address student-selected vocabulary as well as predetermined vocabulary upon subsequent encounters with the text. However, in some cases and with some students, preteaching selected vocabulary may be necessary.

- Text-dependent questions can be answered only by referring explicitly back to the text being read. This encourages students to reread the text for further analysis and allows for a deeper understanding.

B. Jigsaw Part 2: Group Discussion to Determine Whether the Issues Are "Inside Out" or "Back Again" (13 minutes)

- Refocus the whole group. Inform students that they will now share with their numbered heads group. Ask them to take their Text-Dependent Questions, Part B, handout with them.

- Give students about 5 minutes to share within their groups. Encourage them to record new evidence from other poems on their question sheets.

- In the last few minutes of this part of the agenda, be sure that groups discuss and record answers to the synthesis questions at the bottom of the handout:

  - "The final sentence of this paragraph of the informational text says, 'Perhaps the greatest threat to these children is not the stress of belonging to two cultures but the stress of belonging to none.' What is the author saying is the biggest problem, bigger than all the others in this paragraph? Is the author saying this will always be the case? What evidence do you have to answer that question?"

- Ask volunteers from each group to share their group's discussion with the whole class. Encourage students to focus on the word *perhaps* when looking for evidence, because it suggests that this might not always be the case.

Closing and Assessment

A. Adding to the Inside Out and Back Again Anchor Charts (5 minutes)

- Ask volunteers to share some of their details from the informational text and the poem and to justify whether they think the details show turning "inside out" or "back again."

- Record on Inside Out or Back Again Anchor Charts, according to student suggestions.

Meeting Students' Needs

Anchor charts serve as note-catchers when the class is co-constructing ideas.

Homework

Complete a first read of pages 248–260. Take notes (in your journals) using the Structured Notes Graphic Organizer. Focus on key details and the strongest evidence that reveals Ha's dynamic character and the challenges she is facing, plus new or important vocabulary that helps you understand the specific challenges of refugees.

Meeting Students' Needs

- Encourage ELL students or other struggling readers to choose one section from today (related to identity, adaptation, or mourning) and reread it in preparation for deeper work with the text in upcoming lessons. Since they have heard this text read aloud today and have thought about the gist of the text, this second reading will be manageable.

- Consider providing ELL students with a glossary of the terms that were discussed in class today from these three sections of the text.

- Vocabulary can be a source of difficulty for readers who struggle. Provide a brief list with definitions of the challenging vocabulary words from the reading homework. This should be done only for students who need it.

- Most important is to provide words that cannot be easily determined from context. There are few of these in the novel. On pages 248–260, these words might include *intermingling* (mix together) and *glutinous* (sticky like glue in texture).

LESSON 11

Close Reading

Paragraphs 2 and 3 of "Refugee and Immigrant Children: A Comparison" and Introducing the Grades 6–8 Expository Writing Evaluation Rubric

Long-Term Targets Addressed (Based on ELA CCSS)

- I can cite text-based evidence that provides the strongest support for an analysis of literary text. (RI.8.1)
- I can determine a theme or the central ideas of an informational text. (RI.8.2)
- I can analyze the structure of a specific paragraph in a text (including the role of particular sentences in developing and refining a key concept). (RI.8.5)
- I can read above-grade informational texts with scaffolding and support. (RI.8.10)

Supporting Learning Targets

- I can find the gist of paragraphs 2 and 3 of "Refugee and Immigrant Children: A Comparison."
- I can analyze how specific words, phrases, and sentences help me understand what refugee and immigrant children need for successful adaptation.
- I can read a text closely in order to answer text-dependent questions.

Ongoing Assessment

- "Refugee and Immigrant Children: A Comparison": Paragraphs 2 and 3, Text-Dependent Questions, Part A

Agenda

1. Opening
   A. Engaging the Reader: Pages 248–260 of *Inside Out & Back Again* (5 minutes)
   B. Unpacking Learning Targets (2 minutes)

2. Work Time

    A.   Reading Aloud and Rereading for Gist: Paragraphs 2 and 3 of "Refugee and Immigrant Children: A Comparison" (8 minutes)

    B.   Rereading and Text-Dependent Questions (15 minutes)

    C.   Introducing Grades 6–8 Expository Writing Evaluation Rubric, Row 1 (10 minutes)

3. Closing and Assessment

    A.   Analyzing the Model Essay Using the Rubric (5 minutes)

4. Homework

    A.   Complete the homework question at the bottom of "Refugee and Immigrant Children: A Comparison."

Teaching Notes

- This lesson introduces students to the second and third paragraphs of "Refugee and Immigrant Children: A Comparison" in the informational text "Refugee Children in Canada: Searching for Identity," which describes factors that make adaptation successful for refugee and immigrant children.

- This lesson is similar in format to Lesson 9, in which students read the first paragraph of this section of text for gist and answered text-dependent questions to dig deeper into the vocabulary and content.

- In advance: Review the second and third paragraphs of the "Refugee and Immigrant Children: A Comparison" section as well as the note-catchers in both this lesson and Lesson 12.

- Remind students that close reading is a challenge. They can all do it by working at it, and they will rise to the challenge.

- This lesson introduces students to the Grades 6–8 Expository Writing Evaluation Rubric, which has a great deal of academic vocabulary. Students are given a Writer's Glossary (also used in seventh grade). If students have had seventh-grade Module 1, they will be more familiar with these terms and concepts. Make clear that these are words they will return to throughout the year as they develop as writers; this lesson is just a preliminary exposure (or a review, if they learned the terms in seventh grade).

- Post: Inside Out and Back Again Anchor Charts, learning targets.

Lesson Vocabulary

adaptation, at large, to a larger extent, persecution, prolonged stays, atrocities

Materials

- *Inside Out & Back Again* (book; one per student)

- Inside Out Anchor Chart and Back Again Anchor Chart (begun in Lesson 8)

- Sticky notes (one per student)
- "Refugee and Immigrant Children: A Comparison" (from Lesson 9)
- "Refugee and Immigrant Children: A Comparison": Paragraphs 2 and 3, Text-Dependent Questions, Part A (one per student and one to display)
- Grades 6–8 Expository Writing Evaluation Rubric (one per student and one to display)
- Document camera
- Writer's Glossary for Row 1 of the Expository Writing Evaluation Rubric (one per student)
- Model essay: "How Ha's Mother Is Turned 'Inside Out'" (from Lesson 8; one per student and one to display)

Opening

A. Engaging the Reader: Pages 248–260 of *Inside Out & Back Again* (5 minutes)

- Be sure students have their copies of *Inside Out & Back Again*. Invite students to sit in numbered heads groups. Post the **Inside Out** and **Back Again Anchor Charts** where students can see them.
- Give students **sticky notes**. Invite them to record the strongest piece of evidence they found from pages 248–260 that reveals an aspect of Ha's dynamic character. Ask:
  - "How is Ha changing?"
- Then probe:
  - "Does your evidence show Ha turning 'inside out' or 'back again'? Why?"
- Ask students to put their sticky note on the anchor chart to which their evidence is most relevant.
- Review three of the sticky notes with the whole group. As a class, discuss the following:
  - "Why is this strong evidence that reveals an aspect of Ha's dynamic character?"
  - "Do you think these three sticky notes have been placed on the appropriate anchor chart? Why or why not?"

B. Unpacking Learning Targets (2 minutes)

- Focus students on the three learning targets, which are very similar to those from Lesson 9. Inform students that what they'll do with this lesson will be very much like what they did with the first paragraph several days ago. They will keep digging into the next two paragraphs of the informational text. Ask the class to Think-Pair-Share:
  - "Why is focusing on specific words, phrases, or sentences important?"
- Listen for students to recognize that paying attention to specific vocabulary helps them not only make sense of the text as a whole but also really think about important concepts about the world.
- Ask:
  - "How might reading more of this informational text continue to help us understand Ha better?"
- Listen for: "By reading this text, we are building knowledge about the universal refugee experience of turning 'inside out' and 'back again.' This is what Ha is going through."

---

244   **TEACHER GUIDE** · Grade 8 · Module 1 · Unit 2 · Lesson 11

- Remind students that this information helps them learn about the world and will be important when they write their End-of-Unit Assessment essay. Ha is just one unique (although fictional) example of the universal refugee experience.

Meeting Students' Needs

- Learning targets are a research-based strategy that helps all students, but it helps challenged learners the most.

- Posting learning targets enables students to refer to them throughout the lesson to check their understanding. The learning targets also provide a reminder to students and teachers about the intended learning behind a given lesson or activity.

Work Time

A. Reading Aloud and Rereading for Gist: Paragraphs 2 and 3 of "Refugee and Immigrant Children: A Comparison" (8 minutes)

- Invite students to get into numbered heads groups with numbers 1 and 2 pairing up and numbers 3 and 4 pairing up.

- Display the second and third paragraphs of the section **"Refugee and Immigrant Children: A Comparison"** (pages 589–590) and invite students to refer to their own texts.

- Remind them that when a text is challenging, it is often helpful to chunk it into smaller sections. Today, they will hear you read the next couple of paragraphs of this section of the text, and, as they did in Lesson 9, they will have time to think, talk, and annotate for gist.

- Read paragraph 2 in this section aloud as students read silently.

- Invite students to reread the paragraph silently.

- Ask students to Think-Pair-Share:

  - "So what is your initial sense of what paragraph 2 is mostly about?"

- Invite students to annotate paragraph 2 for the gist based on their pair discussion.

- Invite volunteers to share their gist with the whole group. Listen for: "the factors that make refugee and immigrant children adapt successfully."

- Read paragraph 3 in this section aloud as students read silently.

- Invite students to reread the paragraph silently.

- Ask students to Think-Pair-Share:

  - "So what is your initial sense of what paragraph 3 is mostly about?"

- Invite students to annotate paragraph 3 for the gist based on their pair discussion.

- Invite volunteers to share their gist with the whole group. Listen for: "the factors that affect the adaptation of refugee children more than immigrant children."

Meeting Students' Needs

Asking students to identify challenging vocabulary helps them monitor their understanding of a complex text.

B. Rereading and Text-Dependent Questions (15 minutes)

- Refocus the group. Display and distribute **"Refugee and Immigrant Children: A Comparison": Paragraphs 2 and 3, Text-Dependent Questions, Part A**.

- Reread the first sentence of paragraph 2 of this section of the text: "Successful adaptation can bring with it the opportunity for growth."

- Focus on the first text-dependent question:

  1. Invite students to read the question with you.

  2. Direct their attention to the part of the text that the vocabulary was taken from so they can read it in context.

  3. Invite pairs to discuss what they think the answer might be.

  4. Invite pairs to record their ideas on their text-dependent questions handout.

  5. Select a numbered heads group member to share his or her answer with the whole class and clarify what it means where necessary.

  6. Invite students to revise their notes where they are incorrect.

- Ensure that students have a thorough understanding of what *adaptation* means before moving on, as understanding what this word means is crucial to understanding the two paragraphs.

- Repeat the same process for Questions 2–4.

- Reread these sentences from paragraph 3: "First, refugee children often have experienced the tragedy and trauma of war, including persecution, dangerous escapes, and prolonged stays in refugee camps. Some have witnessed killings, torture, and rape—including atrocities against family members."

- Ask students to Think-Pair-Share:

  - "What does *persecution* mean?"

- Students will not be able to figure this out from the context. Some may already know the meaning; if not, either tell them or invite a student to look it up in a dictionary.

- Repeat the numbered questioning process for the final text-dependent questions.

Meeting Students' Needs

- Hearing a complex text read slowly, fluently, and without interruption or explanation promotes fluency for students: They are hearing a strong reader read the text aloud with accuracy and expression, and they are simultaneously looking at and thinking about the words on the printed page. Set clear expectations that students read along silently as you read the text aloud.

- To support ELL students, consider providing definitions of challenging vocabulary in students' home language. Resources such as Google Translate and bilingual translation dictionaries can assist with one-word translations.

- Text-dependent questions can be answered only by referring explicitly to the text being read. This encourages students to reread the text for further analysis and allows for a deeper understanding.

C. Introducing Grades 6–8 Expository Writing Evaluation Rubric, Row 1 (10 minutes)

- Distribute the **Grades 6–8 Expository Writing Evaluation Rubric**. If possible, display a copy of the rubric on a **document camera** so that all students can see when you are circling vocabulary words and discussing the criteria. Inform the students:

  - "This rubric is used to look at student writing for sixth through eighth grades. This rubric tells what we expect students at your grade level to do when they write an essay. In the next few lessons, you are going to learn what is in this rubric. Then we will use it as you write your essay. By doing this, you will have inside information to become a great writer."

- Ask students to pair up with someone in their numbered heads group. Ask the pairs to read only the first row of the rubric and to circle words they do not know or are unsure about.

- Call on several pairs to share the words they identified. Circle these words on your copy on the document camera. Expect that students will not know the meanings of these vocabulary words: *content, extent, conveys, compelling, task, insightful, comprehension, logically,* and its opposite, *illogically.* Do not define the words yet.

- Distribute the **Writer's Glossary for Row 1 of the Expository Writing Rubric**. Point out to students that certain vocabulary words are boldfaced and defined.

- Discuss and illustrate the definitions of the words already on the page, and add any others that students contribute. (See the Writer's Glossary for Row 1 for definitions.) Students may know some of these words as they are used in other ways, so be sure that they understand them as they are used to refer to writing in the rubric.

- Explain to students that these are sophisticated words and concepts about writing and that they will continue to work to understand what these mean throughout the year. Applying criteria to a model often helps make the criteria clear. That is what they will do next.

Closing and Assessment

A. Analyzing the Model Essay Using the Rubric (5 minutes)

- Inform the class: "Now we are going to use the model essay to understand what the rubric is saying writers should do."

- Explain that the first row across the rubric describes how a writer introduces the topic of an essay. (Be sure students are clear that *columns* run up and down, or vertically, from top to bottom, and that *rows* are the horizontal lines from left to right.) Say something like:

  - "We need to look closely at how an essay would follow what the rubric describes so that you know what you have to do to write an effective essay. We are going to be using the model essay to do that."

- Inform students that the numbered boxes on the top row of the rubric describe how well an essay follows the criteria in the left-most column. Box 4 describes the best essay, so inform students that they will look at the model essay to see what this description means. Read aloud Level 4 and say: "This means that the essay should start by telling the reader what the topic will be, but saying it in a way that is interesting so the reader wants to read the rest."

- Display model essay: "How Ha's Mother Is Turned 'Inside Out'" (from Lesson 8) and invite students to refer to their own text. Ask:

  - "Does this paragraph introduce the topic in an interesting, compelling way? If so, which words or phrases spark the reader's interest?"

- Listen for: "Words like *afraid, fleeing,* and being *turned inside out* make the essay sound like it is about scary experiences, which makes it sound interesting."

- Invite students to reread the rest of the essay to see whether they think the writer knows the book well. How can they tell? The student pairs should find three things in the essay that show the writer knows the book. Ask them to number these three items in the margin of their copy of the model essay.

- Once they have finished, cold-call on several pairs to see what they have selected. Then say: "So the model essay does follow the best description of the rubric. It tells the topic early in an interesting way, and it shows that the writer understands the book well. These are two things you want to do in your own essays."

- Remind students that they will work more with this model and rubric in future lessons; be sure they file away these key resources.

Homework

We discussed what *adaptation* means in this lesson. Complete the homework question at the bottom of the "Refugee and Immigrant Children: A Comparison": Paragraphs 2 and 3, Text-Dependent Questions, Part A.

LESSON 12

Analyzing the Significance of the Novel's Title

Connecting the Universal Refugee Experience to *Inside Out & Back Again,* Part 2

Long-Term Targets Addressed (Based on ELA CCSS)

- I can cite text-based evidence that provides the strongest support for my analysis of literary text. (RL.8.1)
- I can cite text-based evidence that provides the strongest support for an analysis of informational text. (RI.8.1)
- I can read above-grade informational texts with scaffolding and support. (RI.8.10)

Supporting Learning Targets

- I can use the strongest evidence from the novel and from the informational text to support my answers to questions.
- I can make connections between evidence of the universal refugee experience and the title of the novel *Inside Out & Back Again.*

Ongoing Assessment

- "Refugee and Immigrant Children: A Comparison": Paragraphs 2 and 3, Text-Dependent Questions, Part B

Agenda

1. Opening
   A. Unpacking Learning Targets (2 minutes)
2. Work Time
   A. Jigsaw Part 1: Reread Paragraphs 2 and 3 of "Refugee and Immigrant Children: A Comparison" and Connect to a Poem from the Novel with Text-Dependent Questions (23 minutes)
   B. Jigsaw Part 2: Group Discussion to Share Answers and Discuss a Synthesis Question (15 minutes)

3. Closing and Assessment

   A. Adding to the Inside Out and Back Again Anchor Charts (5 minutes)

4. Homework

   A. Reread pages 1–17 and collect the strongest evidence you can find to answer a question.

Teaching Notes

- This lesson follows the pattern of Lesson 10. In this lesson, students continue to work with paragraphs 2 and 3 of the section "Refugee and Immigrant Children: A Comparison" in the informational text "Refugee Children in Canada: Searching for Identity." They reread and answer additional text-dependent questions that relate directly to poems in the novel.

- Students participate in a Jigsaw activity in which they work in pairs on different poems from the novel to connect real-life refugees' experiences to Ha's experiences. They find details in the poems that show evidence of the issues discussed in paragraphs 2 and 3 of the "Refugee and Immigrant Children: A Comparison" section of the informational text.

- For the second part of the Jigsaw, students get back into numbered heads groups to answer a synthesis question.

- As a whole group, students then determine whether the details they have collected from paragraphs 2 and 3 and their poem best support the idea of turning "inside out" or coming "back again."

- For homework, students revisit the beginning of the novel to answer the question, "Who is Ha before she is asked to flee?" This helps prepare them for the End-of-Unit Assessment essay. In the essay's introductory paragraph, students will be expected to describe who Ha is before she flees, to serve as a point of reference for writing about how she turns "inside out" and "back again."

- Post: learning targets, directions for Jigsaw Part 1 (see Work Time), homework question.

Lesson Vocabulary

severity, traumatic events, reception, resiliency

"Neighbors": hogwash, puckering, widow, volunteers

"Laugh Back": Students should be familiar with all of the vocabulary in this poem

"NOW!": butcher, motions

Materials

- *Inside Out & Back Again* (book; one per student)

- "Refugee and Immigrant Children: A Comparison" (from Lesson 9)

- Document camera

- "Refugee and Immigrant Children: A Comparison": Paragraphs 2 and 3, Text-Dependent Questions, Part B (one per student and one to display)

- Inside Out and Back Again Anchor Charts (begun in Lesson 8)

- Homework Purpose for Reading: Who Is Ha before She Is Forced to Flee Her Home? (one per student)

- Grades 6–8 Expository Writing Evaluation Rubric (from Lesson 11; one per student and one to display)

Opening

A. Unpacking Learning Targets (2 minutes)

- Post the learning targets and read them aloud as students follow along silently:

  - "I can use the strongest evidence from the novel and from the informational text to support my answers to questions."

  - "I can make connections between evidence of the universal refugee experience and the title of the novel *Inside Out & Back Again*."

- Remind students that they have seen these learning targets in previous lessons, so they should be familiar with them by now.

- Continue to emphasize that now that they are eighth-graders, they are really being challenged to think about which evidence best proves their point. This is what they will have to do in college and in a broad range of career fields, from law, to auto mechanics, to social work.

Meeting Students' Needs

- Posting learning targets enables students to refer to them throughout the lesson to check their understanding. The learning targets also provide a reminder to students and teachers about the intended learning behind a given lesson or activity.

- Discussing and clarifying the language of learning targets help build academic vocabulary.

Work Time

A. Jigsaw Part 1: Reread Paragraphs 2 and 3 of "Refugee and Immigrant Children: A Comparison" and Connect to a Poem from the Novel with Text-Dependent Questions (23 minutes)

- Be sure students have their copies of **Inside Out & Back Again** as well as the informational text section **"Refugee and Immigrant Children: A Comparison."** Using a **document camera**, display paragraphs 2 and 3 of the section "Refugee and Immigrant Children: A Comparison." Remind students that they began to look closely at these same paragraphs in the previous lesson. Emphasize how important and valuable it is to reread challenging text.

- Focus students on the second sentence in paragraph 2: "How well children adapt is influenced by several factors, including age at arrival, severity of previous traumatic events, family background, individual resiliency, and reception by the host community and society."

- Remind students of the homework questions:

  - "Which factors help Ha adapt successfully in Alabama? How does she grow as a person as a result?"

- Invite students to pair up to share their answers with a peer.

- Ask for volunteers to share their answers with the whole group.

- Display and distribute **"Refugee and Immigrant Children: A Comparison": Paragraphs 2 and 3, Text-Dependent Questions, Part B**. Advise students that today, just like a few lessons ago, they are going to use these questions and make notes to dig deeper into paragraphs 2 and 3 to better understand the process of adaptation faced by refugee and immigrant children. They are going to relate challenges faced by real-life refugee and immigrant children to Ha's experiences when she arrives in Alabama.

- Inform students that they will work in pairs for the Jigsaw activity. Each pair will be assigned one poem from the novel to connect to the real-life refugee experiences in "Refugee and Immigrant Children: A Comparison."

- Focus students on the question sheet. Point out the two columns in which students are to record answers. Make it clear that one column is for answers from the informational text, and the other is for details from their assigned poem.

- Pair students with a student from a different numbered heads group. Assign each pair just *one* of the following poems:

  - "Neighbors" (page 162)

  - "Laugh Back" (page 147)

  - "NOW!" (page 217)

- As far as possible, ensure that at least one student in each numbered heads group is working on each of the poems so that when they come back into their groups, they will have a range of poems to discuss.

- Post these directions:

  1. Reread paragraphs 2 and 3 of "Refugee and Immigrant Children: A Comparison."

  2. Think about the questions.

  3. Discuss your thinking with your partner.

  4. Then write down your thinking in the center column.

  5. On your own, reread your pair's assigned poem.

  6. With your partner, discuss your thinking about the key details in the poem.

  7. Then write down your thinking in the right-hand column.

- Ask students to ignore the synthesis question at the bottom of the form for now; they will return to this in the second part of the Jigsaw.

- Circulate to assist students in rereading the second and third paragraphs of the informational text, reading the poem they have been assigned, and identifying details from the poem that are evidence of similar challenges to those faced by the refugees and immigrants.

- This vocabulary from the poems may need to be discussed:

  - "Neighbors": hogwash, puckering, widow, volunteers

  - "Laugh Back": Students should be familiar with all of the vocabulary in this poem.

  - "NOW!": butcher, motions

- As students work, ask probing questions as needed:

  - "Which factors affect how successfully refugee and immigrant children adapt?"

  - "What evidence of those factors can you find experienced by Ha in your poem?"

  - "What is the strongest evidence of those challenges that you can find in your poem?"

Meeting Students' Needs

- ELL students may be unfamiliar with more vocabulary words than are mentioned in this lesson. Check for comprehension of general words that most students would know.

- Consider partnering ELL students who speak the same home language when discussion of complex content is required. This allows students to have more meaningful discussions and to clarify points in their native language.

- For students who struggle to read complex texts, consider previewing these vocabulary words from the text: *society, settlement, crucial, integrate, characteristics,* and *torture.* If you select additional words to preview, focus on those whose meaning may be difficult to determine using context clues from the text. It is important for students to practice using context clues to determine word meaning so that they become more proficient readers.

- Reviewing academic vocabulary words benefits all students developing academic language. Consider allowing students to grapple with a complex text before explicit teaching of vocabulary. After students have read for gist, they can identify challenging vocabulary for themselves. Teachers can address student-selected vocabulary as well as predetermined vocabulary in subsequent encounters with the text. However, in some cases and with some students, preteaching selected vocabulary may be necessary.

- Text-dependent questions can be answered only by referring explicitly back to the text being read. This encourages students to reread the text for further analysis and allows for a deeper understanding.

B. Jigsaw Part 2: Group Discussion to Share Answers and Discuss a Synthesis Question (15 minutes)

- Refocus the whole group. Inform students that they will now share with their numbered heads group. Ask them to take their paragraphs 2 and 3, Text-Dependent Questions, Part B, handout with them.

- Give students about 5 minutes to share within their groups. Encourage them to record new evidence from other poems on their question sheets.

- In the last few minutes of this part of the agenda, be sure that groups discuss and record an answer to the synthesis question at the bottom of their handout:

  - "How do some of the challenges described in these two paragraphs about adaptation differ from Ha's experiences as a refugee?"

- Ask volunteers from each group to share the group discussion with the whole class.

Closing and Assessment

A. Adding to the Inside Out and Back Again Anchor Charts (5 minutes)

- Select volunteers to share some of their details from the informational text and the poem and to justify whether they think the details show turning inside out or back again.

- Record on the **Inside Out Anchor Chart** or the **Back Again Anchor Chart**, according to class suggestions.

- Distribute **Homework Purpose for Reading: Who Is Ha before She Is Forced to Flee Her Home?**

Meeting Students' Needs

Anchor charts serve as note-catchers when the class is co-constructing ideas.

Homework

Remember that for the End-of-Unit Assessment, you will be writing about how the novel's title, *Inside Out & Back Again,* relates to the universal refugee experience of fleeing and finding home, using Ha as an example. To describe how Ha turns "inside out" and "back again," you first need to describe who she is before she is forced to flee her home. Reread pages 1–17, and collect the strongest evidence you can find to answer this question:

- "Who is Ha before she is forced to flee her home?"

LESSON 13

Close Reading

Paragraph 4 of "Refugee and Immigrant Children: A Comparison"

Long-Term Targets Addressed (Based on ELA CCSS)

- I can cite text-based evidence that provides the strongest support for an analysis of literary text. (RI.8.1)

- I can determine a theme or the central ideas of an informational text. (RI.8.2)

- I can analyze the structure of a specific paragraph in a text (including the role of particular sentences in developing and refining a key concept). (RI.8.5)

- I can read above-grade informational texts with scaffolding and support. (RI.8.10)

Supporting Learning Targets

- I can find the gist of paragraph 4 of "Refugee and Immigrant Children: A Comparison."

- I can analyze how specific words, phrases, and sentences help me understand what refugee and immigrant children need for successful adaptation.

- I can read a text closely to answer text-dependent questions.

Ongoing Assessment

- "Refugee and Immigrant Children: A Comparison": Paragraph 4, Text-Dependent Questions, Part A

Agenda

1. Opening
   A. Sharing Evidence from Homework (5 minutes)
   B. Unpacking Learning Targets (2 minutes)

---

2. Work Time

    A. Reading Aloud and Rereading for Gist: Paragraph 4 of "Refugee and Immigrant Children: A Comparison" (8 minutes)

    B. Rereading and Text-Dependent Questions (15 minutes)

    C. Introducing Row 2 of the Grades 6–8 Expository Writing Evaluation Rubric (10 minutes)

3. Closing and Assessment

    A. Analyzing the Model Essay Using the Rubric (5 minutes)

4. Homework

    A. Complete the homework questions at the bottom of the "Refugee and Immigrant Children: A Comparison."

Teaching Notes

- This lesson introduces students to the fourth paragraph of "Refugee and Immigrant Children: A Comparison" in the informational text "Refugee Children in Canada: Searching for Identity," which describes how refugees mourn what they leave behind.

- This lesson is similar in format to Lessons 9 and 11, in which students read the first three paragraphs of this section of text for gist and answered text-dependent questions to dig deeper into the vocabulary and content.

- In advance: Review the fourth paragraph of the "Refugee and Immigrant Children: A Comparison" section as well as the note-catchers in both this lesson and Lesson 14.

- This lesson introduces students to the second row of the Grades 6–8 Expository Writing Evaluation Rubric, which has a great deal of academic vocabulary. As in Lesson 11, students are given a Writer's Glossary (also used in seventh grade). If students have had seventh-grade Module 1, they will be more familiar with these terms and concepts. Make clear that these are words they will return to throughout the year as they develop as writers; this lesson is just a preliminary exposure (or a review, if they learned the terms in seventh grade).

- Post: Inside Out and Back Again Anchor Charts, learning targets.

Lesson Vocabulary

envision (the possibility), typically, at large, mourning

Words from Row 2 of rubric: command, relevant/irrelevant, concrete details, sustain, varied (variety), partially, textual evidence, consistent/inconsistent, minimal, valid/invalid

Materials

- *Inside Out & Back Again* (book; one per student)

- Inside Out and Back Again Anchor Charts (begun in Lesson 8)

- "Refugee and Immigrant Children: A Comparison" (from Lesson 9)

- "Refugee and Immigrant Children: A Comparison": Paragraph 4, Text-Dependent Questions, Part A (one per student and one to display)

- Grades 6–8 Expository Writing Evaluation Rubric (from Lesson 11; one per student and one to display)

- Writer's Glossary for Row 2 of the Expository Writing Rubric (one per student)

- Document camera

- Model essay: "How Ha's Mother Is Turned 'Inside Out'" (from Lesson 8; one per student and one to display)

Opening

A. Sharing Evidence from Homework (5 minutes)

- Be sure students have their copies of *Inside Out & Back Again*. Invite students to sit in numbered heads groups. Pair up number 1s with number 2s and number 3s with number 4s.

- Ask students to share the strongest evidence they found in pages 1–17 to answer the question:

  - "Who is Ha before she is forced to flee her home?"

- Invite students to add any new evidence that their partner found to their own Homework Purpose for Reading: Who Is Ha before She Is Forced to Flee Her Home?

Meeting Students' Needs

- Learning targets are a research-based strategy that helps all students, especially challenged learners.

- Posting learning targets enables students to refer to them throughout the lesson to check their understanding. The learning targets also provide a reminder to students and teachers about the intended learning behind a given lesson or activity.

B. Unpacking Learning Targets (2 minutes)

- Focus students on the three learning targets, which are similar to those from Lessons 9 and 11.

- Advise students that this lesson will be very much like what they have done with the first three paragraphs of text in previous lessons. They will keep digging into the next paragraph of the informational text.

- Ask the class to Think-Pair-Share:

  - "Why is reading a text closely to answer text-dependent questions a useful skill?"

- Listen for students to recognize that to answer text-dependent questions, they have to dig deeply into a text and really understand the meaning, which is something that they will have to do in college and at work to thoroughly understand the texts they will encounter.

- Ask:

  - "How might reading more of this informational text continue to help us understand Ha better?"

- Listen for: "By reading this text, we are building knowledge about the universal refugee experience of turning 'inside out' and 'back again.' This is what Ha is going through."

- Remind students that this information helps them learn about the world and will be important when they write their End-of-Unit Assessment essay. Ha is just one unique (although fictional) example of the universal refugee experience.

Work Time

A. Reading Aloud and Rereading for Gist: Paragraph 4 of "Refugee and Immigrant Children: A Comparison" (8 minutes)

- Invite students to get into numbered heads groups, with number 1s and 4s pairing up and number 2s and 3s pairing up.

- Display the fourth paragraph of the section **"Refugee and Immigrant Children: A Comparison"** (page 590), and invite students to refer to their own texts.

- Remind them that when a text is challenging, it is often helpful to chunk it into smaller sections. Today, they will hear you read the next couple of paragraphs of this section of the text, and, as they did in Lessons 9 and 11, they will have time to think, talk, and annotate for gist.

- Read aloud paragraph 4 in this section as students read silently.

- Invite students to reread the paragraph silently.

- Ask them to Think-Pair-Share:

  - "So what is your initial sense of what paragraph 4 is mostly about?"

- Invite students to annotate paragraph 4 for the gist based on their pair discussion.

- Ask for volunteers to share their gist with the whole group. Listen for: "Refugee children and their families mourn the things they leave behind, but children often don't talk about it, so it isn't recognized."

Meeting Students' Needs

- Hearing a complex text read slowly, fluently, and without interruption or explanation promotes fluency for students: They are hearing a strong reader read the text aloud with accuracy and expression, and they are simultaneously looking at and thinking about the words on the printed page. Set clear expectations that students read along silently as you read the text aloud.

- To support ELL students, consider providing definitions of challenging vocabulary in students' home language. Resources such as Google Translate and bilingual translation dictionaries can assist with one-word translations.

- Asking students to identify challenging vocabulary helps them monitor their understanding of a complex text.

B. Rereading and Text-Dependent Questions (15 minutes)

- Refocus the group. Display and distribute the **"Refugee and Immigrant Children: A Comparison":** **Paragraph 4, Text-Dependent Questions, Part A**.

- Reread the first sentence of paragraph 4 of this section of the text: "Typically, immigrants can, at least, envision the possibility of returning to their countries; most refugees cannot."

- Focus on the first text-dependent question:

  1. Invite students to read the question with you.

  2. Direct their attention to the part of the text that the vocabulary is taken from so they can read it in context.

  3. Invite pairs to discuss what they think the answer might be.

  4. Ask pairs to record their ideas on their text-dependent questions handout.

  5. Select a numbered heads group member to share his or her answer with the whole class and clarify what it means where necessary.

  6. Invite students to revise their notes where they are incorrect.

- Repeat the same process for Questions 2–4.

- Ensure that students have a thorough understanding of what *mourning* means before moving on, as understanding what this word means is crucial to understanding the two paragraphs.

Meeting Students' Needs

Text-dependent questions can be answered only by referring explicitly to the text being read. This encourages students to reread the text for further analysis and allows for a deeper understanding.

C. Introducing Row 2 of the Grades 6–8 Expository Writing Evaluation Rubric (10 minutes)

- Ask students to take out their copy of the **Grades 6–8 Expository Writing Evaluation Rubric**. Ask students to read across Row 2 and circle any words they do not know or are unsure about.

- Distribute the **Writer's Glossary for Row 2 of the Expository Writing Evaluation Rubric**. Invite students to work with their partners to check the words there that they circled and to add any that are not already on the sheet.

- Review the vocabulary words in the Writer's Glossary (*command, relevant* and *irrelevant, concrete details, sustain, varied* [*variety*], *partially, textual evidence, consistent* and *inconsistent, minimal, valid* and *invalid*) and any that students added. Provide simple definitions that fit the context, and/or ask students to contribute definitions for words they know. Explain the words that are matched with their opposites, such as *relevant* and *irrelevant*.

- As you and students provide definitions for the words, talk about what each of the levels (columns) of the Command of Evidence row means in terms of how a student writes. For example, for the Criteria box, you might say: "This row is about how well a writer proves his or her ideas with

---

examples. These examples should come from other sources and provide logical support for the main message the writer wants the reader to understand."

- Once you have modeled how to do this, ask students to volunteer to take one of the level boxes and add the descriptors in their own words. If you think students need to work with a peer here, they can turn and talk about it before they volunteer an answer.

Closing and Assessment

A. Analyzing the Model Essay Using the Rubric (5 minutes)

- Inform the class: "Now we are going to use the model essay to understand what the rubric is saying writers should do." Ask students to Think-Pair-Share:
  - "If we are going to look at the model against the second row of the rubric, what are we going to be focusing on in the model essay?"
- Listen for students to explain that they are going to be looking at the evidence the author has used in the model to support the claims made.
- Remind students that Level 4 is a great piece of writing. Read aloud Level 4 of Row 2 of the rubric and say: "This means that the claims the author has made should be supported with a few different pieces of well-chosen evidence from the text, and there should be evidence all the way through the model essay."
- Using a **document camera**, display the **model essay: "How Ha's Mother Is Turned 'Inside Out'"** (from Lesson 8) and invite students to refer to their own text.
- Focus students on the second paragraph. Ask:
  - "Does this paragraph contain evidence?"
  - "Does the evidence support the claim the author has made?"
  - "Is there more than one piece of evidence to support the claim?"
  - "Does the cited evidence come from different texts?"
- Listen for students to confirm that the evidence contained in paragraph 2 does support the claim the author has made and that there are multiple pieces of evidence from the novel and from the informational text.
- Invite students to reread the rest of the essay one paragraph at a time, and at the end of each paragraph, discuss with their numbered heads group whether the author has used well-chosen evidence from more than one piece of text to support the claims in the paragraph.
- Explain that the opening and concluding paragraphs may not contain any evidence, because those paragraphs are outlining the topic and purpose of the essay rather than getting into the details of the claims.
- Once students have finished, cold-call on several pairs to determine whether the author of the model has used well-chosen evidence from more than one piece of text throughout the essay to support its claims. Then say: "So the model essay does follow the best description of the rubric. It

uses well-chosen evidence from more than one piece of text throughout the essay to support the claims made. This is something I want you to do in your own essays."

- Remind students that they will work more with this model and rubric in future lessons; be sure they file away these key resources.

Homework

We discussed what *mourning* means in this lesson. Complete the homework questions at the bottom of the handout "Refugee and Immigrant Children: A Comparison": Paragraph 4, Text-Dependent Questions, Part A.

LESSON 14

Analyzing the Significance of the Novel's Title

Connecting the Universal Refugee Experience to *Inside Out & Back Again*, Part 3

Long-Term Targets Addressed (Based on ELA CCSS)

- I can cite text-based evidence that provides the strongest support for my analysis of literary text. (RL.8.1)
- I can cite text-based evidence that provides the strongest support for an analysis of informational text. (RI.8.1)
- I can read above-grade informational texts with scaffolding and support. (RI.8.10)

Supporting Learning Targets

- I can use the strongest evidence from the novel and from the informational text to support my answers to questions.
- I can make connections between evidence of the universal refugee experience and the title of the novel *Inside Out & Back Again*.

Ongoing Assessment

- "Refugee and Immigrant Children: A Comparison": Paragraph 4, Text-Dependent Questions, Part B

Agenda

1. Opening
   A. Unpacking Learning Targets (2 minutes)

2. Work Time

   A. Jigsaw Part 1: Pairs Reread Paragraph 4 of "Refugee and Immigrant Children: A Comparison" and Connect to a Poem from the Novel with Text-Dependent Questions (23 minutes)

   B. Jigsaw Part 2: Group Discussion to Share Answers and Revisit Our Prediction (15 minutes)

3. Closing and Assessment

   A. Adding to the Inside Out and Back Again Anchor Charts (5 minutes)

4. Homework

   A. Reread pages 18–49 and continue to collect evidence to answer a question.

Teaching Notes

- This lesson follows the pattern of Lessons 10 and 12. Students continue to work with paragraph 4 of the section "Refugee and Immigrant Children: A Comparison" in the informational text "Refugee Children in Canada: Searching for Identity." They reread and answer additional text-dependent questions that relate directly to poems in the novel.

- Students participate in a Jigsaw activity in which they work in pairs on different poems from the novel to connect real-life refugees' experiences to Ha's experiences. They find details in the poems that show evidence of the process of mourning discussed in paragraph 4.

- Note that in the second part of the Jigsaw, students begin to synthesize their learning from Lessons 9–14. They get back into numbered heads groups to return to the original predictions they made in Lesson 9 about the similarities and differences between how refugees and immigrants adapt.

- Post: learning targets, directions for Jigsaw Part 1 (see Work Time), homework question.

Lesson Vocabulary

Process of mourning

"Not the Same": pouches

"Can't Help": solitude, jasmine, ashy, inhaling, yearning

Materials

- *Inside Out & Back Again* (book; one per student)

- "Refugee and Immigrant Children: A Comparison" (from Lesson 9)

- "Refugee and Immigrant Children: A Comparison": Paragraph 4, Text-Dependent Questions, Part B (one per student and one to display)

- Document camera

- Inside Out Anchor Chart and Back Again Anchor Chart (begun in Lesson 8)

- Homework Purpose for Reading: Who Is Ha before She Is Forced to Flee Her Home? (begun as homework for Lesson 12)

Opening

A. Unpacking Learning Targets (2 minutes)

- Post the learning targets and read them aloud as students follow along silently:

  - "I can use the strongest evidence from the novel and from the informational text to support my answers to questions."

  - "I can make connections between evidence of the universal refugee experience and the title of the novel *Inside Out & Back Again.*"

- Remind students that they have seen these learning targets in previous lessons, so they should be familiar with them by now.

- Continue to emphasize that now that they are eighth-graders, they are really being challenged to think about which evidence best proves their point. This is what they will have to do in college and in a broad range of career fields, from law, to auto mechanics, to social work.

Meeting Students' Needs

- Posting learning targets enables students to refer to them throughout the lesson to check their understanding. The learning targets also provide a reminder to students and teachers about the intended learning behind a given lesson or activity.

- Discussing and clarifying the language of learning targets help build academic vocabulary.

Work Time

A. Jigsaw Part 1: Pairs Reread Paragraph 4 of "Refugee and Immigrant Children: A Comparison" and Connect to a Poem from the Novel with Text-Dependent Questions (23 minutes)

- Be sure students have their article "Refugee Children in Canada: Searching for Identity." Display paragraph 4 of the section **"Refugee and Immigrant Children: A Comparison."** Remind students that they began to look closely at this same paragraph in the previous lesson. Emphasize how important and valuable it is to reread challenging text.

- Focus students on the second sentence in paragraph 4: "It is only natural that refugee children, along with their families, go through a process of mourning those losses."

- Remind students of the homework questions:

  - "What do Ha and her family mourn the loss of? How do you know?"

- Invite students to pair up to share their answers with a peer.

- Ask for volunteers to share their answers with the whole group.

- Distribute **"Refugee and Immigrant Children: A Comparison": Paragraph 4, Text-Dependent Questions, Part B**, and display it using a **document camera**. Inform students that today they are going to use these questions and make notes to dig deeper into paragraph 4 and better understand the mourning process for refugee children. They are going to relate the process of mourning by the real-life refugee children to Ha's experiences when she arrives in Alabama.

- Inform students that they will work in pairs. Each pair will be assigned one poem from the novel to connect to the real-life refugee experiences in "Refugee and Immigrant Children: A Comparison."

- Focus students on the question sheet. Point out the two columns in which they are to record answers. Remind them that, as in Lessons 10 and 12, one column is for answers from the informational text, and the other is for details from their assigned poem.

- Pair up students with a peer from a different numbered heads group to perform the Jigsaw protocol. Assign each pair just *one* of the following poems:

  - "Not the Same" (page 232)

  - "Can't Help" (page 173)

  - "Eternal Peace" (page 251)

- As far as possible, ensure that at least one student in each numbered heads group is working on each of the poems so that when they come back into their groups, they will have a range of poems to discuss.

- Post these directions:

  1. Reread paragraph 4 of "Refugee and Immigrant Children: A Comparison."

  2. Think about the questions.

  3. Discuss your thinking with your partner.

  4. Then write down your thinking in the center column.

  5. On your own, reread your pair's assigned poem.

  6. With your partner, discuss your thinking about the key details in the poem.

  7. Then write down your thinking in the right-hand column.

- Ask students to ignore the synthesis questions at the bottom of the form for now; they will return to this in the second part of the Jigsaw.

- Circulate to assist students in rereading paragraph 4 of the informational text, reading the poem they have been assigned, and identifying details from the poem that are evidence of similar challenges to those faced by the refugees and immigrants.

- This vocabulary from the poems may need to be discussed:

  - "Not the Same": pouches

  - "Can't Help": solitude, jasmine, ashy, inhaling, yearning

  - "Eternal Peace": Students should be familiar with the words in this poem.

- As the class works, ask probing questions as needed:

  - "What evidence of mourning can you find experienced by Ha in your poem?"

  - "What is the strongest evidence of mourning that you can find in your poem?"

Meeting Students' Needs

- ELL students may be unfamiliar with more vocabulary words than are mentioned in this lesson. Check for comprehension of general words that most students would know.

- Consider partnering ELL students who speak the same home language when discussion of complex content is required. This allows students to have more meaningful discussions and to clarify points in their native language.

- For students who struggle to read complex texts, consider previewing this vocabulary word from the text: *grieving*. If you select additional words to preview, focus on those whose meaning may be difficult to determine using context clues from the text. It is important for students to practice using context clues to determine word meaning so that they become more proficient readers.

- Reviewing academic vocabulary words benefits all students developing academic language. Consider allowing students to grapple with a complex text before explicit teaching of vocabulary. After students have read for gist, they can identify challenging vocabulary for themselves. Teachers can address student-selected vocabulary as well as predetermined vocabulary in subsequent encounters with the text. However, in some cases and with some students, preteaching selected vocabulary may be necessary.

- Text-dependent questions can be answered only by referring explicitly back to the text being read. This encourages students to reread the text for further analysis and allows for a deeper understanding.

B. Jigsaw Part 2: Group Discussion to Share Answers and Revisit Our Prediction (15 minutes)

- Refocus the whole group. Inform students that they will now share with their numbered heads group. Ask them to take their Paragraph 4, Text-Dependent Questions, Part B, handout with them.

- Give students about 5 minutes to share within their groups. Encourage them to record new evidence from other poems on their question sheets.

- In the last few minutes of this part of the agenda, be sure that groups discuss and record an answer to the synthesis questions at the bottom of their Text-Dependent Questions, Part B, handout:

  - "Look back at the predictions you made a few lessons ago about the similarities and differences between how refugee and immigrant children adapt. What similarities or differences can you now add to your original list? Which of the differences seem most important? Why?"

- Ask volunteers from each group to share their group's discussion with the whole class.

Closing and Assessment

A. Adding to the Inside Out and Back Again Anchor Charts (5 minutes)

- Ask volunteers to share some of their details from the informational text and the poem and to justify whether they think the details show turning "inside out" or "back again."

- Record on the **Inside Out Anchor Chart** or the **Back Again Anchor Chart**, according to class suggestions.

Homework

Remember that for the End-of-Unit Assessment, you are going to be writing about how the novel's title, *Inside Out & Back Again,* relates to the universal refugee experience of fleeing and finding home, using Ha as an example. To describe how Ha turns "inside out" and "back again," you first need to describe who she is before she is forced to flee. Reread pages 18–49, and on your homework recording form, continue to collect the strongest evidence you can find to answer this question: "Who is Ha before she is forced to flee her home?" (This homework question was distributed in Lesson 12.)

Meeting Students' Needs

Anchor charts serve as note-catchers when the class is co-constructing ideas.

LESSON 15

Connecting the Universal Refugee Experience of Fleeing and Finding Home to the Title of the Novel *Inside Out & Back Again*

Long-Term Targets Addressed (Based on ELA CCSS)

- I can cite text-based evidence that provides the strongest support for my analysis of literary text. (RL.8.1)
- I can analyze how specific dialogue or incidents in a plot propel the action, reveal aspects of a character, or provoke a decision. (RL.8.3)
- I can cite text-based evidence that provides the strongest support for an analysis of informational text. (RI.8.1)

Supporting Learning Targets

- I can make a claim about how the lives of refugees turn "inside out" when they flee home, using the strongest evidence I have collected from both the novel and informational text.
- I can make a claim about how the lives of refugees turn "back again" as they find a new home, using the strongest evidence I have collected from both the novel and informational text.
- I can cite where I found my evidence.

Ongoing Assessment

- Two Forming Evidence-Based Claims Graphic Organizers (one for Body Paragraph 1, "Inside Out," and one for Body Paragraph 2, "Back Again")

Agenda

1. Opening
   A. Unpacking Learning Targets (2 minutes)

2. Work Time

    A. Introducing Citations (8 minutes)

    B. Forming Evidence-Based Claims: Connecting the Idea of Fleeing and Finding Home with "Inside Out" (14 minutes)

    C. Forming Evidence-Based Claims: Connecting the Idea of Fleeing and Finding Home with "Back Again" (10 minutes)

3. Closing and Assessment

    A. Preview Homework: Planning Your Essay Paragraphs 1 and 2—How to Plan (5 minutes)

4. Homework

    A. Complete the Forming Evidence-Based Claims Graphic Organizer.

    B. Complete the Planning Your Essay Graphic Organizer for Body Paragraphs 1 and 2.

Teaching Notes

- In this lesson, students transition to formally planning their End-of-Unit Assessment essay. Throughout the unit, they have read informational texts about refugee experiences and the novel *Inside Out & Back Again,* gathering details from the texts that show how refugees turn "inside out" and then come "back again." Much of this evidence is shown on the Inside Out and Back Again Anchor Charts.

- In this lesson, students use this evidence to begin forming specific claims. They complete two Forming Evidence-Based Claims Graphic Organizers—one about how refugees turn "inside out" and another about how refugees turn "back again." (These graphic organizers are from Odell Education resource.) Students use a relatively inductive process to collect and connect details as a way to come to a claim.

- After having filled in these Forming Evidence-Based Claims Graphic Organizers, students receive a new Planning Your Essay Graphic Organizer to complete for homework. On this, they begin with the claim they came up with inductively earlier in the lesson.

- Post: learning targets, questions for Work Time.

Lesson Vocabulary

strongest evidence, claim, cited/citation, physical, psychological, emotional

Materials

- *Inside Out & Back Again* (book; one per student)

- Document camera

- Model essay: "How Ha's Mother Is Turned 'Inside Out'" (from Lesson 8; one to display)

- Citing Books and Articles Anchor Chart (new; teacher-created)

- Inside Out Anchor Chart and Back Again Anchor Chart (begun in Lesson 8)
- Forming Evidence-Based Claims Graphic Organizer (two per student and one to display)
- Directions for Forming Evidence-Based Claims (one per student)
- Planning Your Essay Graphic Organizer (one per student and one to display)

Opening

Meeting Students' Needs

- Posting learning targets enables students to refer to them throughout the lesson to check their understanding. They also provide a reminder to students and teachers about the intended learning behind a given lesson or activity.
- Discussing and clarifying the language of learning targets help build academic vocabulary.

A. Unpacking Learning Targets (2 minutes)

- Read aloud the learning targets as students follow along silently:
  - "I can make a claim about how the lives of refugees turn 'inside out' when they flee home, using the strongest evidence I have collected from both the novel and informational text."
  - "I can make a claim about how the lives of refugees turn 'back again' as they find a new home, using the strongest evidence I have collected from both the novel and informational text."
  - "I can cite where I found my evidence."
- Point out that the first two targets are almost identical.
- Invite students to Think-Pair-Share:
  - "What is the *strongest evidence*? What does that mean?"
  - "What is a *claim*?"
- Listen for students to explain that the *strongest evidence* is "evidence that best supports a point being made," and a *claim* is "a statement the author is making about a text."

Work Time

A. Introducing Citations (8 minutes)

- Display the first body paragraph in the **model essay: "How Ha's Mother Is Turned 'Inside Out.'"** Remind students that they read this full essay several lessons ago. Read the first body paragraph aloud as students follow along silently.
- Point out the citations in the essay and ask:
  - "What do these notes in parentheses mean?"

- - "Why are they there? What is the purpose?"

  - "What order are they presented in?"

- Listen for students to say: "They tell readers where they can find the evidence listed by providing first the author's last name and then the page number to prove that the evidence really came from where the essay writer said it came from."

- Record on the new **Citing Books and Articles Anchor Chart**: (author's last name, page number).

- Refer to the list of works cited at the end and invite students to Think-Pair-Share:

  - "What does *cited* mean? When you *cite* something, what are you doing?"

  - "Why do you cite the work of others?"

- Listen for students to explain that to *cite* means "to use the work of someone else in your own work. You cite the work of others in support of your own claims to make your claims stronger and more valid."

- Record on the Citing Books and Articles Anchor Chart:

  - Cite the work of others to support your own claims to make them stronger and more valid.

- Invite students to Think-Pair-Share:

  - "So how are the notes in parentheses in the essay and the list in the Works Cited section linked?"

  - "How are the books and articles cited in the Works Cited section?"

  - "In which order are the books and articles cited?"

- Listen for students to say that the full titles of the books and articles cited in parentheses are listed in the Works Cited section so that readers can check the sources if they need to. They are cited in alphabetical order with the author's last name, the title of the book or article, where it was published, when it was published, and the page numbers.

- Record on the Citing Books and Articles Anchor Chart:

  - "Works Cited" are listed in alphabetical order.

- Invite students to Think-Pair-Share:

  - "What is the difference in how articles and books are cited?"

- Listen for students to say that "article titles are in quotation marks, whereas book titles are italicized."

- Point out that the journal or magazine where the article was published is italicized, and that when citing a book, you cite the city of publishing, the publisher, and the year of publishing in parentheses.

- Record on the Citing Books and Articles Anchor Chart:

  - Books: Author name, *title, italicized* (place of publishing: publisher, year).

  - Articles: Author name, "title," *title of the magazine/journal in which it was published, italicized,* date, pages on which it was published.

- Inform students that in their essays, they are going to be using this anchor chart to cite the books and articles they use, so they need to make sure they collect page numbers as they gather evidence in the next couple of lessons.

Meeting Students' Needs

Providing models of expected work supports all learners, especially those who are challenged.

B. Forming Evidence-Based Claims: Connecting the Idea of Fleeing and Finding Home with "Inside Out" (14 minutes)

- Remind students that in their End-of-Unit Assessment, they will analyze how the meaning of the novel's title, *Inside Out & Back Again,* relates to the universal refugee experience of fleeing and finding home and how this experience is revealed in Ha's story.

- Inform students that in this lesson, they will focus on gathering evidence and forming claims related to two questions. Post the questions where everyone can see them:

  - "How do the lives of refugees turn 'inside out' as they flee and find home?"

  - "How do the lives of refugees turn 'back again' as they find a new home?"

- Remind the class that fleeing and finding home is a *physical* process in which refugees leave their country and move to a new one, whereas "inside out" and "back again" are more *psychological* and *emotional* processes that refugees go through as they leave everything they know behind and try to adapt to life in a new country.

- Inform students that today they will work to gather evidence to answer these two questions. This will support their writing of the two body paragraphs of their essay.

- Refer to the displayed first body paragraph of the model essay: "How Ha's Mother Is Turned 'Inside Out.'" Ask students to Think-Pair-Share:

  - "What is this first body paragraph of the model about? What are the main ideas the writer is trying to communicate?"

  - "What evidence has the writer used to support her claims?"

- Listen for: "The writer describes how refugees turn 'inside out' when they flee home and presents evidence from the novel to show how Ha's mother turns 'inside out.'"

- Explain to students that the essay they will be writing is similar to the first body paragraph of the model (read at the beginning of the Work Time), but the model focuses only on turning "inside out." Their essay will have one body paragraph about how refugees turn "inside out" and one body paragraph about how refugees turn "back again."

- Inform students that they are going to use the evidence collected on the Inside Out and Back Again Anchor Charts, along with any other evidence from the informational texts and the novel that they think is relevant, to identify connections between pieces of evidence. This will help them make claims to answer the two questions, which will form the basis of the first and second body paragraphs of their essay.

- Distribute one copy of the **Forming Evidence-Based Claims Graphic Organizer** to each student and display it using the document camera.

- Inform students that this organizer will help them connect the strongest pieces of evidence for each of their two body paragraphs.

- Invite them to pair up in their numbered heads groups: number 1s and 4s together, and number 2s and 3s together.

- Focus students on the Inside Out Anchor Chart. Ask them first to think about evidence they have gathered from the informational texts. Ask pairs to Think-Pair-Share:

  - "Look at the evidence we have recorded from informational texts on the Inside Out Anchor Chart. What is the strongest evidence to explain how the lives of refugees turn 'inside out' when they flee and find home?"

  - "Is there any stronger evidence in any of the informational texts that hasn't been recorded on the anchor chart?"

- Remind students that there isn't a right or wrong answer here; it is up to them to choose, but they need to be able to justify why they think the detail they choose is the strongest example of refugees turning "inside out."

- Ask a few volunteers to share out.

- Model how to begin completing the Forming Evidence-Based Claims Graphic Organizer. For example, students may choose this quote from the "Refugee Children in Canada" text: "Some have lost many members of their families and many have lost everything that was familiar to them." Record this detail in the first Detail box on the displayed recording form.

- Remind students that in their essay, they will cite where their evidence came from. Model this by recording the author and page number with the detail (Fantino and Colak 590). Then ask students to record the detail they selected, along with the author and page number. Explain that pairs do not have to record the same detail.

- Repeat this process, focusing on evidence from the novel about how Ha turns "inside out." Ask pairs to Think-Pair-Share:

  - "Look at the details from the novel collected on the Inside Out Anchor Chart and on your structured notes. Which of Ha's experiences relate to the detail you chose from the informational text?"

  - "Is there any stronger evidence in the novel that hasn't been recorded in your structured notes or on the anchor chart?"

- Remind students again that there are no right or wrong answers here. It is up to them to choose, but they need to be able to justify why they think the details they choose are the strongest evidence of Ha's experiences to support the detail they have chosen from the informational texts.

- Again model briefly. For example, students may suggest these quotes from the novel: "Mostly I wish Father would appear in our doorway and make Mother's lips curl upward, lifting them from a permanent frown of worries" and "Three pouches of papaya dried papaya Chewy Sugary Waxy Sticky Not the same at all. So mad, I throw all in the trash." Record these details in the remaining two Details boxes on the displayed recording form.

- Remind students that in their essay, they will cite where the evidence they have chosen comes from. Model this by recording "(Lai 31)" next to the first detail and "(Lai 232)" next to the second detail.

- Then ask students to record the details they selected from the novel, including the author and page number. Explain that pairs do not have to record the same details.

- Refocus students as a whole group. Focus them on the next row of the Forming Evidence-Based Claims Graphic Organizer. Inform them that their next task is to look across the details and connect them.

- Invite students to Think-Pair-Share:

  - "Why did you choose the detail from the informational text? What is your thinking behind choosing this detail?"

  - "What about the two details from the novel? What is your thinking behind choosing those details?"

  - "How are all the details you have collected on your organizer connected?"

- Model briefly. For example, thinking behind the details already recorded on the displayed recording form could be as follows:

  - Informational text detail: "This detail is about refugees mourning what they leave behind. I think mourning turns refugees 'inside out' because they hurt inside."

  - Novel, first detail: "This detail tells us that Ha mourns the loss of her father, and I think this turns her 'inside out' because she hurts inside."

  - Novel, second detail: "This detail tells that Ha mourns the loss of food from home, like papaya. I think this turns her 'inside out' because she hurts inside."

- An example of the way all of these details are connected could read something like this: "All of these details are about how refugees, and Ha as an example, mourn the loss of the things they leave behind."

- Ask students to record their thinking behind the details they have chosen in the same way. Explain that pairs do not have to record the same thinking.

- Focus the class on the final row of the Forming Evidence-Based Claims Graphic Organizer: Making a Claim. Invite students to Think-Pair-Share:

  - "Based on how your details are connected, what claim are you making about how the lives of refugees can turn 'inside out' when they flee and find home?"

- Model briefly. For example, a claim for the evidence recorded on the displayed recording form could be as follows:

  - "Refugees turn 'inside out' when they mourn the loss of the things they leave behind."

Meeting Students' Needs

- Graphic organizers engage students more actively and provide scaffolding that is especially critical for learners with lower levels of language proficiency and/or learning.

- When you're reviewing the graphic organizers or recording forms, consider using a document camera to display them for students who struggle with auditory processing.

C. Forming Evidence-Based Claims: Connecting the Idea of Fleeing and Finding Home with "Back Again" (10 minutes)

- Invite number 1s to pair up with 2s and number 3s to pair up with 4s.

- Inform students that they are going to repeat the same process they just did, but now using the evidence recorded on the Back Again Anchor Chart and any other evidence they want to include from the informational text and novel. Distribute a new **Forming Evidence-Based Claims Graphic Organizer**. Let them know that they will use this to begin to form a claim for the second body paragraph.

- Focus on the second question: "How do the lives of refugees turn 'back again' when they find a new home?"

- Display and distribute the **Directions for Forming Evidence-Based Claims**. Remind students that they do not need to record the same details or claim as their partner. The partner discussion is to help them think through their ideas before writing them down.

- Circulate to provide support. Ask probing questions:

  - "What do you think is the strongest piece of evidence on the Back Again Anchor Chart to explain how the lives of refugees turn 'back again' when they find home?"

  - "Look at the details from the novel collected on the Back Again Anchor Chart. Which of Ha's experiences support the detail you have chosen from the informational text?"

  - "Why did you choose this detail from the informational text? What is your thinking behind choosing it?"

  - "What about the two details from the novel? What is your thinking behind choosing those?"

  - "How are all the details you have collected on your organizer connected?"

  - "Based on how your details are connected, what claim are you making about how the lives of refugees can turn 'back again' when they find home?"

Meeting Students' Needs

- For students who have trouble following multiple-step directions, consider displaying these directions using a document camera or interactive whiteboard. Another option is to type up the instructions for students to have in hand.

- Many students benefit from having the time available for this activity displayed via a timer or stopwatch.

Closing and Assessment

A. Preview Homework: Planning Your Essay Paragraphs 1 and 2—How to Plan (5 minutes)

- Display and distribute the **Planning Your Essay Graphic Organizer**.

- Inform students that for homework, they will finish gathering details and forming a claim (from Work Time today). They will then start formally planning body paragraphs 1 and 2 using this new organizer.

EXPEDITIONARY
LEARNING

- Ask students to ignore the Introductory Paragraph and Concluding Paragraph boxes for now (they will work on these in Lesson 16).
- Emphasize two key reminders:
  - "Just jot down simple notes; you do not need to write in full sentences."
  - "Cite your evidence on the planning form so you will have these citations when you write your essay."
- As time permits, invite students to begin planning body paragraphs 1 and 2 using the Planning Your Essay Graphic Organizer.

Homework

- Complete the Forming Evidence-Based Claims Graphic Organizer if you did not do so in class.
- Complete the Planning Your Essay Graphic Organizer for body paragraphs 1 and 2. Do not forget to cite the author and page number for your evidence. Remember, for now you don't need to plan the introductory or concluding paragraphs. You will do this in the next lesson.

LESSON 16

Planning the Introductory and Concluding Paragraphs of the End-of-Unit Assessment Essay

Long-Term Targets Addressed (Based on ELA CCSS)

- I can analyze how specific dialogue or incidents in a plot propel the action, reveal aspects of a character, or provoke a decision. (RL.8.3)
- I can write informative/explanatory texts that convey ideas and concepts using relevant information that is carefully selected and organized. (W.8.2)
- I can produce clear and coherent writing that is appropriate to task, purpose, and audience. (W.8.4)
- With support from peers and adults, I can use the writing process to ensure that the purpose and audience have been addressed. (W.8.5)

Supporting Learning Targets

- I can plan effective introductory and concluding paragraphs for my analytical essay.
- I can cite where I found my evidence.

Ongoing Assessment

- Forming Evidence-Based Claims Graphic Organizer (with a claim to answer the question, "Who is Ha before she flees home?")
- Planning Your Essay Graphic Organizer (homework for Lessons 15 and 16)

Agenda

1. Opening
   A. Sharing Homework and Unpacking Learning Targets (7 minutes)

---

2. Work Time

    A. Forming an Evidence-Based Claim: "Who Is Ha before She Has to Flee Her Home?" (10 minutes)

    B. Planning the Introductory Paragraph (10 minutes)

    C. Planning the Concluding Paragraph (10 minutes)

3. Closing and Assessment

    A. Peer Critique of Plans for Introductory and Concluding Paragraphs (8 minutes)

4. Homework

    A. Complete the Planning Your Essay Graphic Organizer.

Teaching Notes

- In this lesson, students plan the introductory and concluding paragraphs of their End-of-Unit Assessment analytical essay.

- The essay's introductory paragraph has two components. First, students introduce their central claim (thesis statement). They then provide brief background to describe Ha's character before she has to flee Vietnam. This context is important so students can then, in the body paragraphs of their essay, explain how Ha's experience is a specific example of the universal refugee experience of being turned "inside out" and then "back again."

- To help students plan their introductory paragraph, they again use the Forming Evidence-Based Claims Graphic Organizer to gather and connect details about who Ha is before she flees her home.

- Students have taken copious notes on Ha's character throughout the module and should also refer to their Who Is Ha? Anchor Chart (used primarily in Unit 1). Continue to reinforce the concept of Ha as a dynamic character: It is important to establish who she is before fleeing so students can then describe how she changes.

- This lesson, which focuses on the essay's introduction and conclusion, includes important new learning for students. Up until this point, they have primarily been writing strong analytical paragraphs (Quick Writes), which are more similar to the two body paragraphs they write in this extended essay.

- This is the final lesson during which students gather evidence and plan their essays. In Lesson 17, they will draft their essays. Encourage students to take home their three Forming Evidence-Based Claims Graphic Organizers and their Planning Your Essay Graphic Organizer to review and revise for homework.

- Post: learning targets, Who Is Ha? Anchor Charts.

Lesson Vocabulary

introductory, introduction, concluding, conclusion, thesis, cite

EXPEDITIONARY
LEARNING

Materials

- Document camera
- Model essay: "How Ha's Mother Is Turned 'Inside Out'" (from Lesson 8; one to display)
- Who Is Ha? Anchor Charts (begun in Unit 1, Lesson 4; students added to this chart throughout Unit 1 in their small groups)
- Forming Evidence-Based Claims Graphic Organizer (one new blank form, the same as from Lesson 15, plus one for display)
- Citing Books and Articles Anchor Chart (from Lesson 15; one per student and one to display)
- Directions for Forming Evidence-Based Claims (one per student)
- Planning Your Essay Graphic Organizer (begun for homework in Lesson 15)
- *Inside Out & Back Again* (book; one per student)
- Grades 6–8 Expository Writing Evaluation Rubric (from Lesson 11)

Opening

A. Sharing Homework and Unpacking Learning Targets (7 minutes)

- Invite number 1s to pair up with number 2s and number 3s to pair up with number 4s.
- Give students 4 minutes to share with their partners the planning they did for body paragraphs 1 and 2 of their essay.
- Circulate to check that all students completed the homework and have now completed their planning of body paragraphs 1 and 2.
- Focus students on the posted learning targets. Ask for several volunteers to read each target aloud:
  - "I write a successful introductory and concluding paragraph."
  - "I can cite where I found my evidence."
- Ask students to Think-Pair-Share:
  - "What is an *introductory* paragraph?"
  - "Where do you find the *introduction* in a piece of writing?"
  - "What does the introduction do?"
- Listen for students to say that the introduction is "at the beginning of a piece of writing and introduces what the writer is going to be discussing. It gives the reader an idea of what to expect."
- Ask students to Think-Pair-Share:
  - "What is a *concluding* paragraph?"
  - "Where do you find the *conclusion* in a piece of writing?"
  - "What does the conclusion do?"
- Listen for students to say that the conclusion is "at the end of a piece of writing and restates the point the author is trying to make, summarizes the main points, and leaves the reader with a final thought."

- Point out that the second target is repeated from Lesson 15. Review, asking students to Think-Pair-Share:
    - "What does *cite* mean?"
    - "Why do you need to cite where you found evidence?"
    - "How do you cite evidence?"
- Listen for students to say that *cite* means "to list where they found the evidence so that they can support their claims and make them stronger. First you list the author's last name, and then the page number."

Meeting Students' Needs

- Posting learning targets enables students to refer to them throughout the lesson to check their understanding. They also provide a reminder to students and teachers about the intended learning behind a given lesson or activity.
- Discussing and clarifying the language of learning targets help build academic vocabulary.

Work Time

A. Forming an Evidence-Based Claim: "Who Is Ha before She Has to Flee Her Home?" (10 minutes)

- Using a **document camera**, display the **model essay: "How Ha's Mother Is Turned 'Inside Out'"** and read the introductory paragraph aloud as students follow along silently.
- Invite students to Think-Pair-Share:
    - "So what is the introduction about? What does it tell you? Why?"
- Listen for students to explain that it tells them "what the essay is about and who Ha's mother is before she has to flee Vietnam." This helps make it clear that she turns "inside out" as a result of having to flee and find home.
- Remind students that for homework in Lessons 12–14, they began to locate the strongest evidence at the beginning of the novel to answer the question, "Who is Ha before she is forced to flee Vietnam?" Ask students to Think-Pair-Share:
    - "Why were you doing this? How is this relevant to the content of our essay?"
- Listen for: "To describe how Ha, as an example of a refugee, turns 'inside out' and 'back again,' we first need to describe who she is before fleeing."
- Draw students' attention to the **Who Is Ha? Anchor Charts** around the room.
- Distribute a new **Forming Evidence-Based Claims Graphic Organizer**. Remind students that they used this same organizer in the previous lesson to make claims for body paragraphs 1 and 2. Today, they will use the same process to form an evidence-based claim to answer the question, "Who is Ha before she has to flee Vietnam?" This will become part of the introductory paragraph of their essay.
- Refer to the **Citing Books and Articles Anchor Chart** to remind students to cite their sources.

- Pair up number 1s with 4s and number 2s with 3s to work on making a claim to answer the question.

- Post and distribute **Directions for Forming Evidence-Based Claims**. Ask students to begin.

- Circulate to provide support. Ask probing questions to guide students through the rows of the Forming Evidence-Based Claims Graphic Organizer:

  - "What are the three strongest pieces of evidence that explain who Ha is before she flees her home?"

  - "Why did you choose those details?"

  - "Where did you find those details?"

  - "How are all the details you have collected on your organizer connected?"

  - "Based on how your details are connected, what claim are you making about who Ha is before she has to flee her country?"

Meeting Students' Needs

- Providing models of expected work supports all learners, especially those who are challenged.

- Graphic organizers engage students more actively and provide scaffolding that is especially critical for learners with lower levels of language proficiency and/or learning.

- When you're reviewing graphic organizers or recording forms, consider using a document camera to display them for students who struggle with auditory processing.

- For students who have trouble with following multiple-step directions, consider displaying these directions using a document camera or interactive whiteboard. Another option is to type up the instructions for students to have in hand.

B. Planning the Introductory Paragraph (10 minutes)

- Be sure students have their copies of *Inside Out & Back Again*. Pair up odd-numbered and even-numbered students.

- Instruct students to refer to the first row of the **Grades 6–8 Expository Writing Evaluation Rubric**, and remind them of the section about introductory paragraphs: "Clearly introduce a topic in a manner that is compelling and follows logically from the task and purpose."

- Invite students to Think-Pair-Share:

  - "So now that you have read the introductory paragraph of the model and the row of the rubric about introductions, what do you think makes the introduction of an essay effective?"

- List student ideas on the board. Ensure that they include the following:

  - Outlines what the essay will be about—gives a clear purpose

  - Outlines the main point you are trying to make and why you are making that point

  - Outlines the evidence you will be using

- Inform students that they will now begin to plan their own introductory paragraph. Focus the class on the **Planning Your Essay Graphic Organizer** (from Lesson 15). Point out the questions that students can use to help them build their central claim or thesis in the Introductory Paragraph box:

  - "What is the essay about?"

  - "What point will you, the author, be making?"

  - "What evidence will you be using? Why?"

- Explain that the thesis statement tells the reader what the essay will be about, what point the student will be making, and the evidence the student will be using to support his or her claims.

- Ask students to think about the three claims they have made so far:

  - Who Ha is before she flees her home

  - How refugees turn "inside out"

  - How refugees turn "back again" as they flee and find home

  - "What point are you going to make in your essay with these claims?"

- Give students 2 minutes to think and discuss ideas with their partner.

- Refocus students on the Planning Your Essay Graphic Organizer, specifically the Introductory Paragraph, Part 1, box. Ask students to record their thinking there. Remind them that this is just a planning organizer, so they don't need to write in full sentences. But their plans should be clear enough for them to follow to write their essay.

- Circulate to identify students who may need additional support refining their thesis statement. Ask probing questions:

  - "What point will you, the author, be making?"

- Ask students to look at the questions next to part 2 of the Introductory Paragraph box on their Planning Your Essay Graphic Organizer. Invite them to read along with you:

  - "Who is Ha before she flees her home?"

  - "Why do we need to know this to understand how she turns 'inside out' and 'back again'?"

- Ask students to use the following resources to finish planning their introductory paragraph on their Planning Your Essay Graphic Organizer:

  - The model essay

  - The criteria (listed on the board)

  - The Forming Evidence-Based Claims Graphic Organizer about "Who is Ha?"

- Remind students that this is just a planning organizer, so they don't need to write in full sentences, but their plans should be clear enough for them to follow to write their essay.

- Refer to the Citing Books and Articles Anchor Chart to remind students to cite their evidence on their planning graphic organizer so that they have everything they need when they begin to write.

- Circulate to offer guidance while students plan.

- Some students may not finish in the time allotted; remind them that they can keep working on their plans for homework.

C. Planning the Concluding Paragraph (10 minutes)

- Display the model essay: "How Ha's Mother Is Turned 'Inside Out'" again. Read aloud the concluding paragraph as students read along silently.

- Invite students to Think-Pair-Share:

  - "What makes this conclusion effective?"

- Record students' ideas on the board. These should include the following:

  - Conclusion should tie everything together.

  - Conclusion should restate the thesis statement.

  - Conclusion should review the main points that have been made.

  - Conclusion should remind the reader of what you have outlined in your writing.

  - The final sentence should be like a final thought.

- Ask students to use the criteria listed on the board and the model essay to plan their essay's concluding paragraph on the Planning Your Essay Graphic Organizer. Remind them again that this is just a planning organizer, so they don't need to write in full sentences.

- Circulate to offer guidance while the class writes. Ask probing questions:

  - "What is your thesis statement?"

  - "What are the main points you make throughout the essay?"

  - "What is your final thought that you want to leave the reader with? Why?"

- If students finish planning their concluding paragraphs, invite them to do the following:

  - Review and revise their Planning My Essay Graphic Organizer.

  - Reread the model essay to see what else they notice that might help them draft their essays in the next lesson.

Meeting Students' Needs

Many students benefit from having the time available for this activity displayed via a timer or stopwatch.

Closing and Assessment

A. Peer Critique of Plans for Introductory and Concluding Paragraphs (8 minutes)

- Invite students to pair up—odd numbers and even numbers—to peer critique their plans for the introductory and concluding paragraphs.

- Ask them to follow these directions for the peer critique:

  1. Decide who will go first.

  2. Partner A, take 2 minutes to talk Partner B through your plan for your essay.

  3. Partner B, tell Partner A one "star" (positive thing) about his or her plan.

---

4. Partner B, ask Partner A one question that will help Partner A think more deeply about one aspect of his or her plan in order to improve it. Examples could include:

- "So which evidence are you using in your essay to support your claims?"
- "Why are you using that evidence?"
- "What is your final thought?"
- "Why have you chosen that final thought?"

5. Partner A, write down one step you will take for homework to improve your plan.

6. Trade roles and repeat.

Meeting Students' Needs

Asking students to provide feedback to their peers based on explicit criteria benefits both students in clarifying the meaning of the learning target.

Homework

Complete, review, and revise your Planning My Essay Graphic Organizer in preparation for writing your essay in the next lesson. Make sure your plans are at the stage that you can use them as a basis for your writing.

LESSON 17

End-of-Unit 2 Assessment, Part 1

First Draft of Analysis Essay

Long-Term Targets Addressed (Based on ELA CCSS)

- I can cite text-based evidence that promotes the strongest support for my analysis of literary text. (RL.8.1)
- I can analyze how specific dialogue or incidents in a plot propel the action, reveal aspects of a character, or provoke a decision. (RL.8.3)
- I can cite text-based evidence that provides the strongest support for an analysis of informational text. (RI.8.1)
- I can analyze full-length novels, short stories, poems, and other genres by authors who represent diverse world cultures. (RL.8.6)
- I can write informative/explanatory texts that convey ideas and concepts using relevant information that is carefully selected and organized. (W.8.2)
- I can produce clear and coherent writing that is appropriate to task, purpose, and audience. (W.8.4)
- I can use evidence from literary texts to support analysis, reflection, and research. (W.8.9)

Supporting Learning Targets

- I can write an essay explaining the universal refugee experience of turning "inside out" and "back again."
- I can cite the strongest evidence from informational texts to support my claims about how refugees turn "inside out" and "back again."
- I can cite the strongest evidence from the novel *Inside Out & Back Again* to support my claims about who Ha is before she flees and how she is turned "inside out" and "back again."
- I can cite where I found my evidence.

Ongoing Assessment

- End-of-Unit 2 Assessment, Part 1: First Draft of Analytical Essay

---

Agenda

1. Opening
    A. Unpacking Learning Targets (3 minutes)
2. Work Time
    A. Drafting the Essay (25 minutes)
    B. Analyzing Grades 6–8 Expository Writing Evaluation Rubric: Row 3 and Self-Assessing Draft Essay (12 minutes)
3. Closing and Assessment
    A. Exit Ticket: Selecting a Refugee Experience for Further Research (5 minutes)
4. Homework
    A. Continue independent reading book.

Teaching Notes

- In this lesson, students pull together all of their graphic organizers and planning notes and draft their essays.

- Be sure students have all of their materials from previous lessons: their novel, informational texts, structured notes, completed Forming Evidence-Based Claims Graphic Organizers, and so forth. Have on hand a few clean copies of the two articles ("Refugees: Who, Where, and Why" and "Refugee Children in Canada").

- If the technology is available, provide computers for students to word-process their essays.

- Emphasize to students that their work today is a draft. They will receive teacher feedback and then will have time in Lesson 20 to revise their essay.

- At the end of this lesson, students choose which research team they would like to be on for their short research project on refugees from three specific times and places in history: Kurdistan, Bosnia, and Afghanistan (which begins in Lesson 18).

- Post: learning targets, Who Is Ha? Anchor Charts, Inside Out Anchor Chart, Back Again Anchor Chart.

Lesson Vocabulary

coherence/incoherence, style, complex ideas, concepts, precise, appropriate/inappropriate, transitions, unified, enhance, exhibit, predominantly

Materials

- End-of-Unit 2 Assessment prompt (introduced in Lesson 8; one per student and one for display)
- *Inside Out & Back Again* (book; one per student)
- Model essay: "How Ha's Mother Is Turned 'Inside Out'" (from Lesson 8)

- Grades 6–8 Expository Writing Evaluation Rubric (from Lesson 11)
- "Refugees: Who, Where, and Why" (from Lesson 4)
- "Refugee Children in Canada" (from Lesson 9)
- Who Is Ha? Anchor Charts (begun in Unit 1, Lesson 4)
- Inside Out Anchor Chart and Back Again Anchor Chart (begun in Lesson 8)
- Citing Books and Articles Anchor Chart (from Lesson 15)
- Writer's Glossary for Row 3 of the Expository Writing Rubric (one per student and one to display)
- Grades 6–8 Expository Writing Evaluation Rubric: Row 3—Conclusion (one per student and one for display)
- Document camera
- Half sheet of paper for Exit Ticket (one per student)

Opening

A. Unpacking Learning Targets (3 minutes)

- Invite the class to read aloud the learning targets with you:
  - "I can write an essay explaining the universal refugee experience of turning 'inside out' and 'back again.'"
  - "I can cite the strongest evidence from informational texts to support my claims about how refugees turn 'inside out' and 'back again.'"
  - "I can cite the strongest evidence from the novel *Inside Out & Back Again* to support my claims about who Ha is before she flees and how she is turned 'inside out' and 'back again.'"
  - "I can cite where I found my evidence."
- Invite students to Think-Pair-Share:
  - "How do today's targets help you know what specifically you will need to focus on as you draft your essay?"
- Listen for students to explain that their essay needs to include the strongest evidence from both informational and literary texts to support their claims.

Meeting Students' Needs

- Posting learning targets enables students to refer to them throughout the lesson to check their understanding. They also provide a reminder to students and teachers about the intended learning behind a given lesson or activity.
- Discussing and clarifying the language of learning targets help build academic vocabulary.

Work Time

A. Drafting the Essay (25 minutes)

- Display the **End-of-Unit 2 Assessment prompt** (introduced in Lesson 8). Remind students that they have had a lot of time over the past few lessons to think, talk, and take notes about what they want to write. Today their job is to write their best full draft on their own.

- Emphasize that students have already gathered their evidence and planned their four paragraphs. Today is about pulling the information together in clear and coherent paragraphs. They will then get feedback from you and have a chance to revise their essay in a few days.

- Ask students to get their planning materials out:

  - *Inside Out & Back Again*
  - Planning Your Essay Graphic Organizer (completed)
  - Three Forming Evidence-Based Claims Graphic Organizers (completed in Lessons 15 and 16)
  - Structured notes
  - **Model essay: "How Ha's Mother Is Turned 'Inside Out'"**
  - **Grades 6–8 Expository Writing Evaluation Rubric**
  - **"Refugees: Who, Where, and Why"**
  - **"Refugee Children in Canada"**

- Draw students' attention to the anchor charts posted around the room:

  - **Who Is Ha? Anchor Charts**
  - **Inside Out Anchor Chart**
  - **Back Again Anchor Chart**

- Explain that the anchor charts are resources that they can use to help draft their essays. Refer to the **Citing Books and Articles Anchor Chart** to remind students to cite sources in their essay correctly and to create a Works Cited list at the end of their essay.

- Let students know that they should raise their hand if they have questions, but otherwise set the expectation that this drafting should be done individually.

- Ask students to begin. As the students work, circulate around the room to observe how well they are using their planning resources for their drafting. Guide them toward using their resources as needed.

- If students finish early, encourage them to reread their essay in a whisper voice to check for the overall flow.

B. Analyzing Grades 6–8 Expository Writing Evaluation Rubric: Row 3 and Self-Assessing Draft Essay (12 minutes)

- Ask students to get out their copy of the Grades 6–8 Expository Writing Evaluation Rubric. Inform them that they will be looking at the rubric criteria for coherence and organization, Row 3, to self-assess parts of their draft essay.

- Remind them of the routine they built in previous lessons: Ask them to read through this row and circle any words they do not know.

- Distribute the **Writer's Glossary for Row 3 of the Grades 6–8 Expository Writing Evaluation Rubric** and compare the words they circled with those that are on the glossary page: *coherence/ incoherence, style, complex ideas, concepts, precise, appropriate/inappropriate, transitions, unified, enhance, exhibit, predominantly*. The glossary page should already have a simple definition for each of the words.

- Have a student volunteer read the words and definitions that are on the glossary page. Define any words as necessary. Be sure to point out the words that are matched with their opposite, such as *coherence/incoherence, appropriate/inappropriate*.

- If students have other words they questioned, ask them to add those to their list and share with the class. See whether they can tell what the words mean; if not, give a simple definition.

- Distribute and display the **Expository Writing Evaluation Rubric: Row 3—Conclusion** using the **document camera**. Ask students to focus on this third section of Row 3 of the rubric: "Provide a concluding statement or section that follows from the topic and information presented."

- Ask students to self-assess their conclusion against this part of the rubric. Invite them to highlight on the rubric where they think the conclusion of their draft essay fits and to justify why on the lines underneath by citing evidence from their essay.

Closing and Assessment

A. Exit Ticket: Selecting a Refugee Experience for Further Research (5 minutes)

- Inform students that in the next lesson, they will begin a short research project about real refugees from several different countries to find out more about life for refugees. Build excitement by explaining that in the next unit, students will have the chance to be creative by using their research to write some "Inside Out" and "Back Again" poems similar to those written by Ha in the novel.

- Distribute **half sheets of paper** for Exit Tickets to students. Ask them to indicate their first and second choices:

    - "Out of the refugee experiences we have learned about, identify which one you would like to learn more about and write why." The choices are a Kurdish refugee, a Bosnian refugee, or an Afghani refugee.

- Collect students' Exit Tickets.

Homework

Continue reading in your independent reading book for this unit.

Note: Prior to Lesson 20, review students' draft essays and provide specific feedback. Focus feedback on strengths and next steps related to the top two rows of the expository writing rubric. In Lesson 20, students will have time to revise their essays.

Lessons 18 and 19 involve research toward the Final Performance Task. Review students' Exit Tickets to form research teams (heterogeneous groups of three to four students). Begin to prepare the research texts (see Lesson 19 Supporting Materials for this list of research texts).

LESSON 18

Introducing the Final Performance Task and Analyzing Statistics

Long-Term Targets Addressed (Based on ELA CCSS)

- I can determine a theme or central idea of literary text. (RL.8.1)
- I can analyze the connections and distinctions between individuals, ideas, or events in a text. (RI.8.3)
- I can effectively engage in discussions with diverse partners about eighth-grade topics, texts, and issues. (SL.8.1)

Supporting Learning Targets

- I can determine the factual details (specific to a time and place in history) that Thanhha Lai uses in the poems "Birthday" and "Saigon Is Gone."
- I can analyze statistics about refugee experiences around the world to notice patterns.

Ongoing Assessment

- Specific Factual Details tickets
- Chalk Talk participation and discussion

Agenda

1. Opening
   A. Unpacking Learning Targets (2 minutes)
   B. Introducing the Performance Task Prompt (8 minutes)
2. Work Time
   A. Identifying Specific Factual Details in Poems from *Inside Out & Back Again* (10 minutes)
   B. Statistics Chalk Talk (20 minutes)

3. Closing and Assessment

    A.   Chalk Talk Gallery Walk (5 minutes)

4. Homework

    A.   Familiarize yourself with the research guide.

    B.   Continue reading independent reading book.

Teaching Notes

- Although this lesson is officially part of Unit 2, in effect it launches the work of Unit 3. (This sequence is designed to give you time to read and give feedback on students' draft End-of-Unit 2 Assessment essays.) Students are formally introduced to the final performance task in this lesson.

- The performance task prompt sets up students to revisit several poems from the novel with the focus on identifying the specific factual details Thanhha Lai includes in her poems about Vietnam at the time and why she includes them. This increases students' awareness of the purpose for researching specific factual details (about a specific time and place in history when refugees fled) to use later when writing their own poems.

- In a Chalk Talk, research teams analyze statistics from the informational texts they read earlier in Unit 2. The goal is for them to begin to recognize more fully that the universal refugee experience has taken place throughout history and around the world.

- Students take home the Research Guide to familiarize themselves with the kind of research information they will be gathering.

- In advance: Using the Exit Tickets from Lesson 17, divide students into research teams of three or four according to the refugee situation they chose to focus on (Kurdish, Bosnian, or Afghani refugees). Mixed-ability student groupings will provide a collaborative and supportive structure for reading complex texts.

- Note that students work with their teams for the first time during Work Time: Be prepared to reinforce classroom norms as students begin to work in these new groups.

- See the Articles for Research Folders (Teacher Reference) in the Lesson 19 Supporting Materials and the Teaching Notes at the end of this lesson. Be sure to prepare these folders before Lesson 19, when students formally launch their short research project.

- Note also the glossary with words from each article; put these glossaries in the folders so students have them for reference as they conduct their research.

- Review the Chalk Talk protocol (see the Appendix).

- Post: learning targets, list of research teams.

Lesson Vocabulary

specific, statistics; vast, uprising, resettling

Materials

- *Inside Out & Back Again* (book; one per student)
- Student-Friendly Performance Task Prompt (one per student)
- Specific Factual Details Task 1 (for half of the students)
- Specific Factual Details Task 2 (for half of the students)
- List of research teams (see Teaching Notes)
- Chalk Talk Statistics (one per student)
- Prefixes Note-Catcher (begun in Lesson 3)
- Chart paper (one piece per research team)
- Chalk Talk Statistics Guidelines (one per student)
- Markers (one per student)
- Research Guide (one per student)

Opening

A. Unpacking Learning Targets (2 minutes)

- Inform students that in this lesson, they will learn more about a short research project they will do in preparation for Unit 3.

- Ask a volunteer to read aloud the first learning target:

    - "I can determine the factual details (specific to a time and place in history) that Thanhha Lai uses in the poems 'Birthday' and 'Saigon Is Gone.'"

- Invite students to Think-Pair-Share:

    - "What does *specific* mean?"

- Listen for students to explain that *specific* means "particular," or based on the historical context Thanhha Lai is writing about.

- Ask another volunteer to read aloud the second target:

    - "I can analyze statistics about refugee experiences around the world in order to notice patterns."

- Ask students to Think-Pair-Share:

    - "What are *statistics*?"

- Listen for students to explain that *statistics* are "numerical representations of facts and data."

- Inform students that they will revisit statistics from some of the informational texts they have read during Unit 2. This will help them continue to notice what makes the refugee experience *universal* and learn more details about specific times and places in history when many people had to flee their home country. Later, in Unit 3, they will also read statistics as a part of their research project.

EXPEDITIONARY
LEARNING

B. Introducing the Performance Task Prompt (8 minutes)

- Display and distribute the **Student-Friendly Performance Task Prompt**. Focus students on part 1. Read it aloud as students read silently.

- Remind them that in the closing of the previous lesson, they selected which place and time in history they would like to research (refugees from Bosnia, Kurdistan, or Afghanistan) and recorded this on an Exit Ticket. Explain that later on in this lesson, they will be teamed with other students who chose the same research focus.

- Ask students to Think-Pair-Share:

  - "According to the prompt, what type of information will you need to gather within your research teams?"

- Listen for students to explain that they need to collect information about why refugees have to flee their homes and settle somewhere else.

- Focus students on part 2 of the performance task prompt. Read it aloud as students read along silently. Students should be quite familiar with the concepts of "inside out" and "back again" based on their analysis essay.

- Invite students to Think-Pair-Share to review the following:

  - "What do you notice?"

  - "What do you wonder?"

  - "How is the 'Inside Out' poem different from the 'Back Again' poem?"

  - "What does turning 'inside out' mean? When do refugees turn 'inside out'?"

  - "What does 'back again' mean? When do refugees turn 'back again'?"

- Listen for students to explain that refugees turn "inside out" when they are forced to flee their home and are new to another country. It means that emotionally, they feel as though their lives have been turned inside out. Refugees turn "back again" when they begin to settle and adapt in their new country and to feel more themselves.

- Inform students that in Unit 3, they will work first on the "Inside Out" poem and then on the "Back Again" poem. Emphasize that although the research is team-based, the poetry writing will be done individually.

Work Time

A. Identifying Specific Factual Details in Poems from *Inside Out & Back Again* (10 minutes)

- Be sure students have their copies of ***Inside Out & Back Again***. Inform them that now that they have seen the prompts, they are going to revisit a few of Thanhha Lai's poems, focusing on how the author uses specific facts that she may have had to research. This will help students see how specific facts can make their own poems more realistic and powerful.

- Ask students to get into numbered heads groups. Partner up number 1s with 2s and number 3s with 4s. For each pair, distribute **Specific Factual Details Task 1** to one student and **Specific Factual Details Task 2** to the other student:

  - Specific Factual Details Task 1: Reread the poem "Birthday" (page 26) in *Inside Out & Back Again*. What specific factual details about Vietnam at the time the novel is set are evident in the poem?

  - Specific Factual Details Task 2: Reread the poem "Saigon Is Gone" (page 67) in *Inside Out & Back Again*. What specific factual details about Vietnam at the time the novel is set are evident in the poem?

- Give students 3 to 4 minutes to do their task individually.

- Then ask students to do the following:

  - "Share with your partner the specific factual details about Vietnam at the time the novel is set that you found in your poem."

  - "Think and then discuss with your partner, 'Why are those specific factual details used in the poem? What is the purpose of those details for the reader?'"

- Refocus students as a whole group. Call on a numbered heads group member to share his or her answers with the whole class. Listen for students to explain that the writer needed to research specific factual, historical information about people and events in the Vietnam War. Those specific facts make the novel seem more realistic and believable for the reader.

- Explain that Thanhha Lai probably uses a lot of the information and facts she knows through her personal experiences to tell the story of Ha, but she also would have had to do research to ensure that the information she uses is factually correct to make the book more realistic and believable.

Meeting Students' Needs

Providing students with time to work individually and then to share out with their peers gives them "think time" that can benefit those who generally need extended time.

B. Statistics Chalk Talk (20 minutes)

- Announce and post the **list of research teams**. Invite students to get into their research teams for the next activity. As needed, remind or reinforce students about classroom norms for collaboration (from Unit 1), since they will be working with new peers for the next few lessons.

- Remind students that in their analysis essay, they discuss the universal refugee experience of turning "inside out" and "back again" as refugees flee and find home. Inform students that today they will think more about many examples of this universal refugee experience before diving in to learn more about one specific time and place in history.

- Display and distribute the **Chalk Talk Statistics**. Point out that these statistics come from the two informational texts they have read during Unit 2: "Refugees: Who, Where, and Why" and the introduction of "Refugee Children in Canada."

- Read the statistics aloud as students follow along silently.

- Distribute a piece of **chart paper**, the **Chalk Talk Statistics Guidelines**, and **markers** to each research team. Read through the protocol as students follow along silently:

  - Remember that Chalk Talks are silent. Use your marker to create a written conversation.

  - Make sure each student in your group has a chance to respond to the question.

  - Ask more questions when you don't understand what another student has written or you need further clarification.

- Write the question for the Chalk Talk discussion on the board:

  - "What do these statistics tell you about refugees?"

- Invite research teams to begin their Chalk Talk. Give teams 10 minutes to work. Circulate to remind students of and reinforce the guidelines.

- After about 10 minutes, refocus the group. Ask students to discuss in their research team:

  - "The text says, 'Every day, nearly 5,000 children become refugees, with a vast number growing up and spending their entire lives in refugee camps.' What does the term *vast* mean?"

- Underline the word *vast* on the displayed text, and invite students to do the same on theirs. Ask for volunteers to share the meaning of the word with the whole group.

- Listen for students to explain that in this context, *vast* means "a large number." Students should be able to figure out the meaning of this word from the context.

- Focus on the statistic about Hungary. Ask students to discuss in their research teams:

  - "In the statistic '1956 Uprisings in Hungary force more than 200,000 people to become refugees,' what does the term *uprising* mean?"

  - "How does your growing knowledge of prefixes help you understand that word? How is an *uprising* different from a *rising*? Why might the author have chosen this specific word?"

- Underline the word *uprising* on the displayed text, and invite students to do the same.

- Select volunteers to share the meaning of the word with the whole group. Listen for students to explain that an *uprising* is "like a revolt against something—lots of people get together to oppose another group, such as the government, to show that they are not happy with something. They use the power of a large group to try to get what they want." An *uprising* is different from *rising* because *rising* means "moving upward," whereas *uprising* means "a group of people who band together against another group to make their voices heard." The author may have chosen this word because a large group of people got together in Hungary to try to get what they wanted.

- Invite students to record the word *uprising* on their **Prefixes Note-Catcher**.

- Focus on the statistic about Canada's role. Invite students to discuss in their research teams:

  - "In the statistic 'Since the end of World War II, Canada has resettled about 800,000 refugees from every region of the world, including Europe, Asia, Africa, the Middle East, and Central and South America,' how is *resettled* different from *settled*? How does the prefix *re* change the meaning of the word?"

  - "What does the word *resettled* imply about Canada's role as a host country?"

- Underline the word *resettled* on the displayed text, and invite students to do the same. Ask for volunteers to share the meaning of the word with the whole group.

- Listen for students to explain that *resettled* means "they have already settled somewhere before and have to settle again." The word *resettled* tells us that Canada has to help the people from overseas settle in and adapt to life in another country as it becomes their permanent home.

- Invite students to record the word *resettled* on their Prefixes Note-Catcher.

Meeting Students' Needs

- Use of protocols (such as Chalk Talk) allows for total student participation. It encourages critical thinking, collaboration, and social construction of knowledge.

- Reviewing academic vocabulary words benefits all students developing academic language. Consider allowing students to grapple with a complex text before explicit teaching of vocabulary.

- Encourage students to use word attack strategies, identifying prefixes, root words, suffixes, cognates, and context.

Closing and Assessment

A. Chalk Talk Gallery Walk (5 minutes)

- Invite students to circulate to read the Chalk Talks from other research teams.

- Ask for volunteers to share their answers to the question with the whole class:

  - "What do these statistics tell you about refugees?"

- Listen for students to notice the key point: People have become refugees throughout history, around the world, and this issue affects a large number of people around the globe.

- Distribute the **Research Guide**. Inform students that part of their homework is to preview this guide to be clear on which types of information they will be gathering during this short research project.

Homework

- Spend time familiarizing yourself with the Research Guide. Consider which details you are going to be looking for when researching in informational texts.

- Continue reading your independent reading book for this unit.

Note: For Lesson 19, prepare Research Folders for each research team. See the Supporting Materials for Lesson 19 for the list of texts that need to go into each folder and instructions for accessing them.

Students color-code their research texts in Lesson 19. Be sure to have red, blue, and green pencils or highlighters (one per student).

LESSON 19

Launching Researching

Reading for Gist and Gathering Evidence Using the Research Guide

Long-Term Targets Addressed (Based on ELA CCSS)

- I can conduct short research projects to answer a question. (W.8.7)
- I can use evidence from informational texts to support analysis, reflection, and research. (W.8.9)
- I can express my own ideas clearly during discussions, and I can build on others' ideas during discussions. (SL.8.1)

Supporting Learning Targets

- I can find the gist of informational texts.
- I can select the strongest evidence in an informational text about who the refugees were, where they fled from, and why they had to flee.

Ongoing Assessment

- Research Guide

Agenda

1. Opening
   A. Unpacking Learning Targets (2 minutes)
   B. Introducing the Research Guide (5 minutes)
2. Work Time
   A. Reading All Research Texts for Gist (15 minutes)
   B. Rereading One Research Text to Identify "Who? Where? and Why?" Details (8 minutes)
   C. Gathering Evidence on Research Guides (10 minutes)

---

3. Closing and Assessment

    A. Sharing Evidence (5 minutes)

4. Homework

    A. Finish recording "Who? Where? and Why?" evidence onto your Research Guide.

Teaching Notes

- Although this lesson is in Unit 2, the research conducted will apply toward the final performance task and assessments in Unit 3. (This sequence is designed to provide you time to read and give feedback on students' draft End-of-Unit 2 Assessment essays.) Students begin working in their research teams to gather information aligned with the final performance task. The students will be using this research to write "Inside Out" and "Back Again" poems about specific refugee experiences from Bosnia, Afghanistan, or Kurdistan.

- Students begin their research with their teams using Research Folders that contain a small number of previously selected research materials for each of the countries identified (see Lesson 19 Supporting Materials for the list of texts).

- In advance: Have these folders ready. Each team needs a Research Folder containing the materials relevant to the group of refugees they have chosen to research, including a glossary of words they may not be familiar with. Have enough copies of each text for every student in the group so students can self-select texts.

- Students read each informational text in their folder, first for gist. It is important that students have a general sense of the article as a whole before they go searching for specific details.

- Students then reread and use a color-coding system to underline evidence answering the "Who? Where? and Why?" questions on the Research Guide.

- Be sure that students are aware that in Unit 3 they will create a fictional narrator for their poems, just as Thanhha Lai does in creating Ha. They will use evidence and details from the research materials as a basis for creating this fictional character, so they need to collect as much strong evidence as possible.

- Help students choose text that will challenge them at the appropriate level. Students also may partner read.

- In advance: Select one text from a research folder to model underlining evidence. See Work Time for more information.

- Post: learning targets, list of research teams (from Lesson 18).

Lesson Vocabulary

gist, strongest evidence; see the glossary in each Research Folder for vocabulary for each of the informational texts

---

EXPEDITIONARY
LEARNING

Materials

- List of research teams (from Lesson 18)
- Research Guide (from Lesson 18)
- Articles for Research Folders (Teacher Reference)
- Research Folders (one copy of each text per student on the research team; see Teaching Notes)
- Research Team Task Card (one per student)
- Informational text (one to display; see Work Time for more information)
- Red, blue, and green colored pencils (one each per student)
- Document camera

Opening

A. Unpacking Learning Targets (2 minutes)

- Post the **list of research teams** (from Lesson 18). Be sure students are sitting with their teams.
- Focus students on the first target and invite them to Think-Pair-Share:
  - "I can find the gist of informational texts."
- Students should be familiar with the term *gist*. Cold-call on a student to remind the class what it means. Listen for: "getting an initial sense of what a text is mostly about."
- Explain to students that real researchers read a lot of texts and need to be able to do a first read just to get a basic sense of the text and determine whether it is relevant to their research questions.
- Focus students on the second learning target and invite them to read it with you:
  - "I can select the strongest evidence in an informational text about who the refugees were, where they fled from, and why they had to flee."
- Ask students to Think-Pair-Share:
  - "What does *strongest evidence* mean?"
- Listen for students to explain that the *strongest evidence* is "the best evidence, or evidence that is most relevant to your particular questions or task."

Meeting Students' Needs

- Learning targets are a research-based strategy that helps all students, especially challenged learners.
- Posting learning targets enables students to refer to them throughout the lesson to check their understanding. They also provide a reminder to students and teachers about the intended learning behind a given lesson or activity.

EXPEDITIONARY
LEARNING

B. Introducing the Research Guide (5 minutes)

- Ask students to refer to their **Research Guide**, with which they familiarized themselves for homework. Invite students to read the headings of the columns on the Research Guide, and then the titles of the rows, with you. Ask students to Think-Pair-Share:

  - "Look at the left-hand column of the Research Guide. What do you think you are going to record in each row of this column? Why?"

- Listen for students to explain that they are going to record the strongest evidence that explains who the refugee is, where the refugee fled from, where the refugee fled to, the time in history when it happened, and why the refugee fled. Students should notice that these are aspects of the universal refugee experience they learned about earlier in the unit (Lessons 4 and 5).

- Highlight the words in brackets and explain that these are the specific details they will be looking for.

- Focus students on the right-hand column, Source Information. Ask them to Think-Pair-Share:

  - "What do you think you are going to record in the right-hand column of the Research Guide? Why?"

- Listen for students to explain that they are going to cite the works they have used, as they did when writing their analysis essay.

Work Time

A. Reading All Research Texts for Gist (15 minutes)

- Provide the research teams with their **Research Folders**. Inform students that in this lesson, they get to dig into the research to find out more about a specific group of refugees. As a research team, they are going to find the gist of the materials within the Research Folders so that they can figure out what the text is mostly about before they begin looking for particular details.

- Distribute **Research Team Task Cards**. Focus students on Part A: Reading for Gist.

- Read the directions aloud as students read silently.

- Emphasize that reading for gist is something real researchers do. Invite students to read the informational texts in their Research Folders for gist.

- Circulate to assist students with reading.

Meeting Students' Needs

- Refer students to the glossary for each of the texts in the Research Folders to help them understand unfamiliar words.

- Providing students with task cards ensures that expectations are consistently available.

- Encourage students to choose a text from the Research Folder that is most appropriate for their reading level—encourage students to challenge themselves within reason.

B. Reading One Research Text to Identify "Who? Where? and Why?" Details (8 minutes)

- Remind students of the "Who? Where? and Why?" questions on the Research Guide. Now that they have gotten a sense of the gist of the various texts in their folders, they will work in pairs to read just one text in more detail.

- Focus students on task card Part B: Rereading for "Who? Where? and Why?" Answer clarifying questions as needed.

- Display one of the informational texts. Follow the directions on the task card to model for students how to underline the text as the task card directs.

- Distribute **colored pencils** (or highlighters) and ask students to follow the part B directions to identify and underline in colored pencils the specific information to answer the "Who? Where? and Why?" questions.

- Circulate to assist students with reading to identify the details. Remind students of the guiding words in brackets on the Research Guide.

Meeting Students' Needs

Graphic organizers and recording forms engage students more actively and provide scaffolding that is especially critical for learners with lower levels of language proficiency and/or learning.

C. Gathering Evidence on Research Guides (10 minutes)

- Remind students that in Unit 3, they will use the answers from their Research Guide to be creative and write "Inside Out" and "Back Again" poems.

- Model how to fill out the first row of the Research Guide using the information from the text you underlined as a model during Work Time. Focus first on the Who? information underlined in red. Transfer the information underlined in red onto the first row of the Research Guide. Show students how underlining in different colors should make scanning the text for this evidence easier.

- Record the details of the text in the second column and explain that next you would move on to the Where? evidence underlined in this same text, and that you would finish working with one text before moving on to another.

- Invite students to follow along silently as you read Part C: Gathering Evidence on Research Guides.

- Invite groups to follow the directions to record evidence in each of the sections of the Research Guide.

- Inform students that they will finish collecting this evidence to answer the "Who? Where? and Why?" questions for homework.

Meeting Students' Needs

When you're reviewing the graphic organizers or recording forms, consider using a document camera to display the document for students who struggle with auditory processing.

Closing and Assessment

A. Sharing Evidence (5 minutes)

- Ask students to bring their texts and Research Guide and gather in their original numbered heads groups (so students who are studying different refugee contexts get to share with one another). Ask students to pair up, number 1s with 2s and number 3s with 4s.

- Invite students to share their answer to the following question, based on the evidence they have collected so far on their Research Guide:

  - "Now that you have looked through the stories of refugees, who are the refugees from this specific time and place in history? What do you know about them?"

- As time permits, invite a few students to share out with the whole group. Push students to keep thinking about the strongest evidence they collected as they researched today:

  - "Which details seem most relevant given the poems you are preparing to write? Why?"

Homework

For the text you read with your partner, finish recording the strongest "Who? Where? and Why?" evidence onto your Research Guide. Read other texts if you choose.

LESSON 20

End-of-Unit 2 Assessment, Part 2

Final Draft of Analytical Essay

Long-Term Targets Addressed (Based on ELA CCSS)

- I can write informative/explanatory texts that convey ideas and concepts using relevant information that is carefully selected and organized. (W.8.2)
- With support from peers and adults, I can use the writing process to ensure that the purpose and audience have been addressed. (W.8.5)
- I can use evidence from literary texts to support analysis, reflection, and research. (W.8.9)

Supporting Learning Targets

I can use teacher feedback to revise my analytical essay to meet the expectations of the Grades 6–8 Expository Writing Evaluation Rubric.

Ongoing Assessment

- End-of-Unit 2 Assessment, Part 2: Final Draft of Analytical Essay

Agenda

1. Opening
   A. Unpacking Learning Target (2 minutes)
   B. Examining Row 4 of the Expository Writing Evaluation Rubric (5 minutes)

---

2. Work Time

    A.   Mini Lesson: Addressing Common Errors (5 minutes)

    B.   Return Draft Essays with Feedback (6 minutes)

    C.   Essay Revision (25 minutes)

3. Closing and Assessment

    A.   Collecting End-of-Unit Assessment Essays (2 minutes)

4. Homework

    A.   Finish the final essay draft.

    B.   Continue independent reading book.

Teaching Notes

- This lesson provides an opportunity for students to review their essays to meet the expectations of the expository writing evaluation rubric.

- In advance: Be sure to have reviewed students' drafts (from Lesson 17). Give specific positive feedback for at least one thing each student did well. Provide at least one specific area of focus for each student's revision.

- This lesson includes 5 minutes to address common mistakes you may have noticed while reviewing student essays. A sample structure is provided here. Focus the lesson on one specific common convention error you noticed as you assessed students' drafts.

- Some students may need more help than others with revising. There is time for this during the revision time.

- If students used computers in Lesson 17, allow them to use computers to revise.

- Some students may not finish their final drafts during this lesson. Consider whether to allow them to finish their essays as homework and hand them in at the beginning of the next lesson.

- Post: learning targets.

Lesson Vocabulary

conventions, standard English grammar, emerging, frequent, hinder

Materials

- *Inside Out & Back Again* (book; one per student)

- Grades 6–8 Expository Writing Evaluation Rubric (from Lesson 11)

- Writer's Glossary for Row 4 of the Expository Writing Evaluation Rubric (one per student)

- Student draft essays (from Lesson 17; with teacher feedback)

- Citing Books and Articles Anchor Chart (from Lesson 16)

- Materials for student writing (computers or lined paper)

Opening

A. Unpacking Learning Target (2 minutes)

- Invite the class to read aloud the learning target with you:
  - "I can use teacher feedback to revise my analytical essay to meet the expectations of the expository writing rubric."
- Ask students to Think-Pair-Share:
  - "Given what you have been learning from looking at the model essay and the expository writing rubric, and from planning your own essay, what do you want to focus on as you revise?"
- Emphasize that writing well is difficult, and revision is important to make your message as clear as possible for your readers. Encourage students and thank them in advance for showing persistence and stamina. Revising is difficult, but it is one of the things that can help make a good essay great.

Meeting Students' Needs

- The review of the learning targets is yet another identifier of what is expected on the student essays.

- Learning targets are a research-based strategy that helps all students, especially challenged learners.

- Posting learning targets enables students to refer to them throughout the lesson to check their understanding. They also provide a reminder to students and teachers about the intended learning behind a given lesson or activity.

B. Examining Row 4 of the Expository Writing Evaluation Rubric (5 minutes)

- Ask students to get out their copy of the **Grades 6–8 Expository Writing Evaluation Rubric** and give each student the **Writer's Glossary for Row 4 of the Expository Writing Evaluation Rubric**.

- The vocabulary words from the learning target and Row 4 of the rubric are already on the Writer's Glossary page. Ask students to read Row 4 of the rubric and add any other words they want to talk about.

- Go through the words on the Writer's Glossary page. First ask students whether they know the meaning of each word. If they do not, provide a brief definition and ask them to write the definitions on their pages.

- When you get to *standard English grammar,* say: "If *standard* means 'the way something must be done,' how would that relate to the English language?"

- If necessary, you could give an example of "standards" in the gas mileage that cars must meet. Once they respond with something similar to "standards must be the rules for English," point out why a language needs to have rules for how words are put together. Explain: "The standards for English mean that anyone in the world can understand what another English speaker is saying or writing if they both know and follow the rules."

- Point out that their essay should be clear to any English speaker and must follow the rules of standard English grammar. Ask them to give you an English grammar rule or two to be sure they understand what you are explaining. If they cannot offer examples, you might offer some examples like these: "Sentences need to have a subject and a verb," or "In English, we capitalize the first word in a sentence."

- It is important that students begin to realize why grammar matters when they write. They may have dialects or local speech patterns and words that are not understandable to English speakers elsewhere. There are many situations—conversations or personal writing—when other forms of English (and of course other languages) are totally fine. However, it is important to distinguish when a situation calls for or requires formal English. When they speak, their friends understand, but when they write, they are writing for a larger audience. As authors, it is their responsibility to be sure that readers can understand what they are saying about a topic. This is part of why they have been looking at the model essay so much—to start to get a feel for this more formal standard English.

Work Time

A. Mini Lesson: Addressing Common Errors (5 minutes)

- Inform students that you noticed a common error in their essay (e.g., comma splices or inconsistent capitalization).

- Display an example of the error. Explain why it is incorrect.

- Model how to revise and correct the error.

- Check for understanding. Ask students to give you a thumbs-up if they understand the error and how to fix it when revising or a thumbs-down if they don't fully understand.

- If many students give a thumbs-down, show another example of the error. Ask students to think about how to fix it.

- Cold-call on a student to suggest how to correct it. If the answer is incorrect, clarify. Again ask students to give you a thumbs-up or thumbs-down. If some students are still struggling, consider checking in with them individually.

B. Return Draft Essays with Feedback (6 minutes)

- Inform students that they will be getting their essay back now with specific feedback. Ask them to look over the comments and make sure they understand them. Invite students to raise their hands to ask questions if they have them. Alternatively, create a "Help List" on the board and invite students to add their names to it if they need questions answered.

- Return **students' draft essays**.

Meeting Students' Needs

The use of leading questions on student essays helps struggling students understand which areas they should improve before submitting their essays again.

C. Essay Revision (25 minutes)

- Be sure students have their copies of *Inside Out & Back Again*. Invite students to apply their learning from Row 4 of the rubric, the mini lesson, and the feedback given on their draft to revise their essay.

- Refer to the **Citing Books and Articles Anchor Chart**, and remind students to cite the last name of the author and page number of their evidence within the essay and to create a Works Cited list at the end of the essay containing all the books and articles they have cited.

- If they are using computers to write their essays, students can review and revise. If they are hand-writing their essay, students will need **lined paper** to write a best copy of their essay, incorporating the feedback and learning from the mini lesson.

- Circulate around the room, addressing questions. Consider checking in first with students who need extra support to make sure they use their time well.

- When a few minutes are left, if students are working on computers, ask them to save their work.

Closing and Assessment

A. Collecting End-of-Unit Assessment Essays (2 minutes)

- Give students specific positive praise for perseverance you observed. Collect the final drafts from those students who think that they have finished (plus all of their organizers and planners).

- Based on whether you want this to be a timed assessment, consider whether to give students who still want more time the option of finishing for homework.

Homework

- If you haven't already, finish the final draft of your essay to turn in tomorrow, along with the first draft, rubric, and planners.

- Continue reading your independent reading book for this unit.

UNIT OVERVIEW

Culminating Project

Free-Verse Poems "Inside Out" and "Back Again"

In Unit 3, students draw upon their study of the universal refugee experience to write two research-based poems that reflect the "inside out" and "back again" aspects of a refugee's experience. Students collaborate in research teams to research the experiences of refugees of a specific culture. They then draw upon the research and their study of the novel and the informational texts to write two poems. Students gather the strongest evidence from informational texts to answer specific questions "Who? Where? and Why?" and use their answers to write an "Inside Out" poem about a fictional character who has experienced some real events the students learn about in their research. This "Inside Out" poem establishes the time, place, and reason for the refugee's fleeing home. As students prepare to write this poem, they return to the novel to study a poem for its craft and structure as well as word choice and figurative language. Students' writing of the poem is also supported through the use of a poem graphic organizer. The Mid-Unit Assessment task is the students' best first draft of this poem. Students then draft their "Back Again" poems, aligned with each student's individual interpretation of informational text and his or her own background knowledge and experiences. Students receive peer critique on both poems to ensure they are setting their poems in a particular scene to give the details and information they are including an appropriate context. Students then write a best draft of their two revised poems and present them to peers from other research teams. This serves as the final performance task, which centers on **CCSS RI.8.1; RI.8.2; W.8.3.a, b, d; W.8.4; W.8.5; W.8.7; W.8.9; L.8.1; L.8.2; and L.8.6.**

Guiding Questions and Big Ideas

- What common themes unify the refugee experience?

- How can we tell powerful stories about people's experiences?

- *Authors select a genre of writing to fully engage the reader.*

- *Characters change over time in response to challenges; this is shared through the use of statistics and working through the review of the individual poems.*

Mid-Unit 3 Assessment

Best First Draft of "Inside Out" Poem

This assessment centers on ELA CCSS RI.8.1; W.8.3.a, b, d; W.8.7; and W.8.9. Students use their Research Guides, which outline the research collected through their research teams, and their "Inside Out" Poem Graphic Organizer, which has specific question prompts aligned to the creation of an "Inside Out" poem, to write a first draft their "Inside Out" poem.

End-of-Unit 3 Assessment

Best First Draft of "Back Again" Poem

This assessment centers on ELA CCSS RI.8.1; W.8.3.a, b, d; W.8.7; and W.8.9. Students draft their "Back Again" poem about their same fictional refugee moving to a new country, sharing the experiences and feelings that the refugee might feel in adapting and mourning while adjusting to his or her new home. As with their "Inside Out" poem, students use a graphic organizer to help them plan.

Final Performance Task

Free-Verse Narrative Poems "Inside Out" and "Back Again"

For the final performance task of Module 1, students draw upon their study of the universal refugee experience to write two research-based poems that reflect the "inside out" and "back again" aspect of a refugee experience. Students collaborate in research teams to research the experiences of refugees of a specific culture. They then draw upon this research as well as their study of the novel and the informational texts to write two poems. The first, an "Inside Out" poem, is based on the research conducted. The second, a more creative "Back Again" poem, is aligned with each student's individual interpretation of informational text as well as his or her own background knowledge and experiences. The students have the opportunity to revise, edit, and share their two poems within the classroom and with other research teams for the final performance task, which centers on **CCSS RI.8.1; RI.8.2; W.8.3.a, b, d; W.8.4; W.8.5; W.8.7; W.8.9; L.8.1; L.8.2; and L.8.6.**

Content Connections

This module is designed to address English Language Arts (ELA) standards. However, the module intentionally incorporates Social Studies content that many teachers may be teaching during other parts of the day. These intentional connections are described below.

Social Studies Connection

Social Studies Themes in Context:

- Individual Development and Cultural Identity
  - Role of social, political, and cultural interactions in the development of identity

- • Personal identity as a function of an individual's culture, time, place, geography, interaction with groups, influences from institutions, and lived experiences
- • Development, Movement, and Interaction of Cultures
  - • Role of diversity within and among cultures

Central Texts

1. Thanhha Lai, *Inside Out & Back Again*. New York: HarperCollins, 2011.
2. Research texts: See Unit 2, Lesson 19 Supporting Materials for a complete list of texts students continue to work with as a part of their short research project.

Unit-at-a-Glance Calendar

This unit is approximately 1.5 weeks, or 6 lessons, of instruction. Note, however, that Lessons 18 and 19 in Unit 2 (research) in effect launch Unit 3.

Lesson	Lesson Title	Long-Term Targets	Supporting Targets	Ongoing Assessment	Anchor Charts and Protocols
1	Finishing "Who? Where? and Why?" Research	• I can conduct short research projects to answer a question. (W.8.7) • I can use evidence from informational texts to support analysis, reflection, and research. (W.8.9)	• I can find the gist of informational texts. • I can select the strongest evidence in an informational text about who the refugees were, where they fled from, and why they had to flee.	• Research Guide • Character Profile on the "Inside Out" Poem Graphic Organizer	• Think-Pair-Share protocol

			• I can express my own ideas clearly during discussion, and I can build on others' ideas during discussions. (SL.8.1)	• I can use the evidence I have gathered in research to create a culturally appropriate fictional character profile for the refugee narrator of my "Inside Out" poem.		
2	Analyzing Poems from *Inside Out & Back Again* to Develop Criteria for an Effective Poem		• I can determine a theme or central ideas of literary text. (RL.8.2) • I can express my own ideas clearly during discussions. (SL.8.1) • I can analyze figurative language, word relationships, and nuances in word meanings. (L.8.5)	• I can identify figurative and descriptive language as well as purposeful word choice in the "Papaya Tree" and "Wet and Crying" poems from *Inside Out & Back Again*. • I can describe the criteria of an effective poem. • I can use figurative and descriptive language as well as purposeful word choice to turn my research notes into free-verse narrative poetry.	• What Makes an Effective Poem? Anchor Chart • "Inside Out" Poem Graphic Organizer	• Think-Pair-Share protocol • What Makes an Effective Poem? Anchor Chart

| 3 | Mid-Unit Assessment: Writing Best First Draft of "Inside Out" Poem | • I can write narrative text about real or imagined experiences using relevant details and event sequences that make sense. (W.8.3)

• I can produce text (print or nonprint) that explores a variety of cultures and perspectives. (W.8.4.a)

• With support from peers and adults, I can use the writing process to ensure that purpose and audience have been addressed. (W.8.5)

• I can conduct short research projects to answer a question. (W.8.7) | • I can write a poem describing how the narrator, a refugee, turns "inside out" when he or she is forced to flee home.

• I can write an "inside out" poem based on factual details about real-life refugees from informational texts.

• I can use figurative and descriptive language as well as purposeful word choice to add tone and meaning to my "Inside Out" poem. | • Mid-Unit 3 Assessment: Best First Draft of "Inside Out" poem | • Peer Critique protocol

• What Makes an Effective Poem? Anchor Chart

• Think-Pair-Share protocol |

		• I can use several sources in my research. (W.8.7) • I can use evidence from informational texts to support analysis, reflection, and research. (W.8.9) • I can effectively engage in discussions with diverse partners about eighth-grade topics, texts, and issues. (SL.8.1)			
4	End-of-Unit Assessment: Writing Best First Draft of "Back Again" Poem	• I can write narrative text about real or imagined experiences using relevant details and event sequences that make sense. (W.8.3)	• I can write a poem describing how the narrator, a refugee, turns "back again" as he or she adapts to life in a new country.	• Mid-Unit 3 Assessment: Best First Draft of "Back Again" poem	• What Makes an Effective Poem? Anchor Chart

		• With support from peers and adults, I can use the writing process to ensure that the purpose and audience have been addressed. (W.8.5) • I can effectively engage in discussions with diverse partners about eighth-grade topics, texts, and issues. (SL.8.1)	• I can create meaning in my "Back Again" poem by using figurative and descriptive language as well as purposeful word choice to convey a certain tone.		
5	Peer Critique of "Inside Out" and "Back Again" Poems	• I can write narrative text about real or imagined experiences using relevant details and event sequences that make sense. (W.8.3) • With support from peers and adults, I can use the writing process to ensure that the purpose	• I can use the "Inside Out" and "Back Again" Poetry Rubric to provide kind, specific, and helpful feedback to my peers.	• Revised "Inside Out" and "Back Again" poems • Stars and Steps for "Inside Out" and "Back Again" poems	• Think-Pair-Share protocol

		and audience have been addressed. (W.8.5) • I can conduct short research projects to answer a question. (W.8.7) • I can use several sources in my research. (W.8.7) • I can use evidence from informational texts to support analysis, reflection, and research. (W.8.9) • I can effectively engage in discussions with diverse partners about eighth-grade topics, texts, and issues. (SL.8.1)	• I can create meaning in my "Inside Out" and "Back Again" poems by using figurative and descriptive language and purposeful word choice to convey a certain tone. • I can use peer feedback to revise my "Inside Out" and "Back Again" poems.		
6	Revision: Best Draft of "Inside Out" and "Back Again" Poems (Final Performance Task)	• I can write narrative text about real or imagined experiences using relevant details and event sequences that make sense. (W.8.3)	• I can write a final draft of two poems describing how the narrator, a refugee, turns "inside out" and "back again" as he or she flees home and adapts to life in a new country.	• Best draft of "Inside Out" and "Back Again" poems	• What Makes an Effective Poem? Anchor Chart • Think-Pair-Share protocol

		• With support from peers and adults, I can use the writing process to ensure that the purpose and audience have been addressed. (W.8.5) • I can effectively engage in discussions with diverse partners about eighth-grade topics, texts, and issues. (SL.8.1) • I can use correct grammar and usage when writing or speaking. (L.8.1) • I can use correct capitalization, punctuation and spelling to send a clear message to my reader. (L.8.2)	• I can create meaning in my "Inside Out" and "Back Again" poems by using figurative and descriptive language and purposeful word choice to convey a certain tone. • I can use correct grammar and punctuation in my "Inside Out" and "Back Again" poems.		

EXPEDITIONARY
LEARNING

Optional: Experts and Fieldwork

Experts

• Invite poets to visit the class to describe to the students how they write poetry and to read some of their poetry for the students.

Fieldwork

• Local libraries sometimes host poetry events. This could be a place for students to hear poetry and/ or read their poetry to others.

Optional: Extensions

• Organize a forum for students to read their poems aloud for an audience. For example, students could host a poetry evening or read their poems to other classes in the school.

• Consider arranging an outside audience to listen to students share their poems in Lesson 6, or they may share at a more formal poetry reading.

• If technology allows, students could record their poems.

Preparation and Materials

• Students will be receiving many recording forms, graphic organizers, and texts throughout this module. It is suggested that students have a binder in which to collect these materials and refer back to them. Alternately, teachers who prefer to use notebooks or journals can use the recording forms and graphic organizers as a template with which to model for students to create these structures independently.

Independent Reading and Reading Response Letter

Some students, especially stronger readers, will finish *Inside Out & Back Again* early in the unit. They should be encouraged to complete independent reading related to the topic of the unit. See the lists of Recommended Texts in Unit 1 and Unit 2, which include texts at many levels. The daily lessons do not include time to check on students' independent reading, but consider how you might support students with this volume of reading. Included is a template for a Reader's Response letter, a format students can use to share their thinking about their reading with you or with their peers. Some teachers create a binder of these letters, and then future students can look through them as they select books to read.

LESSON 1

Finishing "Who? Where? and Why?" Research
Long-Term Targets Addressed (Based on ELA CCSS)

- I can conduct short research projects to answer a question. (W.8.7)
- I can use evidence from informational texts to support analysis, reflection, and research. (W.8.9)
- I can express my own ideas clearly during discussion, and I can build on others' ideas during discussions. (SL.8.1)

Supporting Learning Targets

- I can find the *gist* of informational texts.
- I can select the strongest evidence in an informational text about who the refugees were, where they fled from, and why they had to flee.
- I can use the evidence I have gathered in research to create a culturally appropriate fictional character profile for the refugee narrator of my "Inside Out" poem.

Ongoing Assessment

- Research Guide
- Character Profile on the "Inside Out" Poem Graphic Organizer

Agenda

1. Opening
   A. Review Learning Targets (2 minutes)
   B. Sharing Strongest Evidence (5 minutes)
2. Work Time
   A. Finishing Research (20 minutes)
   B. Review Performance Task Prompt (5 minutes)
   C. Building a Character Profile (8 minutes)

3. Closing and Assessment

   A. Becoming the Character in an Interview (5 minutes)

4. Homework

   A. Get familiar with the "Inside Out" Poem Graphic Organizer.

Teaching Notes

- This is the first lesson in Unit 3. However, students began their research for the performance task in Unit 2, Lessons 18 and 19.

- Students start by sharing with a peer the evidence they collected for homework. This makes students accountable for completing their homework. It also gives them the opportunity to add research to their Research Guide that they may have missed.

- During Work Time, students finish using the informational texts in their Research Folders to gather enough evidence on their Research Guides to plan their "Inside Out" poems. Continue to emphasize with students that this is a very short research project and that they are not expected to know everything about their assigned complex time and place in history. Their goal is simply to be able to tell the story of who, where, why, and how their refugee turned "inside out."

- During this lesson, students are formally introduced to the "Inside Out" Poem Graphic Organizer, which they will use to organize their research into a free-verse narrative poem. Students do not complete the entire "Inside Out" Poem Graphic Organizer in this lesson, though; they fill out only the character profile at the beginning of the organizer.

- Review: Final performance task (see Lesson 18).

- Post: Learning targets, directions for closing activity.

Lesson Vocabulary

culturally appropriate, fictional, character profile

Materials

- Research Guide (from Unit 2, Lesson 18)
- Research Folder (from Unit 2, Lesson 19)
- Research Task Card (from Unit 2, Lesson 19)
- Student-Friendly Performance Task Prompt (from Unit 2, Lesson 18)
- "Inside Out" Poem Graphic Organizer (one per student)

Opening

A. Review Learning Targets (2 minutes)

- Ask the students to read along as you read the learning targets aloud:

  - "I can find the *gist* of informational texts."

- "I can select the strongest evidence in an informational text about who the refugees were, where they fled from, and why they had to flee."

- "I can use the evidence I have gathered in research to create a culturally appropriate fictional character profile for the refugee narrator of my 'Inside Out' poem."

- Students should be familiar with the first two targets because they are the same as the targets for Unit 2, Lesson 19.

- Focus students on the third learning target. Ask them to Think-Pair-Share:

  - "What does *culturally appropriate* mean?"

  - "What does *fictional* mean?"

  - "What is a *character profile*?"

- Listen for students to explain that *culturally appropriate* means "they have considered the culture of their refugee," that *fictional* means "made up," and that a *character profile* is "building an idea of who the character is."

- Use Ha as an example. Remind students that Ha is a fictional character—a young girl from Vietnam who flees with her family to Alabama to escape the dangers of the war. Although Thanhha Lai, the author of *Inside Out & Back Again,* was herself a refugee from Vietnam, she made up a fictional character to tell the story.

Meeting Students' Needs

- Learning targets are a research-based strategy that helps all students, especially challenged learners.

- Discussing and clarifying the language of learning targets help build academic vocabulary.

- Posting learning targets enables students to refer to them throughout the lesson to check their understanding. This also provides a reminder to students and teachers about the intended learning behind a given lesson or activity.

B. Sharing Strongest Evidence (5 minutes)

- Ask students to get into research teams and then get out their research texts and their **Research Guide** (from Unit 2, Lesson 19).

- Remind students that part of their homework in Unit 2, Lesson 19 was to finish collecting the strongest "Who? Where? and Why?" evidence on their Research Guide from the informational text they read in that lesson.

- Invite students to pair up within their research team to work with a peer who read and annotated one of the other informational texts from their **Research Folder**. They are going to share the "Who? Where? and Why?" evidence recorded on their Research Guide, referring back to the texts.

- Encourage students to record any "Who? Where? and Why?" evidence they are missing on their Research Guide as their peers share.

Work Time

A. Finishing Research (20 minutes)

- Inform students that in this lesson they are going to finish collecting evidence from the texts in their Research Folder.

- Invite students to refer to their **Research Task Card** from previous lessons and inform them that, as in the previous lesson, they are going to work on the remaining texts in their Research Folder to find the gist, underline the "Who? Where? and Why?" evidence, and then record that evidence in the appropriate boxes on their Research Guide.

- Advise students that they may all need to work on the same text this time, as they may have only one text left to work with, but they are still to work in pairs.

- Circulate to assist students with reading for the gist and identifying the "Who? Where? and Why?" details. Remind students of the guiding words in brackets on the Research Guide.

Meeting Students' Needs

- Refer students to the glossary for each of the texts in the Research Folder to help them understand unfamiliar words.

- Providing students with task cards ensures that expectations are consistently available.

B. Review Performance Task Prompt (5 minutes)

- Celebrate the work that students have done in collecting the strongest evidence from the informational texts. Remind them that this is something that researchers have to do in the real world when they gather evidence, so it is a very important skill to practice.

- Inform the students that over the next few lessons they will use the evidence recorded on their Research Guide to develop their individual "Inside Out" poem.

- Invite students to reread Part 2 of the **Student-Friendly Performance Task Prompt** (from Unit 2, Lesson 18) silently as you read it aloud: "Imagine that you are a refugee from this specific time and place in history. You, like Ha and the real refugees we have read about, have been forced to flee your home country for your safety. On your own, write two free-verse poems similar to Ha's diary entries in the novel *Inside Out & Back Again*. The first poem will be an 'Inside Out' poem. For this poem, consider these questions:

  - What hardships did you face in your country?

  - Why did you decide to flee your country?

  - What was it like for you after you fled?

  - Where did you go?

  - Where did you find help?

- Where did you settle?

- How was your life turned 'inside out'?"

- Remind students that the questions in the prompt are to help them think about what they know about their refugee. They don't have to answer all of these questions in their poem, because they may not have found all of this information in their research texts, but they should use the questions as guidelines for the kinds of details to include to make their poem more realistic and believable.

- Ask students to Think-Pair-Share:

  - "So what is your 'Inside Out' poem going to be about?"

- Listen for students to explain that they are going to imagine they are a refugee from the country they have researched and they are going to write a poem that answers the questions and explains how their lives turn "inside out" when they have to flee.

C. Building a Character Profile (8 minutes)

- Remind students that even though they have been gathering factual information, they are going to be using it to write a fictional poem, just like the poems in the novel *Inside Out & Back Again*. Advise students that now they are going to begin the creative process by using the evidence they have collected to consider who their refugee is going to be.

- Display and distribute the **"Inside Out" Poem Graphic Organizer.** Give students a minute to read through it.

- Focus their attention on the Character Profile section at the top of the handout, and ask them to read it with you.

- Inform students that in the same way Thanhha Lai created Ha to be the fictional narrator of the poems in *Inside Out & Back Again,* each of them is going to build a profile of a fictional character to be the narrator of their poem. They are going to use the research they have conducted to determine where this person fled from, why he or she fled, and where he or she fled to—but students can decide the age of their refugee and whether this person is male or female.

- Explain that students can name their refugee if they have seen names of people in their research to use; otherwise, they should avoid choosing a name, as people from different places sometimes have different types of names than students are familiar with. It would make their poem unrealistic if the refugee had a culturally inappropriate name.

- Use the example of Ha to model how to fill out the character profile:

  - Who is your refugee? *Ha, a female child.*

  - Where did he/she come from? *Vietnam at the time of the Vietnam War.*

  - Why did he/she flee? *Because there was a war, it was dangerous, and the family was suffering through lack of food.*

  - Where did he/she flee to? *Alabama.*

- Invite students to spend a couple of minutes thinking about who their fictional character is going to be before recording it on their character profile.

- Circulate to assist students in filling out their character profiles. Look in particular for those students who have chosen names that may not be culturally appropriate; ask questions to encourage them to reconsider their choices:

  - "Where is that name in your article?"

  - "How do you know it is culturally appropriate?"

Meeting Students' Needs

- Graphic organizers and recording forms engage students more actively and provide scaffolding that is especially critical for learners with lower levels of language proficiency and/or learning.

- When you're reviewing the graphic organizers or recording forms, consider using a document camera to display the document for students who struggle with auditory processing.

- Modeling provides a clear vision of the expectation for students.

Closing and Assessment

A. Becoming the Character in an Interview (5 minutes)

- Invite students to pair up with a student from another research team. Inform them that they will write their poem as if they are the refugees, just as with Ha's poems, so they are going to practice being the refugee they have developed in their character profile.

- Let them know that they are going to interview their partner and be interviewed using the questions on the character profile. They do not need to speak as if they are reading poetry—they just need to answer the questions, giving as many details as possible, as if they are the refugee.

- Post these directions:

  1. In your pairs, decide who will be number 1 and who will be number 2.

  2. Number 1, use your character profile to pretend to be your character.

  3. Number 2, interview number 1 by asking the following questions:

     - Who are you?

     - Where did you come from?

     - Why did you flee?

     - Where did you flee to?

  4. Switch roles.

Meeting Students' Needs

Consider partnering ELL students who speak the same home language when discussion of complex content is required. This can allow students to have more meaningful discussions and clarify points in their native language.

Homework

Familiarize yourself with the rest of the "Inside Out" Poem Graphic Organizer to get ready for the next lesson. Be clear about what you think should be recorded in each column and why so that you are prepared for a discussion. Do not record anything else on the organizer yet.

LESSON 2

Analyzing Poems from *Inside Out & Back Again* to Develop Criteria for an Effective Poem

Long-Term Targets Addressed (Based on ELA CCSS)

- I can determine a theme or central ideas of literary text. (RL.8.2)
- I can express my own ideas clearly during discussions. (SL.8.1)
- I can analyze figurative language, word relationships, and nuances in word meanings. (L.8.5)

Supporting Learning Targets

- I can identify figurative and descriptive language as well as purposeful word choice in the "Papaya Tree" and "Wet and Crying" poems from *Inside Out & Back Again*.
- I can describe the criteria of an effective poem.
- I can use figurative and descriptive language as well as purposeful word choice to turn my research notes into free-verse narrative poetry.

Ongoing Assessment

- What Makes an Effective Poem? Anchor Chart
- "Inside Out" Poem Graphic Organizer

Agenda

1. Opening
   A. Unpacking Learning Targets (2 minutes)
   B. Introducing the What Makes an Effective Poem? Anchor Chart (8 minutes)

---

2. Work Time

    A. Analyzing "Papaya Tree" for Word Choice, Tone, and Meaning (15 minutes)

    B. Analyzing "Wet and Crying" for Word Choice, Tone, and Meaning (10 minutes)

    C. Applying Learning from Research on "Inside Out" Poem Graphic Organizer (8 minutes)

3. Closing and Assessment

    A. Begin Filling Out "Inside Out" Poem Graphic Organizer (2 minutes)

4. Homework

    A. Finish filling out the Graphic Organizer.

Teaching Notes

- This lesson signals the transition from students' very short research project to the writing of their poem.

- Students analyze two poems from the novel using the same note-catcher they used in Unit 1 to analyze word choice and to make them aware of the use of language in an effective poem. These specific poems have been selected because they contain facts and examples of figurative language and they are linked through subject matter.

- Once they have identified the criteria of an effective poem, students begin to turn their research into poetry ideas on a graphic organizer. This is challenging for students, so it is modeled using the story of Ha as an example. Students finish filling out the graphic organizer for homework to give them plenty of time to work on ideas.

- In advance: Review the poems "Papaya Tree" (pages 8 and 9) and "Wet and Crying" (page 60) from *Inside Out & Back Again*. Focus on the figurative and descriptive language as well as purposeful word choice and how it is anchored in specific content—something that is happening or the character is seeing. Continue to emphasize with students that they need to write about a specific scene.

- Post: Learning targets.

Lesson Vocabulary

figurative language, purposeful word choice, free verse, narrative, tone, stanza, scene

Materials

- *Inside Out & Back Again* (book; one per student)

- What Makes an Effective Poem? Anchor Chart (new; co-created with students during Opening and Work Time; see Supporting Materials)

- What Makes an Effective Poem? Note-Catcher (one per student)

- Word Choice, Tone, and Meaning Note-Catcher (one per student and one to display)

- Document camera
- "Inside Out" Poem Graphic Organizer (from Lesson 1)
- Research Guide (from Unit 2, Lesson 18)

Opening

A. Unpacking Learning Targets (2 minutes)

- Ask students to sit in research teams.
- Invite them to read the learning targets with you:
  - "I can identify figurative and descriptive language as well as purposeful word choice in the 'Papaya Tree' and 'Wet and Crying' poems from *Inside Out & Back Again*."
  - "I can describe the criteria of an effective poem."
  - "I can use figurative and descriptive language as well as purposeful word choice to turn my research notes into free-verse narrative poetry."
- Focus on the first learning target. Invite students to Think-Pair-Share with a peer in their research teams:
  - "What is *figurative language*?"
  - "What does *purposeful word choice* mean?"
- Listen for students to explain that *figurative language* is when you "describe something by comparing it to something else."
- Invite students to Think-Pair-Share:
  - "What is a *free-verse* poem?"
  - "What is a *narrative*?"
  - "So what kind of poem is this going to be?"
- Listen for students to explain that a *free-verse poem* "doesn't follow any particular pattern and doesn't rhyme. It follows the pattern of speech, much like the poems in *Inside Out & Back Again*." A *narrative* is "a story," so their poem is going to tell a story.

Meeting Students' Needs

- Learning targets are a research-based strategy that help all students, especially challenged learners.
- Discussing and clarifying the language of learning targets help build academic vocabulary.
- Posting learning targets enables students to reference them throughout the lesson to check their understanding. This also provides a reminder to students and teachers about the intended learning behind a given lesson or activity.

B. Introducing Anchor Chart: What Makes an Effective Poem? (8 minutes)

- Remind students that they will use information from their research as they write an "Inside Out" poem and later a "Back Again" poem. Post the new **What Makes an Effective Poem? Anchor Chart** and invite students to read the question with you:

  - "Think about the poems you have read in the novel *Inside Out & Back Again*. What makes an effective poem?"

- Distribute the **What Makes an Effective Poem? Note-Catcher**. Give students a couple of minutes to refer to *Inside Out & Back Again* and to think about their response to this question before recording their ideas on the note-catcher.

- Have students sit with their research teams from the previous lessons and invite them to discuss their initial responses to the question with each other.

- Select a student from each team to share with the whole class the ideas the team discussed. As they share, note criteria on the left-hand column of the anchor chart.

- Remind students that identifying criteria for effective poems is the main focus of this lesson, so it's fine if at this point they don't have many ideas about what makes a poem effective.

Meeting Students' Needs

Anchor charts serve as note-catchers when the class is co-constructing ideas.

Work Time

A. Analyzing "Papaya Tree" for Word Choice, Tone, and Meaning (15 minutes)

- Remind the class that before writing, it is often useful to analyze good models to figure out what makes a piece of writing successful. Inform students that for the rest of this lesson, they are going to be analyzing poems from *Inside Out & Back Again* to figure out what makes them effective so that they can add this information to the What Makes an Effective Poem? Anchor Chart for reference when writing their own poems.

- Give students a couple of minutes to reread the poem "Papaya Tree" on pages 8 and 9 of *Inside Out & Back Again* independently. Then ask:

  - "What is this poem about?"

  - "What does it tell us? What is the purpose of this poem?"

- Listen for students to explain that the poem tells the story of a papaya tree that grew from a seed that Ha threw into the garden. In addition to telling us about how the papaya tree grew, the poem introduces us to the ages of Ha's brothers and what they do.

- Invite students to focus on the *scene* of this poem—where it is set. Ask:

  - "We are given these details about Ha's brothers in the context of a particular scene. What is the setting of this scene, which provides the context opportunity for Ha to describe the ages of her brothers?"

- Listen for students to explain that Ha uses the setting of the papaya tree as a context to provide details about the age of her brothers.

- Ask:

  - "So now that we know what 'Papaya Tree' is about and the scene it is set in to give the details a poetic but meaningful context, what criteria can we add to our effective poem anchor chart?"

  - "What evidence from the poem can we add to the Example column on the anchor chart?"

- Add student suggestions to the What Makes an Effective Poem? Anchor Chart. Make sure the following criteria are included:

  - Tells a story. Example: "The tree has grown twice as tall." Content in Context of Scene: Telling us the story of how the tree has grown.

  - Provides details in the context of a scene (the papaya tree) to help us better understand the whole story. Example: "Brother Khoi spotted the first white blossom. Four years older, he can see higher." Content in Context of Scene: Introducing the idea that Brother Khoi is older by describing how he can see the blossom because he is taller and then leading into revealing how much older he is.

- Read the second stanza of "Papaya Tree" and invite students to follow along silently: "A seed like a fish eye, slippery shiny black." Ask students to Think-Pair-Share:

  - "Why has the author chosen to compare the papaya seed to a fish eye?"

- Listen for students to explain that in comparing the seed to a fish eye, it gives the reader who may not have ever seen a papaya seed an idea of what it might look like and builds a visual image.

- Ask students to Think-Pair-Share:

  - "So what do we call it when something is compared to something else, like the papaya seed being compared to a fish eye?"

- Listen for students to explain that it is *figurative language* and that this particular example is a *simile*.

- Focus students' attention on the "slippery shiny black" part of the second stanza. Ask students to Think-Pair-Share:

  - "What kind of words has the author used here to describe the papaya seed? Why?"

- Listen for them to explain that the author has used *descriptive sensory adjectives* that describe how the seed looks and feels so that the reader can build a clear visual image.

- Distribute the **Word Choice, Tone, and Meaning Note-Catcher** and display it using a **document camera**. Remind students that this is similar to the note-catcher they used to analyze word choice, tone, and meaning in Unit 1, so they should be familiar with it.

- Inform students that they are now going to work with their research team to analyze word choice and tone in the poem and begin thinking about how word choice, tone, and meaning make a poem effective. Remind students of the work they did analyzing word choice, tone, and meaning of poems in the novel in Unit 1. Remind them of what the word *tone* means. Ask:

  - "What is *tone*?"

- Listen for students to explain that *tone* means "the feeling a text brings out in a reader, or the attitude an author has toward a subject."

- Review how to fill in the columns on the note-catcher. Ask students to Think-Pair-Share:

  - "What are you going to record in each column? Why?"

- Invite students to pair up within their research team. Give them 10 minutes to analyze and discuss word choice, tone, and meaning in the poem and fill out the note-catcher.

- Circulate and listen in to gauge how well students are connecting the author's word choice with tone and how tone contributes to meaning. Ask probing questions:

  - "What feeling or meaning does this word convey? Why?"

  - "How would you describe the tone? Why?"

  - "What examples of figurative language have you found?"

  - "What examples of descriptive language have you found?"

- Invite pairs to share their notes with the rest of their research team and to add anything new to their note-catchers that they hear from peers.

- Refocus students as a whole group. Cold-call on a few students to share their notes about word choice, tone, and meaning with the whole class.

Meeting Students' Needs

- Providing models of expected work supports all learners, especially challenged learners.

- Asking students to analyze good models to build criteria of an effective poem provides a scaffold for them to follow when writing their own poems.

- Graphic organizers and recording forms engage students more actively and provide the necessary scaffolding that is especially critical for learners with lower levels of language proficiency and/or learning.

- When you're reviewing the graphic organizers or recording forms, consider using a document camera to display the document for students who struggle with auditory processing.

B. Analyzing "Wet and Crying" for Word Choice, Tone, and Meaning (10 minutes)

- Give students a couple of minutes to reread independently the poem "Wet and Crying" on page 60 of *Inside Out & Back Again*. Ask:

  - "What is this poem about? What does it tell us? What is the purpose of this poem?"

  - "What is the connection between this poem and the earlier 'Papaya Tree' poem?"

  - "What is the scene that provides a context for our understanding of particular details about what is going on at the time?"

- Listen for students to explain that the poem tells the story of cutting down the biggest papaya on the papaya tree. It tells us that Ha's mother is worried about difficult times ahead and about how the family doesn't want to leave anything for the "communists" in the context of the scene of papaya tree, just as in the "Papaya Tree" poem.

- Ask:
  - "So knowing what 'Wet and Crying' is about, can we add any new criteria to our effective poem anchor chart?"
  - "What evidence from the poem can we add to the Example column on the anchor chart?"
- Add student suggestions to the What Makes an Effective Poem? Anchor Chart. Make sure the following criterion is included:
  - Gives details about what is going on in that time period in the context of a scene (the papaya tree). Example: "Saying it's better than letting the communists have it." Content in Context of Scene: Describing how Brother Vu wants to cut down the papaya to prevent the communists from getting it.
- Focus students on the layout of the poem. Remind them that each block of text is called a *stanza*; for example, the first stanza begins with, "My biggest papaya is light yellow, still flecked with green."
- Give students 30 seconds to read through the third stanza, beginning with, "Brother Vu chops; the head falls." Then ask:
  - "What do you notice about this stanza?"
  - "Why does the author structure it this way? Why doesn't she just write this on one line like a sentence?"
- Listen for students to explain that this structure makes the poem more dramatic by adding impact to each action described and helps the reader pause in certain places, which adds emphasis to particular words or phrases.
- Ask:
  - "So now that we know why the author has organized that stanza this way, can we add any new criteria to our effective poem anchor chart?"
  - "What evidence from the poem can we add to the Example column on the anchor chart?"
- Add student suggestions to the What Makes an Effective Poem? Anchor Chart. Make sure the following criterion is included:
  - Sentences are broken up to emphasize actions to add more drama and impact. Example: "Brother Vu chops; the head falls; a silver blade slices." Content in Context of Scene: Describing how Brother Vu cut the papaya down from the tree.
- Invite students to pair up with another student in their research team to analyze the word choice, tone, and meaning in "Wet and Crying" using the bottom of the note-catcher. Remind them to include figurative and descriptive language and how it adds meaning.
- Circulate and listen in to gauge how well students are connecting the author's word choice with tone and how tone contributes to meaning. Ask probing questions:
  - "What feeling or meaning does this word convey? Why?"
  - "How would you describe the tone? Why?"

- - "What examples of figurative language have you found?"
  - "What examples of descriptive language have you found?"

- Invite pairs to share their notes with the rest of their research team and to add anything new to their note-catchers that they hear from peers.

- Refocus students as a whole group. Cold-call on a few students to share their notes about word choice, tone, and meaning with the whole class.

- Ask students to discuss in their research team:

  - "So thinking about your analysis of word choice, tone, and meaning, what makes an effective poem? Why?"

- Cold-call on students and add suggestions to the What Makes an Effective Poem? Anchor Chart. Make sure the following criteria are added:

  - Purposeful word choice that makes the reader feel a certain way and conveys a tone and meaning that the author wants the reader to understand. Example: "Wet and Crying." Content in Context of Scene: Describing how Ha is sad to be leaving through a description of the seeds that spill out of the papaya that has been cut down.

  - Figurative language to help the reader understand what something looks like or how big it is. Example: "A seed like a fish eye." Content in Context of Scene: Describing what the papaya seed looks like.

  - Descriptive language (sensory adjectives) to help the reader create a visual image of what something looks and feels like. Example: "Slippery shiny black." Content in Context of Scene: Describing what the seed looks and feels like.

  - Strong, precise verbs that emphasize actions. Example: "Brother Vu chops; the head falls; a silver blade slices." Content in Context of Scene: Describing how the papaya is cut down.

C. Applying Learning from Research on "Inside Out" Poem Graphic Organizer (8 minutes)

- Ask students to get their **"Inside Out" Poem Graphic Organizers** that they started to familiarize themselves with for homework and their **Research Guide** completed in previous lessons.

- Display an "Inside Out" Poem Graphic Organizer and ask students:

  - "Who is Ha?"

- Ask for volunteers to share their suggestions. In the first column of the organizer, record their ideas to include the following:

  - Female child

  - Vietnamese

  - Not communist—doesn't agree with communism

- Ask students to focus on the space for them to record the scene underneath the character profile. Ask:

  - "What is the scene of the 'Papaya Tree' poem?"

  - "What is the scene of the 'Wet and Crying' poem?"

TEACHER GUIDE · Grade 8 · Module 1 · Unit 3 · Lesson 2   **333**

- Listen for students to explain that in both poems, it is the papaya tree.

- Remind students that one of the criteria of an effective poem is that it provides details in the context of a scene (refer to the What Makes an Effective Poem? Anchor Chart).

- Inform students that you have chosen the scene for the poem for the graphic organizer about Ha to be at night, when she is in bed trying to sleep. This is a time when adults often speak about things they don't want children to worry about, so it is a good opportunity to introduce details about what is going on. Record: "At night in the dark when she is in bed" next to the space marked "Scene."

- Remind students that this means that everything that happens in the poem is framed in the context of this scene.

- Ask students to discuss with their research team:

    - "So what do you think you are going to record in the middle column? Why?"

- Listen for students to explain that they are going to put their research details into poetic language in the context of the scene they have chosen using figurative and descriptive language and thinking about word choice, meaning, and tone.

- Invite students to help you model an example of how to turn this information into poetic language in the second column. Ask:

    - "How would you describe who Ha is using figurative or descriptive language or strong word choice in the context of the in-bed-at-night scene?"

- Ask for volunteers to share their suggestions; in the second column, record student ideas. The following are suggestions:

    - Little girls are not supposed to know, but I hear my brother's frantic whispers and mother's scared sobs through the dark blackness of the night.

    - I want to scream at them that I understand that terrible things are happening in my beloved Vietnam.

    - They growl under their breath to each other like a pack of frightened dogs about how the communists will take our things if we don't flee.

- Point out to students that they haven't written the complete poem on the organizer—they have just recorded a few ideas to help them write their poems.

- Ask students to Think-Pair-Share:

    - "Why those words? How do those words affect the meaning and tone of the poem?"

- Ask for volunteers to share their suggestions. In the third column, record student ideas. The following are suggestions:

    - "Little girl" sets up the female child narrator.

    - "Frantic" adds drama and action and tells the reader that something serious is happening.

    - "Scared sobs" tells the reader the mother is afraid of something.

EXPEDITIONARY
LEARNING

Closing and Assessment

A. Begin Filling Out "Inside Out" Poem Graphic Organizer (2 minutes)

- Invite students to begin filling out their "Inside Out" Poem Graphic Organizer in the same way that you modeled. Ask them to begin by thinking about the scene that their poem will be set in, as this will determine how they frame the content in the rest of the poem.

- Inform students that they are to finish filling out this "Inside Out" Poem Graphic Organizer for homework.

Homework

Use your completed Research Guide to finish filling out your graphic organizer using figurative and descriptive language as well as purposeful word choice so you can begin turning the information you have gathered through research into poetry.

Note: Hold on to the "Inside Out" Poem Graphic Organizer that you used to model in this lesson, because you will use it again in Lesson 3.

LESSON 3

Mid-Unit Assessment

Writing Best First Draft of "Inside Out" Poem

Long-Term Targets Addressed (Based on ELA CCSS)

- I can write narrative text about real or imagined experiences using relevant details and event sequences that make sense. (W.8.3)
- With support from peers and adults, I can use the writing process to ensure that the purpose and audience have been addressed. (W.8.5)
- I can conduct short research projects to answer a question. (W.8.7)
- I can use several sources in my research. (W.8.7)
- I can use evidence from informational texts to support analysis, reflection, and research. (W.8.9)
- I can effectively engage in discussions with diverse partners about eighth-grade topics, texts, and issues. (SL.8.1)

Supporting Learning Targets

- I can write a poem describing how the narrator, a refugee, turns "inside out" when he or she is forced to flee home.
- I can write an "Inside Out" poem based on factual details about real-life refugees from informational texts.
- I can use figurative and descriptive language as well as purposeful word choice to add tone and meaning to my "Inside Out" poem.

Ongoing Assessment

- Mid-Unit 3 Assessment: Best First Draft of "Inside Out" Poem

Agenda

1. Opening
    A. Unpacking Learning Targets (2 minutes)
    B. Sharing Homework in Research Teams (6 minutes)
2. Work Time
    A. Introduce "Inside Out" and "Back Again" Poetry Rubric (5 minutes)
    B. Draft "Inside Out" Poem (20 minutes)
    C. Introducing "Back Again" Poem (10 minutes)
3. Closing and Assessment
    A. Beginning to Plan "Back Again" Poem (2 minutes)
4. Homework
    A. Complete the "Back Again" Poem Graphic Organizer.

Teaching Notes

- In this lesson, students draft their "Inside Out" poems as the Mid-Unit Assessment. Note that they will revise this poem during Lesson 6 (as a part of their Final Performance Task).

- For the Mid-Unit Assessment, focus on just Row 2 (Command of Evidence in "Inside Out" poems only) of the "Inside Out" and "Back Again" Poetry Rubric (see Supporting Materials).

- Before Lesson 6, plan to give students specific feedback on their draft poem. In Lesson 6, they will revise both poems based on teacher and peer feedback (their Final Performance Task).

- At the end of the lesson, students begin to consider the "Back Again" poem they will write in the next lesson. Students will complete the graphic organizer for this poem at home for homework; they should be familiar with how to plan using the graphic organizer, since it is the same as the organizer they used to plan their "Inside Out" poems in Lesson 2.

- The "Back Again" poem is not research-based, although students can use the experiences of Ha in the novel *Inside Out & Back Again* and the experiences of real-life refugees in the "Refugees in Canada" informational text as inspiration.

- If the technology is available, provide computers for students to word-process their essays.

- In advance: Review the poem "But Not Bad" on page 233 of the novel, focusing on how it shows that Ha is turning "back again."

- Post: Learning targets, What Makes an Effective Poem? Anchor Chart.

Lesson Vocabulary

free verse, narrative

Materials

- What Makes an Effective Poem? Anchor Chart (from Lesson 2)
- "Inside Out" and "Back Again" Poetry Rubric (one per student)
- Document camera
- Mid-Unit 3 Assessment: Best First Draft of "Inside Out" Poem (one per student)
- Lined paper (two sheets per student)
- "Inside Out" Poem Graphic Organizer (from Lesson 2)
- "Back Again" Poem Graphic Organizer (one per student and one to display)
- Model "Inside Out" Poem Graphic Organizer (filled in by the teacher as a model for students during Lesson 2)

Opening

A. Unpacking Learning Targets (2 minutes)

- Students should be sitting with their research teams. Invite students to read the learning targets with you:
  - "I can write a poem describing how the narrator, a refugee, turns 'inside out' when he or she is forced to flee home."
  - "I can write an 'Inside Out' poem based on factual details about real-life refugees from informational texts."
  - "I can use figurative and descriptive language as well as purposeful word choice to add tone and meaning to my 'Inside Out' poem."
- Inform students that today they will be writing the first draft of their "Inside Out" poems for their Mid-Unit Assessment. Explain that this Mid-Unit Assessment is working toward the final performance task of writing their "Inside Out" and "Back Again" poems.

Meeting Students' Needs

- Learning targets are a research-based strategy that helps all students, especially challenged learners.
- Discussing and clarifying the language of learning targets help build academic vocabulary.
- Posting learning targets enables students to reference them throughout the lesson to check their understanding. This also provides a reminder to students and teachers about the intended learning behind a given lesson or activity.

B. Sharing Homework in Research Teams (6 minutes)

- Focus student attention on the **What Makes an Effective Poem? Anchor Chart** from the previous lesson. Invite students to read silently as you read the criteria aloud.

- Invite students to pair up within their research team and inform them that they will be swapping **"Inside Out" Poem Graphic Organizers** to get feedback from their peers.

- Give students 2 minutes to consider a specific question they would like to pose to their partner about something they would like feedback about, and ask them to write the question at the top of their poem graphic organizer.

- Invite students to swap their graphic organizers with their partner. Give them 2 minutes to read through their partner's organizer, thinking about the question posed and the criteria on the anchor chart.

- Give students another minute in silence to consider how to answer the question posed by their partner and to think of a question they would like to ask their partner that will help them revise their work. Give them an example: "Could you add a sensory adjective here about how it looks to make it more descriptive?"

- Invite students to share their question with their partner.

- When students are done, remind them to thank their partner. Also remind them that they don't necessarily have to follow the advice they have been given if they don't think it works—emphasize that the question posed by their partner may be useful in helping them revise, but it may not.

- Give students 2 minutes to revise their organizer if they choose.

Meeting Students' Needs

- Learning targets are a research-based strategy that helps all students, but it helps challenged learners the most.

- Posting learning targets for students enables them to refer to them throughout the lesson to check their understanding. The learning targets also provide a reminder to students and teachers about the intended learning behind a given lesson or activity.

Work Time

A. Introduce Poem Rubric (5 minutes)

- Refocus the whole group. Distribute the **"Inside Out" and "Back Again" Poetry Rubric** and display it using a **document camera**. Remind students that it is based on the expository writing rubric they used in the previous unit, so it should look familiar.

- Invite students to spend a couple of minutes reading through the rubric.

- Invite them to share notices and wonders. This rubric should look somewhat familiar to them, based on their more extensive work with the analytic rubric in Unit 2. Point out to students that the rubric has been adapted to suit this specific writing task: free-verse narrative poems.

- Address any clarifying questions. Remind students that they should have these criteria in mind as they draft their "Inside Out" poem today. They will get to revise this poem in Lesson 6, as a part of their Final Performance Task.

Meeting Students' Needs

Providing students with the rubric you will be using to assess their work sets expectations up front and provides them with clear criteria to follow to be successful.

B. Draft "Inside Out" Poem (20 minutes)

- Students use their Research Guides, which outline the research collected through their research team, and the "Inside Out" Poem Graphic Organizer, which has specific question prompts aligned to the creation of an "Inside Out" poem, to write the best first draft of their "Inside Out" poem.

- Refocus the whole group. Distribute the **Mid-Unit 3 Assessment: Best First Draft of "Inside Out" Poem**. Point out that this assessment is identical to the first paragraph of the Student-Friendly Performance Task Prompt they saw in Unit 2, Lesson 18.

- Read the assessment prompt aloud, and answer any clarifying questions. Remind students that the questions in the prompt are to help them think about what they know about their refugee. They don't have to answer all of these questions in their poem, as they may not have found all of this information in their research texts, but they should use them as a guideline for the kinds of details to include to make their poem more realistic and believable.

- Remind students of what *free-verse* and *narrative* mean, and refer them to the poems in the novel to remind them of the kind of poem they will be writing.

- Inform students that they are now going to use their "Inside Out" Poem Graphic Organizer, the What Makes an Effective Poem? Anchor Chart, and the "Inside Out" and "Back Again" Poetry Rubric to write the first draft of their "Inside Out" poem.

- Set the parameter that the poem should be no more than four verses or stanzas long and that each verse should contain no more than six lines of poetry. This will encourage students to be more precise.

- Remind them that because this is an assessment, they are to do this work independently in silence. If students are not able to work on computers, distribute **lined paper**. Invite students to draft their "Inside Out" poems.

- Circulate to take this opportunity to make informal assessments of students' work. Make sure students are using their research to create the narrative experience of their refugee.

C. Introducing "Back Again" Poem (10 minutes)

- Inform students that now that they have finished their "Inside Out" poem, they are going to start thinking about their "Back Again" poem.

- Ask students to refer to the final paragraph of their Student-Friendly Performance Task Prompt about the "Back Again" poem: "The second poem will be a 'back again' poem. For this poem, consider these questions:
  - What adaptations have you made as you settle into your new home?
  - What are you mourning from your old life?
  - How is your identity changing?
  - How are you coming 'back again'? Use the details in the poetry graphic organizer to help you plan and draft your poems."

- Share with students that the "Back Again" poem requires less of a research focus and more creativity. They will share the experiences of a refugee who is adapting, mourning, and facing the realities of being "back again."

- Ask students to reread a poem from the novel *Inside Out & Back Again* that shows Ha turning "back again." Give students 2 minutes to reread "But Not Bad" on page 233 independently.

- Ask students to Think-Pair-Share:
  - "What is this poem about?"
  - "What scene is the poem set in?"
  - "How does it show Ha turning 'back again'?"

- Listen for students to explain that the poem is about how Ha is initially very disappointed with the dried papaya and mourns the fresh papayas in Vietnam, but she realizes that it can actually taste good if it is soaked in water. The poem's scene is at home overnight and early the next morning. It shows Ha turning "back again" by accepting that although the papaya isn't as good as fresh papaya back in Vietnam, it is a reasonable substitute.

- Distribute the **"Back Again" Poem Graphic Organizer** and display it using a document camera. Ask students to Think-Pair-Share:
  - "What do you notice?"
  - "What do you wonder?"

- Highlight that, this time, the structure of their poem is not set out for them as it was in the "Inside Out" poem, so although they still have to write a narrative story poem, they can be creative about the structure as long as they answer the questions in the left column and set their answers in the context of a scene.

- Inform students that their "Back Again" poem needs to follow from their "Inside Out" poem. It is the same narrator explaining how his or her life has turned back again, so students need to make sure the details in both poems match up. For example, it would confuse the reader if in the "Inside Out" poem the narrator discusses having two younger brothers but in the "Back Again" poem mentions an older sister.

- Display the **Model "Inside Out" Poem Graphic Organizer**. Remind students that the scene is Ha in bed at night listening to her mother and brother whispering and worrying about the communists and the future.

- Ask students to Think-Pair-Share with a peer on their team:

  - "How could the 'Back Again' poem link to that 'inside out' scene to show Ha turning 'back again'?"

- Provide the following suggestion to guide students if they don't think of the ideas themselves:

  - Ha could be in bed at night reflecting on her life in Alabama, and now she can hear her brothers and mother laughing.

- Inform students that for homework they are going to fill in the organizer to get ready to begin writing the first draft of their "Back Again" poem in the next lesson.

- Ask them to begin by thinking of a scene that their poem will be set in and then to continue by answering the questions in the first column. They will do this by being creative, but they can consider Ha's experiences and what they learned about the adaptation/settling-in process in Unit 2 from the "Refugee Children in Canada" text to answer the questions. Advise students to take their "Refugee Children in Canada" text home with them for reference.

- Emphasize that this is not a research-based poem, so students are only to refer to the informational text and Ha's experiences in the novel for inspiration.

- As with the "Inside Out" Poem Graphic Organizer, they then need to think about how they are going to set these ideas in a specific scene using figurative and descriptive language as well as purposeful word choice in poetry form. In the final column, they then need to justify why they have made those word/text choices based on how they affect the meaning and tone.

- Remind students that this "Back Again" poem will be a continuation of their "Inside Out" poem, so the narrator is the same.

Meeting Students' Needs

- Providing models of expected work supports all learners, especially challenged learners.

- Asking students to analyze good models to build criteria of an effective poem provides a scaffold for them to follow when writing their own poems.

- Graphic organizers and recording forms engage students more actively and provide the necessary scaffolding that is especially critical for learners with lower levels of language proficiency and/or learning.

- When you're reviewing the graphic organizers or recording forms, consider using a document camera to display the document for students who struggle with auditory processing.

Closing and Assessment

A. Beginning to Plan "Back Again" Poem (2 minutes)

Invite students to follow the directions to begin planning their "Back Again" poem. Remind them that the first thing they should do is choose a scene, preferably one that links to the scene in their "Inside Out" poem in some way.

Homework

Follow the directions to complete the "Back Again" Poem Graphic Organizer in preparation for writing the first draft of your "Back Again" poem in the next lesson.

Note: Before Lesson 6, assess students' first draft "Inside Out" poems based on Row 2 of the "Inside Out" and "Back Again" Poetry Rubric. Provide specific feedback: Name one clear strength, and suggest a specific next step. In Lesson 6, students will apply this feedback to write a final best draft of this poem as well as their "Back Again" poem (which they will draft in Lesson 4).

LESSON 4

End-of-Unit Assessment

Writing Best First Draft of "Back Again" Poem

Long-Term Targets Addressed (Based on ELA CCSS)

- I can write narrative text about real or imagined experiences using relevant details and event sequences that make sense. (W.8.3)

- With support from peers and adults, I can use the writing process to ensure that the purpose and audience have been addressed. (W.8.5)

- I can effectively engage in discussions with diverse partners about eighth-grade topics, texts, and issues. (SL.8.1)

Supporting Learning Targets

- I can write a poem describing how the narrator, a refugee, turns "back again" as he or she adapts to life in a new country.

- I can create meaning in my "Back Again" poem by using figurative and descriptive language as well as purposeful word choice to convey a certain tone.

Ongoing Assessment

- Draft "Back Again" poem

Agenda

1. Opening
   A. Unpacking Learning Targets (2 minutes)
   B. Sharing Homework in Research Teams (6 minutes)

2. Work Time

    A.   Draft "Back Again" Poem (20 minutes)

    B.   Self-Assessment Based on the Rubric (10 minutes)

3. Closing and Assessment

    A.   Making Revisions (7 minutes)

4. Homework

    A.   Finish both poems.

Teaching Notes

- This lesson follows a format similar to that of Lesson 3. Students draft their "Back Again" poems for the End-of-Unit Assessment.

- For the assessment, focus on just Row 1 of the "Inside Out" and "Back Again" Poetry Rubric.

- As with the "Inside Out" poem, plan to give students specific feedback on their draft poem before Lesson 6. In Lesson 6, they will revise both poems based on teacher and peer feedback (their Final Performance Task).

- After drafting their "Back Again" poem, students self-assess their draft against particular rows on the rubric and justify how they have scored themselves. This self-assessment activity helps raise student awareness of the issues in their own writing to improve the first draft of their poem before they hand it in at the end of the lesson.

- If the technology is available, provide computers for students to word-process their essays.

- Students will peer critique both of their poems in Lesson 5.

- Post: Learning targets, What Makes an Effective Poem? Anchor Chart.

Lesson Vocabulary

free verse

Materials

- What Makes an Effective Poem? Anchor Chart (from Lesson 2)

- "Back Again" Poem Graphic Organizer (from Lesson 3)

- End-of-Unit 3 Assessment: Best First Draft of "Back Again" Poem (one per student)

- "Inside Out" and "Back Again" Poetry Rubric (from Lesson 3)

- Lined paper (two sheets per student)

- Rows 1 and 3 of "Inside Out" and "Back Again" Poetry Rubric (one per student)

Opening

A. Unpacking Learning Targets (2 minutes)

- Students should be sitting with their research teams. Invite students to read the learning targets with you:

  - "I can write a poem describing how the narrator, a refugee, turns 'back again' as he or she adapts to life in a new country."

  - "I can create meaning in my 'Back Again' poem by using figurative and descriptive language as well as purposeful word choice to convey a certain tone."

  - "I can use the 'Inside Out' and 'Back Again' Poetry Rubric to provide kind, specific, and helpful feedback to my peers."

- Inform students that today they will be writing the first draft of their "Back Again" poems for their End-of-Unit Assessment. Explain that as with the Mid-Unit Assessment, the End-of-Unit assessment is working toward the final performance task of writing the "Inside Out" and "Back Again" poems.

Meeting Students' Needs

- Learning targets are a research-based strategy that helps all students, especially challenged learners.

- Discussing and clarifying the language of learning targets help build academic vocabulary.

- Posting learning targets enables students to refer to them throughout the lesson to check their understanding. This also provides a reminder to students and teachers about the intended learning behind a given lesson or activity.

B. Sharing Homework in Research Teams (6 minutes)

- Focus student attention on the **What Makes an Effective Poem? Anchor Chart** from the previous lesson. Invite students to read along silently as you read the criteria aloud.

- Invite students to pair up within their research teams; inform them that they are going to be swapping **"Back Again" Poem Graphic Organizers** to get feedback from their peers.

- Give students 2 minutes to consider a question they would like to pose to their partner about something they would like specific feedback about, and ask them to write the question at the top of their poem organizer.

- Invite students to swap "Back Again" Poem Graphic Organizers with their partner. Give them 2 minutes to read through their partner's organizer, thinking about the question posed and the criteria on the anchor chart.

- Give students another minute in silence to consider how to answer the question posed by their partner and to think of a question they would like to ask their partner that will help them revise their work. Give them an example: "How does this work in the context of the scene you have chosen?"

- Invite students to share their question with their partner.

- When students are done, remind them to thank their partner. Also remind them that they don't necessarily have to follow the advice they have been given if they don't think it works—emphasize that the question posed by their partner may be useful in helping them revise, but it may not.

- Give students 2 minutes to revise their organizer if they choose.

Work Time

A. Draft "Back Again" Poem (20 minutes)

- Refocus the whole group. Distribute their **End-of-Unit 3 Assessment: Best First Draft of "Back Again" Poem**. Point out that this assessment is identical to the second poem of the Student-Friendly Performance Task Prompt they saw in Unit 2, Lesson 18.

- Read the assessment prompt aloud, and answer any clarifying questions. Remind students of what *back again* actually means—it means "emotionally on the way to being settled and adapting to life in a new country." Clarify that it does not mean they are returning home.

- Remind students that their "Back Again" poem needs to follow from their "Inside Out" poem. It is the same narrator explaining how his or her life has turned back again, so students need to make sure the details in both poems match up. For example, it would confuse the reader if in the "Inside Out" poem the narrator discusses having two younger brothers but in the "Back Again" poem mentions an older sister.

- Inform students that they are now going to refer to their "Back Again" Poem Graphic Organizer, the What Makes an Effective Poem? Anchor Chart, and the **"Inside Out" and "Back Again" Poetry Rubric** as they write the first draft their "Back Again" poem.

- Set the same parameter as with the "Inside Out" poem: The "Back Again" poem should be no more than four verses or stanzas long, and each verse should contain no more than six lines of poetry. This will encourage students to be more precise.

- Remind students that because this is an assessment, they are to work independently in silence. If students are not able to work on computers, distribute **lined paper**. Ask students to draft their "Back Again" poem.

- Circulate to take this opportunity to do informal assessments of students' work. Make sure they are setting the details they want to include in the context of a scene.

Meeting Students' Needs

Providing students with the rubric you will be using to assess their work sets expectations up front and provides them with clear criteria to follow to be successful.

B. Self-Assessment Based on the Rubric (10 minutes)

- Inform students that now that they have drafted their "Back Again" poem, they have an opportunity to self-assess their writing.

- Distribute **Rows 1 and 3 of the "Inside Out" and "Back Again" Poetry Rubric**. Invite students to read the directions at the top of the rubric as you read aloud. Ask them to focus on just these two rows at this point; it is often helpful, as a writer, to focus on just a few things at a time.

- Invite students to follow the directions to self-assess their first draft of their "Back Again" poem. Circulate to ask students to justify their scoring choices on the rubric.

Meeting Students' Needs

Developing self-assessment and reflection supports all learners by giving them the opportunity to identify how they can improve their own work.

Closing and Assessment

A. Making Revisions (7 minutes)

- Invite students to use their self-assessment against the rubric to make final revisions to their first draft "Back Again" poem. Remind them that they should be aiming to score as highly on the rubric as possible.

- Collect the End-of-Unit Assessment and all the student materials: the "Back Again" Poem Graphic Organizer, the first draft of their "Back Again" poem, their self-assessment, and the revision.

Homework

If you have not finished both of your poems, take them home to finish them.

Note: Before Lesson 6, assess students' first-draft "Back Again" poem to provide specific feedback. Focus feedback on strengths and next steps using Row 1 of the "Inside Out" and "Back Again" Poetry Rubric. In Lesson 6, students will apply this feedback to write a final best draft of their poem.

In Lesson 5, students will need both of their first-draft poems for a peer critique.

Meeting Students' Needs

Students who have not yet finished the first drafts of their "Inside Out" and "Back Again" poems in class will need to finish them at home. If necessary, plan to collect these drafts at the end of Lesson 5 to assess.

LESSON 5

Peer Critique of "Inside Out" and "Back Again" Poems

Long-Term Targets Addressed (Based on ELA CCSS)

- I can write narrative text about real or imagined experiences using relevant details and event sequences that make sense. (W.8.3)
- With support from peers and adults, I can use the writing process to ensure that the purpose and audience have been addressed. (W.8.5)
- I can conduct short research projects to answer a question. (W.8.7)
- I can use several sources in my research. (W.8.7)
- I can use evidence from informational texts to support analysis, reflection, and research. (W.8.9)
- I can effectively engage in discussions with diverse partners about eighth-grade topics, texts, and issues. (SL.8.1)

Supporting Learning Targets

- I can use the "Inside Out" and "Back Again" Poetry Rubric to provide kind, specific, and helpful feedback to my peers.
- I can create meaning in my "Inside Out" and "Back Again" poems by using figurative and descriptive language and purposeful word choice to convey a certain tone.
- I can use peer feedback to revise my "Inside Out" and "Back Again" poems.

Ongoing Assessment

- Revised "Inside Out" and "Back Again" poems
- Stars and Steps for "Inside Out" and "Back Again" poems

Agenda

1. Opening
   A. Unpacking Learning Targets (2 minutes)

---

2. Work Time

    A. Mini-Lesson: Word Choice (10 minutes)

    B. Peer Critique: Draft "Inside Out" Poem (13 minutes)

    C. Peer Critique: Draft "Back Again" Poem (10 minutes)

3. Closing and Assessment

    A. Making Revisions Based on Peer Feedback (10 minutes)

4. Homework

    A. No homework.

Teaching Notes

- Students peer critique the first drafts of their "Inside Out" and "Back Again" poems using the Stars and Steps process. Be sure to outline expectations clearly before this activity to ensure that students can peer critique carefully without making others feel bad and also to help students give each other feedback that is sufficiently specific and precise. Students will then use this feedback to revise their poems.

- Although you may be still in the process of assessing the "Inside Out" and "Back Again" poems for the Mid-Unit and End-of-Unit Assessments, students need to work with their poems in this lesson, so ensure that you have them ready to hand out. Also ensure that you collect all poems at the end of the lesson to continue assessing them, and be ready to provide students with feedback on both of their poems in Lesson 6.

- Post: Learning targets, anchor charts.

Lesson Vocabulary

peer critique

Materials

- Using Strong Action Verbs (one per student)
- Document camera
- Peer-Critique Guidelines (new; teacher-created)
- Thesaurus (enough copies for students to be able to use them for quick reference)
- Stars and Steps: "Inside Out" Poem Recording Form (one per student)
- Stars and Steps: "Back Again" Poem Recording Form (one per student)

EXPEDITIONARY
LEARNING

Opening

A. Unpacking Learning Targets (2 minutes)

- Invite students to read through the learning targets with you:
  - "I can use the 'Inside Out' and 'Back Again' Poetry Rubric to provide kind, specific, and helpful feedback to my peers."
  - "I can create meaning in my 'Inside Out' and 'Back Again' poems by using figurative and descriptive language and purposeful word choice to convey a certain tone."
  - "I can use peer feedback to revise my 'Inside Out' and 'Back Again' poems."
- Inform students that today they are going to peer critique another student's poems to provide feedback. Ask students to Think-Pair-Share:
  - "What does *peer critique* mean?"
- Listen for students to explain that a *peer critique* is "when you look over another student's work, focusing on something specific, and provide advice on how he or she could improve the work."

Meeting Students' Needs

- Learning targets are a research-based strategy that helps all students, especially challenged learners.
- Discussing and clarifying the language of learning targets help build academic vocabulary.
- Posting learning targets enables students to refer to them throughout the lesson to check their understanding. This also provides a reminder to students and teachers about the intended learning behind a given lesson or activity.

Work Time

A. Mini-Lesson: Word Choice (10 minutes)

- Inform students that as you have been looking through some of their Mid-Unit and End-of-Unit Assessments, you have noticed that some of them could improve their word choice in their poems. This is something they have paid attention to as readers throughout this module. Today is one last chance for them to think about this as writers before they revise the word choice in their poems.
- Distribute **Using Strong Action Verbs** and display it using a **document camera**. Invite students to spend a minute reading it. Ask:
  - "What do you notice?"
  - "What do you wonder?"
- Focus students on the first row. Ask students to Think-Pair-Share:
  - "What do you notice about the words in the column on the right next to *dislike*?"

- Listen for students to explain that the words in the column on the right next to *dislike* are more powerful, descriptive, and emotional ways of saying *dislike*.

- Write this poetry example on the board:
  - *I don't like*
  - the dried papaya
  - in Alabama,
  - I like
  - the fresh papaya
  - in Vietnam

- Ask students to Think-Pair-Share:
  - "What could Ha say instead to make this stanza of poetry more powerful and descriptive?"
  - "How can you convey that she really doesn't like the papaya in Alabama but really likes the papaya in Vietnam?"
  - "Which words could you change to improve the way it sounds?"

- Encourage students to use the handout to help them with word choice. Continue to emphasize that writers, particularly writers of poetry, choose words carefully to influence both the meaning and the tone of what they are writing. The goal is to be precise. They will keep working on this all year.

- Select students to read the stanza aloud to the whole group, substituting the words they would change. An appropriate example would be:
  - *I despise*
  - the dried papaya
  - in Alabama,
  - I adore
  - the fresh papaya
  - in Vietnam

- Inform students that now they are going to think about how to make this same stanza more powerful to create a strong visual image in the mind of the reader.

- Ask students to Think-Pair-Share:
  - "How could we improve 'the dried papaya' line of this stanza?"
  - "What adjectives (describing words) could we add to make it more descriptive?"
  - "What figurative language could we add?"

- Select students to read the stanza aloud to the whole group, substituting the words they would change. Appropriate examples might be
  - the rubbery, dried papaya
  - papaya so dry it is like eating leather

- Ask students to Think-Pair-Share:
  - "How could we improve 'the fresh papaya' line of this stanza?"
  - "What adjectives (describing words) could we add to make it more descriptive?"
  - "What figurative language could we add?"
- Ask for volunteers to read the stanza aloud to the whole group, substituting the words they would change. Appropriate examples would be:
  - the fresh, juicy papaya
  - the fresh papaya, so ripe and juicy
- Give students a few minutes to revise the word choice in their poems in the same way they helped revise the word choice in this stanza. Inform them that they will have more time for revisions at the end of the lesson, after they have received more feedback from their peers.
- Remind them to use the handout, or they can use a **thesaurus** if they want. (Caution: Often when students use a thesaurus, they end up choosing words with slightly off meanings. Provide guidance as needed.)

Meeting Students' Needs

Set up peer critiquing very carefully to ensure that students feel safe giving and receiving feedback. Students must be given a set of clear guidelines for behavior, and they need to see the teacher model how to do it successfully. Asking students to provide feedback to their peers based on explicit criteria benefits both students in clarifying what a strong piece of writing should look like. Students can learn from both the strengths and weaknesses that they notice in the work of peers.

B. Peer Critique: Draft "Inside Out" Poem (13 minutes)

- Explain that peer critiquing must be done carefully, because we want to be helpful to our peers so they can use our suggestions to improve their work. We don't want to make them feel bad. Post the **Peer Critique Guidelines**.
- Using the document camera, display the "Inside Out" and "Back Again" Poetry Rubric, and ask students to refer to their own copies.
- For students' "Inside Out" poem, ask them to focus their feedback on the degree to which the poem is "research-based." Focus students on Row 1, Content and Analysis. In the Level 3 column, highlight/underline this section: "The poem clearly introduces who the refugee is, where he/she is fleeing from, why he/she has to flee, and how he/she has turned 'inside out' in the context of a compelling scene."
- Focus students on Row 2, Command of Evidence. In the Level 4 column, highlight/underline this section: "Who the refugee is, where he/she is fleeing from, and why he/she has to flee are developed with relevant facts from informational texts."
- Invite students to read aloud each of these sections of the rubric with you. Inform them that during the peer-critique time, they will be focusing on these two specific elements of the poem.

- Distinguish *peer critique* from *proofreading*. It is fine if they catch errors in each other's work, but the goal is to make the thinking in the writing as strong as possible.

- Inform students that they will present feedback in the form of Stars and Steps. They will give three "stars" (one related to Row 1 of the rubric, the other related to Row 2, and another about word choice) and three "steps" (one related to Row 1, the other related to Row 2, and another about word choice).

- Briefly model how to give three "kind, specific, helpful" stars. Be sure to connect your comments directly to each row of the rubric. For example: "It is clear who the refugee is, and you have used well-chosen facts about Vietnam at that time. I like your use of the word 'disturbed' here."

- Repeat, briefly modeling how to give three "kind, specific, helpful" steps. For example: "Where did the refugee flee from? Do you have a detail from the informational texts about why the refugee had to flee? Could you use a more descriptive word than 'dislike'?"

- Emphasize that it is especially important to be kind when giving steps. Asking a question of the writer is often a good way to do this: "I wonder if . . . ?" and "Have you thought about . . . ?"

- Distribute the **Stars and Steps: "Inside Out" Poem Recording Form**. Explain that today students will record the Stars and Steps feedback for their partner on this sheet so that their partner can remember the feedback. They are to write the name of their partner at the top of their form.

- Pair up students. Instruct pairs to swap poems and to spend 3 minutes reading them in silence.

- Ask students to record Stars and Steps for their partner on the recording form. This form is designed to help them remember the feedback they want to give to their partner from the peer critique. Circulate to assist students who may struggle with recording their feedback.

- Ask students to return the poem and Stars and Steps recording form to their partner and to explain the Stars and Steps they recorded for their partner. Invite students to question their partner if they don't understand the Stars and Steps they received.

C. Peer Critique: Draft "Back Again" Poem (10 minutes)

- Refocus students on the "Inside Out" and "Back Again" Poetry Rubric, and ask them to refer to their own copies.

- Remind students that their "Back Again" poem is not as research-based, so their critique will have a slightly different focus.

- Focus students on Row 1 again, but this time on the part about the "Back Again" poem. In the Level 4 column, highlight/underline this section: "The poem clearly introduces how the refugee has had to adapt, what he/she mourns, and how he/she has turned 'back again' in the context of a compelling scene."

- Focus students on Row 3, Cohesion, Organization, and Style. In the Level 3 column, highlight/ underline this section: "The poem has a beginning, middle, and end that connect to each other to create a unified poem."

- Invite students to read aloud each of these sections of the rubric with you. Inform them that during the peer-critique time, they will be focusing on these two specific elements of the poem and word choice.

- If necessary, briefly model again how to give three "kind, specific, helpful" Stars. Be sure to connect your comments directly to each row of the rubric. For example: "Your poem is set in a clear scene, and the answers to those questions are given in the context of the scene. It also has a clear beginning, middle, and end that flows well. I like your use of the word 'devoured.'"

- Repeat, briefly modeling how to give three "kind, specific, helpful" Steps. For example:

  - "Have you thought about describing what the refugee is mourning? I wonder if you could find a way to improve the flow between these two stanzas."

  - "Have you thought about using a more powerful verb instead of 'like'?"

- Reiterate that it is especially important to be kind when giving steps. Asking a question of the writer is often a good way to do this. "I wonder if . . . ?" and "Have you thought about . . . ?"

- Distribute the **Stars and Steps: "Back Again" Poem Recording Form**.

- Pair up students with a different partner. Invite pairs to swap poems and to spend 3 minutes reading them in silence.

- Ask students to record Stars and Steps for their partner on the recording form. This form is designed to help them remember the feedback they want to give to their partner from the peer critique. Circulate to assist students who may struggle with recording their feedback.

- Ask students to return the poem and Stars and Steps recording form to their partner and to explain the Stars and Steps they recorded. Invite students to question their partner if they don't understand the Stars and Steps they have been given.

Closing and Assessment

A. Making Revisions Based on Peer Feedback (10 minutes)

- Invite students to use the Stars and Steps suggested in their peer critique to revise their poems.

- Circulate to assist students in revising their poems. Ensure that they understand their peer feedback. Ask:

  - "What feedback did your partner give you? Why?"

  - "So what are you changing? Where? Why?"

- Collect revised poems to continue assessing them in preparation to give feedback in Lesson 6.

Homework

No homework.

LESSON 6

Revision

Best Draft of "Inside Out" and "Back Again" Poems (Final Performance Task)

Long-Term Targets Addressed (Based on ELA CCSS)

- I can write narrative text about real or imagined experiences using relevant details and event sequences that make sense. (W.8.3)
- With support from peers and adults, I can use the writing process to ensure that purpose and audience have been addressed. (W.8.5)
- I can use correct grammar and usage when writing or speaking. (L.8.1)
- I can use correct capitalization, punctuation, and spelling to send a clear message to my reader. (L.8.2)

Supporting Learning Targets

- I can write a final draft of two poems describing how the narrator, a refugee, turns "inside out" and "back again" as he or she flees home and adapts to life in a new country.
- I can create meaning in my "Inside Out" and "Back Again" poems by using figurative and descriptive language and purposeful word choice to convey a certain tone.
- I can use correct grammar and punctuation in my "Inside Out" and "Back Again" poems.

Ongoing Assessment

- Best draft of "Inside Out" and "Back Again" poems

Agenda

1. Opening
   A. Unpacking Learning Targets (2 minutes)
   B. Return "Inside Out" and "Back Again" Poems with Feedback (6 minutes)

---

2. Work Time

    A. Poetry Share in Research Teams (10 minutes)

    B. Writing Best Draft of "Inside Out" and "Back Again" Poems (20 minutes)

3. Closing and Assessment

    A. Poetry Share with Student from Another Research Team (7 minutes)

4. Homework

    A. Write a short review of *Inside Out & Back Again*.

Teaching Notes

- In this lesson, students begin by reviewing teacher feedback on their "Inside Out" and "Back Again" poems (from the Mid-Unit Assessment and the End-of-Unit Assessment). They then use the relevant parts of this feedback to guide their revisions to both poems.

- Students then share their "Inside Out" and "Back Again" poems with peers in their research team. The focus of this poetry share is on alignment of details between the two poems and on making sure it sounds as though the two poems have been written by the same narrator. Students provide feedback on these points by questioning.

- Students then write their best draft of their "Inside Out" and "Back Again" poems. At the end of the lesson, they share their best draft poems with students from another research team to learn more about a refugee from somewhere else in the world. They synthesize their learning from this poetry sharing by returning to the idea that refugees come from all over the world and different places in time.

- If students used computers in Lessons 3 and 4, allow them to use computers to revise.

- Post: Learning targets, anchor charts.

Lesson Vocabulary

align

Materials

- "Inside Out" and "Back Again" Poetry Rubric (from Lesson 3)

- Student-Friendly Performance Task Prompt (from Unit 2, Lesson 18)

- Lined paper (two sheets per student)

- What Makes an Effective Poem? Anchor Chart (from Lesson 2)

- Poetry Share Task Card (one per student)

- Homework: *Inside Out & Back Again* Review (one per student)

Opening

A. Unpacking Learning Targets (2 minutes)

- Invite students to read through the learning targets with you:

    - "I can write a final draft of two poems describing how the narrator, a refugee, turns 'Inside out' and 'back again' as he or she flees home and adapts to life in a new country."

    - "I can create meaning in my 'Inside Out' and 'Back Again' poems by using figurative and descriptive language and purposeful word choice to convey a certain tone."

    - "I can use correct grammar and punctuation in my 'Inside Out' and 'Back Again' poems."

- Focus on the final learning target, and invite students to read to Row 4 of their **"Inside Out" and "Back Again" Poetry Rubric**. Remind them that even though this is a poem, they still need to use the appropriate grammar and punctuation.

Meeting Students' Needs

- Learning targets are a research-based strategy that helps all students, especially challenged learners.

- Discussing and clarifying the language of learning targets help build academic vocabulary.

- Posting learning targets enables students to refer to them throughout the lesson to check their understanding. This also provides a reminder to students and teachers about the intended learning behind a given lesson or activity.

B. Return "Inside Out" and "Back Again" Poems with Feedback (6 minutes)

- Hand out the "Inside Out" and "Back Again" poems completed in Lessons 3 and 4 with feedback.

- Give students time to read the feedback carefully. Circulate to answer any questions students might have about the feedback they have been given.

Meeting Students' Needs

Providing specific and focused feedback helps students set concrete goals for reaching learning targets.

Work Time

A. Poetry Share in Research Teams (10 minutes)

- Inform the students that, one at a time, they are going to read both of their poems aloud to their research team.

- Post the following questions for students to see:

    - "Do both of the poems sound as though they have been written by the same narrator?"

    - "Do the details in both poems align?"

- Ask students to Think-Pair-Share:

  - "What does *align* mean? What does it mean to make sure the details in both poems align?"

- Listen for students to explain that *align* means "to make sure the details line up between the two poems—there shouldn't be any details that conflict or confuse the reader."

- Inform students that they are going to be listening to the work of their peers for flow between the poems, focusing on whether it sounds as though they have been written by the same narrator and also whether there are any details that don't match or might cause confusion between the two poems. Give the example that the "Inside Out" poem might suggest that the refugee has two younger sisters, whereas the "Back Again" poem might suggest that the refugee has an older brother, which could confuse the reader and make the reader question how realistic and believable the two poems are.

- Inform students that as they listen to their peers read their two poems, they should consider the two questions that have been posted and also think of one question they could ask the writer to help him or her improve the way the poems read so that they sound more like the words of one narrator or ensure that the details align.

- Invite students to share their poems with the research team.

Meeting Students' Needs

Asking students to provide feedback to their peers based on explicit criteria benefits both students in clarifying the meaning of the learning target.

B. Writing Best Draft of "Inside Out" and "Back Again" Poems (20 minutes)

- Ask students to take out their **Student-Friendly Performance Task Prompt** and to reread the final paragraph of Part 2: Writing Free-Verse Narrative Poetry.

- If computers are unavailable, distribute **lined paper**. Inform students that they are now going to write the best drafts of their "Inside Out" and "Back Again" poems.

- Remind students to refer to the feedback from their Mid-Unit and End-of-Unit Assessments, the Stars and Steps feedback from their peer critique in the previous lesson, feedback from the share with their research team, the **"Inside Out" and "Back Again" Poetry Rubric**, the **What Makes an Effective Poem? Anchor Chart**, and the revised drafts of their poems to write the best drafts of their "Inside Out" and "Back Again" poems.

- Circulate around the room, addressing questions. Consider checking in first with students who need extra support to ensure they use their time well.

- When a few minutes are left, if students are working on computers, ask them to save their work.

Closing and Assessment

A. Poetry Share with Student from Another Research Team (7 minutes)

- Ask students to pair up with a student from another research team. Distribute the **Poetry Share Task Card**.

- Invite students to read the instructions with you.

- Invite students to follow the directions to share their "Inside Out" and "Back Again" poems.

- Refocus the whole group. Ask students to Think-Pair-Share:

  - "So what do you now know about refugees?"

  - "Where do they come from in terms of place?"

  - "When do they come from in terms of time?"

  - "What do you know about the possible emotional journey of refugees, as they turn 'inside out' and 'back again'?"

- Listen for students to explain that refugees come from all over the world and from different places in time and that they often turn "inside out" as they flee and find home and turn "back again" as they begin to adapt and settle in to life in their new country.

- Be prepared for students to mention that perhaps not all refugees do turn "back again." If this occurs, ask students to Think-Pair-Share:

  - "Why do you think some refugees do not turn 'back again'?"

  - "From what you have read in the informational texts, how can we help refugees turn 'back again'?"

- Collect the "Inside Out" and "Back Again" poems and all the student materials: Research Guide, poem organizers, and rough drafts of both poems.

- Distribute **Homework: *Inside Out & Back Again* Review**.

Meeting Students' Needs

Task cards support students who struggle with following multiple-step directions.

Homework

Write a short review (no more than three paragraphs) of the novel *Inside Out & Back Again* for someone who is thinking about reading it. Answer these questions in your review:

- What is the book about?

- What do you think of the book? Why?

- How effective is the use of poetry in conveying this particular refugee experience?

- Why do you think this author may have chosen to include both "inside out" and "back again"?

- Would you recommend this book to someone? Why or why not?